FOREWORD BY GREGG WALLA
FROM BBC'S MASTERCHEF

T0023340

The Ultimate Book of

CAKES & COOKIES

365 MUCH-LOVED CLASSICS
AND NEW FAVOURITES

Hannah Miles

W

To Katie and Charlotte, two beautiful girls

The Big Book of Cakes & Cookies
Hannah Miles

First published in the United Kingdom and Ireland in 2009
by Duncan Baird Publishers Ltd
This edition published in the UK and USA in 2022
by Watkins, an imprint of Watkins Media Limited
Unit 11, Shepperton house, 83–93 Shepperton Road,
London N1 3DF

Copyright © Watkins Media Limited 2009, 2022
Text copyright © Hannah Miles 2009, 2022
Photography copyright © Watkins Media Limited 2009, 2022

The right of Hannah Miles to be identified as the Author of this
text has been asserted in accordance with the Copyright, Designs
and Patents Act of 1988.

All rights reserved. No part of this book may be reproduced in
any form or by any electronic or mechanical means, including
information storage and retrieval systems, without permission in
writing from the publisher, except by a reviewer who may quote
brief passages in a review.

Managing Editors: Grace Cheetham, Deirdre Headon,
    Ella Chappell
Editor: Alison Bolus
Assistant Editor: Brittany Willis
Managing Designer: Karen Smith
Designer: Alice Claire Coleman
Studio Photography: William Lingwood
Photography Assistant: Sally Hamer
Food Stylist: Bridget Sargeson
Assistant Food Stylists: Stella Sargeson, Jack Sargeson
Prop Stylist: Rachel Jukes

British Library Cataloguing-in-Publication Data:
A CIP record for this book is available from the British Library

ISBN: 978-1-84899-257-3

10 9 8 7 6 5 4 3 2 1

Typeset in Gill Sans MT
Printed in China

Publisher's Note:
While every care has been taken in compiling the recipes for
this book, Watkins Media Limited, or any other persons who
have been involved in working on this publication, cannot accept
responsibility for any errors or omissions, inadvertent or not,
that may be found in the recipes or text, nor for any problems
that may arise as a result of preparing one of these recipes. If
you are pregnant or breastfeeding or have any special dietary
requirements or medical conditions, it is advisable to consult
a medical professional before following any of the recipes
contained in this book. Ill or elderly people, babies, young
children and women who are pregnant or breastfeeding should
avoid any recipes containing uncooked egg whites.

Notes on the recipes – unless otherwise stated:
• Use whole milk
• A large egg is the equivalent of a US extra large egg
• Do not mix metric and imperial measurements
• Pack brown and muscovado sugar firmly into cups, if using
• 1 tsp = 5ml • 1 tbsp = 15ml • 1 cup = 250ml

Author's acknowledgments:
Thanks to John, Mum, Dad, Liz, Mike, Gareth, Amy, Hunter, Bowen,
Jane, Geoff, and my friends and family for their love, support and
endless baking. Heartfelt gratitude to those who have made this
book possible: Heather and Elly at HHB; Grace, Deirdre, Suzanne
and all at DBP, including Alison Bolus for her unending patience
during editing; William Lingwood and his team for the beautiful
photographs; Bridget Sargeson and her team for making and
displaying the cakes and cookies so elegantly; Gregg Wallace,
particularly for the kind foreword and support during the writing
of this book, John Torode, Karen Ross and all at Shine/Masterchef;
Giancarlo and Katie Caldesi; Kathy and Simon Brown; Chris
Lee at the Bildeston Crown; Fitzbillies in Cambridge and my
wonderful recipe testers: Tina, Maren, Jess, Josh, Rosie, Miles, Nick,
Sophie, Henry, Alfred, Abena, Amelia, Zara, Deidre, Charlotte,
Freddie, Elaine, Fay, Lisa, Tommy, Mags, Ishan, Sonya, Jane, Jenny, Jo,
Kath, Louisa, Madeleine, Sarah, Jonathan, Susan, Pam, Clare, Mark,
William, Anna, Bree, Alison, Ella, Torin, Jackie, Linda, Rita, Premela,
Sheila, Tania, Steven, William, Ben, Charlotte, Kathy, Lucy, David,
Cerys, Vanessa, Rachael, Anna, Liz, Joanne, Premala, Helen, Ed,
Kate, Marian, Ros, the Teesdale boys and our village sewing circle.

CONTENTS

GLUTEN
FREE

DAIRY
FREE

EGG
FREE

FOREWORD

Hannah impressed me from the moment I met her. She has a winning smile and she bakes like an angel. For a man like me with a well-documented sweet tooth, she is simply irresistible!

From the first time she walked into the MasterChef kitchen it was obvious she was a special kind of cook. In the first round, the Invention test, she was half way into a dish when she realized she didn't have all the ingredients to complete the dish. Falling back on her enormous repertoire of sweet things, she managed to knock up the best-tasting cheesecake I've sampled on MasterChef, in less than 12 minutes!

Hannah and I obviously both share a passion for all things sweet and gooey. Hannah is one of the best pastry cooks that I have met, with such generosity of spirit. She wants to make a cake for everybody she meets. She gets real pleasure out of feeding people. I think she takes a naughty delight in watching people indulge themselves. She has presented me with some truly wonderful creations, and I think that everybody should regularly treat themselves to a Hannah work of art.

This book is an absolute joy, as it works on two fronts: it has hundreds of really, really good recipes, but also lots of practical advice from a master of the art. Using this book is like having Hannah standing beside you in the kitchen as you work.

Anybody for another slice? Save me the big bit!

Gregg Wallace, MasterChef

INTRODUCTION

I have enjoyed baking since I was very young, when I baked with my mum, tugging at her apron strings and asking for pieces of dough to make mini loaves for dolls' tea parties. It is no surprise that I enjoy baking – it is a skill I inherited from my Welsh grandpa, who as a baker in the army used to bake loaves in a mobile bake oven. From him I learned how to make perfect loaves of bread and crisp pastry for fruit tarts. During my time on MasterChef, I worked under talented pastry chefs and patissiers at La Cucina Caldesi, at the Savoy and in Paris and have since worked with the wonderful bakers at Fitzbillies in Cambridge and the Bildeston Crown, swapping ideas for unusual flavours and learning secrets of the baking trade.

There is no place I would rather be than in my kitchen, with cakes or biscuits in the oven and a warm scent of baking filling the air. Baking is a skill that can be learned by anyone of virtually any age, and with a little practice, good-quality ingredients and the right equipment, you will easily be able to make delicious home-baked cakes and cookies for family and friends. In this book I have included a wide variety of my favourite cakes and biscuits. In chapters 1 and 2 you will find quick all-in-one cakes, perfect if you are short of time or have unexpected visitors, smalls cakes for packed lunches and picnics as well as Swiss rolls and desserts. There are also traditional favourites such as Lemon Drizzle Cake, Devil's Food Cake, Country Fruitcake and more unusual combinations such as Chocolate & Chilli Cake, Carrot & Courgette Cake and Peshwari Cupcakes. A selection of heavenly desserts make up Chapter 3, most of which can be prepared in advance, which makes them perfect for suppers or dinner parties with friends. Recipes include luscious mousse cakes, cloud cakes with crisp meringue shells and family favourites such as Pineapple Upside-Down Cake. Chapter 4 contains biscuits and cookies of all descriptions – refrigerator cookies that are either rolled and stamped-out or sliced, drops, thins and family favourites such as Melting Moments, Vanilla Shortbread and Coconut Macaroons – as well as delicate meringues, tray bakes and brownies. For birthdays, special events and seasonal celebrations, chapter 5 contains easy-to-assemble but stunning cakes, Ribboned Christmas Tree Biscuits, a Giant Birthday Cookie and party cupcakes. Introducing children to baking at a young age is so important if the tradition of baking is to be carried on from generation to generation. Chapter 6 does just that, containing simple recipes that you can help children to make and also novel ideas for cakes and biscuits for children's parties. (The Magnifying Glass Biscuits with peppermint 'glass' are my particular favourite.) Whatever the occasion, I hope that you will find something in this book to delight you and to encourage you to keep baking.

Top Tips for Baking Success

* Use the best baking ingredients you can afford, such as organic/free-range eggs and chocolate with a high cocoa percentage, as they will improve the flavour of your baking.
* Use eggs at room temperature.
* When making pastry or scones, use chilled butter for easy rubbing in. When creaming, use butter at room temperature, as this will allow you to put more air into the mixture.
* Beat lots of air in when creaming butter and sugar, as this will help your cakes to rise.
* Make sure raising agents such as baking powder, bicarbonate of soda/baking soda and self-raising flour are not out of date, as this could affect the rising of your cakes.
* Sift flour, icing/powdered sugar and other powdered ingredients to remove lumps and to add as much air as possible.
* Smooth out cake mixture in the tins evenly with a spatula or metal spoon so that the cakes rise evenly.
* Roll cookie dough out evenly to ensure even cooking.
* Preheat your oven so that it comes to temperature before the food goes in, otherwise more cooking time may be required. Check the temperature with an oven thermometer – some ovens can vary as much as 50°C/120°F from their stated dials.

* Use the tin size specified in the recipe. Using a smaller or larger tin will mean the cooking time needs to be adjusted.
* Grease your baking tins and trays well with butter to prevent cakes and biscuits sticking. Once you have greased a tin, you can choose to add a little flour to the tin and shake. This will enable you to spot any areas that are not greased, as the flour will not stick. The flour also helps the cake not to stick to the tin.
* Line the tins as recommended. Although lining takes a little time, it will ensure that your cakes do not get stuck in the tin.
* Place your cake tin or tray in the centre of the oven to ensure even baking (unless you have a fan oven, in which case the position is unimportant).
* Try to avoid opening the oven door during the early stages when a cake is cooking, as this could cause the cake to sink in the middle. If you are cooking more than one cake with different cooking times, however, and so do need to test a cake, remove the cake and shut the oven door while testing it, to minimize heat loss.
* When nearing the end of the cooking time, check to see if cakes are done at 5-minute intervals to prevent over-cooking or burning. If a cake has not finished cooking and is starting to brown too much on top, cover the top loosely with baking parchment.

* Use two different methods to check a cake is done, as just one method may not always be accurate. First, insert a skewer into the centre of the cake. If the skewer comes out with cake mixture on it, put the cake back in the oven for 5 minutes. If it comes out clean, press the middle of the cake lightly with a finger. If the cake does not spring back to your touch, cook the cake for a little longer, then retest until it does spring back.

* Do not fill or ice your cakes or cookies until they are completely cold, otherwise the icing/frosting and/or filling will melt.

* Store uneaten cakes and cookies in tins or other airtight containers to prolong their life. If they have fresh cream in them, store in a lidded container in the refrigerator.

Baking Ingredients

Here is a basic list of ingredients to get you started:

* plain/all-purpose flour and self-raising flour
* baking powder
* bicarbonate of soda/baking soda
* butter

* eggs
* caster/superfine sugar
* brown sugar
* muscovado sugar
* icing/powdered sugar

* porridge/rolled oats
* chocolate chips
* a selection of food colourings

Set out below are the types of ingredients that appear in this book, their main uses and any possible substitutions. Other than the dairy products, which need to be stored in a refrigerator, many of these ingredients have long sell-by dates and can be kept in the store cupboard so that you can make cakes or biscuits for any unexpected visitors.

Flours

Bread flour/strong flour – Used for making breads and rolls. This flour has a higher gluten content than other flours, making it ideal for bread because it enables the bread to rise evenly. It comes in white or wholemeal as well as in a wide range of more interesting types, such as granary, seeded and mixed grain.

Plain/all-purpose flour – Used in cookies, biscuits and pastry. This flour does not contain any raising agent and should not be used in cakes without an additional raising agent, such as baking powder, being added.

Self-raising flour – Used for cakes and in some cookies. This flour contains baking powder and will allow your baking to rise without the addition of any other raising agent. If you do not have self-raising flour, add 2 tsp baking powder to every 100g/3½oz plain/all-purpose flour to make your own.

Wholemeal/wholewheat flour – This is used for scones and pastry. This flour contains a higher percentage of the grain than white flour, giving it a browner colour and more nutty flavour.

00 Flour – This very fine flour is ideal for sauces, shortbread and biscuits. It does not contain any raising agent.

Raising Agents & Stabilizers

Baking powder – This is a raising agent that can be added to plain/all-purpose or self-raising flour to make cakes rise. It can also be used together with bicarbonate of soda/baking soda, especially in muffins, to ensure a soft crumb.

Bicarbonate of soda/baking soda – This is a raising agent that can be added to plain/all-purpose flour or self-raising flour to make cakes, biscuits or cookies rise. It has an alkaline taste and should be used sparingly otherwise it can taint the flavour of your cakes or cookies.

Cream of tartar – This is used to stabilize whipped egg whites and give them volume.

Yeast – This can be either fresh or dried. There is much debate about which gives the better flavour, but from personal experience I would say there is little to choose between the two. Supermarkets with in-store bakeries will often offer fresh yeast to customers for free or for a nominal charge. If you do manage to buy fresh yeast, cut it into small 30g/1oz blocks, wrap in cling film/plastic wrap and freeze for up to 3 months so that you have a ready supply. The recipes in this book are made with fast action dried yeast, which can be replaced with fresh yeast if desired. (As a rough guide, use twice the amount of fresh yeast to dried yeast and crumble the fresh yeast before use.) Note that I do not add the fast action yeast directly to the dry ingredients, as instructed on the packet, but prefer to reconstitute it with water first, as explained in the recipes.

Dairy Products

Butter (salted) – Commonly used in cakes and cookies and gives a rich taste to baking. It is preferable to use butter in biscuit recipes and also essential to use butter in recipes that call for melted butter.

Butter (unsalted) – Butter that has had no salt added to it. This is frequently used in baking and can be substituted for salted butter in recipes if you wish to reduce the salt content of your baking.

Butter substitutes/margarines – Many spreads and butter substitutes are not suitable for baking, so always check the information on them. Some margarines are suitable for cooking and can be used instead of butter in some cake recipes if you wish.

Buttermilk – This milk does not actually contain any butter but is thicker than normal milk and has a slightly sour taste. It can be added to cake mixtures or used in place of milk to make buttermilk pancakes.

Clotted cream – This rich, thick, yellow cream is made by heating unpasteurized cow's milk. It is the perfect accompaniment to scones and jam and is also used in cheesecakes and to fill sandwich cakes. The cream is very rich and therefore should be saved for special occasions or treats.

Double/heavy cream – This is a thick cream, which is often whisked to soft or stiff peaks. It is a common ingredient in cheesecakes. It can be piped into decorations on cakes and used to fill meringues, cakes and choux pastry. Take care not to overwhip or it will end up curdling and having buttery lumps in it.

Greek yogurt – A very thick, rich, natural yogurt that can be added to cakes to keep them moist.

Natural/plain yogurt – A plain thin yogurt that can be added to cakes to keep them moist.

Single/light cream – This thin cream cannot be whipped. It can be served to pour over puddings.

Sour cream – This cream has a slightly sour taste and can be used in baking. It is excellent added to cake mixtures, resulting in a moist cake when baked. If you do not have sour cream, you can make your own by adding 1 tablespoon lemon juice to 250ml/9fl oz/1 cup double/heavy, single/light or whipping cream. The cream will thicken when the lemon juice is added and stirred.

Whipping cream – Thicker than single/light cream but lighter in texture than double/heavy cream, this cream can be whipped only to soft peaks. It can be piped into decorations on cakes and used to fill meringues, cakes and choux pastry.

Eggs

Unless otherwise stated, all the recipes in this book use large hens' eggs. Use the freshest eggs available, ideally organic or free-range. Eggs from chickens that have had a better diet will have golden yolks, and you will really notice the difference in the colour of sponge cakes if you use top-quality eggs. Use eggs at room temperature rather than chilled for the best results.

Duck eggs can be substituted in recipes but are generally larger and richer than hens' eggs. Generally speaking, substitute two duck eggs for three large hens' eggs.

Sugars & Other Sweeteners

Brown sugar – This is either a light (a golden-coloured) or a dark (a rich dark brown) soft sugar that contains molasses. The difference in colour is determined by the quantity of molasses the sugar contains. Store in an airtight container to stop it drying out.

Caster/superfine sugar – A fine white granular sugar, ideal for cakes and biscuits.

Fondant icing sugar – This icing sugar has added glucose and sets with a glossy finish, making it perfect for icing cupcakes and fondant fancies.

Golden icing sugar – This has the same uses as icing sugar but is unrefined and is therefore a pale brown colour, rather than pure white. It has a slightly caramel taste and can be substituted in place of icing sugar.

Granulated sugar – This is a coarse white sugar. It is mainly used in drinks. It can be used in baking recipes, but best results are obtained by using finer caster sugar.

Honey – A natural sweetener that can be used to sweeten cakes and biscuits. It can be opaque (set) or clear.

Icing/powdered sugar – A fine powdered sugar that can be mixed with water to make a runny icing/frosting to decorate cakes and biscuits. This sugar is often sifted over cakes in a light dusting to decorate them.

Muscovado sugar – A brown sugar with a molasses flavour, also known as Barbados or moist sugar. It comes in light and dark versions and can be a bit lumpy, so crush any lumps before using. Store in an airtight container to prevent it drying out.

Substitute sugars – There are a variety of sugar substitutes available for people suffering from illnesses such as diabetes. They vary in quality and taste. Some have a very strong taste and can taint the delicate flavour of cakes. There are varying opinions on whether sugar substitutes are better or worse than simply using a lesser quantity of ordinary sugar in recipes. Not all sugar substitutes are suitable for baking and you should check the packaging. Always seek medical advice on whether sugar substitutes are suitable for you.

Flavourings, Dried Fruits & Nuts

Chocolate – It is always preferable to use good-quality chocolate for its intensity of flavour. However, dark/bittersweet chocolate with a high cocoa content such as 70 per cent is not cheap, and so is best reserved for those recipes in which it will really make a difference. For other recipes, plain/semisweet chocolate with a cocoa content of around 40 per cent is fine and will still give a wonderful result.

To make chocolate curls for decoration, rub a bar of chocolate against a coarse cheese grater for short curls; alternatively, shave a vegetable peeler along a bar of chocolate for longer curls. White, milk and dark chocolate can be chopped and added to cake mixtures and biscuit/cookie dough for extra flavour and texture.

Citrus – Juices and zests of lemons, limes and oranges are used frequently in this book. The finely grated zest can be added to cake mixture or biscuit/cookie dough and the juice can be heated with icing/powdered sugar to make a tangy drizzle to pour over cakes.

Culinary lavender – Dried lavender buds (stalks removed) that are pesticide free can be used to add a wonderful floral scent to cakes and biscuits. Buy in delis or online.

Dried fruits – Dried apricots, sultanas, raisins and currants can be added to cake mixtures to give a rich fruity flavour. They can either be used in their dried form or can be rehydrated in water, tea or alcohol. Generally, soaked fruits will increase the cooking time required as they add extra moisture to the cake.

Glacé/candied cherries – These come in two colours: either bright red or a natural dark red. They can be added to cake mixtures or be used as decoration.

Nuts – A wide variety of nuts are used throughout this book. Nuts can be used whole, chopped or even ground into nut pastes. They can be added to cake mixtures to add flavour and texture and also to biscuits/cookies. Ground almonds can be used in place of plain/all-purpose flour in some recipes and a few drops of almond extract will add a wonderful flavour to cakes. Nuts keep well if stored in airtight containers. Use by their best-before date.

Spices – A variety of spices, both whole and ground, are used throughout this book. Ground cinnamon, mixed/pumpkin pie spice, cardamom, nutmeg and ginger are all wonderful for adding flavour to cakes, biscuits and desserts. These spices are available from supermarkets and wholefood shops. They should be stored in airtight containers and used before the best-before date, otherwise they can lose the intensity of their flavour.

Vanilla or vanilla bean powder or paste – Vanilla extract or essence will give a good vanilla flavour in baking and can be added to cake mixtures and cookie doughs. However, the flavour you get from using vanilla pods/beans is far better. To remove the seeds from a vanilla pod, place the pod on a chopping board and use a sharp knife to cut the pod in half lengthways. Scrape out the seeds from the inside of each half of the pod using a teaspoon. The leftover pod, if not needed for the recipe, can be placed in a jar of caster/superfine sugar to make vanilla sugar or can be added to fruit sauces for a wonderful vanilla aroma.

Violet and Rose syrup and liqueurs – Violet and rose flavourings give cakes and biscuits a delicate floral perfume and can be added to cake mixtures or to whipped creams, icings/frostings or buttercreams to fill cakes, biscuits/cookies or choux pastry. Rose and violet syrups are available in specialist food stores and violet and rose liqueur can be found on the internet.

Baking Equipment

Here is a basic list of the kitchen equipment you will need to make most of the cakes and cookies in this book.

- ☆ 2 sandwich cake tins
- ☆ loaf tin
- ☆ 20cm/8in or 23cm/9in springform cake tin
- ☆ 12-hole bun tin and/or muffin tin
- ☆ paper cake/muffin cases/liners
- ☆ mixing bowl
- ☆ scissors

- ☆ baking parchment
- ☆ foil
- ☆ fine-mesh sieve
- ☆ wire rack
- ☆ weighing scales or cups
- ☆ electric hand mixer or wooden spoon (to use for beating)/balloon whisk (to use for whisking)

- ☆ spatula
- ☆ large metal spoon
- ☆ oven gloves
- ☆ pastry brush
- ☆ citrus peeler, zester and grater
- ☆ lemon squeezer
- ☆ icing/frosting bag and nozzles/tips

Cake Tins & Baking Trays

There is a wide variety of cake tins and baking trays available from kitchen shops or on the internet. The following types are used in this book:

Angel food cake tin – A very deep ring pan with sloping sides and a narrow hole in the centre used for making angel food cake: a light, tall, meringue-like sponge cake.

Baking tin – A rectangular tin with deep sides, perfect for tray bakes and slices.

Baking tray/sheet – A rectangular tray used for baking cookies and meringues.

Bun tin – A baking tray with 12 round holes to take cake cases/liners for cupcakes.

Bundt tin – A ring tin with a decorative pattern embossed in it, which creates a patterned cake. A ring tin can be substituted for a bundt tin.

Flan tin – A round tin with a fluted edge, deep sides and a removable base.

Flowerpots – Clean, new mini terracotta flowerpots make novel cake tins. Wash before use and line with cake cases/liners or baking parchment.

Friand tin – A small oval tin (about 6cm/2¼in in length), often with a decorative pattern in the base.

Heart-shaped cake tin – Either deep with straight sides or shallow with a fluted edge like a flan tin. Either version is suitable for the heart cake in this book.

Loaf tin/mini loaf tin – Small, deep rectangular tins used for making loaf cakes or mini loaf cakes, depending on the size. These pans can also be used to make bread.

Madeleine tin – A tin with usually 12 shell-shaped depressions.

Muffin tin/mini muffin tin – A baking tray with 12 large deep or small shallow round holes to take muffin or mini muffin cases/liners.

Rectangular cake tin – A rectangular deep tin, similar to a baking tin.

Ring tin – Either a one-piece tube-shaped tin, as used for a savarin, or a springform tin with a separate funnel centre, which can be used together to create a ring shape.

Sandwich cake tins – Shallow round cake tins used in pairs to make sandwich cakes, such as Victoria sponges.

Sponge flan tin – A round tin with a fluted edge, deep sides and a raised base in the centre. When the cake is turned out, you have a cake with high sides and a cut-away section in the centre which you can fill with a variety of fruits and creamy fillings.

Springform cake tin – A cake tin with sides that clip around a base. This type of tin is useful for a wide variety of cakes, including cheesecakes.

Square cake tin – A deep square tin, usually with a loose bottom.

Swiss/jelly roll tin – A rectangular cake tin with shallow sides used for Swiss/jelly rolls and roulades.

Lining Tins & Trays

Most tins will need to be lined as well as greased to stop food sticking to them. Sometimes just the base needs covering with baking parchment ('base-lined'), for which you simply need to stand the tin on a sheet of baking parchment and draw around it with a pencil, then cut out the marked shape. Grease the base of the tin (see page 13) and place the piece of paper on the greased surface, smoothing it into position. If you are using a raised-base flan tin, only the raised area needs to be covered.

At other times the sides of cake tins will also need to be covered ('lined'). The technique for this varies according to the type of tin or tray, as follows:

Shallow square or rectangular tins – Cut a sheet of baking parchment slightly larger than the size of your tin. Grease the base and sides of the tin with butter. Place the tin in the centre of the paper and, using small scissors, cut diagonally from the corners of the paper to the corresponding corners of the tin. Place the paper in the greased tin and overlap the cut corners so that the paper fits neatly.

Round tins/deep square and rectangular tins – Cut a long strip of baking parchment 2.5cm/1in deeper than the tin and long enough to go all around the sides. Fold the strip along its length so that the extra 2.5cm/1in is on one side of the fold. Snip small incisions at frequent intervals along this side of the strip up to the fold line. Cut a circle or square/rectangle of baking parchment the size of the bottom of the tin. Grease the base and sides of the tin with butter. Press the strip of baking parchment around the inside of the sides of the tin so that the snipped fringe lies flat on the base of the tin. Continue until all the paper is in place and the paper overlaps slightly at the join. Place the baking parchment circle or square over the fringe to cover the base.

Other Equipment

In addition to a good supply of tins and trays, the following items will be of help.

Bain marie – This is a water bath, which enables you to cook delicate dishes such as cheesecakes in the oven without the dish receiving direct heat. Wrap the cheesecake in its tin in cling film/plastic wrap to make sure it is watertight, then place the tin in a baking tin half-filled with water. The cheesecake in its bain marie can then be placed in the oven to cook.

Baking parchment – Culinary paper with a non-stick finish, which eliminates the need to grease the paper. Use for lining tins and trays.

Double boiler – A set of two saucepans, one containing the ingredient to be melted on top of the other containing simmering water. Ideal for melting chocolate and butter.

Basic Baking Methods

Different types of cakes and cookies use different methods, which are explained below.

All-in-one method – All the ingredients are placed in a bowl and mixed together, making these the easiest types of cakes and cookies to make.

Creaming method – This can be used for either cakes or cookies. At the start of preparing the cake or cookie mixture, the butter and sugar are beaten together with an electric hand mixer or wooden spoon until they are light and creamy. This process adds air to the mixture, which helps cakes to rise and binds cookie dough together well.

Melted method – In this method, the wet ingredients (butters and fats, syrups, etc.) are heated together until the butter or fat has melted. This liquid is then stirred into the dry ingredients (flours, sugars, spices and raising agents). This method makes chewy cookies and is also used for making gingerbread.

Refrigerator dough – This cookie dough is made either using the creaming method or the rubbing-in method. The dough is then chilled in the refrigerator before being either cut into slices (from a preformed cylinder of the dough) or rolled out and the cookies stamped out with cutters.

Rubbing-in method – This method requires you to rub the fat into the dry ingredients with your fingertips until the mixture resembles fine breadcrumbs. The mixture is then bound together with liquid, usually milk, for scones, some biscuits and pastry or left dry for crumble toppings.

Whisked egg-white method – Eggs are separated and the whites are whisked to stiff peaks and then folded into the cake or biscuit/cookie mixture to add air to the mixture. This method is used for flourless cakes, some extra-light sponge cakes and drop biscuits.

Whisking-in method – Air is added to the mixture by whisking whole eggs and sugar together until they have doubled in size and are light and creamy. Flour and flavourings are then folded into the mixture. This method is mainly used in Swiss/jelly rolls and roulades and other fatless sponges to give a light result. The whisking is best done with an electric mixer, as whisking with a hand whisk can take some time.

Other Cooking Terms

Greasing – This is rubbing the inside of a cake tin or baking tray with butter. It is important that every part of the tin's surface is covered, otherwise your cakes or cookies may stick. If you are greasing a decorative tin, such as a bundt tin, it is best to melt the butter and apply it with a pastry brush. Note that even when a tin has been greased it is still a good idea to slide a knife around the edge of the tin before turning the cake out or, in the case of a springform tin, releasing the clip and removing the cake.

Melting chocolate – Put pieces of broken chocolate in the top part of a double boiler or in a heatproof bowl set over a pan of simmering water (but not touching the water) and stir occasionally until they have melted into a thick cream. Chocolate can also be melted in a microwave: put the broken pieces of chocolate in a microwave-proof bowl and cook on full power for 1–1½ minutes, stopping every 10–20 seconds to stir the chocolate to prevent it burning. (You may need longer than this time depending on the quantity of chocolate you are melting or on the power of your microwave.) Note that the microwave method is unsuited to white chocolate.

If you have a range cooker, you can melt chocolate by placing it in a heatproof bowl and placing it at the back of the range for 30 minutes.

Melting butter – This can be done as for chocolate. If using a microwave, allow about 1 minute on full power, depending on quantity.

Melting butter and chocolate – This can be done as for chocolate. If using a microwave, allow 1–1½ minutes on medium power, stirring every 10–20 seconds.

Preheating – It is important that an oven is allowed to heat up to the correct temperature before food is put inside to bake. If it is not at full temperature, this may affect the baking time. An oven will usually take about 10 minutes to come to the set temperature.

Softened – This term is primarily used to refer to butter, and it means that the product should be brought to room temperature before being used. This is essential when creaming butter, because cold butter from the refrigerator is difficult to cream and may result in lumps of butter in your cake mixture or icing/frosting.

Whipping cream to peaks – Double/heavy cream can be whipped to soft or stiff peaks and is perfect as a filling for pavlovas and flans with fresh fruit. Whipping cream, which has a slightly lower fat content, gives similar, but lighter, results. To whip cream, put the cream in a clean, dry bowl and whip with an electric hand mixer or a whisk until the cream is stiff enough to stand in soft peaks (which flop slightly) or stiff peaks (which are very firm) when you lift the beaters/whisk out of the mixture.

Whisking egg whites to peaks – To whisk egg whites, put the whites in a clean, dry bowl and whisk with an electric hand mixer or a whisk until the whites are stiff enough to stand in soft peaks (which flop slightly) or stiff peaks (which are very firm) when you lift the beaters or whisk out of the mixture. Note that if you have used the mixer or whisk earlier in the recipe, you must wash and dry it thoroughly before using it to whisk the whites.

Baking for Those With Allergies

Nowadays I often find myself cooking for people with allergies and although this can seem daunting at first there are many gluten free and dairy free products now that can be easily substituted into recipes. The recipes in this book are marked as gluten free, dairy free and egg free to help you make easy recipe selections.

If you are baking for a coeliac it is important to check for wheat in some products that you would not naturally associate with cereals. Manufacturers have improved in recent years and now generally use rice flour in place of wheat flour but do make sure you read the ingredients label carefully for any allergy ingredients. Products to be careful of are chocolates (which can contain milk powders, some of which contain wheat), cocoa, dried fruits and glacé/candied cherries, as anti-sticking agents used to commonly contain wheat. Also check any alcohol you are using is gluten free as some colourants can contain wheat traces.

Trouble Shooting

If your cakes or cookies don't look or taste quite right, it may be there was a problem in their making or baking. Use the list below to identify and remedy the problem.

Cookie/biscuit dough is too sticky or wet – Add extra sifted flour, a little at a time, until the dough becomes firmer and easier to handle. Alternatively, wrap the dough in cling film/plastic wrap and place it in the refrigerator for 30 minutes before cooking.

Cake mixture curdles when you add the eggs – Curdling is the separating of eggs and the butter not mixing together properly. Although this can look serious, it will not generally affect the finished product and is easy to remedy: just whisk in 1–2 tablespoons flour.

Cookie/biscuit dough is too crumbly – Add 1–2 tablespoons milk or water gradually until the dough comes together and can be formed into a ball.

Cake starts to brown too much – Cover the top with a piece of baking parchment or turn the temperature down and cook for a little longer than the stated time.

Cake sinks when you take it out of the oven –
There are several potential causes of a sinking cake: the cake may not have been baked for long enough; the oven temperature may be too low; the cake tin may be too small, meaning that the mixture will be deeper and so may require more cooking; any raising agent used, such as self-raising flour or baking powder, may have been out of date.

Cake doesn't rise – There are several potential causes of a flat cake: the cake tin may be too large, which will give a flatter-than-expected cake; the mixture may have been over-beaten; the air may have been knocked out of the mixture when the flour was folded in; any raising agent, such as self-raising flour or baking powder, may have been out of date.

Cake sticks in the tin – The cake tin was not greased properly. Make sure that every part of the tin is covered with a thin layer of butter.

Cake has a crumbly or dry texture – The cake does not contain enough liquid or the eggs and sugar have not been creamed together for long enough. Creaming should take 3–4 minutes with an electric hand mixer and longer with a wooden spoon.

Icing/frosting melts when applied – Icing must be applied to completely cooled cakes and biscuits. If you are in a hurry to ice and the weather is fine, place the cake or cookies on a wire rack in the garden under a mesh food cover, which will speed up the cooling.

Oven Types & Range Cookers

There is a large selection of ovens available, all of which will have slightly different cooking styles. Over time, you will get to know your oven and how best to use it for baking.

Oven Types

Even within the same type of oven, temperatures, cooking styles and heat distribution can vary. For best results you should buy an oven temperature thermometer, which will enable you to check the actual temperature of your oven and so that you can adjust your dials accordingly if they are not at the correct temperatures.

Whatever oven type you use, towards the end of the specified cooking time you should regularly check to see whether the cake or cookies are done. The more you cook with your oven, the more familiar you will become with its temperature and where to position cakes and cookies within the oven to achieve the best results.

Electric ovens have a more consistent heat within the oven itself.

Fan-assisted ovens generally cook at a higher temperature then regular ovens, so when using them it is advisable to reduce the oven temperature by 10°C/50°F.

Gas ovens cook with a flame and, depending on the location of the flame, are generally hotter at the bottom of the oven than the top.

Range Cookers

With a range cooker you have very limited control over the temperature, and if your range cooker is like mine, the oven temperature varies from day to day depending on how much I have cooked and the weather outside. It is worth investing in an oven thermometer so that you can know the actual temperature of each of the ovens.

A four-door range cooker has a designated baking oven. This is a moderately hot oven that is ideal for baking cakes and cookies and can be used in the same way as a regular oven. If you have a two-door range cooker, you will need to invest in a cool shelf to use in the roasting oven. The roasting oven is generally very hot (about 200°C/400°F) and without using a cool shelf it will harm cakes. Inserting the cool shelf will lower the temperature in the roasting oven below the shelf. Although you can buy specialist cake baking kits for range cookers, I usually bake using normal cake tins without any difficulties. It is best to buy good-quality tins, however, as cheaper tins will warp in the heat of a range cooker. The side of the cooker that is nearest to the burner will be hotter, and therefore it is important to rotate your cake tin or baking tray 180 degrees halfway through cooking to ensure even browning.

For cakes that take over 1 hour to cook, it is advisable to bake them in the roasting oven for 15–20 minutes and then transfer them to the simmering oven for 1–2 hours until the cake is cooked, testing with both the skewer and finger-pressing tests (see page 6).

For quick-cooking cakes, bake in the roasting oven below a cool shelf. Watch the cakes carefully and rotate if they start to brown too much on one side or cover with baking parchment. Depending on the temperature of your range cooker, you may need to reduce the cooking time.

Range cooker temperatures do not drop when you open the oven doors, so until you are familiar with the temperatures of your oven it is best to check the progress of cakes or biscuits on a regular basis. Each range cooker is different and you will need to get to know where it cooks hottest. In my range cooker, if I am making a pair of sponge cakes, I bake both on the same shelf and swap over from front to back halfway through.

Although you can vary the temperature of your range cooker by controlling the flow of fuel to the cooker, the temperature increase will not usually be instant. With my cooker, it takes at least 2 hours to boost the temperature, so forward planning is required.

Range cookers can be temperamental, and in the summer you may need a second cooker to cook on to avoid having a boiling hot kitchen, but they are very much part of a home and can be used for drying cloths and warming mugs of tea, as well as providing cosy warmth for a sleepy cat. It is said that once you have owned a range cooker you will never be without one, and I think that is probably true.

Freezing Cakes & Cookies

* To freeze cakes, leave them to cool completely and then double-wrap in cling film/plastic wrap and place in the freezer. Most cakes can be frozen for up to 3 months. For best results, prepare the cake filling after defrosting, rather than icing and filling before freezing.

* Freeze brownies or slices in one piece. Wrap in cling film/plastic wrap and then cover in foil. They will freeze for up to 3 months. Defrost completely and then cut into slices to serve.

- Freeze cookies at the uncooked stage, rather than when cooked. The dough will freeze for about 1 month. Once the dough has defrosted, follow the cooking instructions.
- For refrigerator cookies, roll the dough into a cylinder and double-wrap in cling film/plastic wrap before freezing. Defrost completely, then cut into slices and cook.
- For drop cookies or ball cookies, form the dough into balls and wrap individually in cling film/plastic wrap before freezing. When ready to cook, defrost completely and place the balls on a tray, then cook according to the recipe instructions.
- For cut-out cookies, roll the prepared dough into a ball and double-wrap in cling film/plastic wrap before freezing. To use, defrost completely, then roll out to the required thickness using a rolling pin, cut out your cookies and bake.

Storage

Apart from fruit cakes, which keep well and improve with age, cakes are best eaten on the day or day after you make them. However, if you do want to store a cake for a little longer (though 2–3 days is the maximum I would recommend for freshness), note:

- Leave cakes to cool completely before storing or wrapping them.
- Wrap un-iced/frosted cakes in greaseproof paper or cling film/plastic wrap.
- Place iced/frosted cakes in cake tins or other containers with tight-fitting lids.
- Store any cakes or cookies containing fresh cream or fresh dairy products such as cream cheese in the refrigerator.
- Store biscuits/cookies in an airtight container; they will generally keep for at least 1 week.

Packaging

Cakes and cookies make perfect gifts for friends and family. Cakes can be packaged in tins tied with ribbons or be placed in wicker baskets lined with a napkin and wrapped in clear florist's wrap tied with a bow. A wide variety of clear and coloured plastic bags are available, which can be filled with freshly baked cookies and tied with a ribbon.

Why not give a tin filled with your favourite cookies and small cakes as a present? Cookies can also be used to decorate presents, so try some Gift Tag Cookies on page 244.

Finishing Techniques

While most cakes and cookies are delicious on their own with a cup of tea, adding a finishing touch in the form of icing/frosting or just a simple dusting of icing/powdered sugar can transform many of the cakes and cookies in this book.

Drizzling – Using either melted chocolate or a runny icing/frosting made with icing/powdered sugar, water and any flavouring of your choice, drizzle over the cookie or biscuit using a fork to make thin lines, flicking the fork backwards and forwards between your fingers quickly to make thin patterns. Alternatively, put the chocolate or icing/frosting in a piping bag with a small plain nozzle/tip and pipe backwards and forwards over your cake or biscuits to make a more regular pattern than with a fork. Allow the icing or chocolate to set before serving.

Dusting – This is the simplest method of decorating. Place icing/powdered sugar in a sieve and tap the side of the sieve gently over the cake or cookies so that they are covered in a light and even layer of icing sugar. For a cake containing spices, you can sift icing sugar with 2 teaspoons ground cinnamon added, while for a chocolate cake combine equal quantities of cocoa powder and icing sugar to dust over. For more fancy dusting decoration, place a doily or a cake decoration template on top of your cake, dust with icing sugar and then carefully remove the doily or template to leave a pretty pattern on the top of the cake.

Icing – Plain biscuits such as simple shortbread and rolled-out cookies that do not spread during cooking have a flat surface, as do cupcakes and muffins, which are ideal for covering with a runny icing/frosting. Use a thick but not too stiff icing made with icing/powdered sugar, water and liquid food colouring or use fondant icing sugar for a shiny, glossy finish. Place 1 teaspoon of the icing/frosting in the centre of the biscuit or cake and spread it out to the edges using a round-bladed knife, adding more icing if you need it. Decorate with sprinkles, glitter or sweets/candies for an effective but simple finish. Allow the icing to set before serving.

Piping – Whether you are piping fresh cream, buttercream or royal icing, place the icing bag in the palm of your hand with the nozzle/tip pointing towards the base of your wrist. Fold 2.5cm/1in around the top of the bag over your fingers. Use a spatula or spoon to fill the bag with icing/frosting. Once filled, pull the folded-over top of the bag up and twist together to squeeze the icing into the bag tightly. This will ensure that you have even pressure when you ice. Using a large star or plain nozzle, you can easily cover the top of a cupcake with a large swirl of icing, then decorate it with some sugar sprinkles to create a very impressive effect that is actually easy to achieve. Different shaped nozzles will create different patterns of icing. The best idea is to make some buttercream and then experiment with each of your nozzles, using them upright and at an angle to see the different effects you can achieve. There are many wonderful books on icing techniques and you will find local courses on cake decorating if you wish to develop your skills further. Piped icing can be used to decorate both cakes and biscuits/cookies.

Icings & Decorations

Buttercream icing/frosting – Cakes can be sandwiched and topped (or even completely coated) with many varieties of buttercream or cream cheese icing. You can vary the flavours easily by adding dissolved coffee, cocoa powder or citrus zest and juice.

Rolled fondant icing/Marzipan – Traditional celebration fruit cakes are covered with marzipan and rolled fondant icing (sold as ready-to-roll or in pre-rolled-out sheets) and then decorated. For best results, the cake will need to be covered with a thin layer of warm apricot jam/jelly to allow the marzipan to stick; the jam layer is then repeated on the marzipan so that the rolled icing sticks when laid on top of the marzipan. Roll out the marzipan and icing on an icing/powdered sugar-dusted surface. To lift the marzipan or rolled icing on to the cake, place your cake as close as possible to where you have rolled out your icing to reduce the lifting distance, place the rolling pin in the centre of the icing and then fold the icing in half over the rolling pin. Lift the rolling pin and position it over the centre of the cake, then gently unfold the icing so that it covers the top and sides of the cake. Using the palms of your hands, gently flatten and smooth the icing around the sides. Any excess icing sugar can simply be brushed away with your hands.

Royal icing – This icing is made from icing/powdered sugar and egg whites and will set hard. It is usually used over a layer of marzipan, particularly for Christmas and wedding cakes because it preserves both well. The icing is spread over the sides and top of the cake and then can either be smoothed with a spatula or rubber scraper or, for Christmas cakes, can be lifted into snow peaks using a fork. This icing can also be used in piping bags to pipe decoration on to cakes and cookies and is good for writing celebration messages on cakes or cookies.

Whipped cream – A simple method of finishing cakes is to fill them with fresh cream and fruit, such as strawberries or raspberries, or with a good-quality jam/jelly or lemon curd.

Decorations – Even the most plainly iced/frosted cake can be transformed into something spectacular with just a few decorations. Most supermarkets and cake-decorating shops have a wide selection of cake decorations, including edible silver balls, hundreds and thousands, chocolate sprinkles and chocolate chips. In addition, sweets/candies can form ideal cake decorations, and are very popular with children. Plastic-backed floral foam pads can be filled with fresh flowers and placed on top of a fondant-iced cake, though it is important to ensure that the foam does not touch the icing itself. Brightly coloured ribbons can be wrapped around cakes and tied in bows or threaded through holes made in cookies before baking, while edible glitter adds the perfect twinkling finish to any cake or cookie. Ideal for a finishing touch on cakes or desserts, chocolate curls can be made easily by grating the chocolate on a coarse grater for short curls or by pulling a vegetable peeler along the side of the chocolate for longer curls.

Decorating Equipment

Often the prospect of decorating a cake can seem daunting, but with a few simple pieces of equipment and some practice you will be amazed by the results you can achieve. If you are not used to icing/frosting, prepare a batch of buttercream or royal icing and spend some time experimenting with piping different shapes, piping patterns around the edge of a plate and writing words and names. Do not worry if you cannot master all types of icing skills – just find a method that you feel comfortable with and use that for your cakes.

Cake boards – These silver or gold boards come in rounds, squares or rectangles of many sizes. These are ideal for serving cakes. A plate can be used as an alternative.

Cake turntable – Although not essential, it can be useful to have a turntable to place your cake on when decorating. This enables you to rotate your cake and ice evenly.

Candles – It is always useful to have a pack of birthday candles in your store cupboard.

Food colourings and food pastes – Liquid food colourings are available in most supermarkets. As a minimum, blue, yellow and red colourings are required, which you can combine to make other colours. The colours from food colourings are not as vibrant as the colour you will obtain from using colouring pastes, which are available from most cake decorating shops. Food colouring pastes are best for colouring rolled fondant icing as they are easier to mix in than liquid colourings.

Icing/piping bags – Fabric icing bags come in several different sizes and can be used with large icing nozzles/tips directly or with small icing nozzles fitted to the bag with a coupler (normally sold with the bag). Fabric bags can retain some moisture when washed and should be used only when they are completely dry, otherwise the icing can be affected. Disposable icing bags are plastic bags that you fill with icing and can then dispose of when you have finished decorating. They are ideal when you are icing with several different colours of icing, as it saves washing and drying a fabric bag between uses. You can also make icing bags yourself using folded greaseproof paper or baking parchment.

Icing/piping nozzles/tips – It is worth investing in a set of icing nozzles as these will enable you to decorate in many different ways. The sizes and styles of nozzles required for decoration in this book are: 3mm/⅛in, 13mm/½in, 15mm/⅝in and 2cm/¾in plain and 6mm/¼in, 13mm/½in and 15mm/⅝in star.

Palette knife – Palette knives are used to spread out icing/frosting smoothly on cakes and cookies. If you do not have one of these, you can use a round-bladed knife.

Rolling pin – For rolling out ready-to-roll fondant icing.

* Always slice on a level surface using a sharp serrated knife. Specific cake slices with a blade and handle on each side are available and ensure level cutting.
* If your cake is not level, use a sharp knife to cut the top of the cake level if you are going to ice it. The icing will cover the cut-away part of the cake and leave you with a perfect finish.
* When cutting cakes to serve, the first slice is always the most difficult to remove. Cut two lines meeting in the centre of the cake. Slide the knife or a palette knife under the slice of cake and gently lift away.
* Before filling a cake, place the bottom layer of the cake on your desired serving plate or cake board. Place a little of the filling on the plate and place the bottom cake on top. This will secure your cake in place and will ensure that it does not move if you need to transport the cake.

* When filling a cake, place the filling in the centre of the cake and, using a palette knife or spatula, gently work the filling out to the edges of the cake.
* When icing the sides of a cake, place the icing/frosting on top of the cake and, using a palette knife, smooth small amounts of icing from the top of the cake and down the sides, working quickly so that you cover as much of the sides of the cake as possible.
* When icing a cake on top of a wire rack, place a sheet of foil or baking parchment under the wire rack to collect the icing that runs off. If there are no crumbs in it, the icing can be reused on the cake if necessary.

RECIPE 245 | VIOLET MERINGUES

BASIC RECIPES

FROSTED ROSE PETALS

MAKES 20   **PREPARATION TIME** 30 minutes

**20 unblemished, fresh and
   pesticide-free rose petals**

**I large egg white
5 tbsp caster/superfine sugar**

1   Remove the bottom point of each petal, where it joins the stem, as this has a rather bitter flavour.
2   Whisk the egg white well with a whisk in a shallow bowl. Place the caster sugar on a plate. Using
    a paintbrush, brush the egg white over the rose petals one at a time. Place the petals in the caster
    sugar and cover lightly, ensuring that each petal is completely covered in sugar.
3   Transfer to a wire rack or a sheet of baking parchment and repeat with all the remaining petals.
    Leave to dry in a warm place for 24 hours. These can be stored for 2 days in a tin.

CHOCOLATE GANACHE

MAKES 250g/9oz   **PREPARATION TIME** 10 minutes

**200g/7oz plain/semisweet chocolate
75ml/2½fl oz/⅓ cup double/heavy cream**

30g/1oz butter

1   Place all the ingredients in a double boiler or a bowl set over (but not touching) a pan of simmering
    water and stir until melted. Alternatively, place the ingredients in a microwave-proof bowl and melt
    on high power for 1 minute, then stir and heat again at 10-second intervals until the chocolate
    has melted.

GLACÉ ICING

MAKES 200g/7oz   **PREPARATION TIME** 5 minutes

200g/7oz/1⅓ cups icing/powdered sugar, sifted

1   Place the sifted icing sugar in a bowl. Gradually add 1–2 tablespoons cold water, while stirring with
    a large metal spoon, until you have a smooth, thick icing/frosting. Add a few drops of liquid food
    colouring, if you wish.

LAVENDER SUGAR

MAKES 1 jar   **PREPARATION TIME** 10 minutes

1   Layer caster/superfine sugar with pesticide-free lavender flowers in a jam jar in alternate layers. Seal the jar and leave for 2 weeks to infuse. You can use the sugar with the lavender still in or sieve the flowers out if you prefer. (For a more intense lavender flavour, grind the sugar and flowers using a pestle and mortar.)

SHORTCRUST PASTRY

MAKES 550g/1lb 4oz   **PREPARATION TIME** 10 minutes, plus chilling

350g/12oz/2¼ cups plain/all-purpose flour, sifted   **175g/6oz chilled butter, chopped**
1 tsp salt

1   Place the flour and salt in a large mixing bowl and rub the butter into the flour with your fingertips until the mixture resembles fine breadcrumbs. Add 2–3 tablespoons chilled water a little at a time, mixing with a flat-bladed knife until you have a soft dough.
2   Bring the dough together in a ball with your hands and wrap in baking parchment or cling film/plastic wrap. Chill in the refrigerator for at least 1 hour.

VANILLA BUTTERCREAM

MAKES 350g/12oz   **PREPARATION TIME** 10 minutes

225g/8oz/1½ cups icing/powdered sugar, sifted
125g/4½oz butter, softened

1 tsp vanilla extract
2 tbsp milk

1   Place all the ingredients in a mixing bowl and beat with an electric hand mixer or wooden spoon for 4–5 minutes to form a light and creamy icing/frosting.

VARIATIONS To make Chocolate Buttercream, replace 30g/1oz icing sugar with the same amount of sifted cocoa powder. To make Coffee Buttercream, replace the vanilla extract with 1 tablespoon instant coffee granules dissolved in 1 tablespoon hot water and cooled. To make Rose or Violet Buttercream, replace the vanilla extract with 1 tablespoon rose or violet syrup.

ROSE PETAL PASTE

MAKES 2–3 tbsp   **PREPARATION TIME** 10 minutes

40–50 fresh and pesticide-free
   rose petals

1 tbsp rose syrup or rosewater
2 tbsp icing/powdered sugar

1   Remove the bottom point of each petal where it joins the stem, as this has a rather bitter flavour. Place the petals in a blender and chop finely. Add the rose syrup and sugar and blitz again. Use this paste soon after making it, as the petals will discolour over time.

ROYAL ICING

MAKES 900g/2lb   **PREPARATION TIME** 15 minutes

900g/2lb/6 cups icing/powdered sugar, sifted
4 large egg whites

1 tsp glycerine

1   Place the sifted icing sugar and egg whites in a large bowl and whisk with an electric hand whisk for 10 minutes until you have a stiff icing/frosting. Add the glycerine and whisk again.

ITALIAN MERINGUE BUTTERCREAM

MAKES enough for 20–24 cupcakes   **PREPARATION TIME** 15 minutes   **COOKING TIME** 5–10 minutes

4 large egg whites
230g/8oz/1¼ cups caster/superfine sugar
90ml/3fl oz/scant ½ cup water

1 tsp vanilla extract
a pinch vanilla salt or white salt
350g/12oz butter, chilled and cut into cubes

1   Whisk the egg whites in a dry mixing bowl to stiff peaks using an electric mixer or whisk.
2   Heat the sugar with the water in a saucepan with the vanilla extract and salt and bring to
    112°C/235°F, measuring using a sugar thermometer.
3   While whisking, slowly pour a thin stream of the sugar syrup into the egg whites, until all of the sugar
    syrup is incorporated. Whisk for a few minutes until the mixture starts to cool.
4   Add the butter, a small cube at a time, and whisk until all the butter is incorporated. Depending on
    the temperature of your room, egg whites and butter, the mixture may seem a little runny. If it does,
    place in the refrigerator for about an hour to firm up. Whisk again and then spoon into a piping bag
    and use according to the recipe instructions.

NUT BUTTERS

MAKES 100g/3½oz   **PREPARATION TIME** 15 minutes

90g/3¼oz/⅔ cup pistachio nuts or
     hazelnuts, toasted

2 tbsp sunflower or coconut oil
3 heaped tbsp icing/powdered sugar

1   Place the nuts, oil and icing sugar in a blender and grind to a smooth paste. Store in a sterilized jar in
    the refrigerator for up to 1 week.

Chapter 1

LARGE CAKES

There is something very special about being able to offer family, friends and visitors a slice of homemade cake still warm from the oven, and it always amazes me that something so delicious can be created so quickly and easily with the simple ingredients of flour, eggs, butter and sugar. Everyone loves cake – whether a traditional Dundee or Battenberg, an indulgent chocolate creation or a refreshing gateau covered with fresh seasonal fruits. From classic favourites, such as Victoria Sandwich, Strawberry & Vanilla Swiss Roll and Lemon Drizzle Cake, to more unusual modern recipes, such as Chocolate & Chilli Pound Cake, Carrot & Courgette Cake and Caramelized Mango Upside-Down Cake and a wide assortment of cakes containing nuts, such as Sticky Toffee Nut Upside-Down Cake and delicious Pistachio Marzipan Ring, there is a cake for everyone in this chapter. So put on your apron and bake a cake today.

001 LEMON DRIZZLE CAKE

PREPARATION TIME 20 minutes **COOKING TIME** 25–30 minutes **SERVES** 8

225g/8oz butter, softened, plus extra
    for greasing
225g/8oz/scant 1 cup caster/superfine sugar
4 large eggs, lightly beaten

225g/8oz/1½ cups self-raising flour, sifted
juice and finely grated zest of 2 lemons
1 heaped tbsp icing/powdered sugar

1 Preheat the oven to 180°C/350°F/gas 4. Grease and line a 20cm/8in springform cake tin.
2 Put the butter and caster sugar in a mixing bowl and beat using an electric hand mixer or wooden spoon until the mixture is light and creamy. Add the eggs gradually, beating after each addition. Add the flour and lemon zest and gently fold them into the mixture, using a large metal spoon. Scrape the mixture into the tin using a spatula.
3 Bake for 25–30 minutes until the cake springs back when pressed lightly and a skewer inserted into the middle of the cake comes out clean.
4 Just before the cake comes out of the oven, heat the lemon juice with the icing sugar in a saucepan until the sugar has dissolved, then boil for 1 minute to create a syrup. Remove the cake from the oven and pour the syrup over the cake. Leave the cake to cool in the tin, then turn out on to a serving plate.

002 LIME & CARDAMOM DRIZZLE CAKE

PREPARATION TIME 20 minutes **COOKING TIME** 25–30 minutes **SERVES** 8

225g/8oz butter, softened, plus extra
    for greasing
225g/8oz/scant 1 cup caster/superfine sugar
4 large eggs, lightly beaten

225g/8oz/1½ cups self-raising flour
1 tsp ground cardamom
juice and finely grated zest of 4 limes
2 tbsp icing/powdered sugar, sifted

1 Preheat the oven to 180°C/350°F/gas 4. Grease and line a 20cm/8in springform cake tin.
2 Put the butter and caster sugar in a mixing bowl and beat using an electric hand mixer or wooden spoon until the mixture is light and creamy. Add the eggs gradually, beating after each addition. Sift in the flour and cardamom and fold them into the mixture with the lime zest, using a large metal spoon. Scrape the mixture into the tin using a spatula.
3 Bake for 25–30 minutes until the cake springs back when pressed lightly and a skewer inserted into the middle of the cake comes out clean.
4 Just before the cake comes out of the oven, heat the lime juice with the icing sugar in a saucepan until the sugar has dissolved, then boil for 1 minute to create a syrup. Remove the cake from the oven and pour the syrup over the cake. Leave the cake to cool in the tin, then turn out on to a serving plate.

003 MADEIRA CAKE

PREPARATION TIME 20 minutes **COOKING TIME** 45–50 minutes **SERVES** 8

225g/8oz butter, softened, plus extra
    for greasing
1 pinch saffron stamens
1 tbsp warm milk
115g/4oz/scant ½ cup caster/superfine sugar
115g/4oz/½ cup light soft brown sugar

4 large eggs, lightly beaten
225g/8oz/1½ cups plain/all-purpose flour
2 tsp baking powder
finely grated zest of 1 lemon,
    1 lime and 1 orange
100g/3½oz/scant ⅔ cup mixed/candied peel

1 Preheat the oven to 180°C/350°F/gas 4. Grease and line a deep 23cm/9in springform cake tin. Put the saffron stamens and the milk in a bowl and leave to infuse for 5 minutes.

2 Put the butter, caster sugar and light brown sugar in a mixing bowl and beat using an electric hand mixer or wooden spoon until the mixture is light and creamy. Add the eggs gradually, beating after each addition. Sift in the flour and baking powder and gently fold them into the mixture with the lemon, lime and orange zests, mixed peel and soaked saffron and milk, using a large metal spoon. Scrape the mixture into the tin using a spatula.

3 Bake for 30 minutes, then turn the temperature down to 170°C/325°F/gas 3 for a further 15–20 minutes until the cake springs back when pressed lightly and a skewer inserted into the middle of the cake comes out clean. Remove the cake from the oven and leave to stand for 5 minutes, then turn out on to a wire rack and leave to cool.

004 MARMALADE & WHISKY CAKE

PREPARATION TIME 20 minutes, plus soaking **COOKING TIME** 35–40 minutes **SERVES** 8

100g/3½oz/½ cup sultanas/golden raisins
3 tbsp whisky
240g/8½oz butter, softened, plus extra
    for greasing
115g/4oz/scant ½ cup caster/superfine sugar
115g/4oz/½ cup dark soft brown sugar

4 large eggs, lightly beaten
225g/8oz/1½ cups self-raising flour, sifted
3 tbsp thin-shred marmalade
finely grated zest of 1 orange
2 tbsp demerara sugar
4 tbsp plain/all-purpose flour, sifted

1 Soak the sultanas in the whisky overnight.

2 Preheat the oven to 180°C/350°F/gas 4. Grease and line a deep 23cm/9in springform cake tin.

3 Put 225g/8oz of the butter, the caster sugar and dark brown sugar in a mixing bowl and beat using an electric hand mixer or wooden spoon until the mixture is light and creamy. Add the eggs gradually, beating after each addition. Add the self-raising flour, marmalade and the soaked sultanas and whisky and gently fold them into the mixture, using a large metal spoon. Scrape the mixture into the tin using a spatula.

4 Put the orange zest, remaining butter, the demerara sugar and plain flour in a mixing bowl and rub together with your fingertips to form a crumble topping. Sprinkle the crumble over the cake mixture.

5 Bake for 35–40 minutes until the cake springs back when pressed lightly and a skewer inserted into the middle of the cake comes out clean. Remove the cake from the oven and leave to stand for 5 minutes, then turn out on to a wire rack and leave to cool.

005 CHERRY CAKE

PREPARATION TIME 20 minutes   **COOKING TIME** 35–40 minutes   **SERVES** 8

225g/8oz butter, softened, plus extra
   for greasing
225g/8oz/scant 1 cup caster/superfine sugar
4 large eggs, lightly beaten
225g/8oz/1½ cups self-raising flour, sifted

1 tsp vanilla extract
200g/7oz/1 cup glacé/candied cherries, halved
200g/7oz/1⅓ cups icing/powdered
   sugar, sifted
1–2 tbsp cherry juice

1 Preheat the oven to 180°C/350°F/gas 4. Grease and line a 20cm/8in springform cake tin.

2 Put the butter and caster sugar in a mixing bowl and beat using an electric hand mixer or wooden spoon until the mixture is light and creamy. Add the eggs gradually, beating after each addition. Add the flour, vanilla extract and cherries and gently fold them into the mixture, using a large metal spoon. Scrape the mixture into the tin using a spatula.

3 Bake for 35–40 minutes until the cake springs back when pressed lightly and a skewer inserted into the middle of the cake comes out clean. Remove the cake from the oven and leave to stand for 5 minutes, then turn out on to a wire rack and leave to cool.

4 Put the icing sugar in a bowl and gradually stir in the cherry juice, adding a little at a time until you have a smooth thick icing/frosting. You may not need all of the cherry juice. Spoon the icing over the top of the cake, smoothing it out with a palette knife or round-bladed knife. Leave the icing to set before serving.

006 APPLE STREUSEL CAKE

PREPARATION TIME 25 minutes   **COOKING TIME** 50–60 minutes   **SERVES** 8

2 large cooking/baking apples, peeled,
   cored and chopped
2 tbsp light soft brown sugar
115g/4oz butter, softened, plus extra
   for greasing
115g/4oz/scant ½ cup caster/superfine sugar

2 large eggs, lightly beaten
115g/4oz/¾ cup self-raising flour
1 tsp baking powder
2 tsp ground cinnamon
custard, to serve

FOR THE STREUSEL

175g/6oz/heaped 1 cup plain/all-purpose
   flour, sifted
115g/4oz chilled butter, chopped

85g/3oz/⅓ cup caster/superfine sugar
1 tsp ground cinnamon

1 Put the apples, light brown sugar and 100ml/3½fl oz/scant ½ cup water in a saucepan and
   simmer for 10 minutes until the apples are very soft. Drain off any water and set aside to cool.
2 Preheat the oven to 180°C/350°F/gas 4. Grease and line a 20cm/8in springform cake tin.
3 Put the butter and caster sugar in a mixing bowl and beat using an electric hand mixer or
   wooden spoon until the mixture is light and creamy. Add the eggs gradually, beating after
   each addition. Sift in the flour, baking powder and ground cinnamon and gently fold them
   into the mixture, using a large metal spoon. Scrape the mixture into the tin using a spatula.
4 For the streusel, put the plain flour in a mixing bowl and rub in the chilled butter using
   your fingertips. Add the caster sugar and ground cinnamon and stir in to make a crumble
   mixture. Spoon the apples over the cake mixture in the tin and top with the streusel.
5 Bake for 55–60 minutes until a skewer inserted into the middle of the cake comes out with
   no cake mixture on it, and the streusel topping is golden brown. Remove the cake from the
   oven and leave to cool in the tin, then turn out on to a serving plate. Serve with custard.

007 PEAR & PECAN UPSIDE-DOWN CAKE

PREPARATION TIME 20 minutes   **COOKING TIME** 35–40 minutes   **SERVES** 8

185g/6½oz butter, softened,
plus extra for greasing
2 tbsp golden syrup
185g/6½oz/1 cup lightly packed
dark muscovado sugar
4 ripe pears, peeled, cored
and quartered

100g/3½oz/heaped ½ cup pecan nuts,
coarsely chopped
3 large eggs, lightly beaten
175g/6oz/heaped 1 cup self-raising flour
2 tsp ground cinnamon

1 Grease and line a 20cm/8in springform cake tin.
2 Put the syrup, 15g/½oz of the butter and 1 tablespoon of the sugar in a saucepan and heat
for about 5 minutes over a gentle heat, stirring, until the sugar has dissolved, then pour
into the tin. Place the pear quarters over the toffee sauce and sprinkle the pecans over
the top. Leave to cool.
3 Preheat the oven to 180°C/350°F/gas 4. Put the remaining butter and sugar in a mixing
bowl and beat using an electric hand mixer or wooden spoon until the mixture is light
and creamy. Add the eggs gradually, beating after each addition. Sift in the flour and ground
cinnamon and gently fold them into the mixture, using a large metal spoon. Scrape the
mixture on top of the pears using a spatula.
4 Bake for 30–35 minutes until the cake springs back when pressed lightly and a skewer
inserted into the middle of the cake comes out clean. Remove the cake from the oven and
leave to stand for 10 minutes. Remove the springform sides of the tin and put a serving
plate on top of the cake. Holding both plate and tin base securely, tip the cake upside
down so that it is inverted on to the plate. Remove the tin base and serve.

008 BLACKBERRY & APPLE UPSIDE-DOWN CAKE

PREPARATION TIME 20 minutes   **COOKING TIME** 40–45 minutes   **SERVES** 8

225g/8oz butter, softened,
plus extra for greasing
3 dessert apples
130g/4½oz/heaped ½ cup light soft
brown sugar
juice of 1 small lemon
200g/7oz/scant 2 cups blackberries

115g/4oz/scant ½ cup caster/superfine sugar
4 large eggs, lightly beaten
225g/8oz/1½ cups self-raising flour
2 tsp ground cinnamon
6 tbsp sour cream
whipped cream, to serve

1 Preheat the oven to 180°C/350°F/gas 4. Grease and line a 20cm/8in springform cake tin.

2 Peel, core and thinly slice 2 of the apples and put in a bowl with 1 tablespoon of the light brown sugar and all the lemon juice, tossing them to make sure they are all coated. Grate the remaining apple, discarding the core. Lay the apple slices and half the blackberries in a pattern on the bottom of the tin.

3 Put the butter, remaining light brown sugar and the caster sugar in a mixing bowl and beat using an electric hand mixer or wooden spoon until the mixture is light and creamy. Add the eggs gradually, beating after each addition. Sift in the flour and ground cinnamon and gently fold them into the mixture with the grated apple, remaining blackberries and sour cream, using a large metal spoon. Scrape the mixture on top of the fruit using a spatula.

4 Bake for 40–45 minutes until the cake springs back when pressed lightly and a skewer inserted into the middle of the cake comes out clean. Remove the cake from the oven and leave to stand for 10 minutes. Remove the springform sides of the tin and put a serving plate on top of the cake. Holding both plate and tin base securely, tip the cake upside down so that it is inverted on to the plate. Remove the tin base and serve with whipped cream.

009 BAKED APPLE CAKE

PREPARATION TIME 30 minutes   **COOKING TIME** 1 hour 25 minutes–1 hour 40 minutes   **SERVES** 8

225g/8oz butter, softened,
   plus extra for greasing
2 large eating apples
2 tbsp sultanas/golden raisins
2 tbsp golden syrup

225g/8oz/scant 1 cup caster/superfine sugar
4 large eggs, lightly beaten
225g/8oz/1½ cups self-raising flour
2 tsp ground cinnamon
2 tbsp sour cream

1 Preheat the oven to 180°C/350°F/gas 4. Grease and line a 23cm/9in springform cake tin.

2 Wash and core the apples using an apple corer and score a horizontal line around the edge of each apple with a sharp knife to prevent the skins splitting while cooking. Place the apples in a baking dish and fill the centre of each apple with half the sultanas and half the syrup. Add 2 tablespoons water to the dish.

3 Bake for 45–55 minutes until the apples are soft. Turn off the oven and leave the apples to cool, then remove the apple skins to leave a soft apple purée with sultanas.

4 Put the butter and sugar in a mixing bowl and beat using an electric hand mixer or wooden spoon until the mixture is light and creamy. Add the eggs gradually, beating after each addition. Sift in the flour and ground cinnamon and gently fold them into the mixture with the sour cream and cooled apple purée, using a large metal spoon. Scrape the mixture into the tin using a spatula.

5 Bake for 40–45 minutes until the cake springs back when pressed lightly and a skewer inserted into the middle of the cake comes out clean. Remove the cake from the oven and leave to stand for 5 minutes, then turn out on to a wire rack and leave to cool.

010 DUTCH APPLE CAKE

PREPARATION TIME 20 minutes   **COOKING TIME** 50–55 minutes   **SERVES** 8

4 dessert apples, peeled,
   cored and chopped
I tsp vanilla extract
225g/8oz butter, softened, plus extra
   for greasing
225g/8oz/scant I cup caster/superfine sugar

4 large eggs, lightly beaten
225g/8oz/I ½ cups self-raising flour
I tsp ground cinnamon
55g/2oz/½ cup ground almonds
100g/3½oz/⅔ cup flaked/sliced almonds
icing/powdered sugar, for dusting

1   Put the apples, vanilla extract and 3 tablespoons water in a saucepan. Cover and simmer for 20 minutes until the apples are soft and have absorbed the water, adding more water if necessary. Set aside to cool.

2   Preheat the oven to 180°C/350°F/gas 4. Grease and line a deep 23cm/9in springform cake tin.

3   Put the butter and sugar in a mixing bowl and beat using an electric hand mixer or wooden spoon until the mixture is light and creamy. Add the eggs gradually, beating after each addition. Sift in the flour and ground cinnamon and gently fold them into the mixture with the ground almonds, using a large metal spoon.

4   Scrape half of the cake mixture into the tin using a spatula, cover with the apple purée and top with the remaining cake mixture. Sprinkle over the flaked almonds.

5   Bake for 30–35 minutes until the cake springs back when pressed lightly and a skewer inserted into the middle of the cake comes out clean. Remove the cake from the oven and leave to cool in the tin, then turn out on to a serving plate and dust with icing sugar before serving.

011 SPICED HONEY & PEAR UPSIDE-DOWN CAKE

PREPARATION TIME 20 minutes   **COOKING TIME** 40–50 minutes   **SERVES** 8

175g/6oz butter, softened,
   plus extra for greasing
4 small pears, peeled, cored and thinly sliced
I tbsp dark soft brown sugar
juice of I lemon
175g/6oz/scant ¾ cup caster/superfine sugar
3 large eggs, lightly beaten

175g/6oz/heaped I cup self-raising flour
2 tsp ground cinnamon
I tsp mixed/pumpkin pie spice
¼ tsp freshly grated nutmeg
100ml/3½fl oz/scant ½ cup sour cream
I tbsp clear honey
whipped cream, to serve

1   Preheat the oven to 180°C/350°F/gas 4. Grease and line a deep 20cm/8in springform cake tin.

2 Put the pear slices in a bowl with the dark brown sugar and lemon juice and toss with your hands to ensure they are all coated. Arrange the pears in a circular pattern on the bottom of the tin.

3 Put the butter and caster sugar in a mixing bowl and beat using an electric hand mixer or wooden spoon until the mixture is light and creamy. Add the eggs gradually, beating after each addition. Sift in the flour and spices and fold in with the sour cream and honey, using a large metal spoon. Scrape the mixture over the pears using a spatula.

4 Bake for 40–50 minutes until the cake springs back when pressed lightly and a skewer inserted into the middle of the cake comes out clean. Remove the cake from the oven and leave to stand for 10 minutes. Remove the springform sides of the tin and put a serving plate on top of the cake. Holding both plate and tin base securely, tip the cake upside down so that it is inverted on to the plate. Remove the tin base and serve with whipped cream.

012 PEACH & AMARETTO CAKE

PREPARATION TIME 20 minutes   COOKING TIME 40–45 minutes   SERVES 8

175g/6oz butter, softened, plus extra
   for greasing
175g/6oz/scant ¾ cup caster/superfine sugar
3 large eggs, lightly beaten
175g/6oz/heaped 1 cup self-raising
   flour, sifted
55g/2oz/heaped ⅓ cup toasted
   flaked/sliced almonds

1 tsp almond extract
2 ripe peaches, stones removed,
   1 finely chopped and 1 sliced
1 tbsp almond liqueur, such as amaretto
1 tbsp peach or apricot jam/jelly

1 Preheat the oven to 180°C/350°F/gas 4. Grease and line a 24 x 12cm/9½ x 4½in loaf tin.

2 Put the butter and sugar in a mixing bowl and beat using an electric hand mixer or wooden spoon until the mixture is light and creamy. Add the eggs gradually, beating after each addition. Add the flour, flaked almonds, almond extract and chopped peach and gently fold them into the mixture, using a large metal spoon. Scrape the mixture into the tin using a spatula. Arrange the peach slices decoratively on top of the cake.

3 Bake for 35–40 minutes until the cake springs back when pressed lightly and a skewer inserted into the middle of the cake comes out clean.

4 Remove the cake from the oven and leave to stand for 5 minutes, then turn out on to a wire rack. Heat the amaretto and jam in a small saucepan until the jam has melted, then brush the glaze over the top of the cake, using a pastry brush. Leave to cool.

013 SUMMER BERRY MERINGUE CAKE

PREPARATION TIME 30 minutes   **COOKING TIME** 50–60 minutes   **SERVES** 8

115g/4oz butter, softened, plus extra
    for greasing
280g/10oz/1 cup caster/superfine sugar
2 large eggs, lightly beaten, plus 3 large
    egg whites
85g/3oz/heaped ½ cup self-raising
    flour, sifted
30g/1oz/heaped ¼ cup ground almonds

1 tsp almond extract
1 tbsp cornflour/cornstarch dissolved in
    1 tbsp white wine vinegar
200g/7oz/1⅓ cups raspberries
150ml/5fl oz/scant ⅔ cup double/heavy
    cream, whipped to stiff peaks
400g/14oz/3½ cups combined strawberries,
    blackberries and redcurrants

1 Preheat the oven to 140°C/275°F/gas 1. Grease and line a deep 23cm/9in springform cake tin.
2 Put the butter and 115g/4oz/scant ½ cup of the sugar in a mixing bowl and beat using an electric hand mixer or wooden spoon until the mixture is light and creamy. Add the whole eggs gradually, beating after each addition. Add the flour, ground almonds and almond extract and gently fold them into the mixture, using a large metal spoon. Scrape the mixture into the tin using a spatula and set aside while you make the meringue.
3 Put the egg whites in a clean, dry bowl and whisk with an electric hand mixer or a whisk until they form stiff peaks. Whisk in the remaining sugar one-third at a time, incorporating all the sugar before you add more. The meringue should become smooth and glossy. When all the sugar has been added, pour in the cornflour mixture and whisk again. Scatter the raspberries on top of the cake mixture and cover with the meringue.
4 Bake for 50–60 minutes until the meringue is crisp and lightly golden. Remove the cake from the oven and leave to cool in the tin, then turn out on to a serving plate. Just before serving the cake, spoon the cream on top of the meringue and cover with the berries.

014 STICKY PLUM CAKE

PREPARATION TIME 20 minutes   **COOKING TIME** 50–60 minutes   **SERVES** 8

175g/6oz butter, softened, plus extra
    for greasing
175g/6oz/scant ¾ cup caster/superfine sugar
3 large eggs, lightly beaten
6 tbsp sour cream
175g/6oz/heaped 1 cup self-raising flour
2 tsp ground cinnamon
2 tbsp soft plum jam/jelly

6 plums, halved and stones removed
100g/3½oz cream cheese

FOR THE TOPPING
115g/4oz/¾ cup plain/all-purpose flour
85g/3oz chilled butter, chopped
140g/5oz/⅔ cup dark soft brown sugar
1 tsp ground cinnamon

1   Preheat the oven to 180°C/350°F/gas 4. Grease and line a deep 23cm/9in springform cake tin.
2   Put the butter and the sugar in a mixing bowl and beat using an electric hand mixer or wooden spoon until the mixture is light and creamy. Add the eggs and sour cream gradually, beating after each addition. Sift in the flour and ground cinnamon and gently fold them into the mixture, using a large metal spoon, then stir in the plum jam. Scrape the mixture into the tin using a spatula. Place the plum halves cut-side down on top of the cake mixture and place small spoonfuls of the cream cheese in between the plums.
3   For the topping, put the flour in a mixing bowl and rub in the butter with your fingertips until the mixture resembles fine breadcrumbs. Stir in the sugar and ground cinnamon to form a crumble topping, then sprinkle it over the plums.
4   Bake for 50–60 minutes until the cake springs back when pressed lightly and a skewer inserted into the middle of the cake comes out clean. Remove the cake from the oven and leave to cool in the tin, then turn out on to a serving plate.

015 ST CLEMENT'S UPSIDE-DOWN CAKE

PREPARATION TIME 30 minutes   **COOKING TIME** 1 hour–1 hour 10 minutes   **SERVES** 8

250g/9oz butter, softened, plus extra
    for greasing
1 lemon
1 large orange
55g/2oz/¼ cup light soft brown sugar
115g/4oz/¾ cup pre-cooked
    polenta/cornmeal grains

225g/8oz/scant 1 cup caster/superfine sugar
3 large eggs, lightly beaten
115g/4oz/1 cup ground almonds
whipped cream, to serve

1   Grease and line a 20cm/8in springform cake tin.
2   Grate the zest from the lemon and orange and set aside. In a small saucepan, heat the brown sugar and 30g/1oz of the butter and simmer until the sugar has dissolved to make a caramel syrup. Pour the syrup over the base of the cake tin. Remove the peel from the orange and lemon and cut the fruit into thick slices, removing any pips. Place the fruit slices in rings on top of the caramel sauce in the tin and leave the caramel to cool.
3   Preheat the oven to 180°C/350°F/gas 4. Simmer the polenta in 500ml/17fl oz/2 cups water for 5 minutes until the grains have absorbed all the water and become a thick paste. Leave to cool for 5 minutes.
4   Meanwhile, put the remaining butter and the caster sugar in a mixing bowl and beat using an electric hand mixer or wooden spoon until the mixture is light and creamy. Add the eggs gradually, beating after each addition. Add the orange and lemon zests, ground almonds and polenta and fold in, using a large metal spoon. Scrape the mixture over the fruit using a spatula.

5 Bake for 50–60 minutes until the cake springs back when pressed lightly and a skewer inserted into the middle of the cake comes out clean. Remove the cake from the oven and leave to stand for 10 minutes. Remove the springform sides of the tin and put a serving plate on top of the cake. Holding both plate and tin base securely, tip the cake upside down so that it is inverted on to the plate. Remove the tin base and serve with whipped cream.

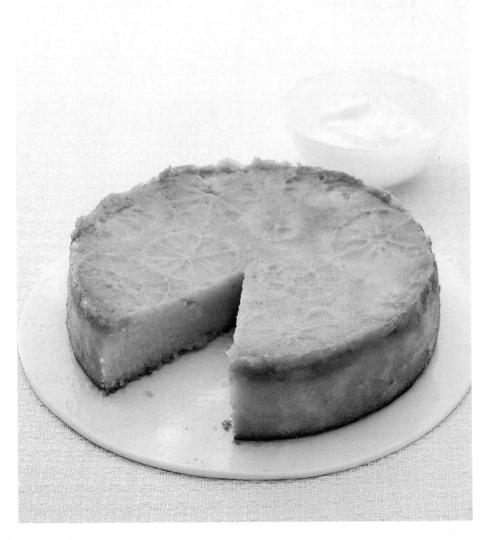

016 CARAMELIZED BANANA UPSIDE-DOWN CAKE

PREPARATION TIME 30 minutes　**COOKING TIME** 1 hour 5 minutes–1 hour 15 minutes　**SERVES** 8

250g/9oz butter, softened,
　plus extra for greasing
2 tbsp dark muscovado sugar
2 tbsp golden syrup
1 tsp ground cinnamon
3 bananas, peeled and sliced

225g/8oz/1 cup light soft brown sugar
4 large eggs, lightly beaten
225g/8oz/1½ cups self-raising flour, sifted
55g/2oz/heaped ½ cup desiccated/dried
　shredded coconut
2 tbsp coconut milk

1　Grease and line a deep 23cm/9in springform cake tin.
2　Put 30g/1oz of the butter, the muscovado sugar, syrup and ground cinnamon in a saucepan and simmer gently until the sugar has dissolved to make a caramel sauce. Pour the sauce over the base of the cake tin and arrange the banana slices on top. Set aside to cool.
3　Preheat the oven to 180°C/350°F/gas 4. Put the remaining butter and the light brown sugar in a mixing bowl and beat using an electric hand mixer or wooden spoon until the mixture is light and creamy. Add the eggs gradually, beating after each addition. Add the flour, desiccated coconut and coconut milk and gently fold them into the mixture, using a large metal spoon. Scrape the mixture into the tin using a spatula.
4　Bake for 60–70 minutes until the cake springs back when pressed lightly and a skewer inserted into the middle of the cake comes out clean. Remove the cake from the oven and leave to stand for 10 minutes. Remove the springform sides of the tin and put a serving plate on top of the cake. Holding both plate and tin base securely, tip the cake upside down so that it is inverted on to the plate. Remove the tin base and serve.

017 MANGO UPSIDE-DOWN CAKE

PREPARATION TIME 25 minutes　**COOKING TIME** 45–50 minutes　**SERVES** 8

200g/7oz butter, softened, plus extra
　for greasing
55g/2oz/¼ cup dark soft brown sugar
1 tbsp golden syrup
1 large ripe mango, peeled, stone removed
　and flesh cut into thin slices

175g/6oz/¾ cup light soft brown sugar
3 large eggs, lightly beaten
175g/6oz/heaped 1 cup self-raising flour,
　sifted
100g/3½oz/1¼ cups desiccated/dried
　shredded coconut

1　Preheat the oven to 180°C/350°F/gas 4. Grease and line a deep 23cm/9in springform cake tin.
2　Put 25g/1oz of the butter, the dark brown sugar and syrup in a small saucepan and simmer until the sugar has dissolved to make a caramel sauce. Pour the sauce over the base of the tin. Arrange the mango slices on top of the caramel in patterns. Set aside to cool.

3 Put the remaining butter and the light brown sugar in a mixing bowl and beat using an electric hand mixer or wooden spoon until the mixture is light and creamy. Add the eggs gradually, beating after each addition. Add the flour and coconut and gently fold them into the mixture, using a large metal spoon. Scrape the mixture over the top of the mango using a spatula.

4 Bake for 40–45 minutes until the cake springs back when pressed lightly and a skewer inserted into the middle of the cake comes out clean. Remove the cake from the oven and leave to stand for 10 minutes. Remove the springform sides of the tin and put a serving plate on top of the cake. Holding both plate and tin base securely, tip the cake upside down so that it is inverted on to the plate. Remove the tin base and serve.

018 TOASTED COCONUT & CARAMEL CAKE

PREPARATION TIME 20 minutes   **COOKING TIME** 30–40 minutes   **SERVES** 8

175g/6oz butter, softened, plus extra
  for greasing
115g/4oz/1¼ cups desiccated/dried
  shredded coconut
85g/3oz/⅓ cup light soft brown sugar
85g/3oz/⅓ cup light muscovado sugar

3 large eggs, lightly beaten
175g/6oz/heaped 1 cup self-raising
  flour, sifted
3 tbsp toffee sauce
100g/3½oz/⅔ cup icing/powdered
  sugar, sifted

1 Preheat the oven to 180°C/350°F/gas 4. Grease and line a 20cm/8in springform cake tin.

2 Put the desiccated coconut in a dry saucepan and heat until it starts to turn golden brown, stirring all the time to ensure it does not burn. Tip into a dish to cool.

3 Put the butter, light brown sugar and muscovado sugar in a mixing bowl and beat using an electric hand mixer or wooden spoon until the mixture is light and creamy. Add the eggs gradually, beating after each addition. Add the flour, two-thirds of the toasted coconut and 2 tablespoons of the toffee sauce and gently fold them into the mixture, using a large metal spoon. Scrape the mixture into the tin using a spatula.

4 Bake for 30–40 minutes until the cake springs back when pressed lightly and a skewer inserted into the middle of the cake comes out clean. Remove the cake from the oven and leave to stand for 5 minutes, then turn out on to a wire rack and leave to cool.

5 Mix together the icing sugar, remaining toffee sauce and 1 tablespoon water to form a smooth icing/frosting and spread this over the top of the cake. Sprinkle the remaining toasted coconut over the cake to decorate.

019 FIG & VANILLA UPSIDE-DOWN CAKE

PREPARATION TIME 30 minutes **COOKING TIME** 30–35 minutes **SERVES** 8

flavourless oil, for greasing
200g/7oz/¾ cup granulated sugar
seeds from 1 vanilla pod/bean (retain the
    pod for the caramel)
5 figs, thinly sliced

3 large eggs, lightly beaten
125g/4½oz/½ cup caster/superfine sugar
125g/4½oz/scant 1 cup plain/all-purpose flour
1 tsp baking powder

1 Preheat the oven to 180°C/350°F/gas 4. Grease and line a 20cm/8in springform cake tin.
2 Put the granulated sugar in a saucepan with 3 tablespoons water and the vanilla pod (but not the seeds) and heat until the sugar has dissolved and turned golden brown. Remove from the heat immediately the caramel starts to colour, otherwise it may burn.
3 Remove and discard the vanilla pod and pour the caramel into the base of the tin. Place the fig slices in patterns on top of the caramel.
4 Put the eggs in a mixing bowl and whisk until they are doubled in size using an electric hand mixer or a whisk, then gradually whisk in the caster sugar. Sift in the flour and baking powder and gently fold them into the mixture with the vanilla seeds, using a large metal spoon. Scrape the mixture on top of the figs using a spatula.
5 Bake for 20–25 minutes until the cake springs back when pressed lightly and a skewer inserted into the middle of the cake comes out clean. Remove the springform sides of the tin and put a serving plate on top of the cake. Holding both plate and tin base securely, tip the cake upside down so that it is inverted on to the plate. Be careful because the hot caramel could spill out and burn you as you turn the tin. Remove the tin base and serve.

020 TROPICAL PINEAPPLE CAKE

PREPARATION TIME 20 minutes **COOKING TIME** 35–40 minutes **SERVES** 8

225g/8oz butter, softened, plus extra
    for greasing
225g/8oz/1½ cups self-raising flour, sifted,
    plus extra for dusting
225g/8oz/scant 1 cup caster/superfine sugar
4 large eggs, lightly beaten

55g/2oz/heaped ½ cup desiccated/dried
    shredded coconut
6 canned pineapple rings, finely chopped
200g/7oz/1 cup glacé/candied cherries, halved
1 tsp almond extract

1 Preheat the oven to 180°C/350°F/gas 4. Grease a 23cm/9in ring tin and dust with flour.
2 Put the butter and sugar in a mixing bowl and beat using an electric hand mixer or wooden spoon until the mixture is light and creamy. Add the eggs gradually, beating after

each addition. Add the flour and the remaining ingredients and gently fold them into the mixture, using a large metal spoon. Scrape the mixture into the tin using a spatula.

3 Bake for 35–40 minutes until the cake springs back when pressed lightly and a skewer inserted into the cake comes out clean. Remove the cake from the oven and leave to stand for 5 minutes, then turn out on to a wire rack and leave to cool.

021 STICKY TOFFEE NUT UPSIDE-DOWN CAKE

PREPARATION TIME 20 minutes   **COOKING TIME** 40–45 minutes   **SERVES** 8

190g/6¾oz butter, softened, plus extra
   for greasing
2 tbsp golden syrup
1 tbsp double/heavy cream
85g/3oz/⅓ cup dark soft brown sugar

300g/10½oz/2 cups mixed unsalted nuts,
   one-third chopped finely
85g/3oz/⅓ cup caster/superfine sugar
3 large eggs, lightly beaten
175g/6oz/heaped 1 cup self-raising
   flour, sifted

1 Preheat the oven to 180°C/350°F/gas 4. Grease and line a 20cm/8in springform cake tin.
2 In a saucepan, heat 15g/½oz of the butter, the syrup, cream and 1 tablespoon of the dark brown sugar gently until the sugar has dissolved to make a thick caramel sauce. Sprinkle the whole nuts over the tin base and pour the caramel over the top. Leave until cold.
3 Put the remaining butter and brown sugar with the caster sugar in a mixing bowl and beat using an electric hand mixer or wooden spoon until the mixture is light and creamy. Add the eggs gradually, beating after each addition. Add the flour and chopped nuts and fold them into the mixture, using a large metal spoon. Scrape the mixture into the tin using a spatula.
4 Bake for 35–40 minutes until the cake springs back when pressed lightly. Remove the springform sides of the tin and put a serving plate on top of the cake. Holding both plate and tin base securely, tip the cake upside down so that it is inverted on to the plate. Remove the tin base and serve.

022 CINNAMON MACADAMIA CAKE

PREPARATION TIME 20 minutes   **COOKING TIME** 40–45 minutes   **SERVES** 8

225g/8oz butter, softened, plus extra
   for greasing
225g/8oz/1 cup light soft brown sugar
4 large eggs, lightly beaten
225g/8oz/1½ cups self-raising flour

2 tsp ground cinnamon
1 tsp vanilla extract
200g/7oz/heaped 1 cup macadamia nuts
icing/powdered sugar, for dusting

1 Preheat the oven to 180°C/350°F/gas 4. Grease and line a 23cm/9in springform cake tin.
2 Put the butter and sugar in a mixing bowl and beat using an electric hand mixer or wooden spoon until the mixture is light and creamy. Add the eggs gradually, beating after each addition. Sift in the flour and ground cinnamon and gently fold them into the mixture with the vanilla extract and macadamia nuts, using a large metal spoon. Scrape the mixture into the tin using a spatula.
3 Bake for 40–45 minutes until the cake springs back when pressed lightly and a skewer inserted into the middle of the cake comes out clean. Remove the cake from the oven and leave to stand for 5 minutes, then turn out on to a wire rack and leave to cool. Dust with icing sugar before serving.

023 WHITE CHOCOLATE, APRICOT & PISTACHIO CAKE

PREPARATION TIME 20 minutes   **COOKING TIME** 35–45 minutes   **SERVES** 8

225g/8oz butter, softened, plus extra
for greasing
225g/8oz/scant 1 cup caster/superfine sugar
4 large eggs, lightly beaten
225g/8oz/1½ cups self-raising flour, sifted
100g/3½oz white chocolate, chopped

50g/1¾oz/scant ⅓ cup dried
apricots, chopped
75g/2½oz/heaped ½ cup pistachio
nuts, chopped
2 tbsp apricot jam/jelly
juice of 1 lemon

1 Preheat the oven to 180°C/350°F/gas 4. Grease and line a 20cm/8in springform cake tin.
2 Put the butter and sugar in a mixing bowl and beat using an electric hand mixer or wooden spoon until the mixture is light and creamy. Add the eggs gradually, beating after each addition. Add the flour, chocolate, apricots and pistachios and fold them into the mixture, using a large metal spoon. Scrape the mixture into the tin using a spatula.
3 Bake for 35–45 minutes until the cake springs back when pressed lightly and a skewer inserted into the middle comes out clean. Remove the cake from the oven and leave to stand for 5 minutes, then turn out on to a wire rack. Heat the jam and lemon juice in a saucepan until the jam melts, strain through a fine-mesh sieve to remove any fruit pieces, then brush the glaze over the top of the cake using a pastry brush. Leave to cool.

024 WHITE CHOCOLATE & PEANUT BUTTER CAKE

PREPARATION TIME 20 minutes   **COOKING TIME** 30–35 minutes   **SERVES** 8

200g/7oz butter, softened, plus extra
   for greasing
250g/9oz/1⅔ cups self-raising flour, sifted,
   plus extra for dusting
2 heaped tbsp smooth peanut butter
225g/8oz/scant 1 cup caster/superfine sugar

4 large eggs, lightly beaten
100g/3½oz white chocolate, melted
   and cooled slightly
100g/3½oz/heaped ½ cup plain/semisweet
   chocolate chips

1　Preheat the oven to 180°C/350°F/gas 4. Grease a 23cm/9in ring tin and dust with flour.
2　Put the butter, peanut butter and sugar in a mixing bowl and beat using an electric hand mixer or wooden spoon until the mixture is light and creamy. Add the eggs gradually, beating after each addition. Add the flour, melted chocolate and chocolate chips and gently fold them into the mixture, using a large metal spoon. Scrape the mixture into the tin using a spatula.
3　Bake for 30–35 minutes until the cake springs back when pressed lightly and a skewer inserted into the cake comes out clean. Remove the cake from the oven and leave to stand for 5 minutes, then turn out on to a wire rack and leave to cool.

025 FLOURLESS CHOCOLATE CAKE

PREPARATION TIME 20 minutes   **COOKING TIME** 20–30 minutes   **SERVES** 8

100g/3½oz butter, chopped, plus extra
   for greasing
250g/9oz dark/bittersweet chocolate (gf)
   (70% cocoa solids), broken into pieces
4 large eggs, separated

175g/6oz/heaped 1 cup icing/powdered sugar,
   sifted, plus extra for dusting
1 tsp ground cinnamon
cocoa powder, for dusting

1　Preheat the oven to 190°C/375°F/gas 5. Grease and line a 23cm/9in springform cake tin.
2　Melt the chocolate and butter together. Leave to cool. Put the egg yolks and icing sugar in a bowl and whisk with an electric hand mixer or a whisk until the mixture is light and creamy and has doubled in size and the whisk leaves a trail when lifted up. Note that the mixture will be quite stiff to start with.
3　Fold the melted chocolate and butter mixture and the ground cinnamon into the egg yolks and sugar, using a large metal spoon. Put the egg whites in a clean, dry bowl and whisk with an electric hand mixer or a whisk until they form soft peaks, then fold into the mixture, making sure they are incorporated. Scrape the mixture into the tin using a spatula.
4　Bake for 20–30 minutes until the cake has formed a crust but still feels quite soft when

pressed lightly. Remove the cake from the oven and leave to cool in the tin, then turn out on to a serving plate and dust with icing sugar and cocoa.

026 RASPBERRY & CLOTTED CREAM CAKE

PREPARATION TIME 25 minutes **COOKING TIME** 20–25 minutes **SERVES** 8

225g/8oz butter, softened, plus extra
    for greasing
225g/8oz/scant 1 cup caster/superfine sugar
4 large eggs, lightly beaten
175g/6oz/heaped 1 cup self-raising flour,
    sifted
55g/2oz/½ cup ground almonds

1 tsp almond extract
5 tbsp almond liqueur, such as amaretto
300g/10½oz clotted cream
3 tbsp raspberry jam
400g/14oz/3 cups raspberries
icing/powdered sugar, for dusting

1 Preheat the oven to 180°C/350°F/gas 4. Grease and base-line two 20cm/8in sandwich cake tins.
2 Put the butter and sugar in a mixing bowl and beat using an electric hand mixer or wooden spoon until the mixture is light and creamy. Add the eggs gradually, beating after each addition. Add the flour, ground almonds and almond extract and gently fold them into the mixture, using a large metal spoon. Divide the mixture between the tins using a spatula.
3 Bake for 20–25 minutes until the cakes spring back when pressed lightly and a skewer inserted into the middle of each cake comes out clean. Remove the cakes from the oven and leave to stand for 5 minutes, then turn out on to a wire rack and leave to cool.
4 Place one of the cakes on a serving plate, drizzle with half the amaretto and top with half the clotted cream and all the jam. Top with the second cake, drizzle with the remaining amaretto and top with the remaining clotted cream. Arrange the raspberries on top, dust with icing sugar and serve immediately. Any cake not eaten straight away should be stored in a lidded container in the refrigerator as it contains fresh cream.

027 VICTORIA SANDWICH

PREPARATION TIME 20 minutes **COOKING TIME** 20–25 minutes **SERVES** 8

225g/8oz butter, softened, plus extra
    for greasing
225g/8oz/scant 1 cup caster/superfine sugar,
    plus extra for dusting
4 large eggs, lightly beaten

225g/8oz/1½ cups self-raising flour, sifted
1 tsp vanilla extract
1 recipe quantity Vanilla Buttercream
    (see page 24)
3 tbsp raspberry jam/jelly

1   Preheat the oven to 180°C/350°F/gas 4. Grease and base-line two 20cm/8in sandwich cake tins.
2   Put the butter and sugar in a mixing bowl and beat using an electric hand mixer or wooden spoon until the mixture is light and creamy. Add the eggs gradually, beating after each addition. Add the flour and vanilla extract and gently fold them into the mixture, using a large metal spoon. Divide the mixture between the tins using a spatula.
3   Bake for 20–25 minutes until the cakes spring back when pressed lightly and a skewer inserted into the middle of each cake comes out clean. Remove the cakes from the oven and leave to stand for 5 minutes, then turn out on to a wire rack and leave to cool. Sandwich the cakes with the buttercream and jam and dust the top with caster sugar.

028 ALL-IN-ONE VANILLA SPONGE

PREPARATION TIME 15 minutes   **COOKING TIME** 20–30 minutes   **SERVES** 8

225g/8oz butter, softened, plus extra
   for greasing
225g/8oz/1½ cups self-raising flour
1 tsp baking powder
225g/8oz/scant 1 cup caster/superfine sugar
4 large eggs, lightly beaten

1 tsp vanilla extract
2 tbsp plum jam/jelly
150ml/5fl oz/scant ⅔ cup whipping cream,
   whipped to stiff peaks
icing/powdered sugar, for dusting

1   Preheat the oven to 180°C/350°F/gas 4. Grease and base-line two 20cm/8in sandwich cake tins.
2   Sift the flour and baking powder into a mixing bowl and add the sugar, butter, eggs and vanilla extract. Beat using an electric hand mixer or wooden spoon until everything is incorporated. Divide the mixture between the tins using a spatula.
3   Bake for 20–30 minutes until the cakes spring back when pressed lightly and a skewer inserted into the middle of each cake comes out clean. Remove the cakes from the oven and leave to stand for 5 minutes, then turn out on to a wire rack and leave to cool. Sandwich the cakes with the jam and whipped cream and dust the top with icing sugar.

029 EGG-FREE VICTORIA SPONGE

PREPARATION TIME 15 minutes   **COOKING TIME** 35–40 minutes   **SERVES** 8

225g/8oz butter, softened, plus extra
   for greasing
225g/8oz/scant 1 cup caster/superfine sugar
350g/12oz/2⅓ cups self-raising flour
½ tsp bicarbonate of soda/baking soda
250ml/9fl oz/1 cup sour cream

100ml/3½fl oz/scant ½ cup milk
2 tbsp strawberry jam/jelly
100ml/3½fl oz/scant ½ cup whipping cream,
   whipped to soft peaks
icing/powdered sugar, for dusting

1 Preheat the oven to 180°C/350°F/gas 4. Grease and base-line two 20cm/8in sandwich cake tins.
2 Put the butter and sugar in a mixing bowl and beat using an electric hand mixer or wooden spoon until the mixture is light and creamy. Sift in the flour and bicarbonate of soda and gently fold them into the mixture with the sour cream and milk, using a large metal spoon. Divide the mixture between the tins using a spatula.
3 Bake for 35–40 minutes until the cakes spring back when pressed lightly and a skewer inserted into the middle of each cake comes out clean. Remove the cakes from the oven and leave to stand for 5 minutes, then turn out on to a wire rack and leave to cool. Sandwich the cakes with the jam and whipped cream and dust the top with icing sugar.

030 LEMON CURD CAKE

PREPARATION TIME 20 minutes   **COOKING TIME** 20–30 minutes   **SERVES** 8

225g/8oz butter, softened, plus extra
   for greasing
225g/8oz/1 cup light soft brown sugar
4 large eggs, lightly beaten
225g/8oz/1½ cups self-raising flour, sifted
finely grated zest of 2 lemons
edible silver balls, to decorate (optional)

FOR THE FILLING
6 tbsp lemon curd
375ml/13fl oz/1½ cups double/heavy cream,
   whipped to stiff peaks

FOR THE ICING/FROSTING
200g/7oz/1⅓ cups icing/powdered sugar, sifted
1–2 tbsp lemon juice

1 Preheat the oven to 180°C/350°F/gas 4. Grease and base-line two 20cm/8in sandwich cake tins.
2 Put the butter and sugar in a mixing bowl and beat using an electric hand mixer or wooden spoon until the mixture is light and creamy. Add the eggs gradually, beating after each addition. Add the flour and gently fold it and the lemon zest into the mixture, using a large metal spoon. Divide the mixture between the tins using a spatula.

3 Bake for 20–30 minutes until the cakes spring back when pressed lightly and a skewer inserted into the middle of each cake comes out clean. Remove the cakes from the oven and leave to stand for 5 minutes, then turn out on to a wire rack and leave to cool.

4 Cut each cake in half horizontally and sandwich the four layers together using one-third of the lemon curd and one-third of the whipped cream between each layer.

5 For the icing/frosting, mix together the icing sugar and lemon juice to make a smooth, thick icing. Spoon over the top of the cake and decorate with edible silver balls, if using. Leave the icing to set before serving.

031 CHOCOLATE & BLACKCURRANT CAKE

PREPARATION TIME 20 minutes   **COOKING TIME** 20–25 minutes   **SERVES** 8

225g/8oz butter, softened, plus extra
   for greasing
225g/8oz/scant 1 cup caster/superfine sugar
4 large eggs, lightly beaten
200g/7oz/1⅓ cups plain/all-purpose flour
4 tbsp cocoa powder

100g/3½oz dark/bittersweet chocolate
   (70% cocoa solids), grated
3 tbsp blackcurrant jam/jelly
150ml/5fl oz/scant ⅔ cup double/heavy
   cream, whipped to stiff peaks
icing/powdered sugar, for dusting

1 Preheat the oven to 180°C/350°F/gas 4. Grease and base-line two 20cm/8in sandwich cake tins.

2 Put the butter and sugar in a mixing bowl and beat using an electric hand mixer or wooden spoon until the mixture is light and creamy. Add the eggs gradually, beating after each addition. Sift in the flour and cocoa and gently fold them and the grated chocolate into the mixture, using a large metal spoon. Divide the mixture between the tins using a spatula.

3 Bake for 20–25 minutes until the cakes spring back when pressed lightly and a skewer inserted into the middle of each cake comes out clean. Remove the cakes from the oven and leave to stand for 5 minutes, then turn out on to a wire rack and leave to cool.

4 Sandwich the cakes together with the jam and whipped cream and dust the top with icing sugar.

032 COFFEE & WALNUT SANDWICH CAKE

PREPARATION TIME 20 minutes   **COOKING TIME** 20–30 minutes   **SERVES** 8

225g/8oz butter, softened, plus extra
    for greasing
225g/8oz/scant I cup caster/superfine sugar
4 large eggs, lightly beaten
225g/8oz/1½ cups self-raising flour, sifted
100g/3½oz/heaped ½ cup walnut halves,
    8 reserved for decoration

2 tbsp instant coffee granules dissolved in
    2 tbsp boiling water and cooled
150ml/5fl oz/scant ⅔ cup double/heavy
    cream
100g/3½oz/⅔ cup fondant icing sugar, sifted

1   Preheat the oven to 180°C/350°F/gas 4. Grease and base-line two 20cm/8in sandwich
    cake tins.
2   Put the butter and caster sugar in a mixing bowl and beat using an electric hand mixer or
    wooden spoon until the mixture is light and creamy. Add the eggs gradually, beating after
    each addition. Add the flour, walnut halves and 1 tablespoon of the coffee liquid and gently
    fold them into the mixture, using a large metal spoon. Divide the mixture between the tins
    using a spatula.
3   Bake for 20–30 minutes until the cakes spring back when pressed lightly and a skewer
    inserted into the middle of each cake comes out clean. Remove the cakes from the oven
    and leave to stand for 5 minutes, then turn out on to a wire rack and leave to cool.
4   For the filling, whip the double cream and the remaining coffee liquid together to stiff
    peaks using an electric mixer or hand whisk. Use this coffee cream to sandwich the cakes
    together. For the icing/frosting, mix the fondant icing sugar with the remaining coffee liquid
    and 1 tablespoon water to make a thick, smooth icing. (You may not need all the water,
    so add it gradually.) Spoon the coffee fondant icing over the cake and decorate with the
    reserved walnut halves.

033 POLKA DOT CHOCOLATE SANDWICH CAKE

PREPARATION TIME 20 minutes   **COOKING TIME** 20–25 minutes   **SERVES** 8

225g/8oz butter, softened, plus extra
    for greasing
225g/8oz/scant I cup caster/superfine sugar
4 large eggs, lightly beaten
225g/8oz/1½ cups self-raising flour, sifted
100g/3½oz/heaped ½ cup plain/semisweet
    chocolate chips
1 tsp vanilla extract

I recipe quantity Chocolate Buttercream
    (see page 24)
55g/2oz/⅓ cup white chocolate buttons,
    to decorate

1. Preheat the oven to 180°C/350°F/gas 4. Grease and base-line two 20cm/8in sandwich cake tins.
2. Put the butter and sugar in a mixing bowl and beat using an electric hand mixer or wooden spoon until the mixture is light and creamy. Add the eggs gradually, beating after each addition. Add the flour, chocolate chips and vanilla extract and gently fold them into the mixture, using a large metal spoon. Divide the mixture between the tins using a spatula.
3. Bake for 20–25 minutes until the cakes spring back when pressed lightly and a skewer inserted into the middle of each cake comes out clean. Remove the cakes from the oven and leave to stand for 5 minutes, then turn out on to a wire rack and leave to cool.
4. Sandwich the cakes together with half the buttercream. Spread the remaining buttercream over the top and decorate with the white chocolate buttons.

034 CHOCOLATE CHERRY CAKE

PREPARATION TIME 20 minutes   **COOKING TIME** 20–25 minutes   **SERVES** 8

225g/8oz butter, softened, plus extra
   for greasing
225g/8oz/scant 1 cup caster/superfine sugar
4 large eggs, lightly beaten
200g/7oz/1⅓ cups self-raising flour
7 tbsp cocoa powder

100g/3½oz/½ cup milk chocolate chips
½ recipe quantity Chocolate Buttercream
   (see page 24)
200g/7oz plain/semisweet chocolate, melted
   and cooled slightly
12 glacé/candied cherries, to decorate

1. Preheat the oven to 190°C/375°F/gas 5. Grease and base-line two 20cm/8in sandwich cake tins.
2. Put the butter and sugar in a mixing bowl and beat using an electric hand mixer or wooden spoon until the mixture is light and creamy. Add the eggs gradually, beating after each addition. Sift in the flour and cocoa powder and gently fold them into the mixture, using a large metal spoon, then fold in the chocolate chips. Divide the mixture between the tins using a spatula.
3. Bake for 20–25 minutes until the cakes spring back when pressed lightly and a skewer inserted into the middle of each cake comes out clean. Remove the cakes from the oven and leave to stand for 5 minutes, then turn out on to a wire rack and leave to cool.
4. Sandwich the cakes together with the buttercream. Pour the melted chocolate over the top of the cake and swirl it attractively with a round-bladed knife. Place the cherries around the edge of the cake to decorate.

035 EGG-FREE CHOCOLATE CAKE

PREPARATION TIME 15 minutes **COOKING TIME** 40–45 minutes **SERVES** 8

225g/8oz butter, softened, plus extra
    for greasing
225g/8oz/scant 1 cup caster/superfine sugar
280g/10oz/scant 2 cups self-raising flour
55g/2oz/⅓ cup cocoa powder
½ tsp bicarbonate of soda/baking soda
250ml/9fl oz/1 cup sour cream

100g/3½oz/heaped ½ cup milk
    chocolate chips
100ml/3½fl oz/scant ½ cup milk
250ml/9fl oz/1 cup crème fraîche
3 tbsp blackcurrant jam/jelly
icing/powdered sugar, for dusting

1 Preheat the oven to 180°C/350°F/gas 4. Grease and base-line two 20cm/8in sandwich cake tins.
2 Put the butter and sugar in a mixing bowl and beat using an electric hand mixer or wooden spoon until the mixture is light and creamy. Sift in the flour, cocoa powder and bicarbonate of soda and gently fold them into the mixture with the sour cream, chocolate chips and milk, using a large metal spoon. Divide the mixture between the tins using a spatula.
3 Bake for 40–45 minutes until the cakes spring back when pressed lightly and a skewer inserted into the middle of each cake comes out clean. Remove the cakes from the oven, turn out on to a wire rack and leave to cool. Sandwich the cakes together with the crème fraîche and jam and dust with icing sugar.

036 DOUBLE CHOCOLATE CHIP FUDGE CAKE

PREPARATION TIME 25 minutes **COOKING TIME** 25–30 minutes **SERVES** 10

145g/5oz butter, softened, plus extra
    for greasing
175g/6oz/¾ cup light soft brown sugar
55g/2oz/¼ cup dark muscovado sugar
3 large eggs, lightly beaten
150ml/5fl oz/scant ⅔ cup sour cream
200g/7oz/1⅓ cups plain/all-purpose flour
55g/2oz/½ cup cocoa powder
1 tsp bicarbonate of soda/baking soda
1 tsp baking powder
100g/3½oz/heaped ½ cup white
    chocolate chips

FOR THE FILLING
150g/5½oz/1 cup icing/powdered sugar, sifted
100g/3½oz white chocolate, melted
    and cooled slightly
30g/1oz butter, softened
1–2 tbsp milk

FOR THE FROSTING
2 tbsp icing/powdered sugar
2 tbsp cocoa powder
200g/7oz plain/semisweet chocolate, melted
    and cooled slightly
150ml/5fl oz/scant ⅔ cup double/heavy cream

1 Preheat the oven to 190°C/375°F/gas 5. Grease and base-line two 20cm/8in sandwich cake tins.
2 Put 115g/4oz of the butter, the light brown sugar and muscovado sugar in a mixing bowl and beat using an electric hand mixer or wooden spoon until the mixture is light and creamy. Add the eggs gradually, beating after each addition, then beat in the sour cream. Sift in the flour, cocoa, bicarbonate of soda and baking powder and gently fold them into the mixture with the chocolate chips, using a large metal spoon. Divide the mixture between the tins using a spatula.
3 Bake for 25–30 minutes until the cakes spring back when pressed lightly and a skewer inserted into the middle of each cake comes out clean. Remove the cakes from the oven and leave to stand for 5 minutes, then turn out on to a wire rack and leave to cool.
4 For the filling, put all the ingredients in a bowl and beat using an electric hand mixer or wooden spoon until light and creamy. Cut each cake in half and sandwich together the four layers with a third of the white chocolate cream between each layer.
5 For the frosting, sift the icing sugar and cocoa into a bowl, add the melted plain chocolate and beat together using an electric hand mixer or wooden spoon. While still beating, pour in the cream and continue beating until you have a thick fudge frosting. Cover the top and sides of the cake with the frosting.

037 CINNAMON DEVIL'S FOOD CAKE

PREPARATION TIME 20 minutes, plus chilling   **COOKING TIME** 50–55 minutes   **SERVES** 8

115g/4oz butter, melted and cooled,
 plus extra for greasing
55g/2oz/⅓ cup cocoa powder
3 tbsp warm milk
225g/8oz/1½ cups plain/all-purpose flour
1 tsp baking powder
1 tsp bicarbonate of soda/baking soda
225g/8oz/1 cup light soft brown sugar
3 large eggs, separated
200ml/7fl oz/scant 1 cup sour cream
2 tsp ground cinnamon
chocolate sprinkles, to decorate

FOR THE ICING/FROSTING
200g/7oz/heaped ¾ cup caster/superfine
 sugar
115g/4oz butter, softened
115g/4oz plain/semisweet chocolate, broken
 into pieces
250ml/9fl oz/1 cup milk
500g/1lb 2oz/3⅓ cups icing/powdered
 sugar, sifted

1 Preheat the oven to 190°C/375°F/gas 5. Grease and line a 20cm/8in springform cake tin.
2 In a mixing bowl, dissolve the cocoa in the warm milk, ensuring there are no lumps. Sift in the flour, baking powder and bicarbonate of soda, add the melted butter, light brown sugar and egg yolks and beat using an electric hand mixer or wooden spoon until creamy.
3 Put the egg whites in a clean, dry bowl and whisk with an electric hand mixer or a whisk

until they form stiff peaks. Fold them into the cake mixture with the sour cream and ground cinnamon, using a large metal spoon. Scrape the mixture into the tin using a spatula.

4   Bake for 45–50 minutes until the cake springs back when pressed lightly and a skewer inserted into the middle of the cake comes out clean. Remove the cake from the oven and leave to stand for 5 minutes, then turn out on to a wire rack and leave to cool.

5   For the icing/frosting, put the caster sugar, butter, chocolate and milk into a saucepan and heat for 5 minutes, stirring, until the chocolate melts and the sugar dissolves. Bring to the boil, then remove from the heat and leave to cool. When cooled, add the icing sugar and beat vigorously with an electric hand mixer or wooden spoon until the icing becomes thick. This may take up to 15 minutes. Cut the cake in half and sandwich together with a third of the icing, then cover the cake with the remaining icing. Decorate with chocolate sprinkles and refrigerate until the icing has set before serving.

038 VANILLA BUNDT CAKE

PREPARATION TIME 20 minutes   **COOKING TIME** 50–55 minutes   **SERVES** 8

250g/9oz butter, softened, plus extra, melted, for greasing
400g/14oz/2⅔ cups plain/all-purpose flour, plus extra for dusting
400g/14oz/1⅔ cups caster/superfine sugar
4 large eggs, lightly beaten

seeds from 1 vanilla pod/bean (retain the pods for the icing/frosting)
250ml/9fl oz/1 cup milk
2 tsp baking powder
150g/5½oz/1 cup icing/powdered sugar, sifted

1   Preheat the oven to 180°C/350°F/gas 4. Grease a 25cm/10in bundt tin using a pastry brush and the melted butter, and dust with flour.

2   Put the butter and caster sugar in a mixing bowl and beat using an electric hand mixer or wooden spoon until the mixture is light and creamy. Add the eggs gradually, beating after each addition.

3   Add the vanilla seeds and milk to the cake mixture, sift in the flour and baking powder and beat again until the mixture is smooth and creamy. Scrape the mixture into the tin using a spatula.

4   Bake for 45–50 minutes until the cake springs back when pressed lightly and a skewer inserted into the middle of the cake comes out clean. Remove the cake from the oven and leave to stand for 5 minutes, then turn out on to a wire rack and leave to cool completely.

5   When the cake has cooled, heat the icing sugar, 2 tablespoons water and the vanilla pod in a small saucepan, stirring to form a smooth, runny icing/frosting. Simmer for 3–5 minutes to allow the vanilla flavour to infuse, then remove and discard the pod. Spoon the icing over the cake to glaze and leave to set before serving.

039 MINT CHOC CHIP BUNDT CAKE

PREPARATION TIME 20 minutes   **COOKING TIME** 25–30 minutes   **SERVES** 8

225g/8oz butter, softened, plus extra,
  melted, for greasing
225g/8oz/1½ cups self-raising flour, sifted,
  plus extra for dusting
225g/8oz/scant 1 cup caster/superfine sugar

4 large eggs, lightly beaten
1 tsp vanilla extract
100g/3½oz plain/semisweet mint chocolate,
  grated

1   Preheat the oven to 180°C/350°F/gas 4. Grease a 23cm/9in bundt tin using a pastry brush and the melted butter, and dust with flour.
2   Put the butter and sugar in a mixing bowl and beat using an electric hand mixer or wooden spoon until the mixture is light and creamy. Add the eggs gradually, beating after each addition. Add the flour, vanilla extract and mint chocolate and gently fold them into the mixture, using a large metal spoon. Scrape the mixture into the tin using a spatula.
3   Bake for 25–30 minutes until the cake springs back when pressed lightly and a skewer inserted into the middle of the cake comes out clean. Remove the cake from the oven and leave to stand for 5 minutes, then turn out on to a wire rack and leave to cool.

040 SILVER CAKE

PREPARATION TIME 25 minutes   **COOKING TIME** 30–35 minutes   **SERVES** 8

225g/8oz butter, softened, plus extra
  for greasing
175g/6oz/heaped 1 cup self-raising flour,
  sifted, plus extra for dusting

225g/8oz/scant 1 cup caster/superfine sugar
7 egg whites
55g/2oz/½ cup ground almonds

1   Preheat the oven to 180°C/350°F/gas 4. Grease a 23cm/9in ring tin and dust with flour.
2   Put the butter and sugar in a mixing bowl and beat using an electric hand mixer or wooden spoon until the mixture is light and creamy. Put the egg whites in a clean, dry bowl and whisk with an electric hand mixer or a whisk until they form stiff peaks. Fold half of the whisked egg whites into the creamed mixture, using a large metal spoon. Add the flour and ground almonds and fold them in gently with the metal spoon, followed by the remaining egg whites. Scrape the mixture into the tin using a spatula.
3   Bake for 30–35 minutes until the cake springs back when pressed lightly and a skewer inserted into the cake comes out clean. Remove the cake from the oven and leave to stand for 5 minutes, then turn out on to a wire rack and leave to cool.

041 LEMON & POPPY SEED RING CAKE

PREPARATION TIME 20 minutes   **COOKING TIME** 30–35 minutes   **SERVES** 8

225g/8oz butter, softened, plus extra
    for greasing
225g/8oz/1½ cups self-raising flour, sifted,
    plus extra for dusting
225g/8oz/scant 1 cup caster/superfine sugar

4 large eggs, lightly beaten
2 tbsp poppy seeds
2 tbsp natural/plain yogurt
juice and finely grated zest of 2 lemons
2 tbsp icing/powdered sugar

1 Preheat the oven to 180°C/350°F/gas 4. Grease a 23cm/9in ring tin and dust with flour.
2 Put the butter and caster sugar in a mixing bowl and beat using an electric hand mixer or wooden spoon until the mixture is light and creamy. Add the eggs gradually, beating after each addition. Add the flour, poppy seeds, yogurt and lemon zest and gently fold them into the mixture, using a large metal spoon. Scrape the mixture into the tin using a spatula.
3 Bake for 30–35 minutes until the cake springs back when pressed lightly and a skewer inserted into the cake comes out clean.
4 Just before the cake comes out of the oven, put the lemon juice and icing sugar in a saucepan and heat until the sugar has dissolved, then boil for 1 minute to create a syrup. Remove the cake from the oven and pour the syrup over the cake. Leave the cake to cool in the tin, then turn out on to a serving plate.

042 BLUEBERRY YOGURT BUNDT CAKE

PREPARATION TIME 20 minutes   **COOKING TIME** 45–50 minutes   **SERVES** 8

225g/8oz butter, softened, plus extra,
    melted, for greasing
225g/8oz/1½ cups self-raising flour, sifted,
    plus extra for dusting
225g/8oz/scant 1 cup caster/superfine sugar
4 large eggs, lightly beaten

finely grated zest of 2 lemons and
    1–2 tbsp of the juice
2 tbsp natural/plain yogurt
250g/9oz/heaped 1 cup blueberries
100g/3½oz/⅔ cup icing/powdered sugar

1 Preheat the oven to 180°C/350°F/gas 4. Grease a 23cm/9in bundt tin using a pastry brush and the melted butter, and dust with flour.
2 Put the butter and caster sugar in a mixing bowl and beat using an electric hand mixer or wooden spoon until the mixture is light and creamy. Add the eggs gradually, beating after each addition. Add the flour, lemon zest and yogurt and gently fold them into the mixture, using a large metal spoon, then fold in the blueberries. Scrape the mixture into the tin using a spatula.
3 Bake for 45–50 minutes until the cake springs back when pressed lightly and a skewer

inserted into the cake comes out clean. Remove the cake from the oven and leave to stand for 5 minutes, then turn out on to a wire rack and leave to cool.

4 Put the icing sugar and lemon juice in a small bowl and stir to make a thick icing/frosting. Drizzle over the top of the cake and leave to set before serving.

043 LEMON & LIME BUTTER CAKE

PREPARATION TIME 20 minutes   **COOKING TIME** 30–35 minutes   **SERVES** 8

250g/9oz butter, softened, plus extra
  for greasing
175g/6oz/heaped 1 cup self-raising flour,
  sifted, plus extra for dusting
225g/8oz/scant 1 cup caster/superfine sugar

juice and finely grated zest of 1 lemon
4 large eggs, lightly beaten
55g/2oz/½ cup ground almonds
4 tbsp natural/plain yogurt
juice and finely grated zest of 2 limes

1 Preheat the oven to 180°C/350°F/gas 4. Grease a 23cm/9in ring tin and dust with flour.
2 Put 225g/8oz of the butter, the sugar and lemon zest in a mixing bowl and beat using an electric hand mixer or wooden spoon until the mixture is light and creamy. Add the eggs gradually, beating after each addition. Add the flour, ground almonds and yogurt and gently fold them into the mixture using a large metal spoon. Scrape the mixture into the tin using a spatula.
3 Bake for 30–35 minutes until the cake springs back when pressed lightly and a skewer inserted into the cake comes out clean.
4 Just before the cake comes out of the oven, heat the remaining butter in a saucepan with the lime juice and zest and the lemon juice for 2–3 minutes until the butter has melted, then boil for 1 minute. Remove the cake from the oven and pour the citrus butter over the cake. Leave the cake to cool in the tin, then turn out on to a serving plate.

044 LEMON & CHOCOLATE CAKE

PREPARATION TIME 20 minutes   **COOKING TIME** 35–40 minutes   **SERVES** 8

225g/8oz butter, softened, plus extra
  for greasing
225g/8oz/1½ cups self-raising flour,
  sifted, plus extra for dusting
225g/8oz/scant 1 cup caster/superfine sugar

4 large eggs, lightly beaten
finely grated zest of 2 lemons
200g/7oz plain/semisweet chocolate:
  half finely chopped; half melted

1 Preheat the oven to 180°C/350°F/gas 4. Grease a 23cm/9in ring tin and dust with flour.
2 Put the butter and sugar in a mixing bowl and beat using an electric hand mixer or wooden spoon until the mixture is light and creamy. Add the eggs gradually, beating after each addition. Add the flour, lemon zest and chopped chocolate and gently fold them into the mixture, using a large metal spoon. Scrape the mixture into the tin using a spatula.
3 Bake for 35–40 minutes until the cake springs back when pressed lightly and a skewer inserted into the cake comes out clean. Remove the cake from the oven and leave to cool in the tin, then turn out on to a serving plate.

4 When the cake has cooled, drizzle the melted chocolate over the top of the cake, using a fork to form a decorative pattern.

045 CHOCOLATE CHERRY BUNDT CAKE

PREPARATION TIME 20 minutes   **COOKING TIME** 40–50 minutes   **SERVES** 8

225g/8oz butter, softened, plus extra
    for greasing
175g/6oz/heaped 1 cup self-raising flour,
    plus extra for dusting
225g/8oz/1 cup light soft brown sugar
4 large eggs, lightly beaten

55g/2oz/⅓ cup cocoa powder
100g/3½oz plain/semisweet chocolate, grated
1 tsp almond extract
200g/7oz/heaped 1 cup preserved
    cherries, stones removed
icing/powdered sugar, for dusting

1 Preheat the oven to 180°C/350°F/gas 4. Grease a 23cm/9in ring tin or bundt pan and dust with flour.

2 Put the butter and brown sugar in a mixing bowl and beat using an electric hand mixer or wooden spoon until the mixture is light and creamy. Add the eggs gradually, beating after each addition. Sift in the flour and cocoa and gently fold them into the mixture with the grated chocolate and almond extract, using a large metal spoon. Stir in the cherries, folding them lightly through the mixture. Scrape the mixture into the tin using a spatula.

3 Bake for 40–50 minutes until the cake springs back when pressed lightly and a skewer inserted into the cake comes out clean. Remove the cake from the oven and leave to stand for 5 minutes, then turn out on to a wire rack and leave to cool. Dust with icing sugar.

046 CHOCOLATE & CHILLI POUND CAKE

PREPARATION TIME 20 minutes   **COOKING TIME** 45–50 minutes   **SERVES** 8

250g/9oz butter, softened, plus extra
    for greasing
200g/7oz/¾ cup caster/superfine sugar
4 large eggs, lightly beaten
200g/7oz/1⅓ cups self-raising flour
6 tbsp cocoa powder

½ tsp chilli powder
100g/3½oz/heaped ½ cup plain/semisweet
    chocolate chips
200g/7oz plain/semisweet chilli chocolate,
    melted and cooled slightly
red sugar sprinkles, to decorate

1 Preheat the oven to 170°C/325°F/gas 3. Grease a deep 23cm/9in springform cake tin.

2 Put the butter and sugar in a mixing bowl and beat using an electric hand mixer or wooden spoon until the mixture is light and creamy. Add the eggs gradually, beating after each addition. Sift in the flour, cocoa and chilli powder and gently fold them into the mixture with the chocolate chips, using a large metal spoon. Scrape the mixture into the tin using a spatula.

3 Bake for 45–50 minutes until the cake springs back when pressed lightly and a skewer inserted into the cake comes out clean. Remove the cake from the oven and leave in the tin to cool, then turn out on to a serving plate. Drizzle the melted chocolate over the top. Decorate with the sprinkles and leave the chocolate to set before serving.

047 CHOCOLATE MARBLE RING

PREPARATION TIME 20 minutes   **COOKING TIME** 25–30 minutes   **SERVES** 8

225g/8oz butter, softened, plus extra
   for greasing
225g/8oz/1½ cups self-raising flour, sifted,
   plus extra for dusting
225g/8oz/scant 1 cup caster/superfine sugar

4 large eggs, lightly beaten
1 tsp vanilla extract
4 tbsp cocoa powder
100g/3½oz/heaped ½ cup plain/semisweet
   chocolate chips

1 Preheat the oven to 180°C/350°F/gas 4. Grease a 23cm/9in ring tin and dust with flour.

2 Put the butter and sugar in a mixing bowl and beat using an electric hand mixer or wooden spoon until the mixture is light and creamy. Add the eggs gradually, beating after each addition. Add the flour and gently fold it into the mixture, using a large metal spoon.

3 Divide the cake mixture between 2 bowls. Add the vanilla extract to one bowl and fold it in. Add the cocoa and chocolate chips to the other bowl and fold them in gently.

4 Place large spoonfuls of the cake mixtures alternately into the ring tin, using a spatula to get all of the mixtures out of the bowls. Gently pull a knife round the centre of the ring so that the different cake mixtures are slightly swirled together.

5 Bake for 25–30 minutes until the cake springs back when pressed lightly and a skewer inserted into the cake comes out clean. Remove the cake from the oven and leave to stand for 5 minutes, then turn out on to a wire rack and leave to cool.

048 GERMAN SAND CAKE

PREPARATION TIME 20 minutes   **COOKING TIME** 40–45 minutes   **MAKES** 20 slices

200g/7oz butter, melted and cooled,
   plus extra for greasing
75g/2½oz digestive biscuits/graham
   crackers, roughly broken
6 large eggs
225g/8oz/scant 1 cup caster/superfine sugar

125g/4½oz/scant 1 cup plain/all-purpose flour
2 tsp baking powder
100g/3½oz/scant ⅔ cup plain/semisweet
   chocolate chips
6 tbsp natural/plain yogurt
1 tsp vanilla extract

1. Preheat the oven to 180°C/350°F/gas 4. Grease and line a 38 x 25 x 6cm/15 x 10 x 2½in baking tin.
2. Put the broken biscuits in a food processor and pulse to fine crumbs. Alternatively, put them in a plastic bag and crush with a rolling pin. Sprinkle the biscuit crumbs over the base of the tin.
3. Put the eggs and sugar in a mixing bowl and whisk with an electric hand mixer or whisk until doubled in size and very creamy, and the whisk leaves a trail when lifted up. Slowly pour in the melted butter while still whisking. Sift in the flour and baking powder and gently fold them, the chocolate chips, yogurt and vanilla extract into the mixture, using a large metal spoon. Spoon the mixture over the crumb base in the tin using a spatula.
4. Bake for 40–45 minutes until the cake springs back when pressed lightly and a skewer inserted into the middle of the cake comes out clean. Remove the cake from the oven and leave to stand for 5 minutes, then invert on to a wire rack and leave to cool.

049 COFFEE STREUSEL LAYER CAKE

PREPARATION TIME 25 minutes   **COOKING TIME** 1–1½ hours   **SERVES** 8

115g/4oz butter, softened, plus extra
   for greasing
115g/4oz/scant ½ cup caster/superfine sugar
2 large eggs, lightly beaten
175g/6oz/heaped 1 cup self-raising flour, sifted
4 tbsp milk
1 tbsp instant coffee granules dissolved in
   1 tbsp boiling water and cooled
100g/3½oz/⅔ cup icing/powdered sugar, sifted

30g/1oz/¼ cup walnut pieces

FOR THE STREUSEL
85g/3oz/⅔ cup walnut pieces
1 level tbsp instant coffee granules
115g/4oz/½ cup soft brown sugar
2 tbsp plain/all-purpose flour
30g/1oz butter, melted and cooled

1. Preheat the oven to 160°C/325°F/gas 3. Grease and line a 20cm/8in loose-bottomed square cake tin.
2. For the streusel, put the walnuts, coffee granules, sugar and flour into a blender and whizz to a fine powder. Pour the melted butter into the blender and mix together. Set aside.
3. Put the softened butter and caster sugar in a mixing bowl and beat using an electric hand mixer or wooden spoon until the mixture is light and creamy. Add the eggs gradually, beating after each addition. Add the flour and milk and gently fold them into the mixture, using a large metal spoon.
4. Scrape half the cake mixture into the cake tin using a spatula and sprinkle over half the streusel, covering the cake mixture completely. Top with the remaining cake mixture and sprinkle over the remaining streusel.
5. Bake for 1–1½ hours until the cake springs back when pressed lightly and a skewer inserted into the middle of the cake comes out clean. Remove the cake from the oven

and leave to stand for 5 minutes, then turn out on to a wire rack. Meanwhile, in a bowl stir the coffee liquid and the icing sugar together to form a thick, smooth icing/frosting, adding a little more hot water if needed.

6 Drizzle the icing over the top of the cake in lines and sprinkle the walnut pieces over the cake before serving.

050 ORANGE SULTANA DRIZZLE CAKE

PREPARATION TIME 20 minutes **COOKING TIME** 30–35 minutes **SERVES** 8

115g/4oz butter, softened, plus extra
   for greasing
280g/10oz/heaped 1 cup caster/superfine
   sugar
2 large eggs, lightly beaten
225g/8oz/1½ cups self-raising flour, sifted

150ml/5fl oz/scant ⅔ cup milk
175g/6oz/heaped ⅔ cup sultanas/golden
   raisins
55g/2oz/heaped ⅓ cup flaked/sliced almonds
juice and finely grated zest of 1 large orange
juice and finely grated zest of 1 lemon

1 Preheat the oven to 180°C/350°F/gas 4. Grease and line a 23cm/9in loose-bottomed square cake tin.

2 Put the butter and 225g/8oz/scant 1 cup of the sugar in a mixing bowl and beat using an electric hand mixer or wooden spoon until the mixture is light and creamy. Add the eggs gradually, beating after each addition. Add the flour, milk, sultanas, almonds and orange and lemon zests and gently fold them into the mixture, using a large metal spoon. Scrape the mixture into the tin using a spatula.

3 Bake for 25–30 minutes until the cake springs back when pressed lightly and a skewer inserted into the middle of the cake comes out clean. Remove the cake from the oven and turn out on to a wire rack.

4 Put the lemon and orange juice and the remaining sugar in a small saucepan and heat until the sugar has dissolved, then boil for 1 minute to create a syrup. Spoon the syrup over the cake while it is still warm, then leave to cool completely.

051 CINNAMON DRIZZLE CAKE

PREPARATION TIME 20 minutes **COOKING TIME** 35–40 minutes **SERVES** 8

175g/6oz butter, softened, plus extra
   for greasing
85g/3oz/⅓ cup caster/superfine sugar
85g/3oz/⅓ cup dark muscovado sugar
3 large eggs, lightly beaten

175g/6oz/heaped 1 cup self-raising flour
1 heaped tsp ground cinnamon
125ml/4fl oz/½ cup maple syrup
1 cinnamon stick

1 Preheat the oven to 180°C/350°F/gas 4. Grease and line a 24 x 12cm/9½ x 4½in loaf tin.
2 Put the butter, caster sugar and muscovado sugar in a mixing bowl and beat using an electric hand mixer or wooden spoon until the mixture is light and creamy. Add the eggs gradually, beating after each addition. Sift in the flour and ground cinnamon and gently fold them into the mixture, using a large metal spoon. Scrape the mixture into the tin using a spatula.
3 Bake for 35–40 minutes until the cake springs back when pressed lightly and a skewer inserted into the middle of the cake comes out clean.
4 Just before the cake comes out of the oven, put the maple syrup, cinnamon stick and 3 tablespoons water in a small saucepan and heat gently for 5 minutes until the syrup smells of cinnamon. Remove the cinnamon stick.
5 Remove the cake from the oven and pour the syrup over the cake. Leave the cake to cool in the tin, then turn out on to a serving plate.

052 CINNAMON BANANA LOAF CAKE

PREPARATION TIME 20 minutes   **COOKING TIME** 40–45 minutes   **SERVES** 8

115g/4oz butter, softened, plus extra
   for greasing
175g/6oz/¾ cup dark soft brown sugar
3 ripe bananas, peeled and mashed
   with a fork

2 large eggs, lightly beaten
225g/8oz/1½ cups self-raising flour
1 tsp baking powder
1 tsp ground cinnamon
115g/4oz/scant 1 cup chopped walnuts

1 Preheat the oven to 180°C/350°F/gas 4. Grease and line a 24 x 12cm/9½ x 4½in loaf tin.
2 Put the butter and sugar in a mixing bowl and beat using an electric hand mixer or wooden spoon until the mixture is light and creamy. Add the bananas and eggs and beat again.
3 Sift in the flour, baking powder and ground cinnamon and gently fold them and the walnuts into the mixture, using a large metal spoon. Scrape the mixture into the tin using a spatula.
4 Bake for 40–45 minutes until the cake springs back when pressed lightly and a skewer inserted into the middle of the cake comes out clean. Remove the cake from the oven and leave to stand for 5 minutes, then turn out on to a wire rack and leave to cool.

053 DATE & WALNUT LOAF CAKE

PREPARATION TIME 25 minutes   **COOKING TIME** 45–50 minutes   **SERVES** 8

175g/6oz butter, softened, plus extra
   for greasing
175g/6oz/¾ cup light soft brown sugar
3 large eggs, lightly beaten

175g/6oz/heaped 1 cup self-raising flour, sifted
100g/3½oz/heaped ½ cup dates, chopped
100g/3½oz/heaped ½ cup walnuts, chopped
200ml/7fl oz/¾ cup maple syrup

1　Preheat the oven to 180°C/350°F/gas 4. Grease and line a 24 x 12cm/9½ x 4½in loaf tin.

2　Put the butter and sugar in a mixing bowl and beat using an electric hand mixer or wooden spoon until the mixture is light and creamy. Add the eggs gradually, beating after each addition. Add the flour, dates, walnuts and half the maple syrup and gently fold them into the mixture, using a large metal spoon. Scrape the mixture into the tin using a spatula.

3　Bake for 45–50 minutes until the cake springs back when pressed lightly and a skewer inserted into the middle of the cake comes out clean.

4　Just before the cake comes out of the oven, heat the remaining maple syrup in a small saucepan for a few minutes. Remove the cake from the oven and pour the syrup over the cake. Leave the cake to cool in the tin, then turn out on to a serving plate.

054　DATE & RAISIN DRIZZLE CAKE

PREPARATION TIME 20 minutes, plus soaking　　**COOKING TIME** 1–1¼ hours　　**SERVES** 8

150ml/5fl oz/scant ⅔ cup maple syrup
100g/3½oz/½ cup raisins
175g/6oz butter, plus extra for greasing
175g/6oz/¾ cup light soft brown sugar

3 large eggs, lightly beaten
175g/6oz/heaped 1 cup self-raising flour
1 tsp ground cinnamon
100g/3½oz/heaped ½ cup dates, chopped

1　Put the maple syrup in a saucepan with the raisins, bring to the boil, then leave for 1 hour to cool so the raisins become plump with the syrup.

2　Preheat the oven to 180°C/350°F/gas 4. Grease and line a 24 x 12cm/9½ x 4½in loaf tin.

3　Put the butter and sugar in a mixing bowl and beat using an electric hand mixer or wooden spoon until the mixture is light and creamy. Add the eggs gradually, beating after each addition. Sift in the flour and ground cinnamon and gently fold them into the mixture with the dates, using a large metal spoon. Strain the raisins, reserving the maple syrup to glaze the cake, and fold the soaked raisins into the mixture. Scrape the mixture into the tin using a spatula.

4　Bake for 1–1¼ hours until the cake springs back when pressed lightly and a skewer inserted into the middle of the cake comes out clean. Remove the cake from the oven and spoon the maple syrup over the top. Leave the cake to cool in the tin, then turn out on to a serving plate.

055 LAVENDER DRIZZLE CAKE

PREPARATION TIME 20 minutes　**COOKING TIME** 25–35 minutes　**SERVES** 8

225g/8oz butter, softened, plus extra
　for greasing
225g/8oz/scant 1 cup caster/superfine sugar
4 large eggs, lightly beaten
225g/8oz/1½ cups self-raising flour, sifted

juice and finely grated zest of 2 lemons
1 heaped tbsp icing/powdered sugar, sifted
2 tsp culinary lavender

1　Preheat the oven to 180°C/350°F/gas 4. Grease and line a 25cm/10in springform cake tin.
2　Put the butter and caster sugar in a mixing bowl and whisk using an electric hand mixer or wooden spoon until the mixture is light and creamy. Add the eggs gradually, beating after each addition. Add the flour and lemon zest and gently fold them into the mixture, using a large metal spoon. Scrape the mixture into the tin using a spatula.
3　Bake for 25–35 minutes until the cake springs back when pressed lightly and a skewer inserted into the middle of the cake comes out clean.
4　Just before the cake comes out of the oven, heat the lemon juice with the icing sugar and lavender in a saucepan until the sugar has dissolved, then boil for 1 minute to make a syrup. Remove the cake from the oven and pour the syrup over the cake. Leave the cake to cool in the tin, then turn out on to a serving plate.

056 STICKY WHITE CHOCOLATE & MARMALADE LOAF

PREPARATION TIME 15 minutes　**COOKING TIME** 40–45 minutes　**SERVES** 8

175g/6oz butter, softened, plus extra
　for greasing
175g/6oz/¾ cup light soft brown sugar
3 large eggs, lightly beaten
175g/6oz/heaped 1 cup self-raising
　flour, sifted

3 tbsp thin-shred marmalade
finely grated zest of 1 orange
100g/3½oz white chocolate,
　coarsely chopped

1　Preheat the oven to 180°C/350°F/gas 4. Grease and line a 24 x 12cm/9½ x 4½in loaf tin.
2　Put the butter and sugar in a mixing bowl and beat using an electric hand mixer or wooden spoon until the mixture is light and creamy. Add the eggs gradually, beating after each addition. Add the flour and gently fold it into the mixture, using a large metal spoon, then fold in 2 tablespoons of the marmalade, the orange zest and white chocolate. Scrape the mixture into the tin using a spatula.
3　Bake for 35–40 minutes until the cake springs back when pressed lightly and a skewer inserted into the middle of the cake comes out clean.

4 Remove the cake from the oven and leave to stand for 5 minutes, then turn out on to a wire rack. Heat the remaining marmalade in a small saucepan, then brush it over the top of the cake to glaze. Leave to cool.

057 MAPLE APPLE LOAF

PREPARATION TIME 20 minutes   **COOKING TIME** 45–55 minutes   **SERVES** 8

175g/6oz butter, softened, plus extra
   for greasing
175g/6oz/¾ cup light soft brown sugar
3 large eggs, lightly beaten
175g/6oz/heaped 1 cup self-raising
   flour, sifted
2 tbsp natural/plain yogurt

1 large cooking/baking apple, peeled,
   cored and grated
100g/3½oz/heaped ½ cup sultanas/
   golden raisins
55g/2oz/½ cup walnuts, chopped
2 tbsp maple syrup

1 Preheat the oven to 180°C/350°F/gas 4. Grease and line a 24 x 12cm/9½ x 4½in loaf tin.
2 Put the butter and light brown sugar in a mixing bowl and beat using an electric hand mixer or wooden spoon until the mixture is light and creamy. Add the eggs gradually, beating after each addition. Add the flour, yogurt, grated apple, sultanas and walnuts and gently fold them into the mixture, using a large metal spoon. Scrape the mixture into the tin using a spatula.
3 Bake for 45–55 minutes until the cake springs back when pressed lightly and a skewer inserted into the middle of the cake comes out clean.
4 Just before the cake comes out of the oven, warm the maple syrup gently in a saucepan. Remove the cake from the oven and pour the syrup over the cake. Leave the cake to cool in the tin, then turn out on to a serving plate.

058 CARROT LOAF CAKE

PREPARATION TIME 20 minutes   **COOKING TIME** 50–60 minutes   **SERVES** 8

125ml/4fl oz/½ cup vegetable oil,
   plus extra for greasing
2 large eggs, lightly beaten
125ml/4fl oz/½ cup natural/plain yogurt
250g/9oz/1 cup light soft brown sugar
180g/6¼oz/1¼ cups plain/all-purpose flour
1 tsp mixed/pumpkin pie spice
1 tsp ground cinnamon

1 tsp bicarbonate of soda/baking soda
2 large carrots, peeled and grated
½ tsp salt
100g/3½oz/heaped ½ cup pecan nuts,
   roughly chopped
juice and finely grated zest of 1 orange
2 tbsp icing/powdered sugar, sifted
crème fraîche or whipped cream, to serve

1 Preheat the oven to 160°C/325°F/gas 3. Grease and line a 24 x 12cm/9½ x 4½in loaf tin.
2 Put the eggs, oil, yogurt and light brown sugar in a mixing bowl and whisk with an electric hand mixer or a whisk to combine all the ingredients. Sift in the flour, spices and bicarbonate of soda and fold in with the grated carrots, salt, pecans and orange zest, using a large metal spoon. Scrape the mixture into the tin using a spatula.
3 Bake for 50–60 minutes until the cake springs back when pressed lightly and a skewer inserted into the middle of the cake comes out clean.
4 Just before the cake comes out of the oven, heat the orange juice and icing sugar in a small saucepan until the sugar has dissolved, then boil for 1 minute to create a syrup. Remove the cake from the oven and pour the syrup over the cake. Leave the cake to cool in the tin, then turn out on to a serving plate and serve with crème fraîche or cream. To make a dairy free version use dairy free yogurt and omit the crème fraîche or whipped cream to serve.

059 CARROT & COURGETTE CAKE

PREPARATION TIME 25 minutes   **COOKING TIME** 1½–1¾ hours   **SERVES** 8

185ml/6fl oz/¾ cup vegetable oil, plus extra for greasing
3 large carrots, peeled
100g/3½oz/⅔ cup icing/powdered sugar, sifted
3 large eggs, lightly beaten
100ml/3½fl oz/scant ½ cup sour cream
200g/7oz/1 cup lightly packed dark muscovado sugar
150g/5½oz/scant ⅔ cup caster/ superfine sugar
250g/9oz/1⅔ cups plain/all-purpose flour
1 tsp mixed/pumpkin pie spice
1 tsp bicarbonate of soda/baking soda

1 courgette/zucchini, trimmed and grated
100g/3½oz/heaped ½ cup chopped walnuts
finely grated zest of 1 lemon
finely grated zest of 1 orange
100g/3½oz/heaped 1 cup desiccated/dried shredded coconut

FOR THE ICING/FROSTING
150g/5½oz cream cheese
300g/10½oz/2 cups icing/powdered sugar, sifted
55g/2oz butter, softened
1 tbsp lemon juice

1 Preheat the oven to 160°C/325°F/gas 3. Grease and line a deep 23cm/9in springform cake tin.
2 Shred 1 of the carrots into strips using a zester for the candied carrot decoration and put in a saucepan with 100ml/3½fl oz/scant ½ cup water and the icing sugar. Bring to the boil, then drain and set aside to cool.
3 Put the eggs, oil, sour cream, muscovado sugar and caster sugar in a mixing bowl and whisk with an electric hand mixer or a whisk to combine all the ingredients. Sift in the flour, mixed spice and bicarbonate of soda, grate the remaining carrots and add with the courgette, walnuts, lemon and orange zest and coconut and fold them in, using a large

metal spoon until mixed well. Scrape the mixture into the cake tin using a spatula.

4 Bake for about 1½–1¾ hours until the cake springs back when pressed lightly and a skewer inserted into the middle of the cake comes out clean. Remove the cake from the oven and leave to stand for 5 minutes, then turn out on to a wire rack and leave to cool.

5 Put the icing/frosting ingredients in a bowl and beat together using an electric hand mixer or wooden spoon until light and creamy. Spread the icing over the top of the cake and decorate with the candied carrot.

060 FARMHOUSE FRUIT CAKE

PREPARATION TIME 20 minutes **COOKING TIME** 45–60 minutes **SERVES** 8

115g/4oz butter, softened, plus extra
    for greasing
115g/4oz/½ cup light soft brown sugar
3 large eggs, lightly beaten
225g/8oz/1½ cups self-raising flour
1 tsp mixed/pumpkin pie spice

½ tsp salt
175g/6oz/1 cup mixed dried fruit
30g/1oz/scant ¼ cup glacé/candied
    cherries, halved
85g/3oz/½ cup flaked/sliced almonds

1 Preheat the oven to 180°C/350°F/gas 4. Grease and line an 18cm/7in springform cake tin.
2 Put the butter and sugar in a mixing bowl and beat using an electric hand mixer or wooden spoon until the mixture is light and creamy. Add the eggs gradually, beating after each addition. Sift in the flour and mixed spice and gently fold them in with the salt, dried fruit, cherries and almonds, using a metal spoon. Scrape the mixture into the tin using a spatula.
3 Bake for 45–60 minutes until the cake springs back when pressed lightly and a skewer inserted into the middle of the cake comes out clean. Remove the cake from the oven and leave to cool in the tin, then turn out on to a serving plate.

061 DUNDEE CAKE

PREPARATION TIME 20 minutes, plus soaking **COOKING TIME** 2–2¼ hours **SERVES** 8

225g/8oz butter, softened, plus extra
    for greasing
30g/1oz/¼ cup blanched whole almonds
3 tbsp milk
225g/8oz/scant 1 cup caster/superfine sugar
4 large eggs, lightly beaten
280g/10oz/scant 2 cups self-raising flour, sifted
finely grated zest of 1 orange and
    half the juice

juice and finely grated zest of 1 lemon
400g/14oz/2 cups mixed dried fruit, such
    as raisins, currants and sultanas
100g/3½oz/½ cup glacé/candied
    cherries, chopped
100g/3½oz/heaped ½ cup mixed/
    candied peel
1 tsp almond extract
2 tbsp apricot jam/jelly

1 Preheat the oven to 160°C/325°F/gas 3. Grease and line a deep 20cm/8in springform cake tin. Put the almonds in a bowl with the milk and soak for 20 minutes.
2 Put the butter and sugar in a mixing bowl and beat using an electric hand mixer or wooden spoon until the mixture is light and creamy. Add the eggs gradually, beating after each addition. Add the flour, citrus zests, dried fruit, cherries, mixed peel and almond extract and gently fold them in, using a large metal spoon. Scrape the mixture into the tin using a spatula and arrange the soaked almonds over the top of the cake in a circular pattern.

3 Bake for about 2–2¼ hours until the cake springs back when pressed lightly and a skewer inserted into the middle of the cake comes out clean.

4 Remove the cake from the oven and leave to stand for 5 minutes, then turn out on to a wire rack. Put the lemon and orange juice and jam in a small saucepan over a gentle heat and stir until melted, then brush the apricot glaze over the top of the cake using a pastry brush. Leave to cool.

062 EARL GREY TEA BREAD

PREPARATION TIME 20 minutes, plus soaking   **COOKING TIME** 1–1¼ hours   **SERVES** 8

115g/4oz/heaped ½ cup sultanas/
   golden raisins
250ml/9fl oz/1 cup black Earl Grey tea
55g/2oz chilled butter, chopped, plus extra
   for greasing
225g/8oz/1½ cups self-raising flour

1 tsp baking powder
55g/2oz/¼ cup dark soft brown sugar
finely grated zest of 1 lemon
finely grated zest of 1 orange
2 large eggs, lightly beaten

1 Soak the sultanas in the tea for about 3 hours. Preheat the oven to 160°C/325°F/gas 3. Grease and line a 24 x 12cm/9½ x 4½in loaf tin.

2 Sift the flour and baking powder into a mixing bowl. Add the butter and rub it into the flour with your fingertips until the mixture resembles fine breadcrumbs.

3 Stir in the sultanas and tea, the sugar, citrus zests and eggs and beat well with a wooden spoon to combine all the ingredients. Scrape the mixture into the tin using a spatula.

4 Bake for 1–1¼ hours until the tea bread springs back when pressed lightly and a skewer inserted into the middle of the loaf comes out clean. Remove the loaf from the oven and leave to stand for 5 minutes, then turn out on to a wire rack and leave to cool.

063 CUT & COME AGAIN CAKE

PREPARATION TIME 25 minutes   **COOKING TIME** 1¼–1½ hours   **SERVES** 8

115g/4oz chilled butter, chopped,
   plus extra for greasing
225g/8oz/1½ cups self-raising flour
1 tsp baking powder
1 tsp mixed/pumpkin pie spice
1 tsp ground cinnamon
115g/4oz/½ cup light soft brown sugar
200g/7oz/1 cup sultanas/golden raisins

85g/3oz/heaped ⅓ cup dried
   apricots, chopped
85g/3oz/scant ½ cup glacé/candied
   cherries, chopped
2 large eggs, lightly beaten
150ml/5fl oz/scant ⅔ cup milk
2 tbsp natural/plain yogurt

1 Preheat the oven to 180°C/350°F/gas 4. Grease and line a 20cm/8in springform cake tin.

2 Sift the flour, baking powder, mixed spice and ground cinnamon into a mixing bowl and stir well with a wooden spoon. Add the butter and rub it into the flour mixture with your fingertips so that the mixture resembles fine breadcrumbs. Stir in the sugar, sultanas, apricots and cherries, then add the beaten eggs, milk and yogurt and mix well with a large metal spoon. Scrape the mixture into the tin using a spatula.

3 Bake for 1¼–1½ hours until the cake springs back when pressed lightly and a skewer inserted into the middle of the cake comes out clean. Remove the cake from the oven and leave to stand for 5 minutes, then turn out on to a wire rack and leave to cool.

064 ROSEWATER BARA BRITH

PREPARATION TIME 20 minutes, plus soaking   **COOKING TIME** 45–50 minutes   **SERVES** 8

115g/4oz/heaped ½ cup currants
115g/4oz/heaped ½ cup sultanas/
    golden raisins
115g/4oz/heaped ½ cup raisins
400ml/14fl oz/1½ cups hot tea
2 tbsp rosewater
flavourless oil, for greasing

55g/2oz/¼ cup glacé/candied cherries, halved
85g/3oz/⅓ cup light muscovado sugar
3 large eggs, lightly beaten
400g/14oz/2⅔ cups self-raising flour
1 tsp mixed/pumpkin pie spice
1 tsp ground cinnamon
butter or dairy free spread, to serve

1 Soak the currants, sultanas and raisins in the hot tea and rosewater in a mixing bowl overnight so that they become plump and absorb some of the liquid.

2 Preheat the oven to 180°C/350°F/gas 4. Grease and line a 23cm/9in loose-bottomed square cake tin.

3 Strain the fruit, retaining the liquid, and put the fruit in a mixing bowl. Stir in the cherries, sugar and eggs and sift in the flour, mixed spice and ground cinnamon, mixing well with a large metal spoon. Slowly pour in the soaking liquid and mix in well. Scrape the mixture into the tin using a spatula.

4 Bake for 45–50 minutes until the cake springs back when pressed lightly and a skewer inserted into the middle of the cake comes out clean. Remove the cake from the oven and leave to cool in the tin, then turn out on to a serving plate. Serve slices spread with butter or a dairy free alternative.

065 COFFEE BATTENBERG

PREPARATION TIME 40 minutes   **COOKING TIME** 20–30 minutes   **SERVES** 8

250g/9oz butter, softened, plus extra
   for greasing
175g/6oz/scant ¾ cup caster/superfine sugar
3 large eggs, lightly beaten
175g/6oz/heaped 1 cup self-raising flour
1 tsp baking powder

1 tbsp cocoa powder
1 tbsp instant coffee granules dissolved
   in 2 tbsp boiling water, then cooled
150g/5½oz/1 cup icing/powdered sugar,
   sifted, plus extra for dusting
400g/14oz white marzipan

1 Preheat the oven to 180°C/350°F/gas 4. Grease and line two 24 x 12cm/9½ x 4½in loaf tins.
2 Put 175g/6oz of the butter and the sugar in a mixing bowl and beat using an electric hand mixer or wooden spoon until the mixture is light and creamy. Add the eggs gradually, beating after each addition. Sift in the flour and baking powder and gently fold them into the mixture, using a large metal spoon.
3 Scrape half the mixture into one of the tins using a spatula. Add the cocoa and half the coffee liquid to the remaining mixture and scrape that into the other tin.

4   Bake for 20–30 minutes until the cakes spring back when pressed lightly and a skewer inserted into the middle of each cake comes out clean. Remove the cakes from the oven and leave to stand for 5 minutes, then turn out on to a wire rack and leave to cool.

5   Put the icing sugar, remaining butter and remaining coffee liquid in a bowl and beat using an electric hand mixer or wooden spoon to make a smooth buttercream.

6   When the cakes have cooled, cut each cake in half lengthways and trim the four cakes with a knife so you have four equal-size rectangular cakes. Sandwich the cakes together with a thin layer of buttercream in alternate colours to make a checkerboard pattern. Cover the outside of the cake with a thin layer of buttercream.

7   Sift icing sugar on to a clean work surface and roll the marzipan out to 5mm/¼in thick into a rectangle with a width as long as the cake and a length just over four times the width of the cake, using a rolling pin. Trim the edges of the marzipan and wrap it around the cake, smoothing it down with your hands, making a firm join and pinching the corners to neaten them. Place the cake on a serving plate with the join underneath.

066 STRAWBERRY & VANILLA SWISS ROLL

PREPARATION TIME 20 minutes   **COOKING TIME** 10–12 minutes   **SERVES** 8

butter, for greasing
3 large eggs, lightly beaten
100g/3½oz/heaped ⅓ cup caster/
   superfine sugar
125g/4½oz/scant 1 cup self-raising flour, sifted
1 tsp vanilla extract

3 tbsp icing/powdered sugar, sifted
240ml/8fl oz/scant 1 cup double/heavy
   cream, whipped to stiff peaks
3 tbsp strawberry jam/jelly
200g/7oz/2 cups strawberries, hulled
   and sliced

1   Preheat the oven to 180°C/350°F/gas 4. Grease and line a 30 x 20cm/12 x 8in Swiss/jelly roll tin.

2   Put the eggs and caster sugar in a mixing bowl and whisk together using an electric hand mixer or a whisk until they are creamy and pale yellow and the whisk leaves a trail when lifted up. Add the flour and vanilla extract and fold them in, using a large metal spoon.

3   Scrape the mixture into the tin using a spatula and bake for 10–12 minutes until the cake springs back when pressed lightly. Remove from the oven and leave for a few minutes.

4   Put a sheet of baking parchment on a clean work surface and dust with the icing sugar. Turn the cake out on to the sugar-covered paper, cover with a damp dish towel and leave to cool for 10 minutes. Remove the towel and lining paper and cut away the edges of the cake to neaten it. Roll the cake up from a short end using the sugar-covered paper to help you and leave to cool completely. (The paper will end up rolled inside the cake.)

5   Unroll the cake, spread the cream and jam over and cover with the strawberries. Roll the Swiss roll up, using the paper to help you but this time not rolling it inside the cake,

and place on a serving plate. As the Swiss roll contains fresh cream, it should be eaten straight away or stored in a lidded container in the refrigerator. To make a dairy free version, serve with just the jam and strawberries and use flavourless oil for greasing rather than butter.

067 CARAMEL ANGEL FOOD CAKE

PREPARATION TIME 20 minutes   **COOKING TIME** 30–35 minutes   **SERVES** 8

flavourless oil, for greasing
125g/4½oz/scant 1 cup plain/all-purpose flour
375g/13oz/heaped 2 cups golden icing/ powdered sugar, plus extra for dusting

10 large egg whites
½ tsp cream of tartar
3 tbsp maple syrup, plus extra to serve

1 Preheat the oven to 190°C/375°F/gas 5. Grease a 25cm/10in angel food cake tin.
2 Sift the flour and icing sugar together 3 or 4 times until they are very light and airy. Put the egg whites in a clean, dry bowl and whisk with an electric hand mixer or a whisk until they form stiff peaks. Add the cream of tartar and whisk again for 1 minute, then gently fold the egg whites into the flour and sugar mixture, using a large metal spoon. Stir in the maple syrup, then scrape the mixture into the tin using a spatula.
3 Bake for 30–35 minutes until the cake springs back when pressed lightly and a skewer inserted into the middle of the cake comes out clean. Remove the cake from the oven and leave to stand for 5 minutes, then turn out on to a wire rack and leave to cool. Dust the cake with icing sugar and serve slices with extra maple syrup drizzled over.

068 PISTACHIO MARZIPAN RING

PREPARATION TIME 25 minutes, plus rising   **COOKING TIME** 25–30 minutes   **SERVES** 8

55g/2oz butter, melted and cooled, plus extra for greasing and to serve
450g/1lb/3 cups strong white bread flour, sifted, plus extra for dusting
1 tsp salt
2 tsp fast action dried yeast

2 tbsp sugar
2 large eggs, beaten
55g/2oz marzipan, grated or finely chopped
100g/3½oz/heaped ½ cup pistachio nuts, chopped

1 Grease a 23cm/9in ring tin and dust with flour.
2 Put the flour, salt, yeast and sugar in a large mixing bowl and make a well in the middle. Add the beaten eggs, melted butter and 170ml/5½fl oz/scant ¾ cup warm water and bring together with your hands to form a soft dough.

3   Sift flour on to a clean work surface and turn the dough out. Knead well, then leave
    to rest for 10 minutes before adding the grated marzipan and chopped pistachios and
    kneading for a further 5–6 minutes. Put the dough in the tin, cover with a damp dish towel
    and leave in a warm place to rise for about 1 hour or until the dough has doubled in size.
    Preheat the oven to 180°C/350°F/gas 4.
4   Bake for 25–30 minutes until the bread is golden. Remove the cake from the oven and tip
    it out upside down on to a wire rack. Tap it with a knuckle, and, if it sounds hollow, it is
    ready. (If it does not sound hollow, return it to the oven for 5 minutes, then try again.) Turn
    right-way up on the rack and leave to cool slightly, then slice and serve warm with butter.

069 LARDY CAKE

PREPARATION TIME 30 minutes, plus rising   **COOKING TIME** 25–35 minutes   **SERVES** 8

115g/4oz butter: half chilled and chopped;
   half melted, plus extra for greasing
2 tsp fast action dried yeast
225g/8oz/scant 1 cup caster/superfine sugar
125ml/4fl oz/½ cup warm milk
1 pinch saffron stamens

225g/8oz/1½ cups plain/all-purpose flour,
   sifted, plus extra for dusting
1 large egg, lightly beaten
1 tsp ground cinnamon
150g/5½oz/heaped ⅔ cup currants

1   Grease a 20cm/8in loose-bottomed square cake tin.
2   Put the yeast in a cup with 1 tablespoon of the sugar and the warm milk and saffron and
    leave for 10 minutes until the mixture is foamy.
3   Put the flour into a large mixing bowl, add the chilled butter and rub it into the flour with
    your fingertips until the mixture resembles fine breadcrumbs. Add the yeast mixture and
    beaten egg to the flour and mix in with your hands to form a soft dough. Add a little more
    flour if the dough is too sticky.
4   Sift flour on to a clean work surface and knead the dough vigorously for 8 minutes. Roll
    the dough out into a 40 x 20cm/16 x 8in rectangle and brush with a third of the melted
    butter. Sprinkle over a third of the remaining sugar, ground cinnamon and currants. Fold
    the dough in half and seal the sides by pressing tightly with your fingers. Roll the dough
    into a rectangle again and repeat the rolling and folding twice more so that you have made
    3 layers of butter and currants in the dough and finish with a 20cm/8in square of dough.
5   Put the dough in the tin, cover with a damp dish towel and leave in a warm place for about
    1 hour until the dough has doubled in size. Preheat the oven to 180°C/350°F/gas 4.
6   Bake for 25–35 minutes until the cake is golden. Remove the cake from the oven and tip
    it out upside down on to a wire rack. Tap it with a knuckle, and, if it sounds hollow, it is
    ready. (If it does not sound hollow, return it to the oven for 5 minutes, then try again.)
    Turn right-way up on the rack and leave to cool completely.

Chapter 2

SMALL CAKES

This chapter contains a wide variety of small and dainty cakes, perfect for afternoon teas, parties or lunch boxes. Pretty cake stands and plates laden with small cakes and delicacies can't fail to delight – try Amaretto & Hazelnut Fondant Fancies, Banoffi Choux Buns and Chocolate Éclairs. These are afternoon treats that will delight any guest. Cupcakes and muffins are hugely popular and always disappear quickly, especially when served still warm from the oven. From plain but highly flavoured Peshwari Cupcakes to indulgent Rocky Road Cupcakes, and from Toffee Popcorn Muffins to Triple Chocolate Muffins, there is something to suit all tastes. There are traditional Iced Cherry Cupcakes and more unusual Lemongrass & Soured Cream Mini Loaf Cakes, dainty Orange Syrup Friands and scones in a wide variety of flavours. Most of these recipes can be prepared very quickly, making them perfect for visitors, for children coming home from school or to sell at school bazaars and summer fêtes.

070 LEMON & APRICOT MUFFINS

PREPARATION TIME 20 minutes   **COOKING TIME** 20–25 minutes   **MAKES** 10 muffins

250g/9oz/1⅔ cups self-raising flour
2 tsp baking powder
1 tsp bicarbonate of soda/baking soda
100g/3½oz/heaped ⅓ cup caster/
    superfine sugar
100g/3½oz/½ cup dried apricots, chopped

juice and finely grated zest of 1 lemon
150ml/5fl oz/scant ⅔ cup milk
4 tbsp natural/plain yogurt
100g/3½oz butter, melted and cooled
3 tbsp apricot jam/jelly, warmed
2 large eggs, lightly beaten

1   Preheat the oven to 180°C/350°F/gas 4. Put 10 muffin cases/liners in a 12-hole muffin tin.
2   Sift the flour, baking powder and bicarbonate of soda into a mixing bowl, add the sugar and stir well with a wooden spoon. Stir in the apricots and lemon zest.
3   In a separate bowl, whisk together the milk, yogurt, melted butter and 2 tablespoons of the jam with an electric hand mixer or a whisk. Add the eggs and whisk again. Pour the liquid into the bowl containing the dry ingredients and fold in with a large metal spoon. Do not overmix: the mixture should be thick and slightly lumpy. Spoon the mixture into the muffin cases.
4   Bake for 15–20 minutes until the muffins spring back when pressed lightly and a skewer inserted into the middle of a muffin comes out clean. Remove the muffins from the oven and turn out on to a wire rack.
5   Heat the remaining jam with the lemon juice in a small saucepan until the jam has melted, then brush this syrup over the muffins with a pastry brush. Leave to cool.

071 CRANBERRY & ORANGE MUFFINS

PREPARATION TIME 15 minutes   **COOKING TIME** 15–20 minutes   **MAKES** 10 muffins

250g/9oz/1⅔ cups self-raising flour
1 tsp baking powder
1 tsp bicarbonate of soda/baking soda
100g/3½oz/heaped ⅓ cup caster/
    superfine sugar
juice and finely grated zest of 1 small orange

100g/3½oz/¾ cup dried cranberries
150ml/5fl oz/scant ⅔ cup milk
4 tbsp natural/plain yogurt
100g/3½oz butter, melted and cooled
2 large eggs, lightly beaten
2 tbsp icing/powdered sugar, sifted

1   Preheat the oven to 180°C/350°F/gas 4. Put 10 muffin cases/liners in a 12-hole muffin tin.
2   Sift the flour, baking powder and bicarbonate of soda into a mixing bowl, add the caster sugar, orange zest and dried cranberries and stir well with a wooden spoon.
3   In a separate bowl, whisk together the milk, yogurt and melted butter with an electric hand mixer or a whisk, add the eggs and whisk again. Pour the liquid into the bowl

containing the dry ingredients and fold in with a large metal spoon. Do not overmix: the mixture should be thick and slightly lumpy. Spoon the mixture into the muffin cases.

4   Bake for 15–20 minutes until the muffins spring back when pressed lightly and a skewer inserted into the middle of a muffin comes out clean.

5   Just before the muffins are cooked, heat the orange juice with the icing sugar in a small saucepan, stirring until the sugar has dissolved, then boil for 1 minute to make a syrup. Remove the muffins from the oven and drizzle the syrup over them. Leave to cool.

072 BLUEBERRY MUFFINS

PREPARATION TIME 15 minutes   **COOKING TIME** 15–20 minutes   **MAKES** 10 muffins

250g/9oz/1⅔ cups self-raising flour
1 tsp baking powder
1 tsp bicarbonate of soda/baking soda
100g/3½oz/heaped ⅓ cup caster/
    superfine sugar
200g/7oz/heaped 1 cup blueberries

juice and grated zest of 1 large lemon
150ml/5fl oz/scant ⅔ cup milk
4 tbsp sour cream
100g/3½oz butter, melted and cooled
2 large eggs, lightly beaten
150g/5½oz/1 cup icing/powdered sugar, sifted

1   Preheat the oven to 180°C/350°F/gas 4. Put 10 muffin cases/liners in a 12-hole muffin tin. Sift the flour, baking powder and bicarbonate of soda into a mixing bowl, add the caster sugar, blueberries and lemon zest and stir well with a wooden spoon.

2   In a separate bowl, whisk together the milk, sour cream and melted butter with an electric hand mixer or a whisk, add the eggs and whisk again. Pour the liquid into the bowl containing the dry ingredients and fold in with a large metal spoon. Do not overmix: the mixture should be thick and slightly lumpy. Spoon the mixture into the muffin cases.

3   Bake for 15–20 minutes until the muffins spring back when pressed lightly. Remove the muffins from the oven, turn out on to a wire rack and leave to cool.

4   Put the icing sugar and 1–2 tablespoons of the lemon juice in a bowl and stir to form a smooth icing/frosting. Spoon a little of the icing over each muffin. Leave to set before serving.

073 BANANA & COCONUT MUFFINS

PREPARATION TIME 15 minutes   **COOKING TIME** 20–25 minutes   **MAKES** 10 muffins

115g/4oz butter, softened
55g/2oz/¼ cup dark soft brown sugar
55g/2oz/¼ cup caster/superfine sugar
2 large eggs, lightly beaten
1 large, ripe banana, peeled

2 tbsp coconut cream
55g/2oz/heaped ½ cup desiccated/dried
  shredded coconut
115g/4oz/¾ cup self-raising flour, sifted

1   Preheat the oven to 180°C/350°F/gas 4. Put 10 muffin cases/liners in a 12-hole muffin tin.
2   Put the butter and both sugars in a mixing bowl and beat using an electric hand mixer or
    wooden spoon until the mixture is creamy. Add the eggs slowly, beating after each addition.
3   Put the banana and coconut cream in a separate bowl and mash together with a fork, then
    stir into the cake mix with the desiccated coconut and flour. Spoon into the muffin cases.
4   Bake for 20–25 minutes until the muffins spring back when pressed lightly and a skewer
    inserted into the middle of a muffin comes out clean. Remove the muffins from the oven,
    turn out on to a wire rack and leave to cool.

074 COCONUT & CARDAMOM MUFFINS

PREPARATION TIME 15 minutes, plus soaking   **COOKING TIME** 15–20 minutes   **MAKES** 10 muffins

100g/3½oz/heaped 1 cup desiccated/dried
  shredded coconut
125ml/4fl oz/½ cup coconut milk
250g/9oz/1⅔ cups self-raising flour
1 tsp baking powder
1 tsp bicarbonate of soda/baking soda
100g/3½oz/heaped ⅓ cup caster/
  superfine sugar

½ tsp ground cardamom
100g/3½oz/heaped ½ cup white
  chocolate chips
100g/3½oz butter, melted
150ml/5fl oz/scant ⅔ cup milk
4 tbsp natural/plain yogurt
2 large eggs, lightly beaten

1   Preheat the oven to 180°C/350°F/gas 4. Put 10 muffin cases/liners in a 12-hole muffin tin.
    Put the desiccated coconut and coconut milk in a bowl and leave to soak for 20 minutes.
2   Sift the flour, baking powder and bicarbonate of soda into a mixing bowl, add the sugar
    and stir well. Stir in the coconut, coconut milk, cardamom and white chocolate chips.
3   Put the remaining ingredients in a separate bowl and whisk together using an electric hand
    mixer or a whisk. Pour the liquid into the bowl containing the dry ingredients and fold in
    with a large metal spoon. Do not overmix: the mixture should be thick and slightly lumpy.
4   Spoon the mixture into the muffin cases and bake for 15–20 minutes until the muffins spring
    back when pressed lightly. Remove from the oven and turn out on to a wire rack to cool.

075 PISTACHIO FRANGIPANE MUFFINS

PREPARATION TIME 20 minutes   **COOKING TIME** 15–20 minutes   **MAKES** 10 muffins

250g/9oz/1⅔ cups self-raising flour
1 tsp baking powder
1 tsp bicarbonate of soda/baking soda
100g/3½oz/heaped ⅓ cup caster/
   superfine sugar
150ml/5fl oz/scant ⅔ cup milk
4 tbsp natural/plain yogurt
100g/3½oz butter, melted and cooled
2 large eggs
1 tsp vanilla extract
200g/7oz/heaped 1 cup raspberries

FOR THE FRANGIPANE
55g/2oz butter, softened
55g/2oz/¼ cup caster/superfine sugar
55g/2oz/½ cup pistachio nuts
1 large egg
2 tbsp plain/all-purpose flour, sifted

1 Preheat the oven to 180°C/350°F/gas 4. Put 10 muffin cases/liners in a 12-hole muffin tin.

2 Sift the flour, baking powder and bicarbonate of soda into a mixing bowl, add the sugar and stir well with a wooden spoon.

3 In a separate bowl, whisk together the milk, yogurt and melted butter with an electric hand mixer or a whisk, add the eggs and the vanilla extract and whisk again. Pour the liquid into the bowl containing the dry ingredients and fold in with a large metal spoon. Do not overmix: the mixture should be thick and slightly lumpy. Fold in the raspberries. Spoon the mixture into the muffin cases.

4 For the frangipane, in a separate bowl, beat together the softened butter and sugar using an electric hand mixer or a wooden spoon. Grind the pistachios to a powder using a mini blender, add to the mixture with the egg and flour and beat again. Place a heaped spoonful of the pistachio frangipane on top of each muffin.

5 Bake for 15–20 minutes until the muffins spring back when pressed lightly and a skewer inserted into the middle of a muffin comes out clean. Remove the muffins from the oven, turn out on to a wire rack and leave to cool.

076 DATE & SESAME MUFFINS

PREPARATION TIME 15 minutes   **COOKING TIME** 15–20 minutes   **MAKES** 10 muffins

250g/9oz/1⅔ cups self-raising flour

1 tsp baking powder

1 tsp bicarbonate of soda/baking soda

1 tsp ground cinnamon

100g/3½oz/heaped ½ cup pitted
   dates, chopped

2 tbsp sesame seeds

100g/3½oz/heaped ⅓ cup caster/
   superfine sugar

150ml/5fl oz/scant ⅔ cup milk

4 tbsp natural/plain yogurt

100g/3½oz butter, melted

2 large eggs, lightly beaten

1 Preheat the oven to 180°C/350°F/gas 4. Put 10 muffin cases/liners in a 12-hole muffin tin.

2 Sift the flour, baking powder, bicarbonate of soda and ground cinnamon into a mixing bowl, add the chopped dates, sesame seeds and sugar and stir well with a wooden spoon.

3 In a separate bowl, whisk together the milk, yogurt and melted butter with an electric hand mixer or a whisk, add the eggs and whisk again. Pour the liquid into the bowl containing the dry ingredients and fold in with a large metal spoon. Do not overmix: the mixture should be thick and slightly lumpy. Spoon the mixture into the muffin cases.

4 Bake for 15–20 minutes until the muffins spring back when pressed lightly. Remove the muffins from the oven, turn out on to a wire rack and leave to cool.

077 MUESLI MUFFINS

PREPARATION TIME 15 minutes   **COOKING TIME** 15–20 minutes   **MAKES** 10 muffins

250g/9oz/1⅔ cups self-raising flour
2 tsp baking powder
1 tsp bicarbonate of soda/baking soda
1 tsp ground cinnamon
100g/3½oz/heaped ⅓ cup caster/
   superfine sugar
1 small apple, peeled, cored and grated

55g/2oz/⅓ cup dried apricots, chopped
100g/3½oz/scant 1 cup muesli
150ml/5fl oz/scant ⅔ cup milk
4 tbsp natural/plain yogurt
100g/3½oz butter, melted
2 large eggs
1 tbsp clear honey

1   Preheat the oven to 180°C/350°F/gas 4. Put 10 muffin cases/liners in a 12-hole muffin tin.
2   Sift the flour, baking powder, bicarbonate of soda and ground cinnamon into a mixing bowl, add the sugar, grated apple, dried apricots and muesli and stir well with a wooden spoon.
3   In a separate bowl, whisk together the milk, yogurt and melted butter with an electric hand mixer or a whisk, add the eggs and honey and whisk again. Pour the liquid into the bowl containing the dry ingredients and fold in with a large metal spoon. Do not overmix: the mixture should be thick and slightly lumpy. Spoon the mixture into the muffin cases.
4   Bake for 15–20 minutes until the muffins spring back when pressed lightly. Remove the muffins from the oven, turn out on to a wire rack and leave to cool.

078 CRANBERRY MUFFINS

PREPARATION TIME 15 minutes   **COOKING TIME** 15–20 minutes   **MAKES** 10 muffins

250g/9oz/1⅔ cups self-raising flour
1 tsp baking powder
1 tsp bicarbonate of soda/baking soda
1 tsp ground cinnamon
100g/3½oz/heaped ⅓ cup caster/
   superfine sugar

100g/3½oz/heaped ½ cup dried cranberries
150ml/5fl oz/scant ⅔ cup milk
4 tbsp natural/plain yogurt
100g/3½oz butter, melted
2 large eggs, lightly beaten

1   Preheat the oven to 180°C/350°F/gas 4. Put 10 muffin cases/liners in a 12-hole muffin tin.
2   Sift the flour, baking powder, bicarbonate of soda and ground cinnamon into a mixing bowl, add the caster sugar and dried cranberries and stir well with a wooden spoon.
3   In a separate bowl, whisk together the milk, yogurt and butter with an electric hand mixer or a whisk, add the eggs and whisk again. Pour the liquid into the first bowl and fold it in with a large metal spoon. Do not overmix: the mixture should be thick and slightly lumpy.
4   Spoon the mix into the muffin cases and bake for 15–20 minutes until the muffins spring back when pressed lightly. Remove from the oven and turn out on to a wire rack to cool.

079 CIDER APPLE MUFFINS

PREPARATION TIME 20 minutes   **COOKING TIME** 15–20 minutes   **MAKES** 10 muffins

250g/9oz/1⅔ cups self-raising flour
1 tsp baking powder
1 tsp bicarbonate of soda/baking soda
2 tsp ground cinnamon
100g/3½oz/heaped ⅓ cup caster/
   superfine sugar
1 eating apple, peeled, cored and grated

55g/2oz/heaped ⅓ cup sultanas/golden raisins
150ml/5fl oz/scant ⅔ cup milk
2 tbsp natural/plain yogurt
100g/3½oz butter, melted and cooled
2 large eggs, lightly beaten
100ml/3½fl oz/scant ½ cup cider
2 tbsp icing/powdered sugar

1   Preheat the oven to 180°C/350°F/gas 4. Put 10 muffin cases/liners in a 12-hole muffin tin.
2   Sift the flour, baking powder, bicarbonate of soda and ground cinnamon into a mixing bowl, add the caster sugar and stir well with a wooden spoon. Stir in the grated apple and sultanas.
3   In a separate bowl, whisk together the milk, yogurt and melted butter with an electric hand mixer or a whisk, add the eggs and whisk again. Pour the liquid into the bowl containing the dry ingredients and fold in with a large metal spoon. Do not overmix: the mixture should be thick and slightly lumpy. Spoon the mixture into the muffin cases.
4   Bake for 15–20 minutes until the muffins spring back when pressed lightly.
5   Just before the muffins are cooked, heat the cider and icing sugar in a saucepan, stirring, to make a syrup. Remove the muffins from the oven and drizzle the syrup over. Leave to cool.

080 SPICED CHAI MUFFINS

PREPARATION TIME 20 minutes, plus soaking   **COOKING TIME** 20–25 minutes   **MAKES** 20 muffins

1 chai tea bag
115g/4oz/heaped ½ cup sultanas/
   golden raisins
225g/8oz butter, softened
225g/8oz/scant 1 cup caster/superfine sugar

4 large eggs, lightly beaten
225g/8oz/1½ cups self-raising flour
1 tsp baking powder
2 tsp ground cinnamon

1   Put the chai tea bag in a bowl with 250ml/9fl oz/1 cup hot water and the sultanas and leave to soak for 1 hour, then remove the tea bag.
2   Preheat the oven to 180°C/350°F/gas 4. Put 20 muffin cases/liners in two 12-hole muffin tins.
3   Put the butter and sugar in a mixing bowl and beat using an electric hand mixer or wooden spoon until the mixture is light and creamy. Add the eggs gradually, beating after each addition. Sift in the flour, baking powder and ground cinnamon and gently fold them into the mixture, using a large wire whisk. Strain the sultanas and add to the cake mixture, folding in gently. Spoon the mixture into the muffin cases.

4 Bake for 20–25 minutes until the muffins spring back when pressed lightly. Remove the muffins from the oven, turn out on to a wire rack and leave to cool.

081 TRIPLE CHOCOLATE MUFFINS

PREPARATION TIME 15 minutes **COOKING TIME** 15–20 minutes **MAKES** 10 muffins

200g/7oz/scant 1½ cups self-raising flour
4 tbsp cocoa powder
1 tsp baking powder
1 tsp bicarbonate of soda/baking soda
100g/3½oz/heaped ⅓ cup caster/
   superfine sugar

150ml/5fl oz/scant ⅔ cup milk
4 tbsp natural/plain yogurt
100g/3½oz butter, melted
2 large eggs, lightly beaten
100g/3½oz nougat chocolate, chopped
100g/3½oz/⅔ cup white chocolate chips

1 Preheat the oven to 180°C/350°F/gas 4. Put 10 muffin cases/liners in a 12-hole muffin tin.
2 Sift the flour, cocoa, baking powder and bicarbonate of soda into a mixing bowl, add the sugar and stir well with a wooden spoon.
3 In a separate bowl, whisk together the milk, yogurt and melted butter with an electric hand mixer or a whisk, add the eggs and whisk again. Pour the liquid into the bowl containing the dry ingredients and fold in with a large metal spoon. Add the chopped chocolate and white chocolate chips and stir again. Do not overmix: the mixture should be thick and slightly lumpy. Spoon the mixture into the muffin cases.
4 Bake for 15–20 minutes until the muffins spring back when pressed lightly. Remove the muffins from the oven, turn out on to a wire rack and leave to cool.

082 MOCHA WALNUT MUFFINS

PREPARATION TIME 30 minutes **COOKING TIME** 15–20 minutes **MAKES** 20 muffins

450g/1lb butter, softened
225g/8oz/scant 1 cup caster/superfine sugar
4 large eggs, lightly beaten
225g/8oz/1½ cups self-raising flour, sifted
200g/7oz/1 cup walnuts, chopped
1 tbsp instant coffee granules dissolved in
   1 tbsp boiling water, then cooled

100g/3½oz/heaped ½ cup plain/semisweet
   chocolate chips
450g/1lb/3 cups icing/powdered sugar, sifted
225g/8oz cream cheese

1 Preheat the oven to 180°C/350°F/gas 4. Put 20 muffin cases/liners in two 12-hole muffin tins.
2 Put 225g/8oz of the butter and the caster sugar in a mixing bowl and beat using an electric hand mixer or wooden spoon until the mixture is light and creamy. Add the eggs gradually,

beating after each addition. Add the flour, half the walnuts, the coffee liquid and chocolate chips and gently fold them into the mixture, using a large metal spoon. Spoon the mixture into the muffin cases.

3 Bake for 15–20 minutes until the muffins spring back when pressed lightly and a skewer inserted into the middle of a muffin comes out clean. Remove the muffins from the oven, turn out on to a wire rack and leave to cool.

4 In a bowl, beat together the icing sugar, cream cheese and remaining butter with an electric hand mixer or a wooden spoon to form a smooth icing/frosting. Spoon the icing into an icing bag fitted with a 13mm/½in star nozzle and pipe swirls on top of each muffin, then top with the remaining walnuts. (If you do not have an icing bag, spread the icing over each cake using a round-bladed knife.) Leave the icing to set before serving.

083 TOFFEE POPCORN MUFFINS

PREPARATION TIME 25 minutes   **COOKING TIME** 20–25 minutes   **MAKES** 12 muffins

250g/9oz/1⅔ cups self-raising flour
1 tsp baking powder
1 tsp bicarbonate of soda/baking soda
100g/3½oz/heaped ⅓ cup caster/
   superfine sugar
150ml/5fl oz/scant ⅔ cup milk
150g/5½oz butter, melted and cooled

4 tbsp natural/plain yogurt
2 large eggs, lightly beaten
3 tbsp toffee sauce
4 tbsp dark soft brown sugar
2 tbsp golden syrup
50g/1¾oz/5 cups cooked popcorn

1 Preheat the oven to 180°C/350°F/gas 4. Put 12 muffin cases/liners in a 12-hole muffin tin.
2 Sift the flour, baking powder and bicarbonate of soda into a mixing bowl, add the caster sugar and stir well with a wooden spoon.
3 In a separate bowl, whisk together the milk, 100g/3½oz of the melted butter and the yogurt with an electric hand mixer or a whisk, add the eggs and toffee sauce and whisk again. Pour the liquid into the bowl containing the dry ingredients and fold in with a large metal spoon. Do not overmix: the mixture should be thick and slightly lumpy. Spoon the mixture into the muffin cases.
4 Bake for 15–20 minutes until the muffins spring back when pressed lightly and a skewer inserted into the middle of a muffin comes out clean. Remove the muffins from the oven, turn out on to a wire rack and leave to cool.
5 In a saucepan, heat the remaining melted butter, the dark brown sugar and syrup, stirring until the sugar has all dissolved and you have a smooth, thick caramel. Add the popcorn and stir to make sure it is all covered in the caramel. Leave to cool slightly, then place spoonfuls of the toffee popcorn on top of each muffin.

084 MOROCCAN ORANGE & ROSEWATER CUPCAKES

PREPARATION TIME 20 minutes   **COOKING TIME** 15–20 minutes   **MAKES** 20 cakes

225g/8oz butter, softened
225g/8oz/scant 1 cup caster/superfine sugar
4 large eggs, lightly beaten
225g/8oz/1½ cups self-raising flour
2 tsp ground cinnamon
finely grated zest of 1 small orange,
   plus 1–2 tbsp of the juice

3 tbsp rosewater
a few drops of pink food colouring
200g/7oz/1⅓ cups icing/powdered sugar
1 recipe quantity Frosted Rose Petals
   (see page 22), to decorate

1 Preheat the oven to 180°C/350°F/gas 4. Put 20 cake cases/liners in two 12-hole bun tins.
2 Put the butter and sugar in a mixing bowl and beat using an electric hand mixer or wooden spoon until the mixture is light and creamy. Add the eggs gradually, beating after each addition. Sift in the flour and ground cinnamon and gently fold them into the mixture with the orange zest and 2 tablespoons of the rosewater, using a large metal spoon. Spoon the mixture into the muffin cases.
3 Bake for 15–20 minutes until the cakes spring back when pressed lightly and a skewer inserted into the middle of a cake comes out clean. Remove the cakes from the oven, turn out on to a wire rack and leave to cool.
4 Put the orange juice, remaining rosewater, the food colouring and icing sugar in a bowl and mix to a smooth icing/frosting. Spread each muffin with icing and decorate with the frosted rose petals. Leave the icing to set before serving.

085 MARMALADE CUPCAKES

PREPARATION TIME 20 minutes   **COOKING TIME** 20–25 minutes   **MAKES** 20 cakes

225g/8oz butter, softened
115g/4oz/scant ½ cup caster/superfine sugar
115g/4oz/½ cup dark soft brown sugar
4 large eggs, lightly beaten
225g/8oz/1½ cups self-raising flour, sifted

100g/3½oz/heaped ½ cup plain/semisweet chocolate chips
3 tbsp thin-shred marmalade
finely grated zest of 1 orange and 1 tbsp of the juice

1 Preheat the oven to 180°C/350°F/gas 4. Put 20 cake cases/liners in two 12-hole bun tins.
2 Put the butter, caster sugar and dark brown sugar in a mixing bowl and beat using an electric hand mixer or wooden spoon until the mixture is light and creamy. Add the eggs gradually, beating after each addition. Add the flour, chocolate chips, 2 tablespoons of the marmalade and the orange zest and gently fold them into the mixture, using a large metal spoon. Spoon the mixture into the cake cases.
3 Bake for 15–20 minutes until the cakes spring back when pressed lightly and a skewer inserted into the middle of a cake comes out clean. Remove the cakes from the oven and turn out on to a wire rack.
4 Heat the remaining marmalade with the orange juice until the marmalade has melted, then brush this glaze over the cupcakes with a pastry brush. Leave to cool.

086 CINNAMON & CHOCOLATE SOURED CREAM CUPCAKES

PREPARATION TIME 20 minutes   **COOKING TIME** 15–20 minutes   **MAKES** 24 cakes

225g/8oz butter, softened
225g/8oz/scant 1 cup caster/superfine sugar
4 large eggs, lightly beaten
225g/8oz/1½ cups self-raising flour
4 tbsp cocoa powder, plus extra for dusting

2 tsp ground cinnamon
100ml/3½fl oz/scant ½ cup sour cream
200g/7oz plain/semisweet chocolate,
   finely chopped
1 Italian Meringue Buttercream (see page 25)

1 Preheat the oven to 190°C/375°F/gas 5. Put 24 cake cases/liners in two 12-hole bun tins.
2 Put the butter and sugar in a mixing bowl and beat using an electric hand mixer or wooden spoon until the mixture is light and creamy. Add the eggs gradually, beating after each addition. Sift in the flour, cocoa and ground cinnamon and gently fold them into the mixture with the sour cream and chopped chocolate, using a large metal spoon. Spoon the mixture into the cake cases.
3 Bake for 15–20 minutes until the cakes spring back when pressed lightly and a skewer inserted into the middle of a cake comes out clean. Remove the cakes from the oven, turn out on to a wire rack and leave to cool.
4 Place the Italian Meringue into a piping bag fitted with a large star nozzle and pipe a small swirl over each cake, then dust with a little cocoa to serve.

087 COFFEE CUPCAKES

PREPARATION TIME 25 minutes   **COOKING TIME** 15–20 minutes   **MAKES** 12 cakes

115g/4oz butter, softened
115g/4oz/scant ½ cup caster/superfine sugar
2 large eggs, lightly beaten
115g/4oz/¾ cup self-raising flour, sifted
2 tbsp instant coffee granules dissolved
   in 2 tbsp boiling water, then cooled

1 recipe quantity Vanilla Buttercream
   (see page 24)
55g/2oz plain/semisweet chocolate, grated

1 Preheat the oven to 180°C/350°F/gas 4. Put 12 cake cases/liners in a 12-hole bun tin.
2 Put the butter and sugar in a mixing bowl and beat using an electric hand mixer or wooden spoon until the mixture is light and creamy. Add the eggs gradually, beating after each addition. Add the flour and half the coffee liquid and gently fold them into the mixture, using a large metal spoon. Spoon the mixture into the cake cases.
3 Bake for 15–20 minutes until the cakes spring back when pressed lightly and a skewer inserted into the middle of a cake comes out clean. Remove the cakes from the oven, turn out on to a wire rack and leave to cool.

4 Mix the remaining coffee liquid into the buttercream and spoon it into an icing bag fitted with a 13mm/½in star nozzle. Pipe the buttercream in swirls on top of each cooled cake and top with the grated chocolate. (If you do not have an icing bag, spread the frosting over each cake using a round-bladed knife.) Leave the frosting to set before serving.

088 BLACK & WHITE CHOCOLATE CUPCAKES

PREPARATION TIME 30 minutes   **COOKING TIME** 15–20 minutes   **MAKES** 24 cakes

225g/8oz butter, softened
225g/8oz/scant 1 cup caster/superfine sugar
4 large eggs, lightly beaten
200g/7oz/1⅓ cups self-raising flour
4 tbsp cocoa powder
100g/3½oz/heaped ½ cup white
   chocolate chips

150g/5½oz plain/semisweet chocolate,
   melted and cooled slightly
150g/5½oz white chocolate, melted and
   cooled slightly
6 white and 6 plain/semisweet chocolate
   truffles, halved, to decorate

1 Preheat the oven to 180°C/350°F/gas 4. Put 24 cake cases/liners in two 12-hole bun tins.
2 Put the butter and sugar in a mixing bowl and beat using an electric hand mixer or wooden spoon until the mixture is light and creamy. Add the eggs gradually, beating after each addition. Sift in the flour and cocoa and gently fold them into the mixture with the chocolate chips, using a large metal spoon. Spoon the mixture into the cake cases.
3 Bake for 15–20 minutes until the cakes spring back when pressed lightly and a skewer inserted into the middle of a cake comes out clean. Remove the cakes from the oven, turn out on to a wire rack and leave to cool.
4 Cover half of the cakes with the melted plain chocolate and top with half a white truffle in the centre of each. Cover the remaining cakes with the melted white chocolate and top with half a plain chocolate truffle. Leave the chocolate to set before serving.

089 SWIRLED CUPCAKES

PREPARATION TIME 25 minutes   **COOKING TIME** 15–20 minutes   **MAKES** 12 cakes

115g/4oz butter, softened
115g/4oz/scant ½ cup caster/superfine sugar
2 large eggs, lightly beaten
85g/3oz/heaped ½ cup self-raising flour
4 tbsp cocoa powder
100g/3½oz/heaped ½ cup chocolate chips
a few drops of food colouring (optional)

1 recipe quantity Vanilla Buttercream
   (see page 24)
sugar sprinkles or sweets/candies,
   to decorate
¾ Italian Meringue Buttercream
   (see page 25)

1 Preheat the oven to 180°C/350°F/gas 4. Put 12 cake cases/liners in a 12-hole bun tin.

2 Put the butter and sugar in a mixing bowl and beat using an electric hand mixer or wooden spoon until the mixture is light and creamy. Add the eggs gradually, beating after each addition. Sift in the flour and cocoa and gently fold them into the mixture with the chocolate chips, using a large metal spoon. Spoon the mixture into the cake cases.

3 Bake for 15–20 minutes until the cakes spring back when pressed lightly and a skewer inserted into the middle of a cake comes out clean. Remove the cakes from the oven, turn out on to a wire rack and leave to cool.

4 Stir the food colouring, if using, into the buttercream until the colour is uniform, then spoon it into an icing bag fitted with a 13mm/½in star nozzle. Pipe the buttercream in swirls on top of each cake. Shake the sprinkles over the cake or decorate with sweets of your choice. (If you do not have an icing bag, spread the frosting over each cake using a round-bladed knife.) Leave the frosting to set before serving.

090 COCONUT & WHITE CHOCOLATE CUPCAKES

PREPARATION TIME 25 minutes, plus soaking **COOKING TIME** 15–20 minutes **MAKES** 12 cakes

175g/6oz/1½ cups desiccated/dried shredded coconut
2 tbsp coconut milk
115g/4oz butter, softened
115g/4oz/scant ½ cup caster/superfine sugar
2 large eggs, lightly beaten

115g/4oz/¾ cup self-raising flour, sifted
55g/2oz/heaped ⅓ cup plain/semisweet chocolate chips
300g/10½oz white chocolate, melted and cooled slightly
sugar sprinkles, to decorate

1 Preheat the oven to 180°C/350°F/gas 4. Put 12 cake cases/liners in a 12-hole bun tin.

2 Soak 55g/2oz of the desiccated coconut in the coconut milk for 1 hour until soft. Put the butter and sugar in a mixing bowl and beat using an electric hand mixer or wooden spoon until the mixture is light and creamy. Add the eggs gradually, beating after each addition. Add the flour, soaked coconut and chocolate chips and gently fold them into the mixture, using a large metal spoon. Spoon the mixture into the cake cases.

3 Bake for 15–20 minutes until the cakes spring back when pressed lightly and a skewer inserted into the middle of a cake comes out clean. Remove the cakes from the oven, turn out on to a wire rack and leave to cool.

4 Spread half the melted white chocolate over the top of the cakes using a round-bladed knife. Stir the remaining coconut into the rest of the chocolate and place a spoonful of the mixture on top of each cake. Decorate with sugar sprinkles and leave the chocolate to set before serving.

091 SPICED CHOCOLATE ORANGE CUPCAKES

PREPARATION TIME 15 minutes   **COOKING TIME** 15–20 minutes   **MAKES** 24 cakes

225g/8oz butter, softened
225g/8oz/1 cup dark soft brown sugar
4 large eggs, lightly beaten
175g/6oz/heaped 1 cup self-raising flour
4 tbsp cocoa powder
100g/3½oz/heaped ½ cup chocolate chips

1 tsp ground cinnamon
finely grated zest of 1 orange
200g/7oz plain/semisweet chocolate,
  melted and cooled slightly
orange sweets/candies or sugar sprinkles,
  to decorate

1 Preheat the oven to 180°C/350°F/gas 4. Put 24 cake cases/liners in two 12-hole bun tins.
2 Put the butter and sugar in a mixing bowl and beat using an electric hand mixer or
   wooden spoon until the mixture is light and creamy. Add the eggs gradually, beating
   after each addition. Sift in the flour and cocoa and gently fold them into the mixture
   with the chocolate chips, ground cinnamon and orange zest, using a large metal spoon.
   Spoon the mixture into the cake cases.
3 Bake for 15–20 minutes until the cakes spring back when pressed lightly and a skewer
   inserted into the middle of a cake comes out clean. Remove the cakes from the oven,
   turn out on to a wire rack and leave to cool. Cover each cake with melted chocolate
   and decorate with orange sweets or sprinkles. Leave the chocolate to set before serving.

092 MAPLE PECAN CUPCAKES

PREPARATION TIME 30 minutes   **COOKING TIME** 15–20 minutes   **MAKES** 24 cakes

350g/12oz butter, softened
225g/8oz/1 cup light soft brown sugar
4 large eggs, lightly beaten
225g/8oz/1½ cups self-raising flour, sifted
5 tbsp maple syrup

100g/3½oz/heaped ½ cup pecan nuts,
  chopped, plus 24 whole pecan nuts,
  to decorate
250g/9oz/1⅔ cups icing/powdered
  sugar, sifted

1 Preheat the oven to 180°C/350°F/gas 4. Put 24 cake cases/liners in two 12-hole bun tins.
2 Put 225g/8oz of the butter and the light brown sugar in a mixing bowl and beat using an
   electric hand mixer or wooden spoon until the mixture is light and creamy. Add the eggs
   gradually, beating after each addition. Add the flour, 2 tablespoons of the maple syrup and
   the chopped pecans and gently fold them into the mixture, using a large metal spoon.
   Spoon the mixture into the muffin cases.
3 Bake for 15–20 minutes until the cakes spring back when pressed lightly and a skewer
   inserted into the middle of a cake comes out clean. Remove the cakes from the oven, turn
   out on to a wire rack and leave to cool.

4 For the buttercream, put the remaining butter and maple syrup with the icing sugar in a bowl and beat using an electric hand mixer or wooden spoon until the mixture is light and creamy. Spoon the buttercream into an icing bag fitted with a 13mm/½in star nozzle and pipe swirls on top of each cooled cake, then top with the whole pecans. (If you do not have an icing bag, spread the frosting over each cake using a round-bladed knife.) Leave the buttercream to set before serving.

093 BUTTERMILK CUPCAKES

PREPARATION TIME 30 minutes **COOKING TIME** 15–20 minutes **MAKES** 20 cakes

270g/9½oz butter, softened
350g/12oz/1⅓ cups caster/superfine sugar
3 large eggs, lightly beaten
250ml/9fl oz/1 cup plus 2 tbsp buttermilk
seeds from 1 vanilla pod/bean

300g/10½oz/2 cups self-raising flour
1 tsp baking powder
400g/14oz/2⅔ cups icing/powdered
  sugar, sifted
chocolate sprinkles, to decorate

1 Preheat the oven to 180°C/350°F/gas 4. Put 20 cake cases/liners in two 12-hole bun tins.
2 Put 175g/6oz of the butter, the caster sugar and eggs in a mixing bowl and whisk using an electric hand mixer or a whisk until the mixture is light and creamy. Add 250ml/9fl oz/ 1 cup of the buttermilk and the vanilla seeds and whisk again. Sift in the flour and baking powder and gently fold them in, using a large metal spoon. Spoon the mixture into the cake cases.
3 Bake for 15–20 minutes until the cakes spring back when pressed lightly and a skewer inserted into the middle of a cake comes out clean. Remove the cakes from the oven, turn out on to a wire rack and leave to cool.
4 For the buttercream, put the remaining 2 tablespoons of buttermilk, remaining butter and the icing sugar in a bowl and beat with an electric hand mixer or wooden spoon until you have a light and creamy frosting. Spoon the buttercream into an icing bag fitted with a 13mm/½in star nozzle and pipe swirls on top of each cooled cake, then decorate with the chocolate sprinkles. (If you do not have an icing bag, spread the frosting over each cake using a round-bladed knife.) Leave the buttercream to set before serving.

094 ROCKY ROAD CUPCAKES

PREPARATION TIME 20 minutes   **COOKING TIME** 15–20 minutes   **MAKES** 12 cakes

115g/4oz butter, softened
115g/4oz/scant ½ cup caster/superfine sugar
2 tbsp crunchy peanut butter
2 large eggs, lightly beaten
85g/3oz/heaped ½ cup self-raising flour
4 tbsp cocoa powder

100g/3½oz/heaped ½ cup plain/semisweet
   chocolate chips
100g/3½oz/heaped ½ cup pecan nuts,
   chopped, 24 reserved for decorating
200g/7oz plain/semisweet chocolate, melted
   and cooled slightly
24 mini marshmallows, to decorate

1   Preheat the oven to 180°C/350°F/gas 4. Put 12 cake cases/liners in a 12-hole bun tin.
2   Put the butter, sugar and peanut butter in a mixing bowl and beat using an electric hand
    mixer or wooden spoon until the mixture is light and creamy. Add the eggs gradually,
    beating after each addition. Sift in the flour and cocoa and gently fold them into the
    mixture with the chocolate chips and chopped pecans, using a large metal spoon. Spoon
    the mixture into the cake cases.
3   Bake for 15–20 minutes until the cakes spring back when pressed lightly and a skewer
    inserted into the middle of a cake comes out clean. Remove the cakes from the oven, turn
    out on to a wire rack and leave to cool.
4   Spread some of the melted chocolate over the top of each cake using a knife, retaining a
    little of the chocolate to drizzle over the topping. Place 2 mini marshmallows and 2 pecans
    on top of each cake and drizzle with the remaining chocolate. Leave the chocolate to set
    before serving.

095 TOFFEE POP CUPCAKES

PREPARATION TIME 20 minutes   **COOKING TIME** 15–20 minutes   **MAKES** 24 cakes

225g/8oz butter, softened
225g/8oz/1 cup dark soft brown sugar
4 large eggs, lightly beaten
225g/8oz/1½ cups self-raising flour, sifted
3 tbsp toffee sauce

24 chocolate-covered soft caramels
200g/7oz/1⅓ cups icing/powdered sugar
100g/3½oz white chocolate, chopped,
   to decorate

1   Preheat the oven to 180°C/350°F/gas 4. Put 24 cake cases/liners in two 12-hole bun tins.
2   Put the butter and dark brown sugar in a mixing bowl and beat using an electric hand
    mixer or wooden spoon until the mixture is light and creamy. Add the eggs gradually,
    beating after each addition. Add the flour and 2 tablespoons of the toffee sauce and
    gently fold them into the mixture, using a large metal spoon.

3 Spoon half the mixture into the cake cases and place a chocolate caramel in the middle of each, then cover with the remaining mixture, making sure the caramels are covered.

4 Bake for 15–20 minutes until the cakes spring back when pressed lightly and a skewer inserted into the middle of a cake comes out clean. Remove the cakes from the oven, turn out on to a wire rack and leave to cool.

5 To make the icing/frosting, mix the remaining toffee sauce with the icing sugar and 1–2 tablespoons water in a bowl to form a smooth icing. Spread each cake with the icing and sprinkle with the chopped white chocolate. Leave the icing to set before serving.

096 RUM & RAISIN CUPCAKES

PREPARATION TIME 20 minutes   **COOKING TIME** 20–25 minutes   **MAKES** 12 cakes

115g/4oz butter, softened
115g/4oz/scant ½ cup caster/superfine sugar
2 large eggs, lightly beaten
115g/4oz/¾ cup self-raising flour, sifted
100g/3½oz rum and raisin fudge, chopped
   into small pieces

chocolate sprinkles, to decorate

FOR THE ICING/FROSTING
80ml/2½fl oz/⅓ cup rum
350g/12oz/2⅓ cups icing/powdered sugar
55g/2oz butter, chopped

1 Preheat the oven to 180°C/350°F/gas 4. Put 12 cake cases/liners in a 12-hole bun tin.

2 Put the butter and sugar in a mixing bowl and beat using an electric hand mixer or wooden spoon until the mixture is light and creamy. Add the eggs gradually, beating after each addition. Add the flour and fudge and fold them in, using a large metal spoon. Spoon the mixture into the cases.

3 Bake for 15–20 minutes until the cakes spring back when pressed lightly and a skewer inserted into the middle of a cake comes out clean. Remove the cakes from the oven, turn out on to a wire rack and leave to cool.

4 Put the icing/frosting ingredients in a saucepan and heat until the icing sugar has dissolved and the butter has melted. Beat with a wooden spoon to make a smooth icing. Spread the icing on top of each cake using a round-bladed knife and decorate with the chocolate sprinkles. Leave the icing to set before serving.

097 MACADAMIA TOFFEE CUPCAKES

PREPARATION TIME 15 minutes   **COOKING TIME** 15–20 minutes   **MAKES** 24 cakes

225g/8oz butter, softened
225g/8oz/scant 1 cup caster/superfine sugar
4 large eggs, lightly beaten
225g/8oz/1½ cups self-raising flour, sifted
4 tbsp toffee sauce

100g/3½oz/heaped ½ cup macadamia nuts,
   coarsely chopped
200g/7oz/1⅓ cups icing/powdered
   sugar, sifted
chocolate sprinkles, to decorate

1   Preheat the oven to 180°C/350°F/gas 4. Put 24 cake cases/liners in two 12-hole bun tins.
2   Put the butter and caster sugar in a mixing bowl and beat using an electric hand mixer or
    wooden spoon until the mixture is light and creamy. Add the eggs gradually, beating after
    each addition. Add the flour, 2 tablespoons of the toffee sauce and the nuts and fold them
    into the mixture, using a large metal spoon. Spoon the mixture into the cake cases.
3   Bake for 15–20 minutes until the cakes spring back when pressed lightly and a skewer
    inserted into the middle of a cake comes out clean. Remove the cakes from the oven, turn
    out on to a wire rack and leave to cool.
4   To make the icing/frosting, put the icing sugar, remaining toffee sauce and 1 tablespoon
    water in a bowl and mix with a spoon to form a smooth toffee icing. If the icing is too
    stiff, add a further tablespoon of water. Spread the icing over each cake and decorate with
    chocolate sprinkles. Leave the icing to set before serving.

098 HONEY CUPCAKES

PREPARATION TIME 20 minutes   **COOKING TIME** 15–20 minutes   **MAKES** 12 cakes

115g/4oz butter, softened
115g/4oz/scant ½ cup caster/superfine sugar
2 large eggs, lightly beaten
115g/4oz/¾ cup self-raising flour

1 tsp mixed/pumpkin pie spice
1 tsp ground cinnamon
1 tbsp clear honey

1   Preheat the oven to 190°C/375°F/gas 5. Put 12 cake cases/liners in a 12-hole bun tin.
2   Put the butter and sugar in a mixing bowl and beat using an electric hand mixer or wooden
    spoon until the mixture is light and creamy. Add the eggs gradually, beating after each
    addition. Sift in the flour, mixed spice and ground cinnamon and gently fold them into the
    mixture with the honey, using a large metal spoon. Spoon the mixture into the cake cases.
3   Bake for 15–20 minutes until the cakes spring back when pressed lightly and a skewer
    inserted into the middle of a cake comes out clean. Remove the cakes from the oven, turn
    out on to a wire rack and leave to cool.

099 PESHWARI CUPCAKES

PREPARATION TIME 20 minutes **COOKING TIME** 15–20 minutes **MAKES** 24 cakes

55g/2oz/⅓ cup sultanas/golden raisins
55g/2oz/heaped ½ cup desiccated/dried
   shredded coconut
55g/2oz/heaped ⅓ cup pistachio nuts
225g/8oz butter, softened

225g/8oz/scant 1 cup caster/superfine sugar
4 large eggs, lightly beaten
250g/9oz/1⅔ cups self-raising flour, sifted
2 tbsp coconut cream

1 Preheat the oven to 180°C/350°F/gas 4. Put 24 cake cases/liners in two 12-hole bun tins.
2 Put the sultanas, desiccated coconut and pistachios in a blender and whizz to chop finely. Set aside while you prepare the cake mixture.
3 Put the butter and sugar in a mixing bowl and beat using an electric hand mixer or wooden spoon until the mixture is light and creamy. Add the eggs gradually, beating after each addition. Add the flour, nut and sultana mix and the coconut cream and gently fold them into the mixture, using a large metal spoon. Spoon the mixture into the cake cases.
4 Bake for 15–20 minutes until the cakes spring back when pressed lightly and a skewer inserted into the middle of a cake comes out clean. Remove the cakes from the oven, turn out on to a wire rack and leave to cool.

100 STEM GINGER CREAM CUPCAKES

PREPARATION TIME 20 minutes **COOKING TIME** 15–20 minutes **MAKES** 24 cakes

225g/8oz butter, softened
225g/8oz/1 cup light soft brown sugar
4 large eggs, lightly beaten
250g/9oz/1⅔ cups self-raising flour, sifted
3 tbsp sour cream

2 tbsp chopped stem/preserved ginger in
   syrup, plus extra to decorate (optional)
1 tsp ground ginger
5 tbsp syrup from the stem ginger

1 Preheat the oven to 180°C/350°F/gas 4. Put 24 cake cases/liners in two 12-hole bun tins.
2 Put the butter and sugar in a mixing bowl and beat using an electric hand mixer or wooden spoon until the mixture is light and creamy. Add the eggs gradually, beating after each addition. Add the flour, sour cream and chopped and ground ginger and gently fold them into the mixture, using a large metal spoon. Spoon the mixture into the cake cases.
3 Bake for 15–20 minutes until the cakes spring back when pressed lightly and a skewer inserted into the middle of a cake comes out clean.
4 Just before the cakes are done, heat the ginger syrup in a saucepan. Remove the cakes from the oven and drizzle with the syrup, then turn out on to a wire rack and leave to cool. Decorate with a little extra chopped stem ginger, if you wish.

101 NUTELLA & HAZELNUT CUPCAKES

PREPARATION TIME 20 minutes   **COOKING TIME** 15–20 minutes   **MAKES** 24 cakes

225g/8oz butter, softened
225g/8oz/scant 1 cup caster/superfine sugar
4 large eggs, lightly beaten
225g/8oz/1½ cups self-raising flour, sifted

100g/3½oz/heaped ½ cup chopped
   roasted hazelnuts
2 heaped tbsp **Nutella** or chocolate
   hazelnut spread

1   Preheat the oven to 180°C/350°F/gas 4. Place 24 cake cases/liners in two 12-hole bun tins.
2   Put the butter and sugar in a mixing bowl and beat using an electric hand mixer or wooden spoon until the mixture is light and creamy. Add the eggs gradually, beating after each addition and whisk in the Nutella. Add the flour and hazelnuts and gently fold them into the mixture, using a large metal spoon. Spoon the mixture into the cake cases.
3   Bake for 15–20 minutes until the cakes spring back when pressed lightly and a skewer inserted into the middle of a cake comes out clean. Remove the cakes from the oven, turn out on to a wire rack and leave to cool.

102 TREACLE CUPCAKES

PREPARATION TIME 20 minutes   **COOKING TIME** 15–20 minutes   **MAKES** 12 cakes

115g/4oz butter, softened
55g/2oz/¼ cup caster/superfine sugar
55g/2oz/¼ cup dark muscovado sugar
2 tsp treacle
2 large eggs, lightly beaten

115g/4oz/¾ cup self-raising flour
1 tsp ground cinnamon
1 tsp mixed/pumpkin pie spice
55g/2oz/⅓ cup sultanas/golden raisins
55g/2oz cream cheese

1   Preheat the oven to 180°C/350°F/gas 4. Put 12 cake cases/liners in a 12-hole bun tin.
2   Put the butter, caster sugar, muscovado sugar and treacle in a mixing bowl and beat using an electric hand mixer or wooden spoon until the mixture is light and creamy. Add the eggs gradually, beating after each addition. Sift in the flour, ground cinnamon and mixed spice and gently fold them into the mixture with the sultanas, using a large metal spoon.
3   Put 1 tablespoon of the mixture into each cake case, top with 1 teaspoon of the cream cheese and cover with the remaining cake mixture so the cheese is completely covered.
4   Bake for 15–20 minutes until the cakes spring back when pressed lightly and a skewer inserted into the middle of a cake comes out clean. Remove the cakes from the oven, turn out on to a wire rack and leave to cool.

103 CHERRY & ALMOND CUPCAKES

PREPARATION TIME 20 minutes   **COOKING TIME** 15–20 minutes   **MAKES** 24 cakes

225g/8oz butter, softened
225g/8oz/scant 1 cup caster/superfine sugar
4 large eggs, lightly beaten
225g/8oz/1½ cups self-raising flour, sifted
200g/7oz/heaped 1 cup preserved morello
   cherries, 12 halved and reserved to
   decorate

3 tbsp natural/plain yogurt
1 tsp almond extract
1 recipe quantity Chocolate Buttercream
   (see page 24)
100g/3½oz white chocolate, melted and
   cooled slightly, to decorate

1 Preheat the oven to 180°C/350°F/gas 4. Put 24 cake cases/liners in two 12-hole bun tins.
2 Put the butter and sugar in a mixing bowl and beat using an electric hand mixer or wooden spoon until the mixture is light and creamy. Add the eggs gradually, beating after each addition. Add the flour, cherries, yogurt and almond extract and gently fold them into the mixture, using a large metal spoon. Spoon the mixture into the cake cases.
3 Bake for 15–20 minutes until the cakes spring back when pressed lightly and a skewer inserted into the middle of a cake comes out clean. Remove the cakes from the oven, turn out on to a wire rack and leave to cool.
4 Spoon the buttercream into an icing bag fitted with a 13mm/½in star nozzle and pipe a star on each cake, then place half a cherry on top. Dip a fork into the melted white chocolate and drizzle it over the top of each cake. Leave the chocolate to set before serving.

104 ICED CHERRY CUPCAKES

PREPARATION TIME 20 minutes   **COOKING TIME** 15–20 minutes   **MAKES** 24 cakes

225g/8oz butter, softened
225g/8oz/scant 1 cup caster/superfine sugar
4 large eggs, lightly beaten
225g/8oz/1½ cups self-raising flour, sifted
2 tbsp natural/plain yogurt

100g/3½oz/½ cup glacé/candied cherries,
   chopped, plus 12, halved, to decorate
1 tsp vanilla extract
400g/14oz/2⅔ cups icing/powdered sugar

1 Preheat the oven to 180°C/350°F/gas 4. Put 24 cake cases/liners in two 12-hole bun tins.
2 Put the butter and caster sugar in a mixing bowl and beat using an electric hand mixer or wooden spoon until the mixture is light and creamy. Add the eggs gradually, beating after each addition. Add the flour, yogurt, chopped glacé cherries and vanilla extract and gently fold them into the mixture, using a large metal spoon. Spoon the mixture into the cake cases.

3 Bake for 15–20 minutes until the cakes spring back when pressed lightly and a skewer inserted into the middle of a cake comes out clean. Remove the cakes from the oven, turn out on to a wire rack and leave to cool.

4 Mix the icing sugar with 3–4 tablespoons water in a small bowl to form a smooth, thick icing/frosting and spread it over the tops of the cakes using a round-bladed knife. Place half a cherry on each cake. Leave the icing to set before serving.

105 PEACHES & CREAM CUPCAKES

PREPARATION TIME 25 minutes   **COOKING TIME** 20–25 minutes   **MAKES** 20 cakes

225g/8oz butter, softened
225g/8oz/scant 1 cup caster/superfine sugar
4 large eggs, lightly beaten
250g/9oz/1⅔ cups self-raising flour, sifted
3 tbsp sour cream

3 tbsp peach jam/jelly
2 ripe peaches, stones removed and
   cut into 40 thin slices
1 tbsp lemon juice

1 Preheat the oven to 180°C/350°F/gas 4. Put 20 cake cases/liners in two 12-hole bun tins.

2 Put the butter and sugar in a mixing bowl and beat using an electric hand mixer or wooden spoon until the mixture is light and creamy. Add the eggs gradually, beating after each addition. Add the flour, sour cream and 2 tablespoons of the jam and gently fold them into the mixture, using a large metal spoon. Spoon the mixture into the cake cases and place 2 peach slices on top of each cake.

3 Bake for 15–20 minutes until the cakes spring back when pressed lightly and a skewer inserted into the middle of a cake comes out clean.

4 Remove the cakes from the oven and turn out on to a wire rack. Heat the remaining jam with the lemon juice in a small saucepan until the jam has melted, then brush the peach glaze over the top of the cakes with a pastry brush. Leave to cool.

106 TUTTIFRUTTI CUPCAKES

PREPARATION TIME 20 minutes   **COOKING TIME** 15–20 minutes   **MAKES** 24 cakes

225g/8oz butter, softened
225g/8oz/scant 1 cup caster/superfine sugar
4 large eggs, lightly beaten
225g/8oz/1½ cups self-raising flour, sifted
2 tbsp peach jam/jelly
55g/2oz/⅓ cup raisins
55g/2oz/⅓ cup sultanas/golden raisins

30g/1oz/¼ cup mixed/candied peel
30g/1oz/scant ¼ cup glacé/candied cherries,
   chopped
30g/1oz/¼ cup pistachio nuts, chopped
icing/powdered sugar, for dusting

1. Preheat the oven to 180°C/350°F/gas 4. Put 24 cake cases/liners in two 12-hole bun tins.
2. Put the butter and sugar in a mixing bowl and beat using an electric hand mixer or wooden spoon until the mixture is light and creamy. Add the eggs gradually, beating after each addition. Add the flour, jam, raisins, sultanas, mixed peel, cherries and pistachios and gently fold them in, using a large metal spoon. Spoon the mixture into the cake cases.
3. Bake for 15–20 minutes until the cakes spring back when pressed lightly and a skewer inserted into the middle of a cake comes out clean. Remove the cakes from the oven, turn out on to a wire rack and leave to cool. Dust with icing sugar to serve.

107 JELLY BEAN CUPCAKES

PREPARATION TIME 25 minutes   **COOKING TIME** 15–20 minutes   **MAKES** 24 cakes

225g/8oz butter, softened
225g/8oz/scant 1 cup caster/superfine sugar
4 large eggs, lightly beaten
225g/8oz/1½ cups self-raising flour, sifted
1 tsp vanilla extract

3 tbsp strawberry jam/jelly
400g/14oz/2⅔ cups icing/powdered
    sugar, sifted
jelly beans, to decorate

1. Preheat the oven to 180°C/350°F/gas 4. Put 24 cake cases/liners in two 12-hole bun tins.
2. Put the butter and caster sugar in a mixing bowl and beat using an electric hand mixer or wooden spoon until the mixture is light and creamy. Add the eggs gradually, beating after each addition. Add the flour and gently fold it into the mixture with the vanilla extract and jam, using a large metal spoon. Spoon the mixture into the cake cases.
3. Bake for 15–20 minutes until the cakes spring back when pressed lightly and a skewer inserted into the middle of a cake comes out clean. Remove the cakes from the oven, turn out on to a wire rack and leave to cool.
4. Mix together the icing sugar and 3–4 tablespoons water to form a smooth, thick icing/ frosting and spread it over each cake using a round-bladed knife. Top each cake with a few jelly beans and leave the icing to set before serving.

108 TURKISH DELIGHT CUPCAKES

PREPARATION TIME 20 minutes   **COOKING TIME** 15–20 minutes   **MAKES** 12 cakes

115g/4oz butter, softened
115g/4oz/scant ½ cup caster/superfine sugar
2 large eggs, lightly beaten
140g/5oz/1 cup self-raising flour, sifted
2 tbsp sour cream

150g/5½oz chocolate-covered Turkish
    Delight, chopped
200g/7oz white chocolate, melted
    and cooled slightly

1 Preheat the oven to 180°C/350°F/gas 4. Put 12 cake cases/liners in a 12-hole bun tin.
2 Put the butter and sugar in a mixing bowl and beat using an electric hand mixer or wooden spoon until the mixture is light and creamy. Add the eggs gradually, beating after each addition. Add the flour, sour cream and two-thirds of the Turkish Delight and gently fold them into the mixture, using a large metal spoon. Spoon the mixture into the cake cases.
3 Bake for 15–20 minutes until the cakes spring back when pressed lightly and a skewer inserted into the middle of a cake comes out clean. Remove the cakes from the oven, turn out on to a wire rack and leave to cool.
4 Spread the melted chocolate over the cakes and top each one with a piece of the remaining chopped Turkish Delight.

109 APPLE & HAZELNUT MINI LOAF CAKES

PREPARATION TIME 15 minutes **COOKING TIME** 20–25 minutes **MAKES** 6 cakes

115g/4oz butter, softened, plus extra
   for greasing
55g/2oz/¼ cup dark muscovado sugar
55g/2oz/¼ cup caster/superfine sugar
2 large eggs, lightly beaten

115g/4oz/¾ cup self-raising flour, sifted
1 apple, peeled, cored and grated
55g/2oz/⅓ cup chopped toasted hazelnuts
4 tbsp maple syrup

1 Preheat the oven to 190°C/375°F/gas 5. Grease and line six 10 x 5 x 5cm/4 x 2 x 2in mini loaf tins.
2 Put the butter, muscovado sugar and caster sugar in a mixing bowl and beat using an electric hand mixer or wooden spoon until the mixture is light and creamy. Add the eggs gradually, beating after each addition. Add the flour, grated apple, hazelnuts and 2 tablespoons of the maple syrup and gently fold them into the mixture, using a large metal spoon. Divide the mixture between the tins using a spatula.
3 Bake for 20–25 minutes until the cakes spring back when pressed lightly and a skewer inserted into the middle of a cake comes out clean.
4 Just before the cakes come out of the oven, heat the remaining maple syrup with 1 tablespoon water in a small saucepan to form a light syrup. Remove the cakes from the oven and drizzle the syrup over the cakes. Leave the cakes to cool in the tins, then turn out on to a serving plate.

110 COCONUT MINI LOAF CAKES

PREPARATION TIME 15 minutes   **COOKING TIME** 20–25 minutes   **MAKES** 6 cakes

115g/4oz butter, softened, plus extra
   for greasing
175g/6oz/scant ¾ cup caster/superfine sugar
2 large eggs, lightly beaten

115g/4oz/¾ cup self-raising flour, sifted
200ml/7fl oz/scant 1 cup coconut cream
55g/2oz/heaped ½ cup desiccated/dried
   shredded coconut

1 Preheat the oven to 180°C/350°F/gas 4. Grease and line six 10 x 5 x 5cm/4 x 2 x 2in mini loaf tins.
2 Put the butter and 115g/4oz of the sugar in a mixing bowl and beat using an electric hand mixer or wooden spoon until the mixture is light and creamy. Add the eggs gradually, beating after each addition. Add the flour, 100ml/3½fl oz/scant ½ cup of the coconut cream and the desiccated coconut and gently fold them into the mixture, using a large metal spoon. Divide the mixture between the tins using a spatula.
3 Bake for 20–25 minutes until the cakes spring back when pressed lightly and a skewer inserted into the middle of a cake comes out clean.
4 Just before the cakes come out of the oven, heat the remaining coconut cream and remaining sugar in a saucepan, stirring to make a syrup until the sugar has completely dissolved. Remove the cakes from the oven and drizzle the syrup over the cakes. Leave the cakes to cool in the tins, then turn out on to a serving plate.

111 LEMONGRASS & SOURED CREAM MINI LOAF CAKES

PREPARATION TIME 15 minutes   **COOKING TIME** 20–25 minutes   **MAKES** 6 cakes

200g/7oz/heaped ¾ cup caster/
   superfine sugar
1 lemongrass stalk, very finely sliced
juice and finely grated zest of 1 large lemon

115g/4oz butter, softened, plus extra
   for greasing
2 large eggs, lightly beaten
115g/4oz/¾ cup self-raising flour, sifted
2 tbsp sour cream

1 Heat half the sugar, the lemongrass, lemon juice and zest in a saucepan until the sugar has dissolved, then boil for 1 minute to make a syrup. Remove from the heat and leave to cool.
2 Preheat the oven to 180°C/350°F/gas 4. Grease and line six 10 x 5 x 5cm/4 x 2 x 2in mini loaf tins.
3 Put the butter and remaining sugar in a mixing bowl and beat using an electric hand mixer or wooden spoon until the mixture is light and creamy. Add the eggs gradually, beating after each addition. Add the flour and sour cream and gently fold them into the mixture, using a large metal spoon. Divide the mixture between the tins using a spatula.

4 Bake for 15–20 minutes until the cakes spring back when pressed lightly and a skewer inserted into the middle of each cake comes out clean.

5 Remove the cakes from the oven and pour the lemon syrup over them. Leave the cakes to cool in the tins, then turn out on to a serving plate.

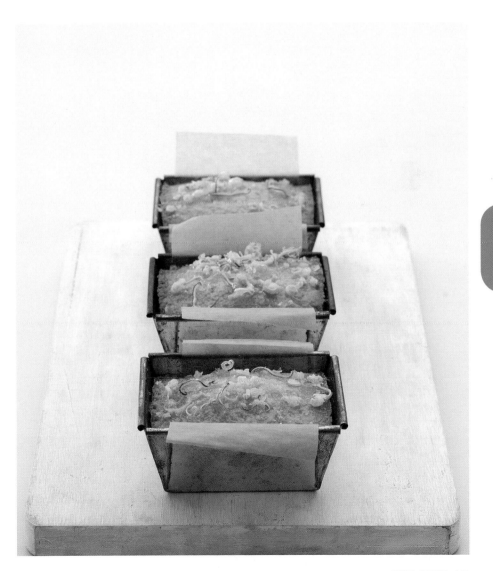

112 STAR ANISE FRIANDS

PREPARATION TIME 20 minutes   **COOKING TIME** 25–30 minutes   **MAKES** 12 friands

100g/3½oz butter, melted and cooled,
  plus extra for greasing
4 large egg whites
100g/3½oz/⅔ cup plain/all-purpose flour
125g/4½oz/scant 1 cup icing/powdered sugar
225g/8oz canned pineapple, finely diced

finely grated zest of 1 lemon
1 tsp ground cinnamon
100ml/3½fl oz/scant ½ cup pineapple
  juice from the can
200g/7oz/heaped ¾ cup caster/superfine sugar
2 star anise

1 Preheat the oven to 180°C/350°F/gas 4. Grease twelve 8cm/3in oval friand tins or a
   12-hole muffin tin.
2 Put the egg whites in a clean, dry bowl and whisk with an electric hand mixer or a whisk
   until they form stiff peaks. Sift in the flour and icing sugar, add the melted butter, pineapple,
   lemon zest and ground cinnamon and fold in gently, using a large metal spoon. Divide the
   mixture between the friand tins and place on a baking tray.
3 Bake for 20–25 minutes until the cakes spring back when pressed lightly and a skewer
   inserted into the middle of a cake comes out clean. Remove the cakes from the oven and
   leave to stand for 5 minutes, then turn out on to a wire rack and leave to cool.
4 Meanwhile, put the pineapple juice, caster sugar, star anise and 100ml/3½fl oz/scant
   ½ cup water in a saucepan and simmer to form a light syrup. Serve the warm friands with
   a drizzle of the star anise syrup over the top.

113 ORANGE SYRUP FRIANDS

PREPARATION TIME 20 minutes   **COOKING TIME** 25–30 minutes   **MAKES** 12 friands

100g/3½oz butter, melted and cooled,
  plus extra for greasing
4 large egg whites
100g/3½oz/⅔ cup plain/all-purpose flour
125g/4½oz/scant 1 cup icing/powdered sugar
1 tsp ground cinnamon

juice and finely grated zest of 1 orange
juice and finely grated zest of 1 lemon
2 tbsp fine-shred marmalade
200g/7oz/heaped ¾ cup caster/
  superfine sugar

1 Preheat the oven to 180°C/350°F/gas 4. Grease twelve 8cm/3in oval friand tins or a
   12-hole muffin tin.
2 Put the egg whites in a clean, dry bowl and whisk with an electric hand mixer or a whisk
   until they form stiff peaks. Sift in the flour, icing sugar and ground cinnamon, add the
   melted butter, orange and lemon zests and marmalade and fold in gently, using a large
   metal spoon. Divide the mixture between the friand tins and place on a baking tray.

3 Bake for 20–25 minutes until the cakes spring back when pressed lightly and a skewer inserted into the middle of a cake comes out clean. Remove the cakes from the oven and leave to stand for 5 minutes, then turn out on to a wire rack and leave to cool.

4 Meanwhile, put the orange and lemon juice, caster sugar and 3 tablespoons water in a small saucepan and simmer to form a light syrup. Drizzle the orange syrup over the friands.

114 GRANDMA'S ROCK CAKES

PREPARATION TIME 10 minutes   **COOKING TIME** 15–20 minutes   **MAKES** 12 cakes

100g/3½oz chilled lard or butter, chopped, plus extra for greasing
225g/8oz/1½ cups self-raising flour, sifted
100g/3½oz/heaped ⅓ cup caster/ superfine sugar

115g/4oz/heaped ½ cup sultanas/ golden raisins
1 large egg, lightly beaten
1 tbsp thin-shred marmalade

1 Preheat the oven to 170°C/325°F/gas 3. Grease a 12-hole muffin tin.

2 Put the flour in a mixing bowl. Add the lard or butter and rub it into the flour with your fingertips until the mixture resembles fine breadcrumbs. Add the remaining ingredients and mix well with a wooden spoon to create a crumbly mixture. Bring it together with your fingers into large crumbly pieces. Divide the mixture between the tin holes.

3 Bake for 15–20 minutes until golden brown. Remove the cakes from the oven and leave to cool in the tin, then turn out on to a serving plate.

115 AUNTY BETTY'S WELSH CAKES

PREPARATION TIME 10 minutes   **COOKING TIME** 8–16 minutes   **MAKES** 20 cakes

225g/8oz/1½ cups self-raising flour, plus extra for dusting
½ tsp baking powder
¼ tsp ground ginger
1 tsp mixed/pumpkin pie spice
100g/3½oz chilled butter, chopped, plus extra for greasing

85g/3oz/⅓ cup caster/superfine sugar, plus extra for dusting
55g/2oz/⅓ cup sultanas/golden raisins
55g/2oz/⅓ cup currants
55g/2oz/¼ cup glacé/candied cherries, chopped
1 large egg, lightly beaten
1 tbsp milk (optional)

1 Sift the flour, baking powder, ginger and mixed spice into a mixing bowl. Add the butter and rub it in with your fingertips until the mixture resembles fine breadcrumbs. Add the sugar, sultanas, currants, cherries and egg and bring the mixture together with your hands to form a very firm dough, adding the milk if the mixture is too dry.

2 Sift flour on to a clean work surface and roll the dough out to 1cm/⅜in thick using a rolling pin. Cut out 20 circles using a 7cm/2½in round cutter.

3 Grease a large bakestone, cast-iron griddle or heavy frying pan with a little butter and then put on the hob/stovetop over a gentle heat. Cook the Welsh cakes in batches for 2 minutes on each side, turning every minute to ensure that the cakes brown nicely but do not burn, and adding more butter to the pan before cooking each batch. When the cakes are cooked, remove from the pan and sprinkle with caster sugar. Serve warm.

116 MAPLE DROP SCONES

PREPARATION TIME 10 minutes   **COOKING TIME** 20 minutes   **MAKES** 24 drop scones

225g/8oz/1½ cups plain/all-purpose flour
1 tsp bicarbonate of soda/baking soda
1 tsp cream of tartar
1 large egg, beaten

300ml/10½fl oz/scant 1¼ cups milk
2 tbsp maple syrup
butter, for frying

1 Sift the flour, bicarbonate of soda and cream of tartar into a mixing bowl and make a well in the middle. Add the egg, milk and maple syrup and mix with an electric hand blender or a whisk to form a smooth, thick batter.

2 Heat a little butter in a large frying pan and put 6 separate tablespoons of the batter in the pan. Cook for about 3 minutes, then turn over and cook for a further 2 minutes until golden brown. Set aside the cooked pancakes and keep warm while you cook the remainder of the batter in the same way, adding a little more butter to the pan each time.

117 LEMON MADELEINES

PREPARATION TIME 15 minutes   **COOKING TIME** 10–12 minutes   **MAKES** 24 madeleines

100g/3½oz butter, melted and cooled,
   plus extra for greasing
100g/3½oz/⅔ cup plain/all-purpose flour,
   plus extra for dusting
3 large eggs

100g/3½oz/heaped ⅓ cup caster/
   superfine sugar
1 tsp baking powder
finely grated zest of 1 lemon
icing/powdered sugar, for dusting

1 Preheat the oven to 180°C/350°F/gas 4. Grease two 12-hole madeleine tins very well with some melted butter, using a pastry brush, and dust with flour.

2 Put the eggs and caster sugar in a mixing bowl and whisk using an electric hand mixer or a whisk until very light and creamy. Sift in the flour and baking powder, pour in the butter and add the lemon zest, then fold them in gently with a large metal spoon.

3   Put spoonfuls of the mixture in the tin holes and bake for 10–12 minutes until the cakes spring back when pressed lightly and a skewer inserted into the middle of a cake comes out clean. Remove the cakes from the oven and leave to cool in the tins, then turn out on to a serving plate and dust with icing sugar.

118 CHOCOLATE CHIP LAMINGTONS

PREPARATION TIME 30 minutes, plus chilling   **COOKING TIME** 30–35 minutes   **MAKES** 15 slices

225g/8oz butter, softened, plus extra
    for greasing
200g/7oz/heaped ¾ cup caster/
    superfine sugar
4 large eggs, lightly beaten
400g/14oz/2⅔ cups self-raising flour
1 tsp bicarbonate of soda/baking soda
2 tsp cream of tartar
250ml/9fl oz/1 cup milk
100g/3½oz/heaped ½ cup plain/semisweet
    chocolate chips

FOR THE COATING
1 tbsp butter, melted and cooled
1 tbsp cocoa powder
250g/9oz/1⅔ cups icing/powdered sugar
125ml/4fl oz/½ cup milk
175g/6oz/heaped 2 cups desiccated/dried
    shredded coconut

1   Preheat the oven to 180°C/350°F/gas 4. Grease a 25 x 20cm/10 x 8in cake tin.
2   Put the butter and sugar in a mixing bowl and beat using an electric hand mixer or wooden spoon until the mixture is light and creamy. Add the eggs gradually, beating after each addition. Sift in the flour, bicarbonate of soda and cream of tartar and gently fold them into the mixture with the milk and chocolate chips, using a large metal spoon. Scrape the mixture into the tin using a spatula.
3   Bake for 30–35 minutes until the cake springs back when pressed and a skewer inserted into the middle comes out clean. Remove the cake from the oven and leave to stand for 5 minutes, then turn out on to a wire rack and leave to cool. Refrigerate for 2 hours.
4   For the coating, put the melted butter, cocoa and icing sugar in a bowl and stir in as much of the milk as is needed to make a smooth, thin icing/frosting. Put the desiccated coconut on a large plate. Cut the cake into 15 rectangles, dunk each one into the icing and then cover it completely with coconut. Put the coated cakes on a wire rack to drip, and leave until the coating is dry before serving.

119 AMARETTO & PISTACHIO FONDANT FANCIES

PREPARATION TIME 40 minutes, plus chilling   **COOKING TIME** 30–35 minutes   **MAKES** 16 cakes

175g/6oz butter, softened

175g/6oz/scant ¾ cup caster/superfine sugar

3 large eggs, lightly beaten

175g/6oz/heaped 1 cup self-raising
  flour, sifted

1 recipe quantity Vanilla Buttercream
  (see page 24)

2 tbsp Pistachio Butter (see page 25)

4 tbsp almond liqueur, such as amaretto

750g/1lb 10oz/5 cups fondant icing
  sugar, sifted

a few drops of food colouring

sweets/candies, to decorate

1   Preheat the oven to 180°C/350°F/gas 4. Grease and line a 20cm/8in loose-bottomed
    square cake tin.

2   Put the butter and caster sugar in a mixing bowl and beat using an electric hand mixer or
    wooden spoon until the mixture is light and creamy. Add the eggs gradually, beating after
    each addition. Add the flour and gently fold it into the mixture, using a large metal spoon.
    Scrape the mixture into the tin using a spatula.

3   Bake for 25–30 minutes until the cake springs back when pressed lightly and a skewer
    inserted into the middle of the cake comes out clean. Remove the cake from the oven and
    leave to stand for 5 minutes, then turn out on to a wire rack and leave to cool.

4   Put the buttercream and pistachio butter in a bowl and mix together. Using a sharp
    knife, cut away the edges of the cake, then slice the cake in half and remove the top
    layer. Drizzle the amaretto over the bottom layer and spread over a thin layer of the
    pistachio buttercream. Place the second cake layer on top and cover the whole cake in the
    remaining pistachio buttercream, smoothing along the sides. Refrigerate for at least 1 hour
    to set, as this will make it easier for the fondant icing to stick to the buttercream.

5   Heat the fondant icing sugar in a saucepan with 100ml/3½fl oz/scant ½ cup water and the
    food colouring. (You may not need all the water, so add it gradually until you reach a thick
    consistency.) Cut the cake into 16 squares and place them on a wire rack set over a piece
    of greaseproof paper to catch the icing. Spoon the warm fondant icing over each cake,
    leave to set for a few minutes and then decorate each cake with a sweet. When the icing
    has set completely, cut the cakes away from the rack with a sharp knife and place in cake
    cases/liners to serve.

120 CRISPY CHOCOLATE & BERRY CAKES

PREPARATION TIME 15 minutes   **COOKING TIME** 10 minutes   **MAKES** 24 cakes

200g/7oz plain/semisweet chocolate, chopped
200g/7oz white chocolate: half chopped;
   half melted and cooled
4 tbsp golden syrup

85g/3oz butter, chopped
200g/7oz/7 cups cornflakes (gf)
300g/10½oz/2 cups combined raspberries
   and blueberries

1 Put 24 cake cases/liners in two 12-hole bun tins.
2 Put the plain and white chopped chocolate, syrup and butter in a large saucepan and heat, stirring with a wooden spoon, over a gentle heat until the chocolate and butter have melted. Remove from the heat, add the cornflakes and stir well to make sure they are coated. Fill each cake case with chocolate cornflakes and top with the fresh berries.
3 Drizzle the melted white chocolate over the cakes and leave to set.

121 TRADITIONAL SCONES

PREPARATION TIME 15 minutes   **COOKING TIME** 12–15 minutes   **MAKES** 10 scones

115g/4oz chilled butter, chopped,
   plus extra for greasing
450g/1lb/3 cups self-raising flour,
   plus extra for dusting
1 tsp baking powder

1 tsp salt
55g/2oz/¼ cup caster/superfine sugar,
   plus extra for sprinkling
200ml/7fl oz/scant 1 cup milk, plus
   extra for brushing

1 Preheat the oven to 190°C/375°F/gas 5. Grease a 30cm/12in baking tray.
2 Sift the flour and baking powder into a mixing bowl, add the salt and butter and rub the butter into the flour with your fingertips until the mixture resembles fine breadcrumbs. Add the sugar and milk and mix to form a soft dough, adding more milk if necessary.
3 Sift flour on to a clean work surface and roll the dough out to 2.5cm/1in thick using a rolling pin. Cut out 10 scones with a 6cm/2½in round cutter, gathering up the trimmings and re-rolling as necessary, but handling the dough as little as possible. (Dipping the cutter in a small bowl of flour between cutting each scone helps them to rise.)
4 Place the scones on the baking tray so that they are touching each other, which helps the scones to rise up straight. Brush the tops of the scones with milk using a pastry brush and sprinkle with caster sugar.
5 Bake for 12–15 minutes until the scones are golden brown and sound hollow when you pick one up with an oven glove and tap it on the bottom. Remove from the oven and transfer to a wire rack with a palette knife to cool a little. Serve warm.

122 MINI CHEESE & POPPY SEED SCONES

PREPARATION TIME 15 minutes   **COOKING TIME** 12–15 minutes   **MAKES** 60 scones

115g/4oz chilled butter, chopped,
    plus extra for greasing
450g/1lb/3 cups self-raising flour,
    plus extra for dusting
1 tsp baking powder
1 tsp salt

1 tbsp caster/superfine sugar
115g/4oz Cheddar cheese, grated
2 tbsp poppy seeds
200ml/7fl oz/scant 1 cup milk
1 large egg, beaten

1 Preheat the oven to 190°C/375°F/gas 5. Grease two 30cm/12in baking trays.
2 Sift the flour and baking powder into a mixing bowl, add the salt and butter and rub the butter into the flour with your fingertips until it resembles fine breadcrumbs. Add the sugar, cheese, poppy seeds and milk and mix to form a soft dough, adding more milk if needed.
3 Sift flour on to a clean work surface and roll the dough out to 2.5cm/1in thick using a rolling pin. Cut out 60 scones with a 2.5cm/1in round cutter, gathering up the trimmings and re-rolling as necessary, but handling the dough as little as possible. (Dipping the cutter in a small bowl of flour between cutting each scone helps them to rise.)
4 Place the scones a little distance apart on the tray and brush the tops with the beaten egg.
5 Bake for 12–15 minutes until the scones are golden brown and sound hollow when you pick one up with an oven glove and tap it on the bottom. Remove from the oven and transfer to a wire rack with a palette knife to cool a little. Serve warm.

123 CHERRY SCONES

PREPARATION TIME 15 minutes   **COOKING TIME** 12–15 minutes   **MAKES** 10 scones

115g/4oz chilled butter, chopped,
    plus extra for greasing
450g/1lb/3 cups self-raising flour,
    plus extra for dusting
1 tsp baking powder
1 tsp salt

55g/2oz/¼ cup caster/superfine sugar,
    plus extra for sprinkling
200g/7oz/1 cup glacé/candied cherries,
    chopped
200ml/7fl oz/scant 1 cup milk, plus
    extra for brushing

1 Preheat the oven to 190°C/375°F/gas 5. Grease a 30cm/12in baking tray.
2 Sift the flour and baking powder into a mixing bowl, add the salt and butter and rub the butter into the flour with your fingertips until the mixture resembles fine breadcrumbs. Add the sugar, cherries and milk and mix to form a soft dough, adding a little more milk if the mixture is too dry.

3 Sift flour on to a clean work surface and roll the dough out to 2.5cm/1in thick using a rolling pin. Cut out 10 scones with a 6cm/2½in round cutter, gathering up the trimmings and re-rolling as necessary, but handling the dough as little as possible. (Dipping the cutter in a small bowl of flour between cutting each scone ensures a clean cut of the dough, which helps them to rise.)

4 Place the scones on the baking tray so that they are touching each other, which helps the scones to rise up straight. Brush the tops of the scones with milk using a pastry brush and sprinkle with caster sugar.

5 Bake for 12–15 minutes until the scones are golden brown and sound hollow when you pick one up with an oven glove and tap it on the bottom. Remove from the oven and transfer to a wire rack with a palette knife to cool a little. Serve warm.

124 WHOLEMEAL SCONES

PREPARATION TIME 15 minutes   **COOKING TIME** 12–15 minutes   **MAKES** 10 scones

115g/4oz chilled butter, chopped,
    plus extra for greasing
250g/9oz/1⅔ cups self-raising wholemeal/
    wholewheat flour, plus extra for dusting
200g/7oz/1⅓ cups self-raising flour
1 tsp baking powder

1 tsp salt
55g/2oz/¼ cup caster/superfine sugar,
    plus extra for sprinkling
200ml/7fl oz/scant 1 cup milk
1 large egg, beaten

1 Preheat the oven to 190°C/375°F/gas 5. Grease a 30cm/12in square baking tray.
2 Sift both flours and the baking powder into a mixing bowl (tipping in the bran left in the sieve), add the salt and butter and rub the butter into the flour with your fingertips until the mixture resembles fine breadcrumbs. Add the sugar and milk and mix to form a soft dough, adding a little more milk if the mixture is too dry.
3 Sift flour on to a clean work surface and roll the dough out to 2.5cm/1in thick using a rolling pin. Cut out 10 scones with a 6cm/2½in round cutter, gathering up the trimmings and re-rolling as necessary, but handling the dough as little as possible. (Dipping the cutter in a small bowl of flour between cutting each scone ensures a clean cut of the dough, which helps them to rise.)
4 Place the scones on the baking tray so that they are touching each other, which helps the scones to rise up straight. Brush the tops of the scones with the beaten egg using a pastry brush and sprinkle with caster sugar.
5 Bake for 12–15 minutes until the scones are golden brown and sound hollow when you pick one up with an oven glove and tap it on the bottom. Remove from the oven and transfer to a wire rack with a palette knife to cool a little. Serve warm.

125 LAVENDER SCONES

PREPARATION TIME 15 minutes   **COOKING TIME** 12–15 minutes   **MAKES** 10 scones

115g/4oz chilled butter, chopped,
    plus extra for greasing
450g/1lb/3 cups self-raising flour,
    plus extra for dusting
1 tsp baking powder
1 tsp salt

55g/2oz/¼ cup caster/superfine sugar,
    plus extra for sprinkling
1 tsp culinary lavender, ground using
    a pestle and mortar
200ml/7fl oz/scant 1 cup milk,
    plus extra for brushing

1 Preheat the oven to 190°C/375°F/gas 5. Grease a 30cm/12in square baking tray.
2 Sift the flour and baking powder into a mixing bowl, add the salt and butter and rub

the butter into the flour with your fingertips until the mixture resembles fine breadcrumbs. Add the sugar, lavender and milk and mix to form a soft dough, adding a little more milk if the mixture is too dry.

3 Sift flour on to a clean work surface and roll the dough out to 2.5cm/1in thick using a rolling pin. Cut out 10 scones with a 6cm/2½in round cutter, gathering up the trimmings and re-rolling as necessary, but handling the dough as little as possible. (Dipping the cutter in a small bowl of flour between cutting each scone ensures a clean cut of the dough, which helps them to rise.)

4 Place the scones on the baking tray so that they are touching each other. This will help the scones to rise up straight. Brush the tops of the scones with milk using a pastry brush and sprinkle with caster sugar.

5 Bake for 12–15 minutes until the scones are golden brown and sound hollow when you pick one up with an oven glove and tap it on the bottom. Remove from the oven and transfer to a wire rack with a palette knife to cool a little. Serve warm.

126 DATE & WALNUT SCONES

PREPARATION TIME 15 minutes   **COOKING TIME** 12–15 minutes   **MAKES** 10 scones

115g/4oz chilled butter, chopped, plus extra for greasing
250g/9oz/1⅔ cups self-raising flour, plus extra for dusting
200g/7oz/1⅓ cups self-raising wholemeal/wholewheat flour
1 tsp baking powder

1 tsp salt
55g/2oz/¼ cup light soft brown sugar
200ml/7fl oz/scant 1 cup milk
55g/2oz/⅓ cup pitted dates, chopped
55g/2oz/scant ½ cup walnuts, chopped
1 large egg, beaten
1 tbsp caster/superfine sugar

1 Preheat the oven to 190°C/375°F/gas 5. Grease a 30cm/12in square baking tray.

2 Sift both flours and the baking powder into a mixing bowl (tipping in the bran left in the sieve), add the salt and butter and rub the butter into the flour with your fingertips until the mixture resembles fine breadcrumbs. Add the sugar and milk and mix to form a soft dough, adding a little more milk if the mixture is too dry. Add the chopped dates and nuts.

3 Sift flour on to a clean work surface and roll the dough out to 2.5cm/1in thick using a rolling pin. Cut out 10 scones with a 6cm/2½in round cutter, gathering up the trimmings and re-rolling as necessary, but handling the dough as little as possible. (Dipping the cutter in a small bowl of flour between cutting each scone ensures a clean cut of the dough, which helps them to rise.)

4 Place the scones on the baking tray so that they are touching each other, which helps the scones to rise up straight. Brush the tops of the scones with beaten egg using a pastry brush and sprinkle with caster sugar.

5 Bake for 12–15 minutes until the scones are golden brown and sound hollow when you pick one up with an oven glove and tap it on the bottom. Remove from the oven and transfer to a wire rack with a palette knife to cool a little. Serve warm.

127 ROSEWATER-GLAZED SCONES

PREPARATION TIME 15 minutes   **COOKING TIME** 12–15 minutes   **MAKES** 10 scones

115g/4oz chilled butter, chopped,
   plus extra for greasing
450g/1lb/3 cups self-raising flour,
   plus extra for dusting
1 tsp baking powder
1 tsp salt

55g/2oz/¼ cup caster/superfine sugar,
   plus extra for sprinkling
200ml/7fl oz/scant 1 cup milk,
   plus extra for brushing
1 tbsp rosewater

1 Preheat the oven to 190°C/375°F/gas 5. Grease a 30cm/12in square baking tray.
2 Sift the flour and baking powder into a mixing bowl, add the salt and butter and rub the butter into the flour with your fingertips until the mixture resembles fine breadcrumbs. Add the sugar and the milk and mix to form a soft dough, adding a little more milk if the mixture is too dry.
3 Sift flour on to a clean work surface and roll the dough out to 2.5cm/1in thick using a rolling pin. Cut out 10 scones with a 6cm/2½in round cutter, gathering up the trimmings and re-rolling as necessary, but handling the dough as little as possible. (Dipping the cutter in a small bowl of flour between cutting each scone ensures a clean cut of the dough, which helps them to rise.)
4 Place the scones on the baking tray so that they are touching each other, which helps the scones to rise up straight. Mix the rosewater with a few teaspoons of milk and brush over the tops of the scones. Sprinkle with caster sugar.
5 Bake for 12–15 minutes until the scones are golden brown and sound hollow when you pick one up with an oven glove and tap it on the bottom. Remove from the oven and transfer to a wire rack with a palette knife to cool a little. Serve warm.

128 RASPBERRY DEVONSHIRE SPLITS

PREPARATION TIME 25 minutes, plus rising   **COOKING TIME** 15–20 minutes   **MAKES** 15 splits

2 tsp fast action dried yeast
55g/2oz/¼ cup caster/superfine sugar
300ml/10½fl oz/scant 1¼ cups warm milk
500g/1lb 2oz/scant 3⅓ cups self-raising flour,
    sifted, plus extra for dusting
30g/1oz butter, melted and cooled,
    plus extra for greasing

225g/8oz clotted cream
200g/7oz/heaped 1 cup raspberries
4 tbsp raspberry jam/jelly
icing/powdered sugar, for dusting

1   Put the yeast, 1 tablespoon of the caster sugar and 2 tablespoons of the warm milk in
    a cup and leave to stand for 10–20 minutes until the mixture has become frothy.
2   Put the flour, yeast mixture, remaining sugar, remaining milk and the melted butter into
    a large mixing bowl and bring the mixture together with your hands.
3   Sift flour on to a clean work surface, turn the mixture out and knead for 10 minutes to
    form a soft dough. Add a little more flour if the dough is too sticky. Return the dough to
    the bowl, cover with cling film/plastic wrap and leave in a warm place for about 1 hour
    until the dough has doubled in size. Grease and line two 30cm/12in square baking trays.
4   Tip the dough on to the floured work surface and punch it a few times to knock the
    air out of it, then cut into 15 pieces. Form each piece into a ball and place on the baking
    trays, spaced 2.5cm/1in apart. Cover with a damp dish towel and leave in a warm place
    to rise for about 30 minutes until the buns have doubled in size. Preheat the oven to
    200°C/400°F/gas 6.
5   Bake for 15–20 minutes until the buns are golden brown and sound hollow when you pick
    one up with an oven glove and tap it on the bottom. Remove from the oven and transfer
    to a wire rack with a spatula to cool.
6   Cut each bun in half from top to bottom (but not right through) and fill with clotted
    cream, a few raspberries and 1 teaspoon of the jam. Dust with icing sugar to serve.

129 ICED RASPBERRY BUNS

PREPARATION TIME 25 minutes, plus rising   **COOKING TIME** 15–20 minutes   **MAKES** 24 buns

2 tsp fast action dried yeast
55g/2oz/¼ cup caster/superfine sugar
300ml/10½fl oz/scant 1¼ cups warm milk
500g/1lb 2oz/3⅓ cups strong white bread
    flour, sifted, plus extra for dusting

30g/1oz butter, melted and cooled,
    plus extra for greasing
350g/12oz raspberry jam/jelly
200g/7oz/1⅓ cups fondant icing sugar
a few drops of pink food colouring

1 Put the yeast, 1 tablespoon of the sugar and 2 tablespoons of the milk in a cup and leave to stand for 10–20 minutes until the mixture has become frothy.

2 Put the flour, yeast mixture, remaining sugar, remaining milk and the melted butter in a large mixing bowl and bring the mixture together with your hands.

3 Sift flour on to a clean work surface, turn the mixture out and knead for 10 minutes to form a soft dough. Add a little more flour if the dough is too sticky. Return the dough to the bowl, cover with cling film/plastic wrap and leave in a warm place for about 1 hour until the dough has doubled in size. Grease and line two 30cm/12in square baking trays.

4 Tip the dough on to the floured work surface and punch it a few times to knock the air out of it, then cut into 24 pieces. Form each piece into a sausage shape and place on the baking trays, spaced 2.5cm/1in apart. Cover with a damp dish towel and leave in a warm place to rise for about 30 minutes until the buns have doubled in size. Preheat the oven to 200°C/400°F/gas 6.

5 Bake for 15–20 minutes until the buns are golden brown and sound hollow when you pick one up with an oven glove and tap it on the bottom. Remove from the oven and transfer to a wire rack with a spatula to cool.

6 Push a sharp, thin-bladed knife into each bun from one end, to make a cavity for the jam. Do not push right through the bun, or the jam will come out the other end. Put the raspberry jam into an icing bag and pipe roughly 1 tablespoon into each hole.

7 Mix the fondant icing sugar with 1–2 tablespoons water and the food colouring to form a smooth, thick icing/frosting. Spread the icing over the top of each bun using a round-bladed knife. Leave the icing to set before serving.

130 GLAZED CINNAMON BUNS

PREPARATION TIME 25 minutes, plus rising **COOKING TIME** 15–20 minutes **MAKES** 20 buns

2 tsp fast action dried yeast
90g/3¼oz/⅓ cup caster/superfine sugar
300ml/10½fl oz/scant 1¼ cups
   warm milk
500g/1lb 2oz/3⅓ cups strong white bread
   flour, sifted, plus extra for dusting

200g/7oz/1 cup sultanas/golden raisins
2 tsp ground cinnamon
30g/1oz butter, melted and cooled,
   plus extra for greasing
1 cinnamon stick

1 Put the yeast, 1 tablespoon of the sugar and 2 tablespoons of the milk in a cup and leave to stand for 10–20 minutes until the mixture has become frothy.

2 Put the flour, yeast mixture, 55g/2oz/¼ cup of the sugar, the remaining milk, sultanas, ground cinnamon and melted butter into a large mixing bowl and bring together with your hands.

3 Sift flour on to a clean work surface, turn the mixture out and knead for 10 minutes to form a soft dough. Add a little more flour if the dough is too sticky. Return the dough to

the bowl, cover with cling film/plastic wrap and leave in a warm place for about 1 hour until the dough has doubled in size. Grease and line two 30cm/12in square baking trays.

4 Tip the dough on to the floured work surface and punch it a few times to knock the air out of it, then cut into 20 pieces. Form each piece into a ball and place on the baking trays, spaced 2.5cm/1in apart. Cover with a damp dish towel and leave in a warm place to rise for about 30 minutes until the buns have doubled in size. Preheat the oven to 200°C/400°F/gas 6.

5 Bake for 15–20 minutes until the buns are golden brown and sound hollow when you pick one up with an oven glove and tap it on the bottom. Remove from the oven and turn out on to a wire rack. Heat the remaining sugar, the cinnamon stick and 3 tablespoons water in a small saucepan over a gentle heat until the sugar has dissolved, then bring to the boil. Brush the syrup over the buns with a pastry brush. Serve warm.

131 SAFFRON & ROSEWATER BUNS

PREPARATION TIME 25 minutes   **COOKING TIME** 20–25 minutes   **MAKES** 20 buns

2 tsp fast action dried yeast
90g/3¼oz/⅓ cup caster/superfine sugar
300ml/10½fl oz/scant 1¼ cups warm milk
3 tbsp rosewater
1 level tsp saffron stamens

500g/1lb 2oz/3⅓ cups strong white bread
flour, sifted, plus extra for dusting
30g/1oz butter, melted and cooled,
plus extra for greasing
200g/7oz/1 cup sultanas/golden raisins

1 Put the yeast, 1 tablespoon of the sugar, 2 tablespoons of the milk, 1 tablespoon of the rosewater and the saffron in a cup and leave for 10–20 minutes until the mixture is frothy.

2 Put the flour, yeast mixture, 55g/2oz/¼ cup of the sugar, the remaining milk and the melted butter into a large mixing bowl and bring the mixture together with your hands.

3 Sift flour on to a clean work surface, turn the mixture out and knead for 10 minutes to form a soft dough. Add a little more flour if the dough is too sticky. Return the dough to the bowl, cover with cling film/plastic wrap and leave in a warm place for about 1 hour until the dough has doubled in size. Grease and line two 30cm/12in square baking trays.

4 Tip the dough on to the floured work surface and punch it a few times to knock the air out of it, then add the sultanas and cut into 20 pieces. Form each piece into a ball and place on the baking trays, spaced 2.5cm/1in apart. Cover with a damp dish towel and leave in a warm place to rise for about 30 minutes until the buns have doubled in size. Preheat the oven to 200°C/400°F/gas 6.

5 Bake for 15–20 minutes until the buns are golden brown and sound hollow when you pick one up with an oven glove and tap it on the bottom. Remove from the oven and turn out on to a wire rack. Heat the remaining rosewater and sugar in a small saucepan over a gentle heat until the sugar has dissolved, then bring to the boil. Brush the syrup over the buns with a pastry brush. Serve warm.

132 CHOCOLATE ÉCLAIRS

PREPARATION TIME 25 minutes   **COOKING TIME** 30–35 minutes   **MAKES** 15 éclairs

115g/4oz butter, chopped, plus extra
    for greasing
140g/5oz/1 cup plain/all-purpose flour, sifted
4 large eggs, beaten

200g/7oz plain/semisweet chocolate, melted
    and cooled slightly
300ml/10½fl oz/scant 1¼ cups double/heavy
    cream, whipped to stiff peaks

1   Preheat the oven to 200°C/400°F/gas 6. Grease and line two 30cm/12in square
    baking trays.
2   Put the butter and 250ml/9fl oz/1 cup water in a saucepan and heat until the butter has
    melted. Bring to the boil, then remove from the heat and quickly add the flour all at once.
    Return the pan to the heat and beat the mixture hard with a wooden spoon until the
    mixture forms a ball of dough and leaves the sides of the pan clean. Remove from the heat
    and leave to cool for 10 minutes. Add the eggs gradually, beating after each addition. When
    all the eggs have been incorporated, you should have a smooth, soft paste.
3   Spoon the paste into an icing bag fitted with a 2cm/¾in plain nozzle and pipe 15 lines of
    the choux pastry approximately 10cm/4in in length on the baking trays.
4   Bake for 20–25 minutes until the pastry is golden brown. Remove from the oven and make
    a small slit at the end of each éclair with a knife to allow the steam to escape, then return to
    the oven for a further 5 minutes. Remove from the oven and transfer to a wire rack to cool.
5   Spread a little melted chocolate on each éclair and leave to set. When you are ready to
    serve, spoon the whipped cream into an icing bag and pipe the cream into the hole at the
    end of each éclair to fill. Serve immediately.

133 VIOLET CHOUX BUNS

PREPARATION TIME 25 minutes   **COOKING TIME** 30–35 minutes   **MAKES** 15 buns

115g/4oz butter, chopped, plus extra
    for greasing
140g/5oz/1 cup plain/all-purpose flour, sifted
4 large eggs, beaten
200g/7oz/1⅓ cups fondant icing sugar
2 tbsp violet syrup

¼ tsp purple food colouring paste
2 tbsp violet liqueur
300ml/10½fl oz/scant 1¼ cups
    double/heavy cream
15 purple sugar flowers, to decorate

1   Preheat the oven to 200°C/400°F/gas 6. Grease and line two 30cm/12in square
    baking trays.
2   Put the butter and 250ml/9fl oz/1 cup water in a saucepan and heat until the butter has
    melted. Bring to the boil, then remove from the heat and quickly add the flour all at once.

Return the pan to the heat and beat the mixture hard with a wooden spoon until the mixture forms a ball of dough and leaves the sides of the pan clean. Remove from the heat and leave to cool for 10 minutes. Add the eggs gradually, beating after each addition. When all the eggs have been incorporated, you should have a smooth, soft paste.

3 Place 15 tablespoons of the paste in balls about 5cm/2in in diameter on the trays.

4 Bake for 20–25 minutes until the pastry is golden brown. Remove from the oven and make a small slit in each bun with a knife to allow the steam to escape, then return to the oven for a further 5 minutes. Remove from the oven and transfer to a wire rack to cool.

5 Put the fondant icing sugar, violet syrup and colouring paste in a small bowl and mix to form a thick icing/frosting. Spread the fondant icing over each bun using a round-bladed knife and top with a purple sugar flower. Leave the icing to set.

6 When you are ready to serve, whisk the violet liqueur and double cream to stiff peaks using a mixer or hand whisk. Spoon the violet cream into an icing bag and pipe the cream into the hole at the end of each bun to fill. Serve immediately.

134 BANOFFI CHOUX BUNS

PREPARATION TIME 25 minutes   **COOKING TIME** 35–40 minutes   **MAKES** 15 buns

115g/4oz butter, chopped, plus extra
   for greasing
140g/5oz/1 cup plain/all-purpose flour
4 large eggs, beaten
300ml/10½fl oz/scant 1¼ cups
   double/heavy cream
100g/3½oz/heaped ⅓ cup dark soft
   brown sugar

3 tbsp maple syrup
2 bananas
100g/3½oz/⅔ cup icing/powdered sugar
55g/2oz/heaped ⅓ cup toasted
   flaked/sliced almonds

1 Preheat the oven to 200°C/400°F/gas 6. Grease and line two 30cm/12in square baking trays.

2 Put the butter and 250ml/9fl oz/1 cup water in a saucepan and heat until the butter has melted. Bring to the boil, then remove from the heat and quickly add the flour all at once. Return the pan to the heat and beat the mixture hard with a wooden spoon until the mixture forms a ball of dough and leaves the sides of the pan clean. Remove from the heat and leave to cool for 10 minutes. Add the eggs gradually, beating after each addition. When all the eggs have been incorporated, you should have a smooth, soft paste.

3 Place 15 tablespoons of the paste in balls about 5cm/2in in diameter on the trays.

4 Bake for 20–25 minutes until the pastry is golden brown. Remove from the oven and make a small slit in each bun with a knife to allow the steam to escape, then return to the oven for a further 5 minutes. Remove from the oven and transfer to a wire rack to cool.

5 To prepare the toffee sauce, put 100ml/3½fl oz/scant ½ cup of the double cream in a saucepan with the dark brown sugar and maple syrup and stir over a gentle heat until the sugar has dissolved. Remove from the heat and leave to cool.

6 When you are ready to serve the buns, place the bananas and icing sugar on a large plate and mash using the back of a fork until soft. Whip the remaining cream to stiff peaks using an electric hand mixer or a whisk and gently fold in the mashed banana using a large metal spoon. Slit each bun in half and fill with the banana cream. Spoon the toffee sauce over the top and sprinkle with the flaked almonds. Serve immediately.

Chapter 3

DESSERTS

This chapter contains delicious cakes that are suitable for serving as desserts, and most are prepared in advance, making them ideal for dinner parties. Wow your guests with a Baked Mocha Alaska filled with coffee ice cream, banana and chocolate, topped with a chewy hot meringue; classics such as Sacher Torte and Black Forest Gateau; luxurious cheesecakes made with clotted cream and summer berries; and party favourites Arctic Roulade and gooey Hazelnut Brownies with Chocolate Sauce. Why not try Gregg Wallace's favourite Sticky Toffee Nut Cheesecake – a creamy baked cheesecake topped with nuts in a caramel sauce? From delicate, meringue-shelled cloud cakes, sumptuously filled with cream and berries, to unusual twists on traditional favourites, such as Pecan Pie Cake and Key Lime Mousse Cake, there is a dessert here for every occasion.

135 LEMON & RASPBERRY CLOUD CAKE

PREPARATION TIME 40 minutes, plus chilling **COOKING TIME** 1 hour **SERVES** 8

butter, for greasing
4 large egg whites
½ tsp cream of tartar
250g/9oz/1 cup caster/superfine sugar
3 heaped tbsp lemon curd
juice and finely grated zest of ½ lemon
150g/5½oz cream cheese

2 tbsp lemon liqueur, such as limoncello
400ml/14fl oz/1½ cups double/heavy cream,
   whipped to stiff peaks
400g/14oz/3 cups raspberries
100g/3½oz white chocolate (gf) made into
   curls, to decorate

1 Preheat the oven to 140°C/275°F/gas 1. Grease and base-line a deep 23cm/9in springform cake tin.
2 Put the egg whites in a clean, dry bowl and whisk with an electric hand mixer or a whisk until they form stiff peaks. Add the cream of tartar and whisk again, then add the sugar a little at a time, whisking until the mixture forms a glossy meringue. Spoon the meringue into the cake tin, making a well in the centre so that the higher sides will contain the filling when cooked.
3 Bake for 1 hour until the meringue is crisp. Remove the meringue from the oven and leave to cool in the tin.
4 Put the lemon curd, lemon juice and zest, cream cheese and limoncello in a mixing bowl and beat to form a smooth lemon cream, using an electric hand mixer or wooden spoon. Add the whipped cream and fold the mixtures gently but thoroughly together, using a large metal spoon. Fold in half the raspberries and spoon the cream into the meringue case.
5 Refrigerate for 1 hour. Remove the meringue from the tin and place on a serving plate. Top with the remaining raspberries and the white chocolate curls.

136 STRAWBERRY CLOUD CAKE

PREPARATION TIME 40 minutes, plus chilling **COOKING TIME** 1 hour 10 minutes **SERVES** 8

butter, for greasing
4 large egg whites
½ tsp cream of tartar
350g/12oz/1⅓ cups caster/superfine sugar
1 vanilla pod/bean

400g/14oz/heaped 3 cups strawberries,
   hulled and sliced
1 tbsp powdered gelatine
500ml/17fl oz/2 cups double/heavy cream

1 Preheat the oven to 140°C/275°F/gas 1. Grease and base-line a deep 23cm/9in springform cake tin.
2 Put the egg whites in a clean, dry bowl and whisk with an electric hand mixer or a whisk

until they form stiff peaks. Add the cream of tartar and whisk again, then add 250g/9oz/ 1 cup of the sugar a little at a time, whisking until the mixture forms a glossy meringue. Spoon the meringue into the cake tin, making a well in the centre so that the higher sides will contain the filling when cooked.

3 Bake for 1 hour until the meringue is crisp. Remove the meringue from the oven and leave to cool in the tin.

4 Slit the vanilla pod in half with a sharp knife and put it in a saucepan with half the strawberries, 100ml/3½fl oz/scant ½ cup water and the remaining sugar. Simmer for 10 minutes until the strawberries are soft. Remove and discard the vanilla pod (scraping out any seeds that have not come out during the cooking process). Pour the mixture into a sieve and press out all the juice from the strawberries using a rubber spatula. Discard the contents of the sieve and return the strawberry juice to the pan.

5 Sprinkle the gelatine over the warm strawberry liquid and stir until the gelatine has dissolved. Leave the syrup to cool completely, then strain the mixture through a fine-mesh sieve.

6 Put 290ml/10fl oz/1¼ cups of the cream in a mixing bowl and whip to stiff peaks, using an electric hand mixer or a whisk. Add the cooled strawberry syrup and whisk again. Spoon the strawberry mousse into the meringue case.

7 Refrigerate for 2 hours. Remove the meringue from the tin and place on a serving plate. Whip the remaining cream to stiff peaks and spread over the top of the mousse. Top with the remaining strawberries.

137 COCONUT CREAM CLOUD CAKE

PREPARATION TIME 35 minutes, plus chilling   **COOKING TIME** 1 hour 5 minutes   **SERVES** 8

butter, for greasing
4 large egg whites and 2 large yolks
½ tsp cream of tartar
250g/9oz/1 cup caster/superfine sugar
30g/1oz/heaped ¼ cup desiccated/dried
   shredded coconut

200g/7oz plain/semisweet chocolate (gf),
   melted and cooled slightly
400ml/14fl oz/1½ cups double/heavy cream,
   whipped to soft peaks
2 tbsp coconut cream
2 tbsp coconut rum

1 Preheat the oven to 150°C/300°F/gas 2. Grease and base-line a deep 23cm/9in springform cake tin.

2 Put the egg whites in a clean, dry bowl and whisk with an electric hand mixer or a whisk until they form stiff peaks. Add the cream of tartar and whisk again, then add the sugar a little at a time, whisking until the mixture forms a glossy meringue. Spoon the meringue into the cake tin, making a well in the centre so that the higher sides will contain the filling when cooked. Make sure that the sides are thickly covered.

3 Bake for 1 hour until the meringue is crisp. Remove the meringue from the oven and leave to cool in the tin.

4 Put the desiccated coconut in a dry saucepan and heat until it starts to turn golden brown, stirring all the time to ensure it does not burn. Tip into a dish to cool.

5 Put the egg yolks in a mixing bowl, add the melted chocolate and then fold in half the whipped cream, the coconut cream and rum, using a large metal spoon. Spoon the mixture into the meringue case. Cover with the remaining cream and sprinkle over the coconut. Refrigerate for 2 hours, then remove from the tin and place on a serving plate.

138 SACHER TORTE

PREPARATION TIME 30 minutes, plus chilling   **COOKING TIME** 50–55 minutes   **SERVES** 8

175g/6oz butter, softened, plus extra
   for greasing
400g/14oz plain/semisweet chocolate
175g/6oz/scant ¾ cup caster/superfine sugar
8 large eggs, separated

140g/5oz/1 cup plain/all-purpose flour, sifted
3 tbsp brandy
3 tbsp apricot jam/jelly
4 tbsp double/heavy cream
sugar flowers, to decorate

1 Preheat the oven to 180°C/350°F/gas 4. Grease and line a deep 23cm/9in springform cake tin.

2 Melt 175g/6oz of the chocolate and leave to cool. Put the butter and sugar in a mixing bowl and beat using an electric hand mixer or wooden spoon until the mixture is light and creamy. Stir in the melted chocolate and egg yolks and mix well.

3 Put the egg whites in a clean, dry bowl and whisk with an electric hand mixer or a whisk until they form stiff peaks, then fold them gently but thoroughly into the chocolate mixture, using a large metal spoon. Add the flour and fold that in too. Scrape the mixture into the tin using a spatula.

4 Bake for 45–50 minutes until a crust has formed on top of the torte and a skewer inserted into the middle of the torte comes out clean. Remove the torte from the oven and leave to stand for 5 minutes, then turn out on to a wire rack and leave to cool.

5 Remove the torte from the tin, cut it in half horizontally and place the bottom layer on a serving plate. Drizzle the brandy over the bottom layer and then sandwich the layers together with half the jam. Warm the remaining jam in a little saucepan, then spread over the sides and top of the torte.

6 Melt the remaining chocolate, add the cream and stir until you have a smooth chocolate icing/frosting. Spread the icing over the top and sides of the torte, using a round-bladed knife, and decorate with the sugar flowers.

139 WHITE CHOCOLATE SACHER TORTE

PREPARATION TIME 30 minutes   **COOKING TIME** 50–55 minutes   **SERVES** 8

175g/6oz butter, softened, plus extra
  for greasing
175g/6oz/scant ¾ cup caster/superfine sugar
400g/14oz white chocolate, melted
  and cooled slightly
8 large eggs, separated
140g/5oz/1 cup plain/all-purpose flour, sifted

3 tbsp almond liqueur, such as amaretto
3 tbsp apricot jam/jelly
225g/8oz plain/semisweet chocolate, melted
  and cooled slightly
4 tbsp double/heavy cream
100g/3½oz white chocolate made into curls
sugar flowers, to decorate

1 Preheat the oven to 180°C/350°F/gas 4. Grease and line a deep 23cm/9in springform cake tin.

2 Put the butter and sugar in a mixing bowl and beat using an electric hand mixer or wooden spoon until the mixture is light and creamy. Stir in the melted white chocolate and egg yolks and mix well.

3 Put the egg whites in a clean, dry bowl and whisk with an electric hand mixer or a whisk until they form stiff peaks, then fold them gently but thoroughly into the chocolate mixture, using a large metal spoon. Add the flour and fold that in too. Scrape the mixture into the tin using a spatula.

4 Bake for 45–50 minutes until a crust has formed on top of the torte and a skewer inserted into the middle of the torte comes out clean. Remove the torte from the oven and leave to stand for 5 minutes, then turn out on to a wire rack and leave to cool.

5 Once cool, cut it in half horizontally and place the bottom layer on a serving plate. Drizzle the amaretto over the bottom layer and then sandwich the layers together with half the jam. Warm the remaining jam in a little saucepan, then spread over the sides and top of the torte. Put the melted plain chocolate in a bowl, add the cream and stir until you have a smooth chocolate ganache. Spread the ganache over the top and sides of the torte, using a round-bladed knife, sprinkle with the white chocolate curls and decorate with sugar flowers.

140 CINNAMON TRUFFLE TORTE WITH PLUM COMPOTE

PREPARATION TIME 30 minutes   **COOKING TIME** 40 minutes   **SERVES** 8

100g/3½oz butter, chopped, plus extra
    for greasing
250g/9oz dark/bittersweet chocolate (gf)
    (70% cocoa solids), broken into pieces
4 large eggs, separated
175g/6oz/heaped 1 cup icing/powdered sugar,
    sifted, plus extra for dusting
1 tsp ground cinnamon

10 ripe red plums, stones removed,
    flesh cut into chunks
2 cinnamon sticks
100g/3½oz/heaped ⅓ cup caster/superfine
    sugar, plus extra if necessary
cocoa powder, for dusting
crème fraîche, to serve

1   Preheat the oven to 180°C/350°F/gas 4. Grease and line a deep 23cm/9in springform
cake tin.

2   Melt the butter and chocolate together. Leave to cool.

3   Put the egg yolks and icing sugar in a mixing bowl and beat using an electric hand mixer
or wooden spoon until the mixture is light and creamy. Stir in the melted chocolate and
butter mixture and the ground cinnamon.

4   Put the egg whites in a clean, dry bowl and whisk with an electric hand mixer or a whisk
until they form soft peaks, then fold them gently but thoroughly into the chocolate
mixture, using a large metal spoon. Scrape the mixture into the tin using a spatula.

5   Bake for 20–30 minutes until a crust has formed on top of the torte and a skewer
inserted into the middle of the torte comes out clean. Meanwhile, put the plums,
100ml/3½fl oz/scant ½ cup water, the cinnamon sticks and caster sugar in a saucepan and
simmer for about 30 minutes, until the plums are soft and the liquid has reduced. Taste the
sauce and add a little more sugar if needed. Remove the cinnamon sticks.

6   Remove the torte from the oven and leave to set in the tin. Turn out on to a serving plate
and dust with the cocoa and icing sugar before serving with the plum compote and some
crème fraîche.

141 CHOCOLATE & NECTARINE TORTE

PREPARATION TIME 20 minutes　**COOKING TIME** 30–35 minutes　**SERVES** 8

150g/5½oz butter, chopped, plus extra
　for greasing
250g/9oz dark/bittersweet chocolate
　(70% cocoa solids), broken into pieces
4 large eggs, separated
175g/6oz/heaped 1 cup icing/powdered sugar,
　sifted, plus extra for dusting

3 ripe nectarines, quartered and
　stones removed
100g/3½oz amaretti biscuits/cookies
100g/3½oz marzipan, chopped
200ml/7fl oz/scant 1 cup double/heavy cream
2 tbsp almond liqueur, such as amaretto

1　Preheat the oven to 190°C/375°F/gas 5. Grease and line a deep 23cm/9in springform cake tin.

2　Melt 100g/3½oz of the butter and all the chocolate together. Put the egg yolks and icing sugar in a mixing bowl and beat using an electric hand mixer or wooden spoon until the mixture is light and creamy. Stir in the melted chocolate and butter mixture and mix well.

3　Put the egg whites in a clean, dry bowl and whisk with an electric hand mixer or a whisk until they form stiff peaks, then fold them gently but thoroughly into the chocolate mixture, using a large metal spoon. Scrape the mixture into the tin using a spatula, and top with the nectarine quarters, placed skin side down.

4　Put the amaretti biscuits in a plastic bag and crush them with a rolling pin. In a bowl, mix together the amaretti crumbs with the marzipan. Melt the remaining butter, add it to the bowl and mix with your hands to form a crumble mixture. Sprinkle the mixture in small lumps over the top of the cake.

5　Bake for 25–30 minutes until a crust has formed on the top of the torte and the nectarines are soft and juicy. (The torte will still be very gooey under the crust, but this will set as it cools to give a truffle-like texture.) Remove the torte from the oven and leave to cool in the tin. Put the cream and amaretto in a bowl and whip to stiff peaks, using an electric hand mixer or a whisk. Remove the torte from the tin and place on a serving plate. Serve with the amaretto cream.

142 RASPBERRY & CHOCOLATE TORTE

PREPARATION TIME 30 minutes　**COOKING TIME** 30–35 minutes　**SERVES** 8

100g/3½oz butter, chopped, plus extra
　for greasing
250g/9oz dark/bittersweet chocolate (gf)
　(70% cocoa solids), broken into pieces
4 large eggs, separated

200g/7oz/1⅓ cups icing/powdered
　sugar, sifted
400g/14oz/scant 3 cups raspberries
crème fraîche, to serve

1 Preheat the oven to 180°C/350°F/gas 4. Grease and line a deep 23cm/9in springform cake tin.

2 Melt the butter and chocolate together and leave to cool. Put the egg yolks and 175g/6oz/ heaped 1 cup of the icing sugar in a mixing bowl and beat using an electric hand mixer or wooden spoon until the mixture is light and creamy. Stir in the melted chocolate and butter mixture and mix well.

3 In a separate bowl, whisk the egg whites until they form soft peaks, using an electric hand mixer or a whisk, then fold them gently but thoroughly into the chocolate mixture, using a large metal spoon. Sprinkle half the raspberries over the bottom of the cake tin and spoon the chocolate mixture over them.

4 Bake for 20–30 minutes until a crust has formed on top of the torte and a skewer inserted into the middle of the torte comes out clean. Remove the torte from the oven and leave to set in the tin.

5 Using a fork, crush the remaining raspberries with the remaining icing sugar, then pass through a sieve to remove the seeds. Remove the torte from the tin and place on a serving plate. Serve slices of the torte with a drizzle of the raspberry sauce and some crème fraîche.

143 BLUEBERRY STREUSEL TORTE

PREPARATION TIME 20 minutes   **COOKING TIME** 55–60 minutes   **SERVES** 8

250g/9oz butter, softened, plus extra
    for greasing
200g/7oz/heaped ¾ cup caster/
    superfine sugar
5 large eggs

280g/10oz/scant 2 cups self-raising flour
1 tsp ground cinnamon
300g/10½oz cream cheese
200g/7oz/heaped 1 cup blueberries
55g/2oz/heaped ⅓ cup flaked/sliced almonds

1 Preheat the oven to 180°C/350°F/gas 4. Grease and line a 25cm/10in springform cake tin.

2 Put 175g/6oz of the butter and 175g/6oz/scant ¾ cup of the sugar in a mixing bowl and beat using an electric hand mixer or wooden spoon until the mixture is light and creamy. Add 3 of the eggs and beat again. Sift in 175g/6oz/scant 1¼ cups of the flour and the ground cinnamon and fold them in, using a large metal spoon. Scrape the mixture into the tin using a spatula.

3 In a separate bowl, beat together the cream cheese, remaining eggs and 1 tablespoon of the remaining sugar using an electric hand mixer or wooden spoon, then stir in the blueberries. Spoon on top of the cake mixture.

4 Put the remaining flour in a bowl and rub in the remaining butter with your fingertips to make large crumble pieces. Mix in the remaining sugar and the flaked almonds and sprinkle the crumble topping over the top.

5 Bake for 55–60 minutes until the crumble topping is golden brown, the cream is set and a skewer inserted into the middle of the torte comes out clean. Remove the torte from the oven and leave to cool in the tin for 10 minutes, then place on a serving plate.

144 RHUBARB & CUSTARD FLAN

PREPARATION TIME 30 minutes   **COOKING TIME** 35–40 minutes   **SERVES** 8

175g/6oz butter, softened, plus extra
    for greasing
600g/1lb 2oz rhubarb, peeled and cut into
    2.5cm/1in pieces
185g/6½oz/scant ¾ cup caster/
    superfine sugar
juice of 1 lemon
3 large eggs plus 3 large egg yolks
175g/6oz/heaped 1 cup self-raising flour,
    sifted

100ml/3½fl oz/scant ½ cup buttermilk
30g/1oz/scant ¼ cup cornflour/cornstarch
400ml/14fl oz/1½ cups milk
100g/3½oz white chocolate, melted
    and cooled slightly
1 tsp vanilla extract
500ml/17fl oz/2 cups double/heavy cream,
    whipped to soft peaks
30g/1oz/scant ¼ cup pistachio nuts,
    finely chopped, to decorate

1 Preheat the oven to 190°C/375°F/gas 5. Grease a 23cm/9in raised-base flan tin and line the raised centre of the tin with baking parchment.

2 Put the rhubarb in a baking dish and sprinkle with 1 tablespoon of the sugar and the lemon juice. Set aside.

3 Put the butter and remaining sugar in a mixing bowl and beat using an electric hand mixer or wooden spoon until the mixture is light and creamy. Add the whole eggs and whisk again. Add the flour and buttermilk and fold them into the mixture, using a large metal spoon. Scrape the mixture into the tin using a spatula.

4 Put the flan tin and rhubarb tin in the oven on separate shelves. Bake for 20–25 minutes until a skewer inserted into the middle comes out clean. Remove the flan from the oven, leaving the rhubarb for another 5 minutes. Leave the torte to stand for 5 minutes, then invert on to a wire rack and leave to cool. Remove the rhubarb from the oven.

5 In a separate bowl, whisk together the cornflour and egg yolks with an electric hand mixer or a whisk. The mixture will be stiff at first but it will become lighter as you progress.

6 Put the milk in a saucepan and bring to the boil, then pour it into the egg mixture, whisking all the time. Stir in the melted white chocolate and vanilla extract and whisk well to combine. Pour the mixture back into the saucepan the milk was heated in, and heat gently for a few minutes until the custard thickens, whisking all the time. When it is thick, remove from the heat and set aside to cool. Pass through a sieve to remove any lumps.

7 When you are ready to serve, fold the cooked rhubarb and half the whipped cream into the white chocolate custard, using a large metal spoon. Put the flan case on a serving plate and spoon the rhubarb custard into the sunken area. Spoon the remaining cream into an icing bag fitted with a 13mm/½in star-shaped nozzle and pipe stars all over the rhubarb, then sprinkle with the pistachios.

145 MANGO & PASSION FRUIT TORTE

PREPARATION TIME 30 minutes, plus chilling   **COOKING TIME** 25–30 minutes   **SERVES** 8

115g/4oz butter, softened, plus extra
 for greasing
115g/4oz/scant ½ cup caster/superfine sugar
2 large eggs, lightly beaten
115g/4oz/¾ cup self-raising flour, sifted
2 tbsp natural/plain yogurt

200ml/7fl oz/scant 1 cup crème fraîche
400g/14oz cream cheese
2 tbsp icing/powdered sugar
pulp and seeds from 4 passion fruit
2 ripe mangoes, peeled, pitted and chopped

1 Preheat the oven to 190°C/375°F/gas 5. Grease and line a 20cm/8in springform cake tin.
2 Put the butter and sugar in a mixing bowl and beat using an electric hand mixer or wooden spoon until the mixture is light and creamy. Add the eggs and beat again. Add the flour and fold it into the mixture with the yogurt, using a large metal spoon. Scrape the mixture into the tin using a spatula.
3 Bake for 25–30 minutes until a skewer inserted into the middle of the torte comes out clean. Remove the torte from the oven and leave to cool in the tin.
4 In a separate bowl, mix together the crème fraîche, cream cheese, icing sugar and half the passion fruit pulp and seeds. Pour the mixture on top of the torte in the cake tin and refrigerate for 2 hours. Remove the torte from the tin and place on a serving plate. Top with the chopped mango and the remaining pulp and seeds.

146 TORTE DI MASCARPONE

PREPARATION TIME 30 minutes, plus chilling   **COOKING TIME** 30–35 minutes   **SERVES** 8

115g/4oz butter, softened, plus extra
 for greasing
115g/4oz/scant ½ cup caster/superfine sugar
2 tbsp Pistachio Butter (see page 25)
2 large eggs, lightly beaten
115g/4oz/¾ cup self-raising flour, sifted

3 tbsp almond liqueur, such as amaretto
3 tbsp raspberry jam/jelly
500g/1lb 2oz mascarpone cheese
250ml/9fl oz/1 cup crème fraîche
2 tbsp icing/powdered sugar, sifted
450g/1lb/3 cups raspberries

1 Preheat the oven to 180°C/350°F/gas 4. Grease and line a 20cm/8in springform cake tin.
2 Put the butter and sugar and 1 tablespoon of the pistachio butter in a mixing bowl and beat using an electric hand mixer or wooden spoon until the mixture is light and creamy. Add the eggs and beat again. Add the flour and fold in, using a large metal spoon. Scrape the mixture into the tin using a spatula.
3 Bake for 30–35 minutes until a skewer inserted into the middle of the torte comes out clean. Remove the torte from the oven and leave to stand for 5 minutes, then turn out on to a wire rack and leave to cool a little. Spoon over the amaretto and leave to cool completely, then spread the jam over the torte. Return the torte to the tin.
4 In a separate bowl, mix together the mascarpone cheese, crème fraîche, remaining pistachio butter, icing sugar and a third of the raspberries using an electric hand mixer or wooden spoon. Spoon this mixture over the torte in the tin and refrigerate for 2 hours. Top the torte with the remaining raspberries and transfer to a serving plate.

147 BLACK FOREST GATEAU

PREPARATION TIME 30 minutes, plus chilling   **COOKING TIME** 35–40 minutes   **SERVES** 8

225g/8oz butter, softened, plus extra
   for greasing
225g/8oz/scant 1 cup caster/superfine sugar
4 large eggs, lightly beaten
200g/7oz/1⅓ cups self-raising flour
4 tbsp cocoa powder
4 tbsp cherry liqueur, such as kirsch

3 tbsp black cherry jam/jelly
200g/7oz/1½ cups preserved cherries,
   drained and halved
500ml/17fl oz/2 cups double/heavy cream,
   whipped to stiff peaks
150g/5½oz plain/semisweet chocolate, grated
5 glacé/candied cherries, halved, to decorate

1 Preheat the oven to 180°C/350°F/gas 4. Grease and line a 23cm/9in springform cake tin.
2 Put the butter and sugar in a mixing bowl and beat using an electric hand mixer or wooden spoon until the mixture is light and creamy. Add the eggs gradually, beating after each addition. Sift in the flour and cocoa and gently fold them into the mixture, using a large metal spoon. Scrape the mixture into the tin using a spatula.
3 Bake for 35–40 minutes until the cake springs back when pressed lightly and a skewer inserted into the middle of the cake comes out clean. Remove the cake from the oven and leave to stand for 5 minutes, then turn out on to a wire rack and leave to cool.
4 Cut the cake into 3 layers using a sharp knife. Drizzle the kirsch over the bottom and middle layers and place the bottom layer on a serving plate. Spread half the jam and preserved cherries on the bottom layer and top with a quarter of the whipped cream. Cover with the next cake layer and repeat. When all 3 layers are assembled, cover the sides and top of the cake with the remaining whipped cream, retaining a few spoonfuls. Sprinkle the grated chocolate over the top and sides of the cake, then spoon the

remaining cream into an icing bag fitted with a 13mm/½in star nozzle and pipe around the top of the cake. Top the cream stars with the glacé cherry halves. Refrigerate for 1 hour before serving.

148 COFFEE GATEAU

PREPARATION TIME 20 minutes   **COOKING TIME** 20–30 minutes   **SERVES** 8

225g/8oz butter, softened, plus extra
   for greasing
225g/8oz/scant 1 cup caster/superfine sugar
4 large eggs, beaten
225g/8oz/1½ cups self-raising flour, sifted
1 tbsp instant coffee granules dissolved in
   2 tbsp boiling water, then cooled

200g/7oz coffee chocolate: half chopped;
   half made into large curls
100ml/3½fl oz/scant ½ cup coffee liqueur
100ml/3½fl oz/scant ½ cup double/heavy
   cream, whipped to stiff peaks
200g/7oz/1⅓ cups icing/powdered sugar,
   sifted, plus extra for dusting

1 Preheat the oven to 180°C/350°F/gas 4. Grease and base-line two 20cm/8in sandwich cake tins.
2 Put the butter and sugar in a mixing bowl and beat using an electric hand mixer or wooden spoon until the mixture is light and creamy. Add the eggs gradually, beating after each addition. Add the flour and gently fold it into the mixture with half the coffee liquid and the chopped coffee chocolate, using a large metal spoon. Divide the mixture between the tins using a spatula.
3 Bake for 20–30 minutes until the cakes spring back when pressed lightly and a skewer inserted into the middle of each cake comes out clean. Remove the cakes from the oven and leave to stand for 5 minutes, then turn out on to a wire rack and leave to cool.
4 Drizzle half the coffee liqueur over the top of each cake using a spoon. Fold the remaining liqueur into the whipped cream and use this to sandwich the cakes together. Place the cake on a serving plate.
5 Put the icing sugar in a bowl, add the remaining coffee liquid and 1–2 tablespoons water (gradually) and mix to form a thick icing/frosting. Spoon this over the top of the cake, decorate with the coffee chocolate curls and dust with icing sugar.

149 STRAWBERRY CARAMEL GATEAU

PREPARATION TIME 30 minutes **COOKING TIME** 30–35 minutes **SERVES** 8

600ml/21fl oz/scant 2½ cups double/
   heavy cream
4 tbsp light muscovado sugar
2 tbsp golden syrup
280g/10oz butter, softened, plus extra
   for greasing
225g/8oz/scant 1 cup caster/superfine sugar

4 large eggs, lightly beaten
225g/8oz/1½ cups self-raising flour
1 tsp baking powder
400g/14oz/heaped 3 cups strawberries,
   hulled and thinly sliced
icing/powdered sugar, for dusting

1 Put 200ml/7fl oz/scant 1 cup of the double cream in a saucepan with the muscovado sugar, syrup and 55g/2oz of the butter and simmer for about 5 minutes until the sugar has dissolved to make a caramel sauce. Set aside to cool.
2 Preheat the oven to 180°C/350°F/gas 4. Grease and base-line two 20cm/8in sandwich cake tins.
3 Put the remaining butter and the caster sugar in a mixing bowl and beat using an electric hand mixer or wooden spoon until the mixture is light and creamy. Add the eggs gradually, beating after each addition. Sift in the flour and baking powder and gently fold into the mixture, using a large metal spoon. Divide the mixture between the tins using a spatula.
4 Bake for 25–30 minutes until the cakes spring back when pressed lightly and a skewer inserted into the middle of each cake comes out clean. Remove the cakes from the oven and leave to stand for 5 minutes, then turn out on to a wire rack and leave to cool.
5 Put the remaining cream in a bowl and whisk to stiff peaks using an electric hand mixer or a whisk. Cut each cake in half horizontally and place the bottom layer on a serving plate. Spread a third of the cream over the bottom layer, cover with a third of the strawberries and drizzle over some of the caramel sauce. Repeat with the remaining layers and dust the top layer with icing sugar. Serve with the rest of the caramel sauce on the side.

150 WHITE CHOCOLATE GATEAU

PREPARATION TIME 30 minutes, plus chilling **COOKING TIME** 30–35 minutes **SERVES** 8

225g/8oz butter, softened, plus extra
   for greasing
225g/8oz/scant 1 cup caster/superfine sugar
4 large eggs, lightly beaten
225g/8oz/1½ cups self-raising flour, sifted
4 tbsp sour cream
100g/3½oz/heaped ½ cup white
   chocolate chips

100g/3½oz/1¼ cups desiccated/dried
   shredded coconut
4 tbsp toffee liqueur
1 recipe quantity **Coffee Buttercream**
   (see page 24)
300ml/10½fl oz/scant 1¼ cups double/heavy
   cream, whipped to stiff peaks
100g/3½oz white chocolate curls, to decorate

1 Preheat the oven to 180°C/350°F/gas 4. Grease and base-line two 20cm/8in sandwich cake tins.

2 Put the butter and sugar in a mixing bowl and beat using an electric hand mixer or wooden spoon until the mixture is light and creamy. Add the eggs and beat again. Add the flour, sour cream and white chocolate chips and fold them in, using a large metal spoon. Divide the mixture between the tins using a spatula.

3 Bake for 25–30 minutes until the cakes spring back when pressed lightly and a skewer inserted into the middle of each cake comes out clean. Remove the cakes from the oven and leave to stand for 5 minutes, then turn out on to a wire rack and leave to cool.

4 Put the desiccated coconut in a dry saucepan and heat gently for about 5 minutes until it starts to turn golden brown, stirring all the time to ensure it does not burn. Tip into a dish to cool.

5 Drizzle half the toffee liqueur over each cake and sandwich them together with the buttercream. Place the cake on a serving plate. Cover the sides and top of the cake with the whipped cream and sprinkle the toasted coconut all over it. Top with the white chocolate curls and refrigerate for 1 hour before serving.

151 PEAR & BLACKBERRY CRUMBLE CAKE

PREPARATION TIME 20 minutes   **COOKING TIME** 40–45 minutes   **SERVES** 8

225g/8oz butter, softened, plus extra
  for greasing
3 large pears, peeled, cored and chopped
3 tbsp light soft brown sugar
200g/7oz/heaped ¾ cup caster/
  superfine sugar

3 large eggs, lightly beaten
225g/8oz/1½ cups self-raising flour
1 tsp ground cinnamon
250g/9oz/scant 2 cups blackberries
55g/2oz/½ cup ground almonds

1 Preheat the oven to 180°C/350°F/gas 4. Grease and line a deep 23cm/9in springform cake tin.

2 Put the pears, light brown sugar and 100ml/3½fl oz/scant ½ cup water in a saucepan and simmer for 15 minutes until the pears are soft. Drain off any remaining water and set the pears aside.

3 Put 175g/6oz of the butter and 175g/6oz/scant ¾ cup of the caster sugar in a mixing bowl and beat using an electric hand mixer or wooden spoon until the mixture is light and creamy. Add the eggs gradually, beating after each addition. Sift in 175g/6oz/scant 1¼ cups of the flour and the ground cinnamon and gently fold them into the mixture, using a large metal spoon. Scrape the mixture into the tin using a spatula, then cover with the pears and blackberries.

4 Put the remaining flour and the ground almonds in a bowl and rub in the remaining butter with your fingertips to make large crumble pieces. Mix in the remaining caster sugar with your fingers. Sprinkle the crumble topping over the fruit.

5 Bake for 25–30 minutes until the crumble topping is golden brown. Remove the cake from the oven and leave to stand for 5 minutes, then turn out on to a serving plate and serve while still warm.

152 PINEAPPLE UPSIDE-DOWN CAKE

PREPARATION TIME 25 minutes   **COOKING TIME** 30–35 minutes   **SERVES** 8

280g/10oz butter, softened, plus extra
   for greasing
3 tbsp golden syrup
8 canned pineapple rings in juice, drained
8 glacé/candied cherries
225g/8oz/scant 1 cup caster/superfine sugar

4 large eggs, lightly beaten
225g/8oz/1½ cups self-raising flour
1 tsp ground cinnamon
2 tbsp milk
custard or cream, to serve

1 Preheat the oven to 190°C/375°F/gas 5. Grease and line a 23cm/9in springform cake tin.

2 Put the syrup and 55g/2oz of the butter in a small saucepan and heat gently for about 5 minutes, stirring, until the butter has melted. Pour the mixture into the bottom of the tin. Arrange the pineapple rings on top of the mixture with a cherry in the middle of each one. Set aside.

3 Put the remaining butter and sugar in a mixing bowl and beat using an electric hand mixer or wooden spoon until the mixture is light and creamy. Add the eggs gradually, beating after each addition. Sift in the flour and ground cinnamon and fold them into the mixture with the milk, using a large metal spoon. Scrape the mixture on top of the pineapple using a spatula.

4 Bake for 25–30 minutes until the cake springs back when pressed lightly and a skewer inserted into the middle of the cake comes out clean. Remove the cake from the oven and leave to stand for 5 minutes. Remove the springform sides of the tin and put a serving plate on top of the cake. Holding both plate and tin base securely, tip the cake upside down so that it is inverted on to the plate. Remove the tin base and serve warm with custard or cream.

153 PECAN PIE CAKE

PREPARATION TIME 20 minutes   **COOKING TIME** 50–60 minutes   **SERVES** 8

225g/8oz butter, softened, plus extra
   for greasing
175g/6oz/¾ cup light soft brown sugar
3 large eggs, lightly beaten
175g/6oz/heaped 1 cup self-raising
   flour, sifted

juice and finely grated zest of
   1 large lemon
100g/3½oz/scant 1 cup pecan halves
55g/2oz/¼ cup dark muscovado sugar
2 tbsp golden syrup
custard or cream, to serve

1   Preheat the oven to 150°C/300°F/gas 2. Grease and line a deep 23cm/9in springform cake tin.
2   Put 175g/6oz of the butter and the light brown sugar in a mixing bowl and beat using an electric hand mixer or wooden spoon until the mixture is light and creamy. Add the eggs gradually, beating after each addition. Add the flour and gently fold it into the mixture with the lemon zest, using a large metal spoon. Scrape the mixture into the tin using a spatula and arrange the pecan halves in a circular pattern on top of the cake.
3   Bake for 50–60 minutes until the cake springs back when pressed lightly and a skewer inserted into the middle of the cake comes out clean.
4   Just before the cake is cooked, put the remaining butter, the lemon juice, muscovado sugar and syrup in a saucepan and heat gently, stirring, until the sugar has dissolved, then boil for 1 minute to create a syrup. Remove the cake from the oven and pour the syrup over the cake. Leave the cake to cool in the tin, then turn out on to a serving plate. Serve warm or cold with custard or cream.

154 RHUBARB UPSIDE-DOWN CAKE

PREPARATION TIME 30 minutes   **COOKING TIME** 45–50 minutes   **SERVES** 8

225g/8oz butter, softened, plus extra
   for greasing
400g/14oz rhubarb, peeled and cut into
   2.5cm/1in pieces
juice and finely grated zest of 1 lemon
1 tbsp caster/superfine sugar
225g/8oz/1 cup dark soft brown sugar

4 large eggs, lightly beaten
225g/8oz/1½ cups self-raising flour, sifted
145ml/4¾fl oz/scant ⅔ cup sour cream
100g/3½oz/heaped ½ cup sultanas/
   golden raisins
clotted cream or crème fraîche, to serve

1   Preheat the oven to 180°C/350°F/gas 4. Grease and line a deep 23cm/9in springform cake tin.

2　Put the rhubarb, lemon juice and caster sugar in a roasting tin with a few tablespoons of water. Bake for about 5–10 minutes until the rhubarb is soft but still retains its shape. Cool and then arrange in circles over the base of the tin.

3　Put the butter and dark brown sugar in a mixing bowl and beat using an electric hand mixer or wooden spoon until the mixture is light and creamy. Add the eggs gradually, beating after each addition. Add the flour and gently fold it into the mixture with the sour cream, sultanas and lemon zest, using a large metal spoon. Spoon the mixture over the rhubarb.

4　Bake for 40–45 minutes until the cake springs back when pressed lightly and a skewer inserted into the middle of the cake comes out clean. Remove the cake from the oven and leave to stand for 10 minutes. Remove the springform sides of the tin and put a serving plate on top of the cake. Holding both plate and tin base securely, tip the cake upside down so that it is inverted on to the plate. Remove the tin base and serve the cake warm with clotted cream or crème fraîche.

155 BUTTERED RUM CAKE

PREPARATION TIME 25 minutes　**COOKING TIME** 25–30 minutes　**SERVES** 8

150g/5½oz butter, melted and cooled,
　plus extra for greasing
4 large eggs, separated
100g/3½oz/⅔ cup icing/powdered sugar,
　sifted
100g/3½oz/⅔ cup plain/all-purpose
　flour, sifted

100g/3½oz/scant 1 cup ground hazelnuts
100g/3½oz/scant 1 cup ground almonds
125ml/4fl oz/½ cup rum
3 tbsp dark muscovado sugar
fresh berries and crème fraîche, to serve

1　Preheat the oven to 190°C/375°F/gas 5. Grease and line a deep 23cm/9in springform cake tin.

2　Put the egg yolks and icing sugar in a mixing bowl and beat using an electric hand mixer or wooden spoon until the mixture is light and creamy. Add the flour, 100g/3½oz of the melted butter and the ground nuts and mix well.

3　Put the egg whites in a clean, dry bowl and whisk with an electric hand mixer or a whisk until they form stiff peaks, then gently fold them into the cake mixture, using a large metal spoon. Scrape the mixture into the tin using a spatula.

4　Bake for 25–30 minutes until the cake springs back when pressed lightly and a skewer inserted into the middle of the cake comes out clean.

5　Just before the cake is cooked, heat the rum with the remaining melted butter and muscovado sugar in a small saucepan until the sugar has dissolved, then boil for 1 minute to create a syrup. Remove the cake from the oven and pour the syrup over. Leave the cake to cool in the tin, then turn out on to a serving plate. Serve with fresh berries and crème fraîche.

156 WARM APPLE & CINNAMON YOGURT CAKE

PREPARATION TIME 25 minutes   **COOKING TIME** 50–60 minutes   **SERVES** 8

200g/7oz butter, softened, plus extra
    for greasing
3 dessert apples, peeled, cored
    and thinly sliced
115g/4oz/½ cup dark muscovado sugar
juice of ½ lemon

115g/4oz/scant ½ cup caster/superfine sugar
3 large eggs, lightly beaten
200g/7oz/1⅓ cups self-raising flour
2 tsp ground cinnamon
200ml/7fl oz/scant 1 cup Greek yogurt
    with honey

1 Preheat the oven to 180°C/350°F/gas 4. Grease and line a 20cm/8in springform cake tin.
2 Put the sliced apples in a bowl with 1 tablespoon of the muscovado sugar and the lemon juice and stir well to coat. Place the apples in circles on the bottom of the tin, overlapping them so that the base is completely covered.
3 Put the butter, caster sugar and remaining muscovado sugar in a mixing bowl and beat using an electric hand mixer or wooden spoon until the mixture is light and creamy. Add the eggs gradually, beating after each addition. Sift in the flour and ground cinnamon and gently fold them into the mixture with the yogurt, using a large metal spoon. Gently spoon the cake mixture on top of the apples.
4 Bake for 50–60 minutes until the cake springs back when pressed lightly and a skewer inserted into the middle of the cake comes out clean. (If the top of the cake starts to brown too much, cover it with a piece of baking parchment.) Remove the cake from the oven and leave to stand for 5 minutes, then invert on to a serving plate and serve warm.

157 VIN SANTO & RASPBERRY TRIFLE CAKE

PREPARATION TIME 40 minutes, plus chilling   **COOKING TIME** 35–40 minutes   **SERVES** 8

175g/6oz butter, softened, plus extra
    for greasing
175g/6oz/scant ¾ cup caster/superfine sugar
3 large eggs, lightly beaten
175g/6oz/heaped 1 cup self-raising
    flour, sifted
100g/3½oz/scant 1 cup ground almonds
2 tbsp natural/plain yogurt
1 tsp almond extract

240ml/8fl oz/scant 1 cup vin santo
    or other dessert wine
1 tbsp powdered gelatine
200ml/7fl oz/scant 1 cup ready-made custard
200g/7oz/heaped 1 cup raspberries
200ml/7fl oz/scant 1 cup double/heavy
    cream, whipped to stiff peaks
icing/powdered sugar, for dusting

1 Preheat the oven to 180°C/350°F/gas 4. Grease and line a deep 23cm/9in springform cake tin.

2 Put the butter and sugar in a mixing bowl and beat using an electric hand mixer or wooden spoon until the mixture is light and creamy. Add the eggs gradually, beating after each addition. Add the flour and gently fold it into the mixture with the ground almonds, yogurt and almond extract, using a large metal spoon. Scrape the mixture into the tin using a spatula.

3 Bake for 30–35 minutes until the cake springs back when pressed lightly and a skewer inserted into the middle of the cake comes out clean. Remove the cake from the oven and leave to stand for 5 minutes, then turn out on to a wire rack and leave to cool.

4 Meanwhile, pour 125ml/4¼fl oz/½ cup of the vin santo into a saucepan and heat gently for about 5 minutes. Remove from the heat, sprinkle over the gelatine and stir until it has dissolved. Set aside to cool, then strain through a fine-mesh sieve.

5 Cut the cake in half horizontally, using a sharp knife. Drizzle the remaining vin santo over the cut sides of the cake using a spoon. Return the bottom layer of cake to the tin with the springform side clipped back in place. Fold the custard, gelatine mixture and raspberries gently into the whipped cream, using a large metal spoon. Pour the custard cream into the cake tin and top with the second cake layer. Refrigerate for 2 hours, then gently transfer to a serving plate and dust with icing sugar.

158 KEY LIME MOUSSE CAKE

PREPARATION TIME 35 minutes, plus chilling   **COOKING TIME** 35–40 minutes   **SERVES** 8

175g/6oz butter, softened, plus extra
    for greasing
400g/14oz/1⅔ cups caster/superfine sugar
3 large eggs, lightly beaten
175g/6oz/heaped 1 cup self-raising flour
1 tsp baking powder
400ml/14fl oz/1½ cups double/heavy cream

250g/9oz mascarpone cheese
juice and finely grated zest of 5 limes
juice of 1 small orange
1 tbsp powdered gelatine
a few drops of green food colouring
    (optional)
icing/powdered sugar, for dusting

1 Preheat the oven to 160°C/325°F/gas 3. Grease and line a deep 23cm/9in springform cake tin.

2 Put the butter and 175g/6oz/scant ¾ cup of the sugar in a mixing bowl and beat using an electric hand mixer or wooden spoon until the mixture is light and creamy. Add the eggs gradually, beating after each addition. Sift in the flour and baking powder and gently fold them into the mixture, using a large metal spoon. Scrape the mixture into the tin using a spatula.

3 Bake for 30–35 minutes until the cake springs back when pressed lightly and a skewer inserted into the middle of the cake comes out clean. Remove the cake from the oven and leave to stand for 5 minutes, then turn out on to a wire rack and leave to cool.

4 In a separate bowl, beat the remaining sugar with the cream, mascarpone cheese, lime juice and zest and orange juice to a smooth cream using an electric hand mixer or wooden spoon.

5 Put 2 tablespoons water in a bowl on top of a saucepan half-full of simmering water. Sprinkle the gelatine over the water and stir until the gelatine has dissolved. Do not overheat, otherwise the gelatine will lose its setting quality. Stir the gelatine mixture into the lime cream with the food colouring, if using. Beat again.

6 Cut the cake in half horizontally, using a sharp knife. Return the bottom layer of the cake to the tin with the side clipped back in place. Pour the lime mousse over the cake, then top with the second layer. Refrigerate for 2 hours, then gently transfer to a serving plate, removing the sides and base of the tin, and dust with icing sugar.

159 BLACKCURRANT & CASSIS CAKE

PREPARATION TIME 30 minutes   **COOKING TIME** 35–45 minutes   **SERVES** 8

200g/7oz/heaped 1 cup fresh or thawed
   frozen blackcurrants
55g/2oz/¼ cup light soft brown sugar
175g/6oz butter, softened, plus extra
   for greasing
175g/6oz/scant ¾ cup caster/superfine sugar
3 large eggs, lightly beaten
140g/5oz/1 cup self-raising flour

55g/2oz/heaped ¼ cup cocoa powder
100g/3½oz plain/semisweet chocolate, grated
250g/9oz mascarpone cheese
200ml/7fl oz/scant 1 cup crème fraîche
2 tbsp icing/powdered sugar, sifted, plus
   extra for dusting
4 tbsp blackcurrant liqueur, such as cassis

1 Put the blackcurrants, light brown sugar and 100ml/3½fl oz/scant ½ cup water in a saucepan and simmer for 5–10 minutes until the fruit is soft. Strain and set aside to cool.

2 Preheat the oven to 180°C/350°F/gas 4. Grease and line a deep 23cm/9in springform cake tin.

3 Put the butter and caster sugar in a mixing bowl and beat using an electric hand mixer or wooden spoon until the mixture is light and creamy. Add the eggs gradually, beating after each addition. Sift in the flour and cocoa and gently fold them into the mixture with the grated chocolate, using a large metal spoon. Scrape the mixture into the tin using a spatula.

4 Bake for 30–35 minutes until the cake springs back when pressed lightly and a skewer inserted into the middle of the cake comes out clean. Remove the cake from the oven and leave to stand for 5 minutes, then turn out on to a wire rack and leave to cool.

5 In a bowl, mix together the mascarpone cheese, crème fraîche and icing sugar and gently fold in the poached blackcurrants to create purple swirls of fruit. Cut the cake in half horizontally, using a sharp knife, and drizzle the cassis over the 2 cut sides of the cake. Place the bottom layer on a serving plate, cover with the blackcurrant cream and top with the remaining cake half. Dust with icing sugar before serving.

160 TIRAMISU CAKE

PREPARATION TIME 30 minutes, plus chilling   **COOKING TIME** 30–35 minutes   **SERVES** 8

175g/6oz butter, softened, plus extra
   for greasing
175g/6oz/scant ¾ cup caster/superfine sugar
3 large eggs, lightly beaten
150g/5½oz/1 cup self-raising flour
4 tbsp cocoa powder, plus extra for dusting
250g/9oz mascarpone cheese
200ml/7fl oz/scant 1 cup crème fraîche

3 tbsp icing/powdered sugar, sifted,
   plus extra for dusting
100g/3½oz nougat chocolate,
   coarsely chopped
2 tbsp instant coffee granules dissolved
   in 3 tbsp boiling water, then cooled
5 tbsp almond liqueur, such as amaretto

1 Preheat the oven to 180°C/350°F/gas 4. Grease and line a deep 23cm/9in springform cake tin.

2 Put the butter and sugar in a mixing bowl and beat using an electric hand mixer or wooden spoon until the mixture is light and creamy. Add the eggs gradually, beating after each addition. Sift in the flour and cocoa and gently fold them into the mixture, using a large metal spoon. Scrape the mixture into the tin using a spatula.

3 Bake for 30–35 minutes until the cake springs back when pressed lightly and a skewer inserted into the middle of the cake comes out clean. Remove the cake from the oven and leave to stand for 5 minutes, then turn out on to a wire rack and leave to cool.

4 Meanwhile, put the mascarpone cheese, crème fraîche and icing sugar in a bowl and beat using an electric hand mixer or a wooden spoon. Stir in the nougat chocolate. Set aside

5 Combine the coffee liquid and amaretto. Cut the cake in half horizontally, using a sharp knife, and spoon the coffee mixture over both cut sides of the cake. Return the bottom layer of the cake to the tin with the springform side clipped back in place. Spoon the mascarpone cheese mixture over the base of the cake and smooth with a spatula, then top with the second layer. Refrigerate for 2 hours, then gently turn out on to a serving plate. Dust with icing sugar and cocoa before serving.

161 PLUM & WHITE CHOCOLATE FLAN

PREPARATION TIME 30 minutes   **COOKING TIME** 55–60 minutes   **SERVES** 8

175g/6oz butter, softened, plus extra for greasing	175g/6oz/heaped 1 cup self-raising flour
8 plums, halved and pitted	1 tsp baking powder
2 tbsp clear honey	100g/3½oz white chocolate, grated
2 tsp ground cinnamon	3 tbsp plum jam/jelly
175g/6oz/scant ¾ cup caster/superfine sugar	juice of 1 lemon
3 large eggs, lightly beaten	200ml/7fl oz/scant 1 cup double/heavy cream, whipped to stiff peaks

1 Preheat the oven to 190°C/375°F/gas 5. Grease a 23cm/9in raised-base flan tin and line the raised centre of the tin with baking parchment.

2 Put the plums in a baking dish and bake with the honey, ground cinnamon and 2 tablespoons water for 30 minutes until the plums are soft but still hold their shape. Remove from the oven and leave to cool completely.

3 Put the butter and sugar in a mixing bowl and beat using an electric hand mixer or wooden spoon until the mixture is light and creamy. Add the eggs gradually, beating after each addition. Sift in the flour and baking powder and gently fold them into the mixture with the grated chocolate, using a large metal spoon. Scrape the mixture into the tin using a spatula.

4 Bake for 20–25 minutes until the cake springs back when pressed lightly and a skewer inserted into the middle of the cake comes out clean. Remove the cake from the oven and leave to stand for 5 minutes, then turn out on to a wire rack and leave to cool.

5 Put the jam and lemon juice in a small saucepan and heat gently until the jam has melted. Put the flan on a serving plate. Fill the centre of the flan with the whipped cream and top with the plums. Brush the glaze over the plums using a pastry brush and serve.

162 APPLE & PINE NUT CRUMBLE TART

PREPARATION TIME 30 minutes   **COOKING TIME** 45–50 minutes   **SERVES** 8

85g/3oz chilled butter, chopped,
    plus extra for greasing
115g/4oz/¾ cup plain/all-purpose flour,
    sifted, plus extra for dusting
1 recipe quantity Shortcrust Pastry
    (see page 23)
1 small egg, beaten
4 large cooking/baking apples, peeled,
    cored and thinly sliced

juice of 1 lemon
2 tbsp dark soft brown sugar
200g/7oz mascarpone cheese
55g/2oz/¼ cup caster/superfine sugar
55g/2oz/heaped ⅓ cup pine nuts
icing/powdered sugar, for dusting

1 Preheat the oven to 180°C/350°F/gas 4. Grease a 23cm/9in round loose-bottomed tart tin.

2 Sift flour on to a clean work surface and roll the pastry out to 1cm/⅜in thick using a rolling pin. Line the tin with the pastry and trim the edge neatly using a knife. Brush the pastry case/shell with a thin layer of beaten egg using a pastry brush.

3 Toss the apple slices in the lemon juice and dark brown sugar and spoon into the pastry case. Dot small spoonfuls of the mascarpone cheese over the apples.

4 Put the flour and butter in a mixing bowl and rub the butter into the flour with your fingertips until the mixture resembles fine breadcrumbs, then mix in the caster sugar and pine nuts to form a crumble topping. Sprinkle over the apples.

5 Bake for 45–50 minutes until the apples are cooked and the topping is golden brown. Remove the tart from the oven and leave to cool in the tin, then turn out on to a serving plate. Dust with icing sugar to serve.

163 GLAZED SUMMER FRUIT FLAN

PREPARATION TIME 30 minutes   **COOKING TIME** 25–30 minutes   **SERVES** 8

175g/6oz butter, softened, plus extra
   for greasing
175g/6oz/scant ¾ cup caster/superfine sugar
3 large eggs, lightly beaten
175g/6oz/heaped I cup self-raising flour
I tsp baking powder
I tsp vanilla extract
2 tbsp strawberry jam/jelly

juice of I lime
200ml/7fl oz/scant I cup double/heavy
   cream, whipped to stiff peaks
2 ripe peaches or nectarines,
   pitted and sliced
400g/14oz/scant 3 cups combined
   raspberries and strawberries,
   hulled

1 Preheat the oven to 180°C/350°F/gas 4. Grease a 23cm/9in raised-base flan tin and line the raised centre of the tin with baking parchment.

2 Put the butter and sugar in a mixing bowl and beat using an electric hand mixer or wooden spoon until the mixture is light and creamy. Add the eggs gradually, beating after each addition. Sift in the flour and baking powder and gently fold them into the mixture with the vanilla extract, using a large metal spoon. Scrape the mixture into the tin using a spatula.

3 Bake for 20–25 minutes until the cake springs back when pressed lightly and a skewer inserted into the middle of the cake comes out clean. Remove the cake from the oven and leave to stand for 5 minutes, then turn out on to a wire rack and leave to cool.

4 Heat the jam and lime juice in a small saucepan until the jam has melted, then leave to cool. Place the flan on a serving plate, fill the centre with the whipped cream and top with the peaches or nectarines and the raspberries and strawberries. Brush over the strawberry glaze with a pastry brush and serve immediately.

164 CHOCOLATE CHIP CHEESECAKE

PREPARATION TIME 30 minutes, plus chilling   **COOKING TIME** 50–60 minutes   **SERVES** 8–10

125g/4½oz butter, melted and cooled,
   plus extra for greasing
300g/10½oz chocolate-covered digestive
   biscuits/graham crackers, roughly broken
600g/1lb 5oz cream cheese
3 large eggs and I large egg yolk

150g/5½oz/scant ⅔ cup caster/
   superfine sugar
90ml/3fl oz/scant ½ cup double/heavy cream
seeds from 2 vanilla pods/beans
100g/3½oz/½ cup plain/semisweet
   chocolate chips

1 Preheat the oven to 150°C/300°F/gas 2. Grease and base-line a 25cm/10in springform cake tin. Wrap the sides and base of the tin with cling film/plastic wrap so that it is watertight.

2 Put the broken biscuits in a food processor and pulse to fine crumbs. Alternatively, put them in a plastic bag and crush with a rolling pin. Mix the biscuit crumbs and melted butter together and press tightly into the base of the tin using the back of a spoon.

3 Put the cream cheese, whole eggs and egg yolk, caster sugar, cream and vanilla seeds into a blender and whizz until you have a smooth cream. Add the chocolate chips, then pour the mixture on top of the biscuit base.

4 Half fill a roasting tin with water and place the cheesecake in the tin. Transfer the cheesecake in the bain marie into the oven.

5 Bake for 50–60 minutes until the cheesecake is firm. Remove the cheesecake from the oven and from the bain marie and leave to cool in the tin, then refrigerate for 1 hour. Remove from the tin and place on a serving plate.

165 NEW YORK SOURED CREAM CHEESECAKE

PREPARATION TIME 30 minutes, plus chilling   **COOKING TIME** 1 hour–1 hour 10 minutes   **SERVES** 8–10

125g/4½oz butter, melted and cooled, plus extra for greasing

300g/10½oz digestive biscuits/graham crackers, roughly broken

seeds from 1 vanilla pod/bean

600g/1lb 5oz cream cheese

250ml/9fl oz/1 cup condensed milk

3 large eggs and 1 large egg yolk

150g/5½oz/scant ⅔ cup caster/ superfine sugar

290ml/10fl oz/heaped 1 cup sour cream

2 tbsp icing/powdered sugar, sifted

1 Preheat the oven to 150°C/300°F/gas 2. Grease and base-line a 23cm/9in springform cake tin. Wrap the sides and base of the tin with cling film/plastic wrap so that it is watertight.

2 Put the broken biscuits in a food processor and pulse to fine crumbs. (Alternatively, put them in a plastic bag and crush with a rolling pin.) Add the biscuit crumbs to the melted butter and mix together, then press the mixture firmly into the base of the tin using the back of a spoon.

3 Put the vanilla seeds, cream cheese, condensed milk, whole eggs and egg yolk, caster sugar and 100ml/3½fl oz/scant ½ cup of the sour cream into a blender and whizz until you have a smooth cream. Pour the cheesecake filling on top of the base.

4 Half fill a roasting tin with water and place the cheesecake in the tin. Transfer the cheesecake in the bain marie into the oven.

5 Bake for 50–60 minutes until the cheesecake is firm. In a separate bowl, beat the remaining sour cream with the icing sugar until smooth, using a wooden spoon. Pour over the cheesecake and return to the oven for 10 minutes. Remove the cheesecake from the oven and from the bain marie and leave to cool in the tin, then refrigerate for 1 hour. Remove from the tin and place on a serving plate.

166 BANOFFI CHEESECAKE

PREPARATION TIME 20 minutes, plus chilling   **SERVES** 8–10

125g/4½oz butter, melted and cooled,
   plus extra for greasing
300g/10½oz digestive biscuits/graham
   crackers, roughly broken
2 bananas, peeled and sliced
4 tbsp toffee or caramel sauce

500g/1lb 2oz mascarpone cheese
250ml/9fl oz/1 cup crème fraîche
2 heaped tbsp icing/powdered sugar, sifted
100g/3½oz plain/semisweet chocolate,
   made into curls, to decorate

1   Grease and base-line a 20cm/8in springform cake tin.
2   Put the broken biscuits in a food processor and pulse to fine crumbs. (Alternatively, put them
    in a plastic bag and crush with a rolling pin.) Add the biscuit crumbs to the melted butter and
    mix together, then press the mixture firmly into the base of the tin using the back of a spoon.
3   Place the banana slices on the biscuit crumbs and top with the toffee sauce.
4   In a bowl, beat together the mascarpone cheese, crème fraîche and icing sugar with an
    electric hand mixer or a wooden spoon. Scrape the mixture into the tin using a spatula.
    Top with the chocolate curls and refrigerate for at least 2 hours. Remove from the tin and
    place on a serving plate.

167 GREGG'S STICKY TOFFEE NUT CHEESECAKE

PREPARATION TIME 30 minutes, plus chilling   **COOKING TIME** 55–65 minutes   **SERVES** 8–10

140g/5oz butter, melted and cooled,
   plus extra for greasing
300g/10½oz digestive biscuits/graham
   crackers, roughly broken
100g/3½oz/1 cup ground almonds
400g/14oz cream cheese
150g/5½oz/scant ⅔ cup caster/
   superfine sugar
2 large eggs and 1 egg yolk
1 tsp vanilla extract

100ml/3½fl oz/scant ½ cup double/heavy
   cream
1 tbsp Pistachio or Hazelnut Butter
   (see page 25)

FOR THE TOPPING
1 tbsp light muscovado sugar
15g/½oz butter, softened
1 rounded tbsp golden syrup
350g/12oz/2½ cups mixed unsalted nuts

1   Preheat the oven to 150°C/300°F/gas 2. Grease and base-line a deep 23cm/9in springform
    cake tin. Wrap the sides and base of the tin with cling film/plastic wrap so it is watertight.
2   Put the biscuits in a food processor and pulse to fine crumbs (or put them in a plastic bag
    and crush with a rolling pin). Add the crumbs and ground almonds to the melted butter
    and mix together, then press firmly into the base of the tin using the back of a spoon.

3 Put the cream cheese, sugar, eggs and egg yolk, vanilla extract, cream and nut butter in a blender and whizz until you have a smooth cream. Pour the mixture over the biscuit base.

4 Half fill a roasting tin with water and place the cheesecake in the tin. Transfer the cheesecake in the bain marie into the oven.

5 Bake for 50–60 minutes until the cheesecake is firm. Remove the cheesecake from the oven and from the bain marie and leave to cool in the tin, then refrigerate for 1 hour. Remove from the tin and place on a serving plate.

6 For the topping, put the sugar, butter and syrup in a saucepan and heat gently for about 5 minutes, stirring, until the sugar has dissolved. Add the nuts and stir to coat, then spoon the nut mixture on top of the cheesecake to serve.

168 BLUEBERRY & LEMON CHEESECAKE

PREPARATION TIME 40 minutes, plus chilling   **COOKING TIME** 1 hour 5 minutes–1 hour 20 minutes
SERVES 8–10

30g/1oz chilled butter, chopped,
    plus extra for greasing
140g/5oz/1 cup self-raising flour
1 tsp baking powder
125g/4½oz/½ cup caster/superfine sugar
4 large eggs
1 tbsp milk (optional)

450g/1lb cream cheese
100ml/3½fl oz/scant ½ cup
    double/heavy cream
juice and finely grated zest of 2 lemons
400g/14oz/2½ cups blueberries
2 tbsp light soft brown sugar
icing/powdered sugar, for dusting

1 Preheat the oven to 180°C/350°F/gas 4. Grease and line a deep 23cm/9in springform cake tin. Wrap the sides and base of the tin with cling film/plastic wrap so that it is watertight.

2 Sift the flour and baking powder into a mixing bowl, add the butter and rub it in with your fingertips until the mixture resembles fine breadcrumbs. Add 2 tablespoons of the caster sugar and 1 of the eggs and mix to form a soft dough with your fingers, adding the milk if the dough is too dry. Press the dough over the base of the tin and cover with baking parchment and ceramic baking beans/pie weights or dried pulses.

3 Bake blind for 10–15 minutes until the base (when you lift up the paper and baking beans) has a slight crust but is still pale. Remove the base from the oven, carefully lift out the beans on the paper and leave the base to cool.

4 Put the cream cheese, remaining caster sugar, the double cream, remaining eggs and the juice and zest of one of the lemons in a blender and whizz to form a smooth cream. Pour the mixture into the cake tin and scatter half the blueberries over the top. (They will sink into the cream.)

5 Half fill a roasting tin with water and place the cheesecake in the tin. Transfer the cheesecake in the bain marie into the oven.

6 Bake for 50–60 minutes until the cheesecake is firm. Remove the cheesecake from the oven and from the bain marie and leave to cool in the tin, then refrigerate for 1 hour.

7 Put the remaining blueberries, remaining lemon juice and zest, 100ml/3½fl oz/scant ½ cup water and the light brown sugar in a saucepan and heat until the fruit is very soft. Blitz with a hand blender to form a sauce. Remove the cheesecake from the tin and place on a serving plate. Dust with icing sugar and serve with the sauce.

169 CHERRY CHEESECAKE

PREPARATION TIME 20 minutes, plus chilling   **COOKING TIME** 3–5 minutes   **SERVES** 8–10

125g/4½oz butter, melted and cooled,
  plus extra for greasing
300g/10½oz plain/semisweet chocolate-
  coated digestive biscuits/graham
  crackers, roughly broken
250g/9oz/2 cups preserved or fresh cherries,
  stones removed

3 tbsp cherry jam/jelly
500g/1lb 2oz mascarpone cheese
500ml/17fl oz/2 cups crème fraîche
finely grated zest of 2 lemons plus
  the juice of 1 lemon
2 heaped tbsp icing/powdered sugar

1 Grease and base-line a 20cm/8in springform cake tin.
2 Put the broken biscuits in a food processor and pulse to fine crumbs (or put them in a
   plastic bag and crush with a rolling pin). Add the crumbs to the melted butter and mix
   together, then press the mixture firmly into the base of the tin using the back of a spoon.
3 Put the cherries and jam in a saucepan and heat gently for 3–5 minutes, then set aside to
   cool. Put the mascarpone cheese, crème fraîche, lemon juice and zest and icing sugar in
   a large bowl and beat using an electric hand mixer or wooden spoon until the mixture is
   light and creamy. Scrape the mixture on top of the biscuit base using a spatula. Cover with
   the cooled cherries and refrigerate for 2 hours, then remove from the tin and place on a
   serving plate.

170 PEACH MELBA CHEESECAKE

PREPARATION TIME 40 minutes, plus chilling   **COOKING TIME** 1 hour–1 hour 15 minutes   **SERVES** 8–10

30g/1oz chilled butter, chopped,
  plus extra for greasing
140g/5oz/1 cup self-raising flour
1 tsp baking powder
270g/9½oz/heaped 1 cup caster/
  superfine sugar
5 large eggs, 1 lightly beaten
1 tbsp milk
2 tbsp peach jam/jelly
2 ripe peaches, stones removed and
  thinly sliced

seeds from 1 vanilla pod/bean (retain
  the pod for the fruit sauce)
600g/1lb 5oz cream cheese
100ml/3½fl oz/scant ½ cup
  double/heavy cream
225g/8oz clotted cream
400g/14oz/heaped 3 cups strawberries,
  hulled and sliced
400g/14oz/scant 3 cups raspberries

1 Preheat the oven to 180°C/350°F/gas 4. Grease and base-line a deep 23cm/9in springform
   cake tin. Wrap the sides and base of the tin with cling film/plastic wrap so it is watertight.

2   Sift the flour and baking powder into a mixing bowl, add the butter and rub it in with your fingertips until the mixture resembles fine breadcrumbs. Add 2 tablespoons of the caster sugar and the beaten egg and mix to form a soft dough with your hands, adding the milk if the dough is too dry. Press the dough over the base of the tin and cover with baking parchment and ceramic baking beans/pie weights or dried pulses.

3   Bake blind for 10–15 minutes until the base (when you lift up the paper and baking beans) has a slight crust but is still pale. Remove the base from the oven, carefully lift out the beans on the paper and leave the base to cool.

4   Spread the jam over the base and top with the peach slices. Put the vanilla seeds, cream cheese, 140g/4½oz/heaped ½ cup of the caster sugar, double cream, clotted cream and whole eggs in a blender and whizz to form a smooth cream.

5   Half fill a roasting tin with water and place the cheesecake in the tin. Transfer the cheesecake in the bain marie into the oven.

6   Bake for 50–60 minutes until the cheesecake is firm. Remove the cheesecake from the oven and from the bain marie and leave to cool in the tin, then refrigerate for 1 hour.

7   Meanwhile, put 200g/7oz of the strawberries, 100g/3½oz of the raspberries, the remaining sugar, the vanilla pod and 100ml/3½fl oz/scant ½ cup water in a saucepan and heat until the fruit is very soft. Tip the mixture into a sieve/strainer and press out all the juice from the fruit and pod using the back of a spoon. Discard the contents of the sieve. Leave the sauce to cool. Remove from the tin and place on a serving plate. Cover with the remaining berries and serve with the summer berry sauce drizzled over.

171 COFFEE CHEESECAKE

PREPARATION TIME 30 minutes, plus chilling   **COOKING TIME** 20–25 minutes   **SERVES** 8–10

115g/4oz butter, softened, plus extra
    for greasing
115g/4oz/½ cup light soft brown sugar
2 large eggs, lightly beaten
115g/4oz/¾ cup self-raising flour, sifted
1 tbsp instant coffee granules dissolved
    in 2 tbsp boiling water, then cooled

500g/1lb 2oz mascarpone cheese
500ml/17fl oz/2 cups crème fraîche
3 heaped tbsp icing/powdered sugar, sifted
200g/7oz plain/semisweet chocolate,
    finely grated
4 tbsp coffee liqueur
100g/3½oz white chocolate, made into curls

1   Preheat the oven to 190°C/375°F/gas 5. Grease and base-line a deep 23cm/9in springform cake tin.

2   Put the butter and light brown sugar in a mixing bowl and beat using an electric hand mixer or wooden spoon until the mixture is light and creamy. Add the eggs gradually, beating after each addition. Add the flour and gently fold it into the mixture with half the coffee liquid, using a large metal spoon. Scrape the mixture into the tin using a spatula.

3   Bake for 20–25 minutes until the cake springs back when pressed lightly and a skewer inserted into the middle of the cake comes out clean. Remove the cake from the oven and leave to cool completely.

4   Put the mascarpone cheese, crème fraîche, icing sugar and the remaining coffee liquid in a mixing bowl and beat using an electric hand mixer or wooden spoon until the mixture is light and creamy. Fold in half the grated chocolate. Drizzle the coffee liqueur over the sponge cake and top with the coffee cream, smoothing over the top with a spatula. Scatter the white chocolate curls and remaining grated chocolate over the top to decorate. Refrigerate for at least 2 hours, then remove the cheesecake from the tin and place on a serving plate.

172 POPPY SEED & LEMON CHEESECAKE

PREPARATION TIME 30 minutes, plus chilling   **COOKING TIME** 50–60 minutes   **SERVES** 8–10

125g/4½oz butter, melted and cooled, plus extra for greasing
300g/10½oz digestive biscuits/graham crackers, roughly broken
3 tbsp lemon curd
600g/1lb 5oz cream cheese
250ml/9fl oz/1 cup condensed milk

150g/5½oz/scant ⅔ cup caster/superfine sugar
3 large eggs, lightly beaten
100ml/3½fl oz/scant ½ cup double/heavy cream
juice and finely grated zest of 2 lemons
2 tbsp poppy seeds

1   Preheat the oven to 180°C/350°F/gas 4. Grease and base-line a deep 23cm/9in springform cake tin. Wrap the sides and base of the tin with cling film/plastic wrap so it is watertight.

2   Put the broken biscuits in a food processor and pulse to fine crumbs. (Alternatively, put them in a plastic bag and crush with a rolling pin.) Add the biscuit crumbs to the melted butter and mix together, then press the mixture firmly into the base of the tin using the back of a spoon. Spoon the lemon curd over the top.

3   Put the remaining ingredients in a blender and whizz until you have a smooth cream. Pour the mixture over the biscuit base.

4   Half fill a roasting tin with water and place the cheesecake in the tin. Transfer the cheesecake in the bain marie into the oven.

5   Bake for 50–60 minutes until the cheesecake is firm. Remove the cheesecake from the oven and from the bain marie and leave to cool in the tin, then refrigerate for 1 hour. Remove from the tin and place on a serving plate.

173 SUMMER BERRY CHEESECAKE

PREPARATION TIME 30 minutes, plus chilling   **COOKING TIME** 50–60 minutes   **SERVES** 8–10

125g/4½oz butter, melted and cooled,
   plus extra for greasing
300g/10½oz digestive biscuits/graham
   crackers, roughly broken
seeds from 1 vanilla pod/bean (retain
   the pod for the fruit sauce)
600g/1lb 5oz cream cheese

3 large eggs and 1 large egg yolk
235g/8½oz/scant 1 cup caster/superfine sugar
225g/8oz clotted cream
2 tbsp strawberry jam/jelly
600g/1lb 5oz/5 cups strawberries
200g/7oz/1½ cups raspberries

1   Preheat the oven to 180°C/350°F/gas 4. Grease and base-line a deep 23cm/9in springform
     cake tin. Wrap the sides and base of the tin with cling film/plastic wrap so it is watertight.
2   Put the broken biscuits in a food processor and pulse to fine crumbs. (Alternatively, put them
     in a plastic bag and crush with a rolling pin.) Add the biscuit crumbs to the melted butter and
     mix together, then press the mixture firmly into the base of the tin using the back of a spoon.
3   Put the vanilla seeds, cream cheese, eggs and egg yolk, 140g/4½oz/heaped ½ cup of the
     sugar, the clotted cream and jam into a blender and whizz to form a smooth cream. Scrape
     the mixture over the biscuit base using a spatula.
4   Half fill a roasting tin with water and place the cheesecake into it. Transfer the bain marie
     into the oven. Bake for 50–60 minutes until the cheesecake is firm. Remove the cake from
     the oven and from the bain marie and leave to cool in the tin, then refrigerate for 1 hour.
5   Meanwhile, put 200g/7oz of the strawberries in a saucepan with 100ml/3½fl oz/scant
     ½ cup water, the remaining sugar and the vanilla pod and simmer for 10 minutes until the
     fruit is soft. Strain the mixture through a fine-mesh sieve, pressing all the juice out
     of the strawberries. Discard the contents of the sieve. Remove the cheesecake from the
     tin and place on a serving plate. Arrange the remaining strawberries and the raspberries
     on top of the cheesecake and pour the strawberry sauce over the top.

174 MANGO CHEESECAKE

PREPARATION TIME 30 minutes, plus chilling   **COOKING TIME** 55–65 minutes   **SERVES** 8–10

125g/4½oz butter, melted and cooled,
   plus extra for greasing
300g/10½oz ginger biscuits, roughly broken
400g/14oz cream cheese
150g/5½oz/scant ⅔ cup caster/
   superfine sugar
2 large eggs and 1 large egg yolk

100ml/3½fl oz/scant ½ cup
   double/heavy cream
juice and finely grated zest of 2 limes
½ tsp freshly grated nutmeg
2 large fresh mangoes, peeled,
   pitted and thinly sliced
2 tbsp tropical fruit jam/jelly

1 Preheat the oven to 150°C/300°F/gas 2. Grease and base-line a deep 23cm/9in springform cake tin. Wrap the sides and base of the tin with cling film/plastic wrap so it is watertight.

2 Put the broken biscuits in a food processor and pulse to fine crumbs. (Alternatively, put them in a plastic bag and crush with a rolling pin.) Add the biscuit crumbs to the melted butter and mix together, then press the mixture firmly into the base of the tin using the back of a spoon.

3 Put the cream cheese, sugar, whole eggs and egg yolk, cream, lime zest and nutmeg in a blender and whizz to form a smooth cream. Pour on top of the biscuit base.

4 Half fill a roasting tin with water and place the cheesecake in the tin. Transfer the cheesecake in the bain marie into the oven.

5 Bake for 50–60 minutes until the cheesecake is firm. Remove the cheesecake from the oven and the bain marie and leave to cool in the tin, then refrigerate for 1 hour. Remove from the tin and place on a serving plate. Arrange the mango slices on top in circles.

6 Put the jam and lime juice in a small saucepan and heat gently, stirring, until the jam has melted. Brush the liquid over the mango slices with a pastry brush.

175 REDCURRANT & ROSEWATER CHEESECAKE

PREPARATION TIME 20 minutes, plus chilling   **COOKING TIME** 3–5 minutes   **SERVES** 8–10

125g/4½oz butter, melted and cooled, plus extra for greasing
300g/10½oz digestive biscuits/graham crackers, roughly broken
250g/9oz mascarpone cheese
400g/14oz cream cheese
250ml/9fl oz/1 cup crème fraîche
3 heaped tbsp icing/powdered sugar, sifted

3 tbsp rosewater
finely grated zest of 1 lemon
200g/7oz/heaped 1 cup redcurrants
200g/7oz/heaped 1 cup raspberries
100ml/3½fl oz/scant ½ cup dessert wine
3 tbsp redcurrant jelly
1 tbsp powdered gelatine

1 Grease and base-line a deep 23cm/9in springform cake tin.

2 Put the broken biscuits in a food processor and pulse to fine crumbs. (Alternatively, put them in a plastic bag and crush with a rolling pin.) Add the biscuit crumbs to the melted butter and mix together, then press the mixture firmly into the base of the tin using the back of a spoon.

3 Put the mascarpone cheese, cream cheese, crème fraîche, icing sugar, 1 tablespoon of the rosewater and the lemon zest in a mixing bowl and beat using an electric hand mixer or wooden spoon until the mixture is light and creamy. Scrape the mixture over the biscuit base, smoothing the top with a spatula. Place the redcurrants and raspberries on top of the cheesecake.

4 Put the dessert wine, redcurrant jelly and remaining rosewater in a small saucepan and

heat gently until the jelly dissolves. Sprinkle the gelatine over the warm jelly mixture and stir for 3–5 minutes until the gelatine has dissolved. Leave the jelly to cool, then strain through a fine-mesh sieve and pour over the fruit. Refrigerate for at least 2 hours, then remove from the tin and place on a serving plate.

176 YUZU CHEESECAKE PIE

PREPARATION TIME 20 minutes   **COOKING TIME** 3–5 minutes   **SERVES** 8–10

300g/10½oz digestive biscuits/graham crackers, roughly broken
125g/4½oz butter, melted and cooled, plus extra for greasing

FOR THE FILLING
250g/9oz mascarpone cheese
250ml/9fl oz/1 cup crème fraîche

3 heaped tbsp icing/powdered sugar, sifted
1 tsp vanilla bean paste
2 heaped tbsp yuzu jam/jelly

FOR THE SAUCE
3 tbsp yuzu jam/jelly
Juice of 2 lemons
2 tbsp caster/superfine sugar

1   Grease and base-line a deep 23cm/9in springform cake tin.
2   Put the broken biscuits in a food processor and pulse to fine crumbs. (Alternatively, put them in a plastic bag and crush with a rolling pin.) Add the biscuit crumbs to the melted butter and mix together, then press the mixture firmly into the base of the tin using the back of a spoon.
3   Put the mascarpone cheese, crème fraîche, icing sugar, vanilla bean paste and yuzu jam in a mixing bowl and beat using an electric hand mixer or wooden spoon until the mixture is light and creamy. Spoon the mixture over the biscuit base, smoothing the top with a spatula. Refrigerate for at least 2 hours, then remove from the tin and place on a serving plate.
4   For the sauce, place the yuzu jam, lemon juice and caster sugar in a saucepan and simmer over a gentle heat until the sugar has dissolved. Allow to cool, then serve drizzled over the cheesecake.

177 RASPBERRY & LEMON ROULADE

PREPARATION TIME 30 minutes   **COOKING TIME** 12–15 minutes   **SERVES** 8

butter, for greasing
4 large eggs
115g/4oz/scant ½ cup caster/superfine sugar
115g/4oz/¾ cup plain/all-purpose flour, sifted
finely grated zest of 2 lemons
icing/powdered sugar, for dusting

4 tbsp almond liqueur, such as amaretto
500ml/17fl oz/2 cups double/heavy cream, whipped to stiff peaks
4 tbsp lemon curd
300g/10½oz/2 cups raspberries

1 Preheat the oven to 190°C/375°F/gas 5. Grease and line a 30 x 20cm/12 x 8in Swiss/jelly roll tin.

2 Put the eggs and caster sugar in a mixing bowl and whisk together using an electric hand mixer or a whisk until creamy and pale yellow and the whisk leaves a trail when lifted up. Add the flour and gently fold it into the mix with the lemon zest, using a large metal spoon.

3 Scrape the mixture into the tin using a spatula and bake for 12–15 minutes until the cake springs back when pressed lightly. Remove from the oven and leave for a few minutes.

4 Put a sheet of baking parchment on a clean work surface and dust with icing sugar. Turn the cake out on to the sugar-covered paper, cover with a damp dish towel and leave to cool for 10 minutes. Remove the dish towel and lining paper. Roll the cake up from a short end using the sugar-covered paper to help you and leave to cool completely. (The paper will end up rolled inside the cake.)

5 When the cake has cooled, unroll it gently, but don't worry if it cracks, because the cream will hold it together when it is rolled up again. Drizzle over the amaretto using a spoon. Spread over the cream and lemon curd and cover with the raspberries. Roll the roulade up, using the paper to help you but this time not rolling it inside the cake, and lift on to a serving plate. Dust with icing sugar before serving. As the roulade contains fresh cream, it should be eaten straight away or stored in a lidded container in the refrigerator.

178 ARCTIC ROULADE

PREPARATION TIME 30 minutes   **COOKING TIME** 10–12 minutes   **SERVES** 8

butter, for greasing

3 large eggs

85g/3oz/⅓ cup caster/superfine sugar

85g/3oz/heaped ½ cup self-raising
   flour, sifted

1 tsp vanilla extract

icing/powdered sugar, for dusting

3 tbsp raspberry jam/jelly

500ml/17fl oz/2 cups strawberry
   ice cream, softened

1 Preheat the oven to 200°C/400°F/gas 6. Grease and line a 30 x 20cm/12 x 8in Swiss/jelly roll tin.

2 Put the eggs and caster sugar in a mixing bowl and whisk together using an electric hand mixer or a whisk until the mixture is creamy and pale yellow and the whisk leaves a trail when lifted up. Add the flour and vanilla extract and fold them in, using a large metal spoon.

3 Scrape the mixture into the tin using a spatula and bake for 10–12 minutes until the cake springs back when pressed lightly. Remove from the oven and leave for a few minutes.

4 Put a sheet of baking parchment on a clean work surface and dust with icing sugar. Turn the cake out on to the sugar-covered paper and cut away the edges of the cake to neaten. Roll the cake up from a short end using the sugar-covered paper to help you and leave to cool completely. (The paper will end up rolled inside the cake.)

5 When the cake has cooled, unroll it gently, but don't worry if it cracks, because the ice cream will hold it together when it is rolled up again. Spread over the jam and cover with the ice cream. Roll the roulade up, using the paper to help you but this time not rolling it inside the cake, and lift on to a serving plate. Serve immediately. Any remaining roulade should be wrapped and stored in the freezer.

179 CHESTNUT CREAM ROULADE

PREPARATION TIME 30 minutes   **COOKING TIME** 18–25 minutes   **SERVES** 8

butter, for greasing
5 heaped tbsp cocoa powder, sifted,
    plus extra for dusting
150ml/5fl oz/scant ⅔ cup milk
5 large eggs, separated
140g/4½oz/½ cup caster/superfine sugar
55g/2oz/⅓ cup icing/powdered sugar, sifted,
    plus extra for dusting

4 tbsp coffee liqueur
200g/7oz chestnut purée
200ml/7fl oz/scant 1 cup crème fraîche
100g/3½oz coffee chocolate (gf), melted
    and cooled slightly
500ml/17fl oz/2 cups double/heavy cream,
    whipped to stiff peaks

1 Preheat the oven to 190°C/375°F/gas 5. Grease and line a 37 x 27cm/14½ x 10½in Swiss/jelly roll tin.

2 Heat the cocoa and milk in a saucepan for 3–5 minutes until the cocoa has dissolved. Put the egg yolks and caster sugar in a mixing bowl and whisk together using an electric hand mixer or a whisk until the mixture is creamy and pale yellow and the whisk leaves a trail when lifted up. Stir in the cocoa mixture.

3 Put the egg whites in a clean, dry bowl and whisk with an electric hand mixer or a whisk until they form stiff peaks, then fold into the cake mixture, using a large metal spoon. Scrape the mixture into the tin using a spatula.

4 Bake for 15–20 minutes until the cake springs back when pressed lightly. Remove the cake from the oven and leave for a few minutes.

5 Put a sheet of baking parchment on a clean work surface and dust with icing sugar and cocoa. Turn the cake out on to the sugar- and cocoa-covered paper, cover with a damp dish towel and leave to cool for 10 minutes. Remove the dish towel and lining paper and drizzle the coffee liqueur over the cake using a spoon. Roll up the cake from a short end using the sugar- and cocoa-covered paper to help you and leave to cool completely. (The paper will end up rolled inside the cake.)

6 In a mixing bowl, mix the chestnut purée, crème fraîche and icing sugar together using a whisk, then fold in the melted chocolate and half the whipped double cream.

7 When the cake has cooled, unroll it gently, but don't worry if it cracks, because the cream will hold it together when it is rolled up again. Spread the chocolate filling over the cake, then top with the remaining cream and roll up the roulade, using the paper to help you but this time not rolling it inside the cake, and lift on to a serving plate. As the roulade contains fresh cream, it should be eaten straight away or stored in a lidded container in the refrigerator.

180 BAKED MOCHA ALASKA

PREPARATION TIME 25 minutes   **COOKING TIME** 25–30 minutes   **SERVES** 8

115g/4oz butter, softened, plus extra
   for greasing
280g/10oz/heaped 1 cup caster/
   superfine sugar
2 large eggs and 4 large egg whites
85g/3oz/⅔ cup self-raising flour
4 tbsp cocoa powder

1 tbsp instant coffee granules dissolved
   in 1 tbsp boiling water, then cooled
100ml/3½fl oz/scant ½ cup coffee liqueur
500ml/17fl oz/2 cups good-quality
   coffee ice cream
1 banana, peeled and thinly sliced
55g/2oz plain/semisweet chocolate, grated

1 Preheat the oven to 190°C/375°F/gas 5. Grease and line a 20cm/8in springform cake tin.

2 Put the butter and 115g/4oz/scant ½ cup of the sugar in a mixing bowl and beat using an electric hand mixer or wooden spoon until the mixture is light and creamy. Add the whole eggs one at a time, beating after each addition. Sift in the flour and cocoa and gently fold them into the mixture with the coffee liquid, using a large metal spoon. Scrape the mixture into the tin using a spatula.

3 Bake for 20–25 minutes until the cake springs back when pressed lightly and a skewer inserted into the middle of the cake comes out clean. Remove the cake from the oven and leave to stand for 5 minutes, then turn out on to a wire rack and leave to cool.

4 When you are ready to serve the Alaska, preheat the oven to 240°C/475°F/gas 9. Put the egg whites in a clean, dry bowl and whisk with an electric hand mixer or a whisk until they form stiff peaks. Slowly pour in the remaining sugar, whisking all the time, until the meringue is thick and glossy.

5 Place the cake in the centre of a shallow baking dish that is larger than the cake. Pour over the coffee liqueur. Top the cake with the ice cream in scoops and the banana and sprinkle over the grated chocolate. Cover with the meringue, making sure that the cake and filling are all covered, and swirl the surface into peaks using a spatula. Bake the Alaska for 3–4 minutes until the meringue is lightly golden. Remove the Alaska from the oven and serve immediately.

181 BAKED LEMON ALASKA

PREPARATION TIME 25 minutes   **COOKING TIME** 25–30 minutes   **SERVES** 8

115g/4oz butter, softened, plus extra
   for greasing
280g/10oz/heaped 1 cup caster/superfine sugar
2 large eggs and 4 large egg whites
115g/4oz/heaped ½ cup self-raising
   flour, sifted

juice and finely grated zest of 2 lemons
3 tbsp icing/powdered sugar, sifted
500ml/17fl oz/2 cups good-quality
   lemon sorbet
3 tbsp lemon curd

1 Preheat the oven to 190°C/375°F/gas 5. Grease and line a 20cm/8in springform cake tin.

2 Put the butter and 115g/4oz/scant ½ cup of the caster sugar in a mixing bowl and beat using an electric hand mixer or wooden spoon until the mixture is light and creamy. Add the whole eggs one at a time, beating after each addition. Add the flour and gently fold it into the mixture with the lemon zest, using a large metal spoon. Scrape the mixture into the tin using a spatula.

3 Bake for 20–25 minutes until the cake springs back when pressed lightly and a skewer inserted into the middle of the cake comes out clean. Shortly before the cake is cooked, heat the lemon juice with the icing sugar in a small saucepan until the sugar has dissolved, then boil for 1 minute. Remove the cake from the oven and pour over the lemon syrup. Leave to stand for 5 minutes, then turn out on to a wire rack and leave to cool.

4 When you are ready to serve the Alaska, preheat the oven to 240°C/475°F/gas 9. Put the egg whites in a clean, dry bowl and whisk with an electric hand mixer or a whisk until they form stiff peaks. Slowly pour in the remaining caster sugar, whisking all the time, until the meringue is thick and glossy.

5 Place the lemon cake in the centre of a shallow baking dish that is larger than the cake. Top the cake with the lemon sorbet in scoops and spoon over the lemon curd. Cover with the meringue, ensuring that the cake and filling are all covered, and smooth the surface into swirled peaks using a spatula.

6 Bake the Alaska for 3–4 minutes until the meringue is lightly golden. Remove the Alaska from the oven and serve immediately.

182 HAZELNUT BROWNIES WITH CHOCOLATE SAUCE

PREPARATION TIME 20 minutes   **COOKING TIME** 25–30 minutes   **SERVES** 8

250g/9oz butter, chopped, plus extra
   for greasing
400g/14oz plain/semisweet chocolate:
   350g/11oz broken into pieces;
   50g/2oz chopped
200g/7oz/¾ cup caster/superfine sugar
200g/7oz/¾ cup light soft brown sugar
5 large eggs
1 tsp vanilla extract
200g/7oz/1⅓ cups plain/all-purpose
   flour, sifted
100g/3½oz/½ cup chopped
   toasted hazelnuts
400g/14oz/heaped 2 cups raspberries

FOR THE SAUCE
150g/5½oz plain/semisweet chocolate,
   broken into pieces
30g/1oz butter
2 tbsp golden syrup
100ml/3½fl oz/scant ½ cup
   double/heavy cream

1 Preheat the oven to 180°C/350°F/gas 4. Grease and line a 30 x 23 x 6cm/12 x 9 x 2½in baking tin.
2 Melt the butter and broken chocolate together and leave to cool.
3 Put the caster sugar, light brown sugar, eggs and vanilla extract in a mixing bowl and whisk using an electric hand mixer or a whisk until the mixture has almost doubled in size. While still whisking, gently pour in the melted chocolate and butter mixture until it is all incorporated. Add the flour and fold it in with the nuts and the chopped chocolate. Pour the cake mixture into the tin.
4 Bake for 25–30 minutes until the brownie has formed a crust and a skewer inserted into the middle of the cake comes out clean. Remove the brownie from the oven and leave to cool in the tin before cutting into 16 slices.
5 Meanwhile, in a saucepan heat the sauce ingredients, stirring, until the chocolate and butter have melted to form a smooth chocolate sauce. Serve the brownies with the sauce and raspberries.

183 BAKEWELL PUFF

PREPARATION TIME 20 minutes   **COOKING TIME** 25–30 minutes   **SERVES** 6–8

175g/6oz butter, softened, plus extra
   for greasing
85g/3oz/heaped ½ cup plain/all-purpose
   flour, sifted, plus extra for dusting
500g/1lb 2oz block puff pastry
2 tbsp raspberry jam/jelly

175g/6oz/scant ¾ cup caster/superfine sugar
85g/3oz/¾ cup ground almonds
2 large egg yolks
55g/2oz/heaped ⅓ cup flaked/sliced almonds
icing/powdered sugar, for dusting

1 Preheat the oven to 180°C/350°F/gas 4. Grease and line a large rectangular baking sheet.
2 Sift flour on to a clean work surface and roll the pastry out into a 40 x 20cm/16 x 8in rectangle, 5mm/¼in thick, using a rolling pin. Place the pastry on the tray.
3 Score a line 2cm/¾in in from the edge of the pastry all the way round the rectangle with a sharp knife, taking care not to cut through the pastry. Spread the jam over the pastry, keeping inside the scored lines.
4 Put the butter and sugar in a mixing bowl and beat using an electric hand mixer or wooden spoon until the mixture is light and creamy. Add the ground almonds, egg yolks and flour and beat again. Spread the almond topping over the jam and sprinkle with the flaked almonds.
5 Bake for 25–30 minutes until the topping is golden brown and the pastry is cooked. Remove from the oven and leave to cool on the tray, then dust with icing sugar to serve.

184 TOFFEE CHOUX BUNS WITH CARAMEL SAUCE

PREPARATION TIME 25 minutes   **COOKING TIME** 35–40 minutes   **MAKES** 16 buns

115g/4oz butter, chopped, plus extra
   for greasing
140g/5oz/1 cup plain/all-purpose flour, sifted
4 large eggs, beaten

4 tbsp maple syrup
1 tbsp dark soft brown sugar
400ml/14fl oz/1½ cups double/heavy cream
2 tbsp toffee or Irish cream liqueur

1 Preheat the oven to 200°C/400°F/gas 6. Grease and line two 30cm/12in square baking trays.
2 Put the butter and 250ml/9fl oz/1 cup water in a saucepan and heat until the butter has melted. Bring to the boil, then remove from the heat and quickly add the flour all at once. Return the pan to the heat and beat the mixture hard with a wooden spoon until it forms a ball of dough and leaves the sides of the pan clean.
3 Remove from the heat and leave to cool for 10 minutes. Add the eggs gradually, beating after each addition. When all the eggs have been incorporated, you should have a smooth, soft paste. Place 16 tablespoons of the paste in balls about 5cm/2in in diameter on the trays.

4 Bake for 20–25 minutes until the pastry is golden brown. Remove the buns from the oven and make a small slit in each one with a knife to allow the steam to escape. Return to the oven for a further 5 minutes to crisp. Remove and leave to cool on a wire rack.

5 Heat the maple syrup, dark brown sugar and 150ml/5fl oz/scant ⅔ cup of the cream in a saucepan, stirring, until the sugar has dissolved and you have a runny caramel sauce. Set aside to cool.

6 Put the remaining cream in a bowl and whip to stiff peaks using an electric hand mixer or a whisk, then fold in the liqueur. Fill the buns with the cream and serve with the caramel sauce drizzled over them.

185 RASPBERRY & ALMOND CHOUX RING

PREPARATION TIME 25 minutes   **COOKING TIME** 50 minutes   **SERVES** 6

115g/4oz butter, chopped, plus extra
    for greasing
140g/5oz/1 cup plain/all-purpose flour, sifted
4 large eggs, beaten
55g/2oz/heaped ⅓ cup flaked/sliced almonds
2 tsp almond extract

2 tbsp icing/powdered sugar, sifted,
    plus extra for dusting
400ml/14fl oz/1½ cups double/heavy cream,
    whipped to stiff peaks
200g/7oz/heaped 1 cup raspberries

1 Preheat the oven to 200°C/400°F/gas 6. Grease and line a 30cm/12in square baking tray.

2 Put the butter and 250ml/9fl oz/1 cup water in a saucepan and heat until the butter has melted. Bring to the boil, then remove from the heat and quickly add the flour all at once. Return the pan to the heat and beat the mixture hard with a wooden spoon until it forms a ball of dough and leaves the sides of the pan clean.

3 Remove from the heat and leave to cool for 10 minutes. Add the eggs gradually, beating after each addition. When all the eggs have been incorporated, you should have a smooth, soft paste. Spoon the paste into an icing bag fitted with a 2cm/¾in plain nozzle and pipe a 20cm/8in ring of small balls on the baking tray. Sprinkle with the flaked almonds.

4 Bake for 15 minutes, then turn the temperature down to 180°C/350°F/gas 4 and bake for 30 minutes until the pastry is golden brown. Remove the ring from the oven and make a small slit in it with a knife to allow the steam to escape. Leave to cool.

5 Fold the almond extract and icing sugar into the whipped cream. Cut the ring in half horizontally and fill with the almond cream and raspberries. Top with the other half of the choux ring and dust with icing sugar.

Chapter 4

BISCUITS, COOKIES & SLICES

Delicious biscuits, cookies and slices of all shapes and sizes fill this chapter, and with many of them taking less than 20 minutes to bake, they are ready in no time. Traditional favourites include Orange Butter Cookies, Garibaldi Biscuits and Coconut Macaroons. New twists on old favourites are Lavender Shortbread, Rose & Violet Cream Biscuits and Chocolate & Cinnamon Streusel Cookies. Delicate meringues, such as Mini Chocolate Meringue Kisses and sumptuous Pistachio & Chestnut Meringues, just melt in the mouth. Tray bakes perfect for fêtes and fairs include flapjacks, gingerbreads, brownies and blondies and fruit slices topped with apples, peaches and cream, gooseberries or raspberries. If nuts are your favourite, try the Peanut Cookies, Pine Nut Biscuits, Macadamia Chocolate Cookies or Attwood Cookies, scented with almond extract and rich with white chocolate and sour cherries. With over 80 quick and easy recipes to choose from, there is something for everyone.

186 MALTED CHOCOLATE COOKIES

PREPARATION TIME 20 minutes   **COOKING TIME** 12–15 minutes   **MAKES** 15 cookies

115g/4oz butter, softened, plus extra
    for greasing
55g/2oz/¼ cup light soft brown sugar
1 medium egg, lightly beaten
4 tbsp cocoa powder

175g/6oz/heaped 1 cup plain/
    all-purpose flour
30g/1oz/¼ cup malted milk powder
100g/3½oz/heaped ½ cup plain/semisweet
    chocolate chips

1   Preheat the oven to 180°C/350°F/gas 4. Grease two 30cm/12in square baking trays.
2   Put the butter and sugar in a mixing bowl and beat using an electric hand mixer or
    wooden spoon until the mixture is light and creamy. Beat in the egg. Sift in the cocoa, flour
    and malted milk powder and add the chocolate chips. Mix together with your hands to
    form a soft dough.
3   Divide the dough into 15 walnut-size balls and place on the baking trays, leaving about
    5cm/2in between them for spreading. Press each cookie down slightly using your fingers.
4   Bake for 12–15 minutes until just firm. Remove the cookies from the oven and leave to cool
    on the trays for a few minutes, then transfer to a wire rack with a palette knife to cool.

187 CHOCOLATE PRALINE COOKIES

PREPARATION TIME 20 minutes   **COOKING TIME** 10–12 minutes   **MAKES** 18 cookies

115g/4oz butter, softened, plus extra
    for greasing
140g/4½oz/heaped ½ cup caster/
    superfine sugar
1 heaped tbsp Hazelnut Butter
    (see page 25)

1 medium egg, lightly beaten
210g/7½oz/1⅓ cups plain/all-purpose flour
4 tbsp cocoa powder
1 tsp bicarbonate of soda/baking soda
200g/7oz plain/semisweet chocolate: half
    chopped; half melted and cooled slightly

1   Preheat the oven to 180°C/350°F/gas 4. Grease two 30cm/12in square baking trays.
2   Put the butter, sugar and hazelnut butter in a mixing bowl and beat using an electric hand
    mixer or wooden spoon until the mixture is light and creamy. Beat in the egg. Sift in the
    flour, cocoa and bicarbonate of soda and add the chopped chocolate. Mix together with
    your hands to form a soft, fairly sticky dough. Add a little more flour if it is too sticky.
3   Divide the dough into 18 walnut-size balls and place on the baking trays, leaving about
    5cm/2in between them for spreading. Press each cookie down slightly using your fingers.
4   Bake for 10–12 minutes until just firm. Remove the cookies from the oven and leave to
    cool on the trays for a few minutes, then transfer to a wire rack with a palette knife to cool.
    Drizzle the melted chocolate over the cookies in thin lines to decorate them, using a fork.

188 TOLLHOUSE COOKIES

PREPARATION TIME 15 minutes **COOKING TIME** 14–18 minutes **MAKES** 20 cookies

125g/4½oz butter, chopped, plus extra
   for greasing
350g/12oz/2⅓ cups plain/all-purpose flour
½ tsp bicarbonate of soda/baking soda
2 tsp ground cinnamon
100g/3½oz/heaped ⅓ cup caster/
   superfine sugar

100g/3½oz/heaped ⅓ cup light soft
   brown sugar
1 tbsp golden syrup
1 large egg, lightly beaten
100g/3½oz/heaped ½ cup plain/semisweet
   chocolate chips
100g/3½oz/heaped ½ cup walnuts, chopped

1　Preheat the oven to 180°C/350°F/gas 4. Grease two 30cm/12in square baking trays.
2　Sift the flour, bicarbonate of soda and ground cinnamon into a mixing bowl and add the caster sugar and light brown sugar. Mix together with a wooden spoon. Put the butter and syrup in a saucepan and heat gently until the butter melts. Cool slightly, then beat into the dry ingredients with the egg, chocolate chips and walnuts to form a soft dough.
3　Divide the dough into 20 walnut-size balls and place on the baking trays, leaving about 5cm/2in between them to allow for spreading. Press each cookie down slightly using your fingers.
4　Bake for 12–15 minutes until golden brown and just firm. Remove the cookies from the oven and leave to cool on the trays for a few minutes, then transfer to a wire rack to cool.

189 CHOCOLATE COCONUT COOKIES

PREPARATION TIME 15 minutes **COOKING TIME** 14–18 minutes **MAKES** 24 cookies

125g/4½oz butter, chopped, plus extra
   for greasing
280g/10oz/scant 2 cups self-raising flour
55g/2oz/heaped ¼ cup cocoa powder
85g/3oz/1 cup desiccated/dried
   shredded coconut

200g/7oz/¾ cup caster/superfine sugar
1 tbsp golden syrup
1 large egg, beaten
115g/3½oz chocolate-coated coconut bars,
   chopped into small pieces
1 tbsp milk (optional)

1　Preheat the oven to 180°C/350°F/gas 4. Grease two 30cm/12in square baking trays.
2　Sift the flour and cocoa into a mixing bowl and add the coconut. Heat the butter, sugar and syrup gently in a saucepan until the butter has melted, then pour over the dry ingredients and mix in. Leave the mixture to cool slightly. Mix in the egg and stir in the chocolate-coated coconut pieces to form a soft dough, adding the milk if the mixture is too dry.
3　Divide the dough into 24 walnut-size balls and place on the baking trays, leaving about 5cm/2in between them for spreading. Press each cookie down slightly using your fingers.

4 Bake for 12–15 minutes until just firm. Remove the cookies from the oven and leave to cool on the trays for a few minutes, then transfer to a wire rack with a palette knife to cool.

190 ALL-AMERICAN CHOCOLATE CHUNK COOKIES

PREPARATION TIME 20 minutes, plus chilling   **COOKING TIME** 10–12 minutes   **MAKES** 12 cookies

200g/7oz/scant 1 cup light brown sugar
100g/3½oz/heaped ⅓ cup caster/
   superfine sugar
1 tsp vanilla extract
175g/6oz butter, melted, plus extra
   for greasing
1 large egg and 1 large egg yolk

300g/10½oz/2 cups plain/all-purpose flour,
   plus extra for dusting
½ tsp bicarbonate of soda/baking soda
300g/10½oz milk chocolate, chopped
100g/3½oz/½ cup sultanas/golden raisins
   or chopped hazelnuts

1 Put the light brown sugar, caster sugar, vanilla extract and melted butter in a mixing bowl and beat using an electric hand mixer or wooden spoon until the mixture is light and creamy. Beat in the egg and egg yolk. Sift in the flour and bicarbonate of soda and add the chocolate and sultanas or hazelnuts depending on which you are using. Mix together with your hands to form a soft dough.
2 Sift flour on to a clean work surface and roll the dough into a 7.5cm/3in diameter cylinder. Wrap the cylinder in cling film/plastic wrap and refrigerate for 1 hour.
3 Preheat the oven to 180°C/350°F/gas 4. Grease two 30cm/12in square baking trays. Cut the dough into 12 slices and place on the baking trays, leaving 5cm/2in gaps between them.
4 Bake for 10–12 minutes until golden brown. Remove from the oven and leave to cool on the trays for a few minutes, then transfer to a wire rack with a palette knife to cool.

191 CHOCOLATE & CINNAMON STREUSEL COOKIES

PREPARATION TIME 20 minutes   **COOKING TIME** 10–12 minutes   **MAKES** 10 cookies

150g/5½oz butter, softened, plus extra
   for greasing
100g/3½oz/heaped ⅓ cup caster/
   superfine sugar
1 large egg, lightly beaten
150g/5½oz/1 cup plain/all-purpose flour
½ tsp bicarbonate of soda/baking soda
4 tbsp cocoa powder
1 tsp vanilla extract

100g/3½oz/heaped ½ cup white
   chocolate chips

FOR THE STREUSEL
55g/2oz/⅓ cup plain/all-purpose flour
3 tbsp caster/superfine sugar
45g/1½oz chilled butter, chopped
1 tsp ground cinnamon

1 Preheat the oven to 190°C/375°F/gas 5. Grease two 30cm/12in square baking trays.
2 Put the streusel ingredients in a bowl and rub with your fingertips to form breadcrumbs.
3 Put the butter and sugar in a mixing bowl and beat using an electric hand mixer or wooden spoon until the mixture is light. Add the egg and beat again. Sift in the flour, bicarbonate of soda and cocoa and add the vanilla extract and chocolate chips. Mix to a soft dough.
4 Divide the dough into 10 walnut-size balls and place on the baking trays, leaving about 5cm/2in between them to allow for spreading. Press each cookie down flat with a fork and top with a little of the streusel topping.
5 Bake for 10–12 minutes until just firm. Remove from the oven and leave to cool on the trays for a few minutes, then transfer to a wire rack with a palette knife to cool.

192 SPICED SYRUP OAT COOKIES

PREPARATION TIME 15 minutes   **COOKING TIME** 12–15 minutes   **MAKES** 18 cookies

115g/4oz butter, softened, plus extra for greasing	115g/4oz/¾ cup plain/all-purpose flour
115g/4oz/scant ½ cup caster/superfine sugar	1 tsp baking powder
1 large egg, lightly beaten	1 tsp mixed/pumpkin pie spice
2 tbsp golden syrup	1 tsp ground cinnamon
	115g/4oz/heaped 1 cup porridge/rolled oats

1 Preheat the oven to 180°C/350°F/gas 4. Grease two 30cm/12in square baking trays.
2 Put the butter and sugar in a mixing bowl and beat using an electric hand mixer or wooden spoon until the mixture is light and creamy. Beat in the egg and syrup. Sift in the flour, baking powder, mixed spice and ground cinnamon and add the oats. Mix together with your hands to form a soft dough.
3 Divide the dough into 18 walnut-size balls and place on the baking trays, leaving about 5cm/2in between them to allow for spreading. Press each cookie down slightly using your fingers or a fork.
4 Bake for 12–15 minutes until golden brown and just firm. Remove the cookies from the oven and leave to cool on the trays for a few minutes, then transfer to a wire rack with a palette knife to cool.

193 CHOCOLATE CORNFLAKE CRUNCH COOKIES

PREPARATION TIME 15 minutes   **COOKING TIME** 12–15 minutes   **MAKES** 15 cookies

115g/4oz butter, softened, plus extra
  for greasing
115g/4oz/½ cup soft light brown sugar
1 large egg yolk
100g/3½oz/⅔ cup plain/all-purpose flour

4 tbsp cocoa powder
1 tsp baking powder
100g/3½oz/heaped ½ cup plain/semisweet
  chocolate chips
55g/2oz/scant 2 cups cornflakes

1   Preheat the oven to 190°C/375°F/gas 5. Grease two 30cm/12in square baking trays.
2   Put the butter and sugar in a mixing bowl and beat using an electric hand mixer or
    wooden spoon until the mixture is light and creamy. Beat in the egg yolk. Sift in the flour,
    cocoa and baking powder and add the chocolate chips and cornflakes. Mix together with
    your hands to form a soft dough.
3   Divide the dough into 15 walnut-size balls and place on the baking trays, leaving about
    5cm/2in between them to allow for spreading. Press each cookie down slightly using your
    fingers or a fork.
4   Bake for 12–15 minutes until just firm. Remove the cookies from the oven and leave to
    cool on the trays for a few minutes, then transfer to a wire rack with a palette knife to cool.

194 VICARAGE COOKIES

PREPARATION TIME 15 minutes   **COOKING TIME** 12–15 minutes   **MAKES** 15 cookies

115g/4oz butter, softened, plus extra
  for greasing
200g/7oz/heaped ¾ cup caster/
  superfine sugar
1 large egg, lightly beaten
1 tbsp golden syrup
200g/7oz/1⅓ cups self-raising flour

1 tsp baking powder
150g/5½oz/scant 2 cups porridge/rolled oats
2 wholewheat breakfast biscuits, such as
  wheetabix, crushed
100g/3½oz/heaped ½ cup white
  chocolate chips

1   Preheat the oven to 180°C/350°F/gas 4. Grease two 30cm/12in square baking trays.
2   Put the butter and sugar in a mixing bowl and beat using an electric hand mixer or wooden
    spoon until the mixture is light and creamy. Beat in the egg and syrup. Sift in the flour and
    baking powder and add the oats, crushed biscuits and chocolate chips. Mix together with
    your hands to form a soft dough, adding a little extra flour if the dough is too sticky.
3   Divide the dough into 15 walnut-size balls and place on the baking trays, leaving about
    5cm/2in between them to allow for spreading. Press each cookie down slightly using your
    fingers or a fork.

4 Bake for 12–15 minutes until golden brown and just firm. Remove the cookies from the oven and leave to cool on the trays for a few minutes, then transfer to a wire rack with a palette knife to cool.

195 ATTWOOD COOKIES

PREPARATION TIME 15 minutes   **COOKING TIME** 10–12 minutes   **MAKES** 20 cookies

175g/6oz butter, melted and cooled, plus extra for greasing
1 large egg
115g/4oz/scant ½ cup caster/superfine sugar
1 tsp almond extract
200g/7oz white chocolate, chopped

300g/10½oz/2 cups plain/all-purpose flour, sifted
55g/2oz/heaped ⅓ cup flaked/sliced almonds, plus extra for sprinkling
75g/2½oz/heaped ⅓ cup dried sour/tart cherries

1 Preheat the oven to 180°C/350°F/gas 4. Grease two 30cm/12in square baking trays.
2 Put the egg and sugar in a mixing bowl and beat using an electric hand mixer or wooden spoon until the mixture is light and creamy. Beat in the almond extract and melted butter. Add the chopped chocolate, flour, flaked almonds and dried cherries and mix together with your hands to form a soft dough.
3 Place 20 large spoonfuls of the cookie mixture on the baking trays, leaving about 5cm/2in between them to allow for spreading. Sprinkle over the extra flaked almonds.
4 Bake for 10–12 minutes until golden brown and just firm. Remove the cookies from the oven and leave to cool on the trays for a few minutes, then transfer to a wire rack to cool.

196 BANANA CHIP COOKIES

PREPARATION TIME 15 minutes   **COOKING TIME** 10–12 minutes   **MAKES** 15 cookies

85g/3oz butter, softened, plus extra for greasing
125g/4½oz/½ cup caster/superfine sugar
1 large egg, lightly beaten

125g/4½oz/scant 1 cup plain/all-purpose flour
1 tsp baking powder
55g/2oz/½ cup dried banana chips, chopped
1 tbsp banana milkshake powder

1 Preheat the oven to 180°C/350°F/gas 4. Grease two 30cm/12in square baking trays.
2 Put the butter and sugar in a mixing bowl and beat using an electric hand mixer or wooden spoon until the mixture is light and creamy. Beat in the egg. Sift in the flour and baking powder and add the banana chips and milkshake powder. Mix together with your hands to form a soft dough.
3 Divide the dough into 15 walnut-size balls and place on the baking trays, leaving about

5cm/2in between them to allow for spreading. Press each cookie down slightly using your fingers or a fork.

4 Bake for 10–12 minutes until golden brown and just firm. Remove the cookies from the oven and leave to cool on the trays for a few minutes, then transfer to a wire rack with a palette knife to cool.

197 CHERRY & HAZELNUT COOKIES

PREPARATION TIME 20 minutes, plus chilling **COOKING TIME** 12–15 minutes **MAKES** 20 cookies

115g/4oz butter, softened, plus extra
  for greasing
55g/2oz/¼ cup caster/superfine sugar
175g/6oz/heaped 1 cup plain/all-purpose
  flour, sifted, plus extra for dusting

55g/2oz/¼ cup glacé/candied cherries,
  chopped
1 tbsp milk (optional)
55g/2oz/⅓ cup toasted hazelnuts, chopped

1 Put the butter and sugar in a mixing bowl and beat using an electric hand mixer or wooden spoon until the mixture is light and creamy. Add the flour and cherries and mix together with your hands to form a soft dough, adding the milk if the mixture is too dry.

2 Sift flour on to a clean work surface and roll the dough into a 5cm/2in diameter cylinder. Put the chopped hazelnuts on a sheet of foil or baking parchment and roll the dough in the nuts, to cover. Wrap the cylinder in cling film/plastic wrap and refrigerate for 1 hour.

3 Preheat the oven to 180°C/350°F/gas 4. Grease two 30cm/12in square baking trays.

4 Cut the dough into 20 slices and place on the baking trays. Bake for 12–15 minutes until golden brown and just firm. Remove the cookies from the oven and leave to cool on the trays for a few minutes, then transfer to a wire rack with a palette knife to cool.

198 SOUR CHERRY DROPS

PREPARATION TIME 20 minutes **COOKING TIME** 15–20 minutes **MAKES** 18 cookies

115g/4oz butter, softened, plus extra
  for greasing
115g/4oz/scant ½ cup caster/superfine sugar
2 large eggs, separated

225g/8oz/1½ cups plain/all-purpose
  flour, sifted
115g/4oz/¾ cup dried sour/tart cherries
1 tsp almond extract

1 Preheat the oven to 180°C/350°F/gas 4. Grease two 30cm/12in square baking trays.

2 Put the butter, sugar and egg yolks in a mixing bowl and beat using an electric hand mixer or wooden spoon until the mixture is light and creamy. Beat in the flour, dried cherries and almond extract.

3 Put the egg whites in a clean, dry bowl and whisk with an electric hand mixer or a whisk until they form stiff peaks, then fold gently into the mixture, using a large metal spoon.

4 Place 18 tablespoons of the mixture on the baking trays, leaving about 5cm/2in between them to allow for spreading.

5 Bake for 15–20 minutes until golden brown and just firm. Remove the cookies from the oven and leave to cool on the trays for a few minutes, then transfer to a wire rack with a palette knife to cool.

RECIPE 199 | SPICED SYRUP OAT COOKIES

199 CHOCOLATE, PEANUT & WALNUT COOKIES

PREPARATION TIME 20 minutes   **COOKING TIME** 10–12 minutes   **MAKES** 15 cookies

125g/4½oz butter, softened, plus extra
    for greasing
70g/2½oz/⅓ cup light soft brown sugar
70g/2½oz/scant ⅓ cup caster/
    superfine sugar
1 large egg, lightly beaten

200g/7oz/1⅓ cups plain/all-purpose flour
1 tsp bicarbonate of soda/baking soda
2 tbsp crunchy peanut butter
200g/7oz plain/semisweet chocolate: half
    chopped; half melted and cooled slightly
100g/3½oz/heaped ½ cup chopped walnuts

1   Preheat the oven to 190°C/375°F/gas 5. Grease two 30cm/12in square baking trays.
2   Put the butter, light brown sugar and caster sugar in a mixing bowl and beat using an
    electric hand mixer or wooden spoon until the mixture is light and creamy. Beat in
    the egg. Sift in the flour and bicarbonate of soda and add the peanut butter, chopped
    chocolate and walnuts. Mix together with your hands to form a soft, fairly sticky dough,
    making sure the chocolate and nuts are evenly distributed. Add a little more flour if the
    dough is too sticky.
3   Divide the dough into 15 walnut-size balls and place on the baking trays, leaving about
    5cm/2in between them to allow for spreading.
4   Bake for 10–12 minutes until golden brown and just firm. Remove the cookies from the
    oven and leave to cool on the trays for a few minutes, then transfer to a wire rack with
    a palette knife to cool. Drizzle the melted chocolate over them, using a fork to make
    decorative lines. Alternatively, put the chocolate in an icing bag fitted with a 3mm/⅛in
    plain nozzle and pipe lines across the cookies.

200 PEANUT CARAMEL COOKIES

PREPARATION TIME 15 minutes   **COOKING TIME** 14–18 minutes   **MAKES** 15 cookies

100g/3½oz butter, chopped,
  plus extra for greasing
350g/12oz/2⅓ cups self-raising flour
1 tsp bicarbonate of soda/baking soda
200g/7oz/heaped ¾ cup caster/
  superfine sugar

1 tbsp golden syrup
1 large egg, lightly beaten
2 tbsp caramel sauce
2 tbsp crunchy peanut butter
55g/2oz/scant ½ cup salted peanuts

1   Preheat the oven to 180°C/350°F/gas 4. Grease two 30cm/12in square baking trays.
2   Sift the flour and bicarbonate of soda into a mixing bowl, add the sugar and mix with a
    wooden spoon. Put the butter and syrup in a saucepan and heat gently for 2–3 minutes
    until the butter has melted. Cool slightly, then beat into the dry ingredients with the egg,
    caramel sauce, peanut butter and peanuts to form a soft dough.
3   Divide the dough into 15 walnut-size pieces and place on the baking trays, leaving about
    5cm/2in between them to allow for spreading. Press each cookie down slightly using your
    fingers or a fork.
4   Bake for 12–15 minutes until golden brown and just firm. Remove the cookies from the
    oven and leave to cool on the trays for a few minutes, then transfer to a wire rack to cool.

201 PEANUT COOKIES

PREPARATION TIME 15 minutes   **COOKING TIME** 12–15 minutes   **MAKES** 18 cookies

125g/4½oz butter, chopped, plus extra
  for greasing
350g/12oz/2⅓ cups plain/all-purpose flour
1 tsp bicarbonate of soda/baking soda
200g/7oz/heaped ¾ cup caster/
  superfine sugar

a pinch salt
2 tbsp golden syrup
1 large egg, lightly beaten
2 tbsp smooth peanut butter
100g/3½oz unsalted peanuts

1   Preheat the oven to 190°C/375°F/gas 5. Grease two 30cm/12in square baking trays.
2   Sift the flour and bicarbonate of soda into a mixing bowl, add the sugar and salt and mix
    well with a wooden spoon. Put the butter and syrup in a saucepan and heat gently for 2–3
    minutes until the butter has melted. Cool slightly, then beat into the dry ingredients with
    the egg, peanut butter and peanuts to form a soft dough.
3   Divide the dough into 18 walnut-size balls and place on the baking trays, leaving about
    5cm/2in between them to allow for spreading. Press each cookie down slightly using your
    fingers or a fork.

4 Bake for 10–12 minutes until golden brown and just firm. Remove the cookies from the oven and leave to cool on the trays for a few minutes, then transfer to a wire rack to cool.

202 MACADAMIA CHOCOLATE COOKIES

PREPARATION TIME 15 minutes   **COOKING TIME** 12–15 minutes   **MAKES** 18 cookies

115g/4oz butter, softened, plus extra
   for greasing
55g/2oz/¼ cup caster/superfine sugar
1 large egg, lightly beaten
2 tbsp golden syrup
200g/7oz/1⅓ cups plain/all-purpose flour

1 tsp bicarbonate of soda/baking soda
100g/3½oz/heaped ½ cup plain/semisweet
   chocolate chips
100g/3½oz/scant 1 cup macadamia
   nut halves

1 Preheat the oven to 180°C/350°F/gas 4. Grease two 30cm/12in square baking trays.
2 Put the butter and sugar in a mixing bowl and beat using an electric hand mixer or wooden spoon until the mixture is light and creamy. Beat in the egg and syrup. Sift in the flour and bicarbonate of soda and add the chocolate chips and nuts. Mix together with your hands to form a soft dough.
3 Divide the dough into 18 walnut-size balls and place on the baking trays, leaving about 5cm/2in between them. Press each cookie down slightly using your fingers or a fork.
4 Bake for 12–15 minutes until golden brown and just firm. Remove the cookies from the oven and leave to cool on the trays for a few minutes, then transfer to a wire rack to cool.

203 HONEY & ALMOND CRUNCH COOKIES

PREPARATION TIME 15 minutes   **COOKING TIME** 12–15 minutes   **MAKES** 20 cookies

115g/4oz butter, softened, plus extra
   for greasing
55g/2oz/¼ cup caster/superfine sugar
1 large egg, lightly beaten
1 tbsp clear honey

200g/7oz/1⅓ cups plain/all-purpose flour
1 tsp baking powder
55g/2oz/heaped ⅓ cup flaked/sliced almonds
30g/1oz/1 cup cornflakes

1 Preheat the oven to 180°C/350°F/gas 4. Grease two 30cm/12in square baking trays.
2 Put the butter and sugar in a mixing bowl and beat using an electric hand mixer or wooden spoon until the mixture is light and creamy. Beat in the egg and honey. Sift in the flour and baking powder and add the almonds and cornflakes. Mix to form a soft dough.
3 Divide the dough into 20 walnut-size balls and place on the baking trays, leaving about 5cm/2in between them. Press each cookie down using your fingers or a fork.

4 Bake for 12–15 minutes until golden brown and just firm. Remove from the oven and leave to cool on the trays for a few minutes, then transfer to a wire rack to cool.

204 COFFEE KISSES

PREPARATION TIME 20 minutes   **COOKING TIME** 10–12 minutes   **MAKES** 15 cookies

225g/8oz butter, softened, plus extra
   for greasing
250g/9oz/1⅔ cups icing/powdered
   sugar, sifted

200g/7oz/1⅓ cups plain/all-purpose flour
4 tbsp cocoa powder
1½ tbsp instant coffee granules dissolved
   in 2 tbsp boiling water, then cooled

1 Preheat the oven to 180°C/350°F/gas 4. Grease two 30cm/12in square baking trays.
2 Put 175g/6oz of the butter and 55g/2oz/⅓ cup of the icing sugar in a mixing bowl and beat using an electric hand mixer or wooden spoon until the mixture is light and creamy. Sift in the flour and cocoa, add 1 tablespoon of the coffee liquid and mix again.
3 Spoon the mixture into an icing bag fitted with a 13mm/½in star nozzle and pipe thirty 3cm/1¼in stars on the baking trays, leaving about 5cm/2in between them for spreading.
4 Bake for 10–12 minutes until just firm. Remove the cookies from the oven and leave to cool on the trays for a few minutes, then transfer to a wire rack with a palette knife to cool.
5 For the filling, put the remaining icing sugar, butter and coffee liquid in a bowl and beat using an electric hand mixer or a wooden spoon until the mixture is light and creamy. Sandwich pairs of the biscuits together with the coffee cream and place in cake cases.

205 MOCHA COOKIES

PREPARATION TIME 20 minutes   **COOKING TIME** 10–12 minutes   **MAKES** 14 cookies

175g/6oz butter, softened, plus extra
   for greasing
85g/3oz/⅓ cup dark soft brown sugar
1 large egg, lightly beaten
1 tbsp instant coffee granules, dissolved
   in 1 tbsp boiling water, then cooled

200g/7oz/1⅓ cups plain/all-purpose flour
1 tsp baking powder
4 tbsp cocoa powder
100g/3½oz coffee chocolate, chopped
100g/3½oz/⅔ cup icing/powdered sugar, sifted
chocolate sprinkles, to decorate

1 Preheat the oven to 180°C/350°F/gas 4. Grease two 30cm/12in square baking trays.
2 Put the butter and dark brown sugar in a mixing bowl and beat using an electric hand mixer or wooden spoon until the mixture is light and creamy. Beat in the egg and half of the coffee liquid. Sift in the flour, baking powder and cocoa and add the coffee chocolate. Mix together with your hands to form a soft dough.

3   Divide the dough into 14 walnut-size balls and place on the baking trays, leaving about 5cm/2in between them. Press each cookie down slightly using your fingers or a fork.
4   Bake for 10–12 minutes until just firm. Remove the cookies from the oven and leave to cool on the trays for a few minutes, then transfer to a wire rack with a palette knife to cool.
5   Put the icing sugar into a bowl, add the remaining coffee liquid and mix together to make a runny icing/frosting, adding a little water if it is too thick. Drizzle the icing over the cookies, using a fork to form decorative patterns. Shake the chocolate sprinkles over the icing while it is still wet, then leave to set.

206 FUDGE COOKIES

PREPARATION TIME 20 minutes   **COOKING TIME** 10–12 minutes   **MAKES** 20 cookies

175g/6oz butter, softened, plus extra
    for greasing
115g/4oz/scant ½ cup caster/superfine sugar
100g/3½oz cream cheese
225g/8oz/1½ cups self-raising flour, sifted

100g/3½oz plain/semisweet chocolate,
    chopped
100g/3½oz vanilla fudge, chopped into
    small pieces

1   Preheat the oven to 190°C/375°F/gas 5. Grease two 30cm/12in square baking trays.
2   Put the butter, sugar and cream cheese in a mixing bowl, add the flour and beat using an electric hand mixer or wooden spoon until the mixture is light and creamy. Fold in the chocolate and fudge, making sure the pieces are evenly distributed.
3   Place 20 tablespoons of the mixture on the baking trays, leaving about 5cm/2in between them to allow for spreading.
4   Bake for 10–12 minutes until golden brown and just firm. Remove the cookies from the oven and leave to cool on the trays for a few minutes, then transfer to a wire rack with a palette knife to cool. (Trim away any of the fudge pieces around the edge of the cookies that have oozed during cooking.)

207 CHOCOLATE BEAN COOKIES

PREPARATION TIME 20 minutes   **COOKING TIME** 12–18 minutes   **MAKES** 18 cookies

125g/4½oz butter, chopped, plus extra
    for greasing
350g/12oz/2⅓ cups plain/all-purpose flour
1 tsp bicarbonate of soda/baking soda
a pinch salt

200g/7oz/heaped ¾ cup caster/
    superfine sugar
2 tbsp golden syrup
1 large egg, lightly beaten
1 tbsp milk
115g/4oz sugar-coated chocolate beans

1 Preheat the oven to 180°C/350°F/gas 4. Grease two 30cm/12in square baking trays.

2 Sift the flour, bicarbonate of soda and salt into a mixing bowl with the sugar. Put the butter and syrup in a saucepan and heat gently for 2–3 minutes until the butter has melted. Cool slightly, then beat into the dry ingredients with the egg and milk, using a wooden spoon, to form a soft dough, then gently stir in half the chocolate beans.

3 Divide the dough into 18 walnut-size pieces and place on the baking trays, leaving about 10cm/4in between them to allow for spreading. Press each cookie down slightly using your fingers or a fork. Top with the remaining chocolate beans.

4 Bake for 10–15 minutes until golden brown and just firm. Remove the cookies from the oven and leave to cool on the trays for a few minutes, then transfer to a wire rack with a palette knife to cool.

208 HONEYCOMB COOKIES

PREPARATION TIME 20 minutes   **COOKING TIME** 12–15 minutes   **MAKES** 15 cookies

55g/2oz butter, softened, plus extra for greasing
2 tbsp caster/superfine sugar
1 large egg, lightly beaten
2 tbsp golden syrup

225g/8oz/1½ cups plain/all-purpose flour
1 tsp bicarbonate of soda/baking soda
1 tsp salt
85g/3oz chocolate-covered honeycomb, coarsely chopped

1 Preheat the oven to 180°C/350°F/gas 4. Grease two 30cm/12in square baking trays.

2 Put the butter and sugar in a mixing bowl and beat using an electric hand mixer or wooden spoon until the mixture is light and creamy. Beat in the egg and syrup. Sift in the flour, bicarbonate of soda and salt and add the honeycomb, making sure the pieces are evenly distributed. Mix together with your hands to form a soft dough.

3 Divide the dough into 15 walnut-size pieces and place on the baking trays, leaving about 5cm/2in between them to allow for spreading. Press each cookie down slightly using your fingers or a fork.

4 Bake for 12–15 minutes until golden brown and just firm. Remove the cookies from the oven and leave to cool on the trays for a few minutes, then transfer to a wire rack with a palette knife to cool.

209 CHEWY GINGER COOKIES

PREPARATION TIME 15 minutes   **COOKING TIME** 14–18 minutes   **MAKES** 20 cookies

125g/4½oz butter, chopped, plus extra
    for greasing
350g/12oz/2⅓ cups self-raising flour
½ tsp bicarbonate of soda/baking soda
1 tsp ground ginger
finely grated zest of 1 orange
a pinch salt

200g/7oz/heaped ¾ cup caster/
    superfine sugar
1 tbsp golden syrup
1 large egg, lightly beaten
4 pieces stem/preserved ginger in syrup,
    drained and finely chopped
1 tbsp of the stem ginger syrup

1 Preheat the oven to 180°C/350°F/gas 4. Grease two 30cm/12in square baking trays.
2 Sift the flour, bicarbonate of soda and ground ginger into a mixing bowl and add the orange zest, salt and sugar. Mix together with a wooden spoon. Put the butter and syrup in a saucepan and heat gently for 2–3 minutes until the butter has melted. Cool slightly, then beat into the dry ingredients with the egg, stem ginger and ginger syrup to form a soft dough.
3 Divide the dough into 20 walnut-size pieces and place on the baking trays, leaving about 5cm/2in between them to allow for spreading. Press each cookie down slightly using your fingers or a fork.
4 Bake for 12–15 minutes until golden brown and just firm. Remove the cookies from the oven and leave to cool on the trays for a few minutes, then transfer to a wire rack with a palette knife to cool.

210 CINNAMON SNAPS

PREPARATION TIME 15 minutes   **COOKING TIME** 14–18 minutes   **MAKES** 20 cookies

125g/4½oz butter, chopped, plus extra
    for greasing
200g/7oz/heaped ¾ cup caster/
    superfine sugar
350g/12oz/2⅓ cups plain/all-purpose flour

a pinch salt
½ tsp bicarbonate of soda/baking soda
2 tsp ground cinnamon
1 tbsp golden syrup
1 large egg, lightly beaten

1 Preheat the oven to 180°C/350°F/gas 4. Grease two 30cm/12in square baking trays.
2 Put the sugar in a mixing bowl and sift in the flour, salt, bicarbonate of soda and ground cinnamon. Mix together with a wooden spoon. Put the butter and syrup in a saucepan and heat gently for 2–3 minutes until the butter has melted. Cool slightly, then beat into the dry ingredients with the egg to form a soft dough.

3 Divide the dough into 20 walnut-size pieces and place on the baking trays, leaving about 5cm/2in between them to allow for spreading. Press each cookie down slightly using your fingers or a fork.

4 Bake for 12–15 minutes until golden brown and just firm. Remove the cookies from the oven and leave to cool on the trays for a few minutes, then transfer to a wire rack to cool.

211 GOLDEN CITRUS COOKIES

PREPARATION TIME 15 minutes   **COOKING TIME** 14–18 minutes   **MAKES** 20 cookies

125g/4½oz butter, chopped, plus extra
   for greasing
200g/7oz/heaped ¾ cup caster/
   superfine sugar
finely grated zest of 1 lemon
finely grated zest of 1 orange

350g/12oz/2⅓ cups self-raising flour
a pinch salt
½ tsp bicarbonate of soda/baking soda
1 tbsp golden syrup
1 large egg, lightly beaten
2 tbsp mixed/candied peel

1 Preheat the oven to 180°C/350°F/gas 4. Grease two 30cm/12in square baking trays.

2 Put the sugar and lemon and orange zests in a mixing bowl and sift in the flour, salt and bicarbonate of soda. Mix together with a wooden spoon. Put the butter and syrup in a saucepan and heat gently for 2–3 minutes until the butter has melted. Cool slightly, then beat into the dry ingredients with the egg and mixed peel to form a soft dough.

3 Divide the dough into 20 walnut-size pieces and place on the baking trays, leaving about 5cm/2in between them to allow for spreading. Press each cookie down slightly using your fingers or a fork.

4 Bake for 12–15 minutes until golden brown and just firm. Remove the cookies from the oven and leave to cool on the trays for a few minutes, then transfer to a wire rack to cool.

212 DATE, ORANGE & WALNUT COOKIES

PREPARATION TIME 20 minutes, plus chilling   **COOKING TIME** 12–15 minutes   **MAKES** 18 cookies

115g/4oz butter, softened, plus extra
   for greasing
55g/2oz/¼ cup light soft brown sugar
175g/6oz/heaped 1 cup plain/all-purpose
   flour, sifted plus extra for dusting

55g/2oz/½ cup walnut pieces, chopped
55g/2oz/⅓ cup pitted dates, chopped
finely grated zest of 1 large orange
1 tsp vanilla extract
1 tbsp milk (optional)

1 Put the butter and sugar in a mixing bowl and beat using an electric hand mixer or wooden spoon until the mixture is light and creamy. Add the flour, walnuts, dates, zest and vanilla extract and mix together with your hands to form a soft dough, adding the milk if the mixture is too dry. Wrap in cling film/plastic wrap and refrigerate for 1 hour.

2 Preheat the oven to 180°C/350°F/gas 4. Grease two 30cm/12in square baking trays.

3 Sift flour on to a clean work surface and roll the dough out to about 1cm/⅜in thick using a rolling pin. Cut out 18 rectangles using a 2.5 x 7.5cm/1 x 3in cutter, gathering up the trimmings and re-rolling as necessary. Place the cookies on the baking trays.

4 Bake for 12–15 minutes until golden brown and just firm. Remove the cookies from the oven and leave to cool on the trays for a few minutes, then transfer to a wire rack with a palette knife to cool.

213 GLAZED ORANGE COOKIES

PREPARATION TIME 20 minutes, plus chilling   **COOKING TIME** 12–15 minutes   **MAKES** 15 cookies

115g/4oz butter, softened, plus extra
    for greasing
55g/2oz/¼ cup caster/superfine sugar
175g/6oz/heaped 1 cup plain/all-purpose
    flour, plus extra for dusting
1 tsp ground cinnamon

finely grated zest of 1 orange, plus
    2 tbsp of the juice
1 tbsp milk (optional)
4 heaped tbsp icing/powdered sugar, sifted
a few drops of orange food colouring
chocolate sprinkles, to decorate

1 Put the butter and caster sugar in a mixing bowl and beat using an electric hand mixer or wooden spoon until the mixture is light and creamy. Sift in the flour and ground cinnamon and add the orange zest. Mix together with your hands to form a soft dough, adding the milk if the mixture is too dry. Wrap in cling film/plastic wrap and refrigerate for 1 hour.

2 Preheat the oven to 180°C/350°F/gas 4. Grease two 30cm/12in square baking trays.

3 Sift flour on to a clean work surface and roll the dough out to about 1cm/⅜in thick using a rolling pin. Cut out 15 rounds using a 7.5cm/3in round cutter, gathering up the trimmings and re-rolling as necessary. Place the cookies on the baking trays.

4 Bake for 12–15 minutes until golden brown and just firm. Remove the cookies from the oven and leave to cool on the trays for a few minutes, then transfer to a wire rack to cool.

5 Put the icing sugar, orange juice and food colouring in a bowl and mix to form a thick icing/frosting. Drizzle the icing over the cookies in lines using a fork and decorate with chocolate sprinkles. Leave the icing to set before serving.

214 LEMON & SULTANA COOKIES

PREPARATION TIME 20 minutes, plus chilling   **COOKING TIME** 12–15 minutes   **MAKES** 16 cookies

115g/4oz butter, softened, plus extra
   for greasing
55g/2oz/¼ cup caster/superfine sugar
55g/2oz/⅓ cup sultanas/golden raisins

175g/6oz/heaped 1 cup plain/all-purpose
   flour, sifted, plus extra for dusting
finely grated zest of 1 lemon
1 tbsp milk (optional)

1 Put the butter and sugar in a mixing bowl and beat using an electric hand mixer or wooden spoon until the mixture is light and creamy. Add the sultanas, flour and lemon zest and mix together with your hands to form a soft dough, adding the milk if the mixture is too dry. Wrap in cling film/plastic wrap and refrigerate for 1 hour.

2 Preheat the oven to 180°C/350°F/gas 4. Grease two 30cm/12in square baking trays.

3 Sift flour on to a clean work surface and roll the dough out to about 1cm/⅜in thick using a rolling pin. Cut out 16 cookies using a 7.5cm/3in round cutter, gathering up the trimmings and re-rolling as necessary. Place the cookies on the baking trays.

4 Bake for 12–15 minutes until golden brown and just firm. Remove the cookies from the oven and leave to cool on the trays for a few minutes, then transfer to a wire rack to cool.

215 ORANGE BUTTER COOKIES

PREPARATION TIME 20 minutes, plus chilling   **COOKING TIME** 12–15 minutes   **MAKES** 12 cookies

115g/4oz butter, softened, plus extra
   for greasing
55g/2oz/¼ cup caster/superfine sugar
175g/6oz/heaped 1 cup plain/all-purpose
   flour, sifted, plus extra for dusting

finely grated zest of 1 large orange
1 tbsp milk (optional)

1 Put the butter and sugar in a mixing bowl and beat using an electric hand mixer or wooden spoon until the mixture is light and creamy. Add the flour and orange zest and mix to form a soft dough, adding the milk if the mixture is too dry. Wrap in cling film/plastic wrap and refrigerate for 1 hour.

2 Preheat the oven to 180°C/350°F/gas 4. Grease two 30cm/12in square baking trays.

3 Sift flour on to a clean work surface and roll the dough out to about 1cm/⅜in thick using a rolling pin. Cut out 12 rounds using a 7.5cm/3in round cutter, gathering up the trimmings and re-rolling as necessary. Place the cookies on the baking trays and prick with a fork.

4 Bake for 12–15 minutes until golden brown and just firm. Remove the cookies from the oven and leave to cool on the trays for a few minutes, then transfer to a wire rack with a palette knife to cool.

216 MARGARITA COOKIES

PREPARATION TIME 20 minutes, plus chilling   **COOKING TIME** 12–15 minutes   **MAKES** 18 cookies

115g/4oz butter, softened, plus extra
    for greasing
55g/2oz/¼ cup caster/superfine sugar
175g/6oz/heaped 1 cup plain/all-purpose
    flour, sifted, plus extra for dusting
finely grated zest of 2 limes, plus
    1–2 tbsp of the juice

1 tbsp tequila
4 heaped tbsp icing/powdered sugar, sifted
a few drops of green food colouring
1 tsp coarse-ground sea salt

1   Put the butter and sugar in a mixing bowl and beat using an electric hand mixer or wooden spoon until the mixture is light and creamy. Add the flour and lime zest and mix together with your hands to form a soft dough, adding 1 tablespoon of the lime juice if the mixture is too dry. Wrap in cling film/plastic wrap and refrigerate for 1 hour.
2   Preheat the oven to 180°C/350°F/gas 4. Grease two 30cm/12in square baking trays.
3   Sift flour on to a clean work surface and roll the dough out to about 1cm/⅜in thick using a rolling pin. Cut out 18 rounds using a 5cm/2in round cutter, gathering up the trimmings and re-rolling as necessary. Place the cookies on the baking trays.
4   Bake for 12–15 minutes until golden brown and just firm. Remove the cookies from the oven and leave to cool on the trays for a few minutes, then transfer to a wire rack to cool.
5   In a bowl, mix together the tequila, icing sugar, food colouring and 1 tablespoon of the lime juice to make a runny icing/frosting. Drizzle the icing over the cookies in lines using a fork, then sprinkle with the sea salt. Leave the icing to set before serving.

217 ORANGE & CARDAMOM COOKIES

PREPARATION TIME 20 minutes   **COOKING TIME** 12–15 minutes   **MAKES** 18 cookies

115g/4oz butter, softened, plus extra
    for greasing
55g/2oz/¼ cup caster/superfine sugar
1 large egg, lightly beaten
2 tbsp golden syrup

200g/7oz/1⅓ cups plain/all-purpose flour
1 tsp bicarbonate of soda/baking soda
1 tsp ground cardamom
finely grated zest of 1 orange

1   Preheat the oven to 180°C/350°F/gas 4. Grease two 30cm/12in square baking trays.
2   Put the butter and sugar in a mixing bowl and beat using an electric hand mixer or wooden spoon until the mixture is light and creamy. Beat in the egg and syrup. Sift in the flour, bicarbonate of soda and ground cardamom and add the orange zest. Mix to form a soft dough.

3 Divide the dough into 18 walnut-size balls and place on the baking trays, leaving about 5cm/2in between them. Press each cookie down slightly using your fingers or a fork.

4 Bake for 12–15 minutes until golden brown and just firm. Remove the cookies from the oven and leave to cool on the trays for a few minutes, then transfer to a wire rack to cool.

218 GARIBALDI BISCUITS

PREPARATION TIME 20 minutes   **COOKING TIME** 15–18 minutes   **MAKES** 16 biscuits

55g/2oz chilled butter, chopped, plus extra
   for greasing
115g/4oz/heaped ½ cup sultanas/
   golden raisins
finely grated zest of 1 lemon
1 tsp ground cinnamon

115g/4oz/¾ cup plain/all-purpose flour, plus
   extra for dusting
3 tbsp milk
55g/2oz/¼ cup light soft brown sugar
1 medium egg, beaten
caster/superfine sugar, for sprinkling

1 Preheat the oven to 190°C/375°F/gas 5. Grease two 30cm/12in square baking trays.

2 Put the sultanas and lemon zest in a blender or food processor and chop finely. Set aside.

3 Sift the ground cinnamon and flour into a mixing bowl. Rub the butter into the flour with your fingertips until the mixture resembles fine breadcrumbs. Add the milk and light brown sugar and mix to form a stiff dough.

4 Sift flour on to a clean work surface and roll the dough out into a rectangle 5mm/¼in thick using a rolling pin. Cut the rectangle in half and sprinkle one half with the chopped fruit mixture. Place the other half on top and press down with the rolling pin.

5 Roll the dough sandwich out to about 1cm/⅜in thick and then cut into sixteen 5 x 10cm/ 2 x 4in rectangles with a sharp knife or a rectangular cutter. Place on the baking trays and brush with the beaten egg using a pastry brush, then sprinkle with a little caster sugar.

6 Bake for 15–18 minutes until golden brown and just firm. Remove the biscuits from the oven and leave to cool on the trays for a few minutes, then transfer to a wire rack to cool.

219 ORANGE & STRAWBERRY BISCUITS

PREPARATION TIME 20 minutes   **COOKING TIME** 15–18 minutes   **MAKES** 12 biscuits

115g/4oz butter, plus extra for greasing
55g/2oz/¼ cup caster/superfine sugar
225g/8oz/1½ cups plain/all-purpose flour
1 tsp bicarbonate of soda/baking soda
1 tbsp golden syrup
1 large egg, lightly beaten

55g/2oz dried strawberry pieces
100g/3½oz/heaped ½ cup white
   chocolate chips
finely grated zest of 1 orange

1 Preheat the oven to 180°C/350°F/gas 4. Grease two 30cm/12in square baking trays.
2 Put the sugar in a mixing bowl and sift in the flour and bicarbonate of soda. Mix together with a wooden spoon. Put the butter and syrup in a saucepan and heat gently for 2–3 minutes until the butter has melted. Cool slightly, then beat into the dry ingredients with the egg, strawberry pieces, chocolate chips and orange zest to form a soft dough.
3 Divide the dough into 12 walnut-size pieces and place on the baking trays, leaving about 5cm/2in between them to allow for spreading. Press each biscuit down slightly using your fingers or a fork.
4 Bake for 12–15 minutes until golden brown and just firm. Remove the biscuits from the oven and leave to cool on the trays for a few minutes, then transfer to a wire rack to cool.

220 CHOCOLATE CHIP HEARTS

PREPARATION TIME 20 minutes, plus chilling   **COOKING TIME** 12–15 minutes   **MAKES** 15 biscuits

115g/4oz butter, softened, plus extra
    for greasing
55g/2oz/¼ cup caster/superfine sugar
100g/3½oz/heaped ½ cup chocolate chips

175g/6oz/heaped 1 cup plain/all-purpose
    flour, sifted, plus extra for dusting
1 tbsp milk (optional)

1 Put the butter and sugar in a mixing bowl and beat using an electric hand mixer or wooden spoon until the mixture is light and creamy. Add the chocolate chips and flour and mix together with your hands to form a soft dough, adding the milk if the mixture is too dry. Wrap in cling film/plastic wrap and refrigerate for 1 hour.

2 Preheat the oven to 180°C/350°F/gas 4. Grease two 30cm/12in square baking trays.

3 Sift flour on to a clean work surface and roll the dough out to about 1cm/⅜in thick using a rolling pin. Cut out 15 heart shapes using a 10cm/4in heart cutter or a cardboard template and a knife. Place the biscuits on the baking trays using a palette knife.

4 Bake for 12–15 minutes until golden brown and just firm. Remove the biscuits from the oven and leave to cool on the trays for a few minutes, then transfer to a wire rack to cool.

221 TRIPLE CHOCOLATE CHUNK BISCUITS

PREPARATION TIME 15 minutes   **COOKING TIME** 14–18 minutes   **MAKES** 20 biscuits

250g/9oz/1⅔ cups self-raising flour
100g/3½oz/⅔ cup cocoa powder
a pinch salt
1 tsp bicarbonate of soda/baking soda
200g/7oz/heaped ¾ cup caster/
   superfine sugar

125g/4½oz butter, chopped, plus for greasing
1 tbsp golden syrup
1 large egg, lightly beaten
100g/3½oz white chocolate, chopped
100g/3½oz plain/semisweet chocolate,
   chopped

1 Preheat the oven to 180°C/350°F/gas 4. Grease two 30cm/12in square baking trays.

2 Sift the flour, cocoa, salt and bicarbonate of soda into a mixing bowl and mix in the sugar. Heat the butter with the syrup until the butter has melted, cool slightly and then stir into the dry ingredients. Beat in the egg and chocolate pieces to form a soft dough.

3 Divide the dough into 20 walnut-size pieces and place on the baking trays, leaving about 5cm/2in between them. Press each biscuit down slightly using your fingers.

4 Bake for 12–15 minutes until firm. Remove the biscuits from the oven and leave to cool on the trays for a few minutes, then transfer to a wire rack with a palette knife to cool.

222 COFFEE JAPONAISE CAKES

PREPARATION TIME 15 minutes   **COOKING TIME** 25–30 minutes   **MAKES** 8 cakes

125g/4½oz butter, softened, plus extra
   for greasing
3 egg whites
½ tsp cream of tartar
225g/8oz/scant 1 cup caster/superfine sugar

115g/4oz/¾ cup pistachio nuts
350g/12oz/2⅓ cups icing/powdered
   sugar, sifted
1 tbsp instant coffee granules (gf) dissolved
   in 1 tbsp boiling water, then cooled

1 Preheat the oven to 180°C/350°F/gas 4. Grease and line two 30cm/12in square baking trays.

2 Put the egg whites and cream of tartar in a clean, dry bowl and whisk with an electric hand mixer or a whisk until they form stiff peaks. Gradually add the caster sugar while still whisking until it has all been whisked in. Grind the pistachios using a blender, then gently fold in half of them, using a large metal spoon. Spoon the mixture into an icing bag with a 13mm/½in plain nozzle and pipe sixteen 5cm/2in rounds of meringue on to the trays. (If you do not have an icing bag, make small mounds using 2 teaspoons.)

3 Bake for 25–30 minutes until crisp, then remove from the oven and cool on the trays.

4 Put the butter, icing sugar and coffee liquid in a bowl and beat using an electric hand mixer or wooden spoon until they form a light coffee buttercream. Sandwich pairs of the meringues together with some of the buttercream. Spread a thin layer of buttercream around the sides of each pair and roll in the remaining ground pistachios. Place in cake cases/liners to serve.

223 TOASTED HAZELNUT BISCUITS

PREPARATION TIME 20 minutes, plus chilling   **COOKING TIME** 12–15 minutes   **MAKES** 15 biscuits

115g/4oz butter, softened, plus extra
  for greasing
55g/2oz/¼ cup caster/superfine sugar
175g/6oz/heaped 1 cup plain/all-purpose
  flour, sifted, plus extra for dusting

55g/2oz/heaped ⅓ cup toasted
  hazelnuts, chopped
1 tbsp milk (optional)

1 Put the butter and sugar in a mixing bowl and beat using an electric hand mixer or wooden spoon until the mixture is light and creamy. Add the flour and toasted hazelnuts, then mix together with your hands to form a soft dough, adding the milk if the mixture is too dry. Wrap in cling film/plastic wrap and refrigerate for 1 hour.

2 Preheat the oven to 180°C/350°F/gas 4. Grease two 30cm/12in square baking trays.

3 Sift flour on to a clean work surface and roll the dough out to about 1cm/⅜in thick using a rolling pin. Cut out 15 heart shapes using a 10cm/4in heart cutter or a cardboard template and a knife, gathering up the trimmings and re-rolling as necessary. Place the biscuits on the baking trays using a palette knife.

4 Bake for 12–15 minutes until golden brown and just firm. Remove the biscuits from the oven and leave to cool on the trays for a few minutes, then transfer to a wire rack with a palette knife to cool.

224 ANZAC BISCUITS

PREPARATION TIME 15 minutes   **COOKING TIME** 12–15 minutes   **MAKES** 12 biscuits

115g/4oz butter, chopped, plus extra
  for greasing
100g/3½oz/heaped ⅓ cup light soft
  brown sugar
100g/3½oz/1 cup porridge/rolled oats

100g/3½oz/heaped 1 cup desiccated/dried
  shredded coconut
125g/4½oz/scant 1 cup plain/all-purpose flour
1 level tsp bicarbonate of soda/baking soda
3 tbsp golden syrup

1   Preheat the oven to 180°C/350°F/gas 4. Grease two 30cm/12in square baking trays.
2   Put the sugar, oats and coconut in a mixing bowl, sift in the flour and bicarbonate of soda
    and mix together with a wooden spoon. Put the butter and syrup in a saucepan and heat
    gently for 2–3 minutes until the butter has melted. Cool slightly, then beat into the dry
    ingredients with 1 tablespoon water.
3   Place 12 tablespoons of the biscuit mixture on the baking trays, leaving about 5cm/2in
    between each spoonful to allow for spreading.
4   Bake for 10–12 minutes until golden brown and just firm. Remove the biscuits from the
    oven and leave to cool on the trays for a few minutes, then transfer to a wire rack with
    a palette knife to cool.

225 PINE NUT BISCUITS

PREPARATION TIME 20 minutes   **COOKING TIME** 12–15 minutes   **MAKES** 18 biscuits

115g/4oz butter, softened, plus extra
  for greasing
55g/2oz/¼ cup caster/superfine sugar
175g/6oz/heaped 1 cup plain/all-purpose
  flour, sifted, plus extra for dusting

1 tbsp golden syrup
55g/2oz/⅓ cup pine nuts

1   Preheat the oven to 190°C/375°F/gas 5. Grease two 30cm/12in square baking trays.
2   Put the butter and sugar in a mixing bowl and beat using an electric hand mixer or
    wooden spoon until the mixture is light and creamy. Add the flour, golden syrup and pine
    nuts and mix together with your hands to form a soft dough.
3   Divide the dough into 18 walnut-size balls and place on the baking trays, leaving about
    5cm/2in between them to allow for spreading. Press each biscuit down slightly using your
    fingers or a fork.
4   Bake for 12–15 minutes until golden brown and just firm. Remove the biscuits from the
    oven and leave to cool on the trays for a few minutes, then transfer to a wire rack with
    a palette knife to cool.

226 ROSE & PISTACHIO THINS

PREPARATION TIME 20 minutes, plus chilling **COOKING TIME** 12–15 minutes **MAKES** 20 biscuits

100g/3½oz butter, softened, plus extra
    for greasing
100g/3½oz/heaped ⅓ cup caster/
    superfine sugar
1 medium egg, lightly beaten
1 tbsp milk

1 tbsp rosewater
200g/7oz/1⅓ cups plain/all-purpose flour,
    plus extra for dusting
1 tsp baking powder
30g/1oz pistachio nuts, finely chopped

1   Put the butter and sugar in a mixing bowl and beat using an electric hand mixer or wooden spoon until the mixture is light and creamy. Beat in the egg, milk and rosewater. Sift in the flour and baking powder and add the pistachios. Mix together with your hands to form a soft dough, adding a little extra flour if the dough is too sticky.

2   Sift flour on to a clean work surface and roll the dough into a 5cm/2in cylinder. Wrap the cylinder in cling film/plastic wrap and refrigerate for 1 hour.

3   Preheat the oven to 190°C/375°F/gas 5. Grease two 30cm/12in square baking trays. Cut the dough into 20 slices and place on the baking trays.

4   Bake for 12–15 minutes until golden brown and just firm. Remove the biscuits from the oven and leave to cool on the trays for a few minutes, then transfer to a wire rack with a palette knife to cool.

227 ROSE & VIOLET CREAM BISCUITS

PREPARATION TIME 25 minutes **COOKING TIME** 10–12 minutes **MAKES** 10 biscuits

140g/5oz butter, softened, plus extra
    for greasing
225g/8oz/scant 1 cup caster/superfine sugar
1 large egg, lightly beaten
1 tsp vanilla extract
225g/8oz/1½ cups plain/all-purpose flour
1 tsp baking powder
5 tbsp cocoa powder
100g/3½oz/heaped ½ cup plain/semisweet
    chocolate chips

FOR THE BUTTERCREAM
140g/5oz butter, softened
285g/10oz/scant 2 cups icing/powdered
    sugar, sifted
2 tbsp milk
1 tbsp rose syrup
a few drops of pink and purple
    food colouring
1 tbsp violet syrup or liqueur

1   Preheat the oven to 180°C/350°F/gas 4. Grease two 30cm/12in square baking trays.

2   Put the butter and caster sugar in a mixing bowl and beat using an electric hand mixer or wooden spoon until the mixture is light and creamy. Beat in the egg and vanilla extract.

Sift in the flour, baking powder and cocoa and add the chocolate chips. Mix together with your hands to form a soft dough.

3 Divide the dough into 20 walnut-size balls and place on the baking trays, leaving about 5cm/2in between them to allow for spreading. Press each biscuit down slightly using your fingers or a fork.

4 Bake for 10–12 minutes until just firm. Remove the biscuits from the oven and leave to cool on the trays for a few minutes, then transfer to a wire rack with a palette knife to cool.

5 To make the buttercream, put the butter, icing sugar and 1 tablespoon of the milk in a bowl and beat using an electric hand mixer or wooden spoon for 5 minutes until light and creamy, adding the remaining milk if it is too stiff. Divide the buttercream between 2 bowls. Add the rose syrup and pink food colouring to one bowl and the violet syrup and purple food colouring to the other bowl. Stir both creams well with a spoon to mix in the flavourings and colourings. Sandwich the cookies together in pairs, some with the rose buttercream and some with the violet.

228 TOFFEE PECAN SHORTBREAD

PREPARATION TIME 20 minutes, plus chilling   **COOKING TIME** 12–15 minutes   **MAKES** 12 shortbread

115g/4oz butter, softened, plus extra
   for greasing
55g/2oz/¼ cup light soft brown sugar
1 tbsp toffee sauce

175g/6oz/heaped 1 cup plain/all-purpose
   flour, sifted, plus extra for dusting
55g/2oz/heaped ⅓ cup pecan nuts,
   coarsely chopped

1 Put the butter, sugar and toffee sauce in a mixing bowl and beat using an electric hand mixer or wooden spoon until the mixture is light and creamy. Add the flour and pecans and mix together with your hands to form a soft dough. Wrap in cling film/plastic wrap and refrigerate for 1 hour.

2 Preheat the oven to 180°C/350°F/gas 4. Grease two 30cm/12in square baking trays.

3 Sift flour on to a clean work surface and roll the dough out to about 1cm/⅜in thick using a rolling pin. Cut out 12 circles using a 7.5cm/3in fluted round cutter, gathering up the trimmings and re-rolling as necessary. Place the shortbread on the baking trays.

4 Bake for 12–15 minutes until golden brown and just firm. Remove the shortbread from the oven and leave to cool on the trays for a few minutes, then transfer to a wire rack to cool.

229 LAVENDER SHORTBREAD

PREPARATION TIME 20 minutes, plus chilling   **COOKING TIME** 12–15 minutes   **MAKES** 12 shortbread

115g/4oz butter, softened, plus extra
 for greasing
2 tbsp caster/superfine sugar, plus extra for
 dusting

2 tbsp Lavender Sugar (see page 23)
175g/6oz/heaped 1 cup plain/all-purpose
 flour, sifted, plus extra for dusting
1 tbsp milk (optional)

1   Put the butter, caster sugar and lavender sugar in a mixing bowl and beat using an electric
    hand mixer or wooden spoon until the mixture is light and creamy. Add the flour and mix
    together with your hands to form a soft dough, adding the milk if the mixture is too dry.
    Wrap in cling film/plastic wrap and refrigerate for 1 hour.
2   Preheat the oven to 180°C/350°F/gas 4. Grease two 30cm/12in square baking trays.
3   Sift flour on to a clean work surface and roll the dough out to about 1cm/⅜in thick using
    a rolling pin. Cut out 12 heart shapes using a 10cm/4in heart cutter, gathering up the
    trimmings and re-rolling as necessary. Place the shortbread on the baking trays.
4   Bake for 12–15 minutes until golden brown. Remove from the oven, dust with caster sugar
    and cool on the trays for a few minutes, then transfer to a wire rack, removing any excess
    caster sugar.

230 VANILLA SHORTBREAD

PREPARATION TIME 20 minutes, plus chilling   **COOKING TIME** 12–15 minutes   **MAKES** 12 shortbread

115g/4oz butter, softened, plus extra
 for greasing
55g/2oz/¼ cup caster/superfine sugar
1 tsp vanilla extract

175g/6oz/heaped 1 cup plain/all-purpose
 flour, sifted, plus extra for dusting
1 tbsp milk (optional)

1   Put the butter, sugar and vanilla extract in a mixing bowl and beat using an electric hand
    mixer or wooden spoon until the mixture is light and creamy. Add the flour and mix
    together with your hands to form a soft dough, adding the milk if the mixture is too dry.
    Wrap in cling film/plastic wrap and refrigerate for 1 hour.
2   Preheat the oven to 180°C/350°F/gas 4. Grease two 30cm/12in square baking trays.
3   Sift flour on to a clean work surface and roll the dough out to about 1cm/⅜in thick using
    a rolling pin. Cut out 12 rounds using a 7.5cm/3in round cutter, gathering up the trimmings
    and re-rolling as necessary. Place the shortbread on the baking trays and prick each one
    twice in the middle with a fork.
4   Bake for 12–15 minutes until golden brown and just firm. Remove the shortbread from the
    oven and leave to cool on the trays for a few minutes, then transfer to a wire rack to cool.

231 HONEY SHORTBREAD

PREPARATION TIME 20 minutes, plus chilling   **COOKING TIME** 12–15 minutes   **MAKES** 18 shortbread

115g/4oz butter, softened, plus extra
    for greasing
55g/2oz/¼ cup caster/superfine sugar
1 tbsp clear honey

175g/6oz/heaped 1 cup plain/all-purpose
    flour, sifted, plus extra for dusting
1 tbsp milk (optional)

1 Put the butter, sugar and honey in a mixing bowl and beat using an electric hand mixer or wooden spoon until the mixture is light and creamy. Add the flour and mix together with your hands to form a soft dough, adding the milk if the mixture is too dry. Wrap in cling film/plastic wrap and refrigerate for 1 hour.

2 Preheat the oven to 190°C/375°F/gas 5. Grease two 30cm/12in square baking trays.

3 Sift flour on to a clean work surface and roll the dough out to about 1cm/⅜in thick using a rolling pin. Cut out 18 rounds using a 6cm/2½in round cutter, gathering up the trimmings and re-rolling as necessary. Place the shortbread on the baking trays.

4 Bake for 12–15 minutes until golden brown and just firm. Remove the shortbread from the oven and leave to cool on the trays for a few minutes, then transfer to a wire rack with a palette knife to cool.

232 LEMON & APRICOT SHORTBREAD

PREPARATION TIME 20 minutes, plus chilling   **COOKING TIME** 12–15 minutes   **MAKES** 18 shortbread

115g/4oz butter, softened, plus extra
    for greasing
55g/2oz/¼ cup caster/superfine sugar
175g/6oz/heaped 1 cup plain/all-purpose
    flour, sifted, plus extra for dusting

55g/2oz/⅓ cup chopped dried apricots
finely grated zest of 1 large lemon
1 tbsp milk (optional)

1 Put the butter and sugar in a mixing bowl and beat using an electric hand mixer or wooden spoon until the mixture is light and creamy. Add the flour, apricots and lemon zest and mix together with your hands to form a soft dough, adding the milk if the mixture is too dry. Wrap in cling film/plastic wrap and refrigerate for 1 hour.

2 Preheat the oven to 190°C/375°F/gas 5. Grease two 30cm/12in square baking trays.

3 Sift flour on to a clean work surface and roll the dough out to about 1cm/⅜in thick using a rolling pin. Cut out 18 rounds using a 6cm/2½in round cutter, gathering up the trimmings and re-rolling as necessary. Place the shortbread on the baking trays.

4 Bake for 12–15 minutes until golden brown and just firm. Remove from the oven and leave to cool on the trays for a few minutes, then transfer to a wire rack with a palette knife to cool.

233 CINNAMON VIENNESE WHIRLS

PREPARATION TIME 25 minutes   **COOKING TIME** 10–15 minutes   **MAKES** 12 biscuits

175g/6oz butter, softened
55g/2oz/⅓ cup icing/powdered sugar, sifted,
   plus extra for dusting

175g/6oz/heaped 1 cup plain/all-purpose flour
1 tsp ground cinnamon
4 tbsp plum or cherry jam/jelly

1 Preheat the oven to 180°C/350°F/gas 4. Put 12 cake cases/liners into a 12-hole bun tin.
2 Put the butter and sugar in a mixing bowl and beat using an electric hand mixer or wooden spoon until the mixture is light and creamy. Sift in the flour and ground cinnamon and mix again.
3 Spoon the mixture into an icing bag fitted with a 15mm/⅝in star nozzle. Pipe a swirl of mixture into each cake case. Press an indent into the centre of each whirl and fill with 1 teaspoon of the jam.
4 Bake for 10–15 minutes until golden brown and just firm. Remove the biscuits from the oven and leave to cool on the trays for a few minutes, then transfer to a wire rack with a palette knife to cool. Dust with icing sugar before serving.

234 POPPY SEED SNAPS

PREPARATION TIME 20 minutes   **COOKING TIME** 10–13 minutes   **MAKES** 12 biscuits

55g/2oz butter, chopped, plus extra
   for greasing
150g/5½oz/scant ⅔ cup caster/
   superfine sugar

1 tbsp golden syrup
40g/1½oz/¼ cup plain/all-purpose
   flour, sifted
2 tbsp poppy seeds

1 Preheat the oven to 190°C/375°F/gas 5. Grease two 30cm/12in square baking trays.
2 Put the butter in a saucepan with the sugar and golden syrup and heat gently for 2–3 minutes, stirring, until the butter has melted and the sugar has dissolved. Remove the pan from the heat and stir in the flour and poppy seeds. Place 12 tablespoons of the mixture on the baking trays, leaving about 10cm/4in between them to allow for spreading.
3 Bake for 8–10 minutes until golden brown and just firm. Remove the biscuits from the oven and leave to cool for 2 minutes on the trays, then, working quickly, wrap each biscuit around a thin rolling pin to curl it. Alternatively, use a normal-size rolling pin or a drinking glass for a looser curl. If the biscuits set too quickly, return them to the oven for 1 minute to soften, then curl them again.

235 WALNUT & CINNAMON PALMIERS

PREPARATION TIME 20 minutes   **COOKING TIME** 10–15 minutes   **MAKES** 25 pastries

55g/2oz butter, melted and cooled,
    plus extra for greasing
flour, for dusting
500g/1lb 2oz block puff pastry
100g/3½oz/heaped ⅓ cup dark soft
    brown sugar

100g/3½oz/heaped ½ cup walnuts,
    finely chopped
1 tbsp ground cinnamon
1 tbsp milk
1 heaped tbsp caster/superfine sugar

1   Preheat the oven to 180°C/350°F/gas 4. Grease two 30cm/12in square baking trays.
2   Sift flour on to a clean work surface and roll out the puff pastry into a 40 x 20cm/
    16 x 8in rectangle, 5mm/¼in thick. In a bowl, mix together the dark brown sugar,
    walnuts and ground cinnamon.
3   Brush the pastry with the melted butter and sprinkle over half of the walnut mixture.
    Fold the dough in half lengthways with the walnuts on the inside and roll out again
    into a rectangle. Brush with butter and sprinkle over the remaining walnut mixture.
4   Fold the two long sides into the middle so that they meet at the centre of the rectangle,
    and press down with a rolling pin. Brush with butter. Fold in half lengthways so that you
    have a long, thin piece of dough. Cut crossways into 25 slices about 1cm/⅜in wide and
    place apart on the baking trays, opening the pastry shapes slightly to form heart shapes.
    Brush with the milk and sprinkle with the caster sugar.
5   Bake for 10–15 minutes until the pastry has cooked and is golden. Remove the pastries
    from the oven and leave to cool on the trays for a few minutes, then transfer to a wire
    rack with a palette knife to cool.

236 ALMOND TUILES

PREPARATION TIME 20 minutes   **COOKING TIME** 8–10 minutes   **MAKES** 12 biscuits

55g/2oz butter, melted and cooled,
    plus extra for greasing
55g/2oz/⅓ cup plain/all-purpose flour

55g/2oz/⅓ cup icing/powdered sugar
2 medium egg whites
55g/2oz/heaped ⅓ cup flaked/sliced almonds

1   Preheat the oven to 190°C/375°F/gas 5. Grease two 30cm/12in square baking trays.
2   Sift the flour and icing sugar into a mixing bowl. Mix in the melted butter and egg whites
    and mix together with an electric hand mixer or a whisk until the mixture is light and
    creamy. Place 12 dessertspoons of the mixture on to the trays about 2.5cm/1in apart.
    Sprinkle each biscuit with flaked almonds.

3 Bake for 8–10 minutes until golden brown. Remove the biscuits from the oven and leave to cool for a few minutes, then, working carefully and speedily, curl each biscuit around a rolling pin to give them a curled shape. If the biscuits set too quickly, return them to the oven for 1 minute to soften, then curl them again.

237 APRICOT & PISTACHIO FLORENTINES

PREPARATION TIME 20 minutes   **COOKING TIME** 10–12 minutes   **MAKES** 12 florentines

85g/3oz butter, chopped, plus extra
   for greasing
4 tbsp milk
100g/3½oz/⅔ cup icing/powdered
   sugar, sifted
45g/1½oz/⅓ cup plain/all-purpose
   flour, sifted
85g/3oz/1 cup flaked/sliced almonds

45g/1½oz/heaped ¼ cup pistachio
   nuts, chopped
45g/1½oz/¼ cup glacé/candied cherries,
   chopped
30g/1oz/¼ cup dried apricots, chopped
1 tsp ground cinnamon
150g/5½oz plain/semisweet chocolate,
   melted and cooled slightly

1 Preheat the oven to 190°C/375°F/gas 5. Grease and line two 30cm/12in square baking trays.
2 Put the butter, milk and icing sugar in a saucepan and heat gently until the butter has melted. Add all the remaining ingredients, except the melted chocolate, and mix well with a wooden spoon. Leave to cool completely.
3 Place 12 dessertspoons of the mixture on the baking trays, leaving about 2.5cm/1in between them to allow for spreading. Press each florentine down with the back of a spoon so they are of an even thickness.
4 Bake for 8–10 minutes until lightly browned. Remove the florentines from the oven and leave to cool on the trays.
5 Cover the underside of each florentine with the melted chocolate, using a round-bladed knife to spread it. Leave to set slightly, and then make wavy lines through the chocolate with a fork. Leave the chocolate to set before serving.

238 COCONUT MACAROONS

PREPARATION TIME 10 minutes   **COOKING TIME** 12–15 minutes   **MAKES** 15 macaroons

butter, for greasing
200g/7oz/2½ cups desiccated/dried
   shredded coconut
200ml/7fl oz/scant 1 cup condensed milk
1 tsp vanilla extract

1 tsp almond extract
150g/5½oz/1 cup self-raising flour, sifted

1 Preheat the oven to 180°C/350°F/gas 4. Grease and line two 30cm/12in square baking trays.

2 Put all the ingredients in a mixing bowl and stir well with a wooden spoon. Using 2 teaspoons, place 15 walnut-size mounds of the coconut mixture on to the trays, leaving about 2.5cm/1in between them to allow for spreading.

3 Bake for 12–15 minutes until lightly golden brown and just firm. Remove the macaroons from the oven and transfer to a wire rack with a palette knife to cool.

239 PISTACHIO MACAROONS

PREPARATION TIME 20 minutes   **COOKING TIME** 15–20 minutes   **MAKES** 12 macaroons

flavourless oil, for greasing
55g/2oz/heaped ¼ cup pistachio nuts;
    12 reserved for decoration
2 large egg whites

100g/3½oz/scant 1 cup ground almonds
200g/7oz/heaped ¾ cup caster/
    superfine sugar

1 Preheat the oven to 170°C/325°F/gas 3. Grease and line two 30cm/12in square baking trays.
2 Place the pistachios in a food processor or blender and chop very finely. Put the egg whites in a clean, dry bowl and whisk with an electric hand mixer or a whisk until they form soft peaks. Add the pistachios, ground almonds and sugar and fold them in well.
3 Divide the mixture into 12 walnut-size balls and place on the baking trays, leaving about 5cm/2in between them to allow for spreading. Flatten each ball with your fingers and place a whole pistachio in the centre of each one for decoration.
4 Bake for 15–20 minutes until golden brown and just firm. Remove the macaroons from the oven and transfer to a wire rack with a palette knife to cool.

240 ORANGE FLOWER WATER & CINNAMON MERINGUES

PREPARATION TIME 25 minutes   **COOKING TIME** 1–1¼ hours   **MAKES** 20 meringues

butter, for greasing
3 large egg whites
175g/6oz/scant ¾ cup caster/superfine sugar
2 tsp ground cinnamon

finely grated zest of 1 orange
1 tbsp orange flower water
250ml/9fl oz/1 cup double/heavy cream,
    whipped to stiff peaks

1 Preheat the oven to 140°C/275°F/gas 1. Grease and line two 30cm/12in square baking trays.
2 Put the egg whites and sugar in a heatproof bowl over a saucepan of simmering water. It is important that the bottom of the bowl does not touch the water. Using an electric hand mixer, whisk the egg whites and sugar over the heat for 5 minutes until they form stiff peaks. Remove the bowl from the heat, add the ground cinnamon and orange zest and continue whisking for a further 5 minutes until the meringue is very stiff.
3 Spoon the meringue into an icing bag fitted with a 13mm/½in star nozzle and pipe forty 4cm/1½in meringues on to the baking trays. If you do not have an icing bag, make small mounds of meringue using 2 teaspoons.
4 Bake for about 1–1¼ hours until dried and crisp. Remove the meringues from the oven and leave to cool on the trays. Fold the orange flower water into the whipped cream with a large metal spoon and sandwich pairs of the meringues together with the cream. Place the meringues in cake cases/liners and serve immediately.

241 ALMOND MERINGUE BISCUITS

PREPARATION TIME 10 minutes   **COOKING TIME** 1–1¼ hours   **MAKES** 15 biscuits

butter, for greasing
3 large egg whites
175g/6oz/scant ¾ cup caster/superfine sugar
100g/3½oz/scant 1 cup ground almonds

1 tsp almond extract
30g/1oz/¼ cup flaked/sliced almonds

1 Preheat the oven to 150°C/300°F/gas 2. Grease and line two 30cm/12in square baking trays.
2 Put the egg whites and sugar in a heatproof bowl over a saucepan of simmering water. It is important that the bottom of the bowl does not touch the water. Using an electric hand mixer, whisk the egg whites and sugar over the heat for 5 minutes until they form stiff peaks. Remove the bowl from the heat and continue whisking for a further 5 minutes. Using a spatula, gently fold in the ground almonds and almond extract.
3 Place 15 spoonfuls of the meringue to form small mounds about 5cm/2in in diameter on the baking trays and sprinkle over the flaked almonds.
4 Bake for about 1–1¼ hours until crisp. Remove the biscuits from the oven and leave to cool on the trays for a few minutes, then transfer to a wire rack with a palette knife to cool.

242 COFFEE MERINGUES

PREPARATION TIME 20 minutes   **COOKING TIME** 1–1¼ hours   **MAKES** 20 meringues

butter, for greasing
3 large egg whites
175g/6oz/scant ¾ cup caster/superfine sugar

1 tbsp instant coffee granules (gf) dissolved
in 1 tbsp boiling water, then cooled
250ml/9fl oz/1 cup double/heavy cream,
whipped to stiff peaks

1 Preheat the oven to 140°C/275°F/gas 1. Grease and line two 30cm/12in square baking trays.
2 Put the egg whites and sugar in a heatproof bowl over a pan of simmering water. It is important that the bottom of the bowl does not touch the water. Using an electric hand whisk, whisk the egg whites and sugar over the heat for 5 minutes until they form stiff peaks. Remove the bowl from the heat and whisk for a further 5 minutes until the meringue is very stiff. Gently whisk in half of the coffee liquid.
3 Spoon the meringue into an icing bag fitted with a 13mm/½in plain nozzle and pipe forty 4cm/1½in meringues on to the baking trays. (If you do not have an icing bag, make small mounds of meringue using 2 teaspoons.)
4 Bake for about 1–1¼ hours until dried and crisp. Remove the meringues from the oven and leave to cool on the trays.

5 Fold the remaining coffee liquid into the whipped cream with a large metal spoon and sandwich pairs of the meringues together with the cream. Place the meringues in cake cases/liners to serve.

243 MINI CHOCOLATE MERINGUE KISSES

PREPARATION TIME 20 minutes   **COOKING TIME** 1–1¼ hours   **MAKES** 40 meringues

butter, for greasing
3 large egg whites
175g/6oz/scant ¾ cup caster/superfine sugar

150g/5½oz milk chocolate (gf): half grated; half melted and cooled slightly

1 Preheat the oven to 140°C/275°F/gas 1. Grease and line two 30cm/12in square baking trays.
2 Put the egg whites and sugar in a heatproof bowl over a pan of simmering water. It is important that the bottom of the bowl does not touch the water. Using an electric hand whisk, whisk the egg whites and sugar over the heat for 5 minutes until they form stiff peaks. Remove the bowl from the heat and whisk for a further 5 minutes until the meringue is very stiff. Gently fold in the grated chocolate.
3 Spoon the meringue into an icing bag fitted with a 13mm/½in star nozzle and pipe forty 4cm/1½in meringues on to the baking trays, or make mounds using 2 teaspoons.
4 Bake for about 1–1¼ hours until dried and crisp. Remove the meringues from the oven and leave to cool on the trays. Drizzle the melted chocolate over the meringues in thin lines.

244 CASSIS CREAM MERINGUES

PREPARATION TIME 20 minutes   **COOKING TIME** 1–1¼ hours   **MAKES** 20 meringues

butter, for greasing
3 large egg whites
175g/6oz/scant ¾ cup caster/ superfine sugar

3 tbsp cassis/blackcurrant liqueur
a few drops of purple food colouring
250ml/9fl oz/1 cup double/heavy cream, whipped to stiff peaks

1 Preheat the oven to 140°C/275°F/gas 1. Grease and line two 30cm/12in square baking trays.
2 Put the egg whites and sugar in a heatproof bowl over a pan of simmering water. It is important that the bottom of the bowl does not touch the water. Using an electric hand whisk, whisk the egg whites and sugar over the heat for 5 minutes until they form stiff peaks. Remove the bowl from the heat, add half the cassis and purple food colouring and continue whisking for a further 5 minutes until the meringue is very stiff.

3 Spoon the meringue into an icing bag fitted with a 13mm/½in plain nozzle and pipe forty 4cm/1½in meringues on to the baking trays, or make mounds using 2 teaspoons.

4 Bake for about 1–1¼ hours until dried and crisp. Remove the meringues from the oven and leave to cool on the trays. Fold the remaining cassis into the whipped cream and sandwich pairs of the meringues together with the cream. Place the meringues in cake cases/liners to serve.

245 VIOLET MERINGUES

PREPARATION TIME 20 minutes   **COOKING TIME** 1–1¼ hours   **MAKES** 20 meringues

butter, for greasing
3 large egg whites
175g/6oz/scant ¾ cup caster/superfine sugar
1 tbsp violet liqueur or violet syrup

a few drops of purple food colouring
1 tbsp rose syrup
250ml/9fl oz/1 cup double/heavy cream, whipped to stiff peaks

1 Preheat the oven to 140°C/275°F/gas 1. Grease and line two 30cm/12in square baking trays.

2 Put the egg whites and sugar in a heatproof bowl over a pan of simmering water. It is important that the bottom of the bowl does not touch the water. Using an electric hand whisk, whisk the egg whites and sugar over the heat for 5 minutes until they form stiff peaks. Remove the bowl from the heat and whisk for a further 5 minutes until the meringue is very stiff. Gently whisk in the violet liqueur or syrup and the food colouring.

3 Spoon the meringue into an icing bag fitted with a 13mm/½in star nozzle and pipe forty 4cm/1½in meringues on to the baking trays, or make mounds using 2 teaspoons.

4 Bake for about 1–1¼ hours until dried and crisp. Remove the meringues from the oven and leave to cool on the trays. Fold the rose syrup into the whipped cream and sandwich pairs of meringues together with the cream. Place the meringues in cake cases/liners to serve.

246 PISTACHIO & CHESTNUT MERINGUES

PREPARATION TIME 30 minutes   **COOKING TIME** 1 hour   **MAKES** 10 meringues

butter, for greasing
2 large egg whites
115g/4oz/scant ½ cup caster/superfine sugar
100g/3½oz/⅔ cup pistachio nuts

4 tbsp canned unsweetened
   chestnut purée
2 tbsp icing/powdered sugar, sifted
5 glacé/candied chestnuts, finely chopped
whipped cream, to serve

1 Preheat the oven to 140°C/275°F/gas 1. Grease and line two 30cm/12in square baking trays.
2 Put the egg whites in a clean, dry bowl and whisk with an electric hand mixer or a whisk until they form soft peaks, then whisk in the caster sugar until the mixture is glossy. Spoon ten 3cm/1¼in mounds of meringue on to the trays.
3 Bake for about 1 hour until the shells are crisp and the insides are still gooey.
4 Meanwhile, grind the pistachios using a pestle and mortar, then mix well with the chestnut purée, icing sugar and glacé chestnuts in a bowl, using an electric hand mixer or wooden spoon. Spoon the mixture into an icing bag fitted with a 13mm/½in plain nozzle.
5 Remove the meringues from the oven and carefully pipe the nut mixture into them from the underside while they are still warm. Leave to cool before serving with whipped cream.

247 CARAMEL CHOCOLATE BROWNIES

PREPARATION TIME 20 minutes **COOKING TIME** 25–30 minutes **MAKES** 16 brownies

250g/9oz butter, plus extra for greasing
400g/14oz plain/semisweet chocolate, broken into pieces
200g/7oz/¾ cup caster/superfine sugar
200g/7oz/¾ cup light soft brown sugar
5 large eggs

1 tsp vanilla extract
200g/7oz/1⅓ cups plain/all-purpose flour, sifted
200g/7oz caramel-filled chocolate bar, cut into squares

1 Preheat the oven to 180°C/350°F/gas 4. Grease and line a 30 x 23 x 6cm/12 x 9 x 2½in baking tin.
2 Melt the butter and 350g/12oz of the plain chocolate together. Leave to cool. Chop the remaining plain chocolate and set aside.
3 Put both sugars, eggs and vanilla extract in a mixing bowl and whisk using an electric hand mixer or a whisk until the mixture is very light and has doubled in size.
4 While still whisking, slowly pour in the melted chocolate and butter mixture. Fold in the flour, chopped chocolate and the caramel chocolate squares, using a metal spoon. Pour the cake mixture into the tin.
5 Bake for 25–30 minutes until the brownie has formed a crust and a skewer inserted into the middle of the brownie comes out clean. Remove the brownie from the oven and leave to cool in the tin before cutting into 16 slices.

248 WHITE CHOCOLATE BLONDIES

PREPARATION TIME 20 minutes   **COOKING TIME** 25–35 minutes   **MAKES** 16 blondies

115g/4oz butter, melted and cooled,
    plus extra for greasing
115g/4oz/scant ½ cup caster/superfine sugar
2 large eggs, lightly beaten
1 tsp vanilla extract

150g/5½oz/1 cup plain/all-purpose flour
1 tsp baking powder
100g/3½oz/heaped ½ cup white
    chocolate chips
55g/2oz/⅓ cup macadamia nuts, halved

1   Preheat the oven to 180°C/350°F/gas 4. Grease and line a 30 x 23 x 6cm/12 x 9 x 2½in baking tin.
2   Put the melted butter and sugar in a bowl and beat using an electric hand mixer or wooden spoon until the mixture is light and creamy. Add the eggs and vanilla extract and beat again. Sift in the flour and baking powder and fold in with the chocolate chips and nuts, using a large metal spoon. Pour the cake mixture into the tin.
3   Bake for 25–35 minutes until the blondie has formed a crust and a skewer inserted into the middle of the blondie comes out clean. Remove the blondie from the oven and leave to cool in the tin before cutting into 16 slices.

249 TRIPLE CHOCOLATE MOCHA BROWNIES

PREPARATION TIME 20 minutes   **COOKING TIME** 25–30 minutes   **MAKES** 16 brownies

250g/9oz butter, chopped, plus extra
    for greasing
400g/14oz plain/semisweet chocolate,
    broken into pieces
200g/7oz/¾ cup caster/superfine sugar
200g/7oz/¾ cup light soft brown sugar
5 large eggs

1 tbsp instant coffee granules dissolved in
    1 tbsp boiling water, then cooled
200g/7oz/1⅓ cups plain/all-purpose
    flour, sifted
100g/3½oz/⅔ cup white chocolate chips
100g/3½oz/⅔ cup milk chocolate chips

1   Preheat the oven to 180°C/350°F/gas 4. Grease and line a 30 x 23 x 6cm/12 x 9 x 2½in baking tin.
2   Melt the butter and 350g/12oz of the plain chocolate together and leave to cool. Chop the remaining plain chocolate and set aside.
3   Put the caster sugar, light brown sugar, eggs and coffee liquid in a mixing bowl and whisk using an electric hand mixer or a whisk until the mixture is very light and has doubled in size.
4   While still whisking, slowly pour in the melted chocolate and butter mixture. Add the flour, chopped chocolate and the white and milk chocolate chips, and fold together.

5 Pour the cake mixture into the tin and bake for 25–30 minutes until the brownie has formed a crust and a skewer inserted into the middle of the brownie comes out clean. Remove from the oven and leave to cool in the tin before cutting into 16 slices.

250 NUTTY CHOCOLATE BROWNIES

PREPARATION TIME 20 minutes   **COOKING TIME** 25–30 minutes   **MAKES** 16 brownies

250g/9oz butter, chopped, plus extra
   for greasing
400g/14oz plain/semisweet chocolate,
   broken into pieces
200g/7oz/¾ cup caster/superfine sugar
200g/7oz/¾ cup light soft brown sugar
5 large eggs

1 tsp vanilla extract
200g/7oz/1⅓ cups plain/all-purpose
   flour, sifted
200g/7oz/heaped 1 cup walnuts, chopped
200g/7oz/heaped 1 cup pecan nuts, chopped
100g/3½oz/heaped ½ cup pistachio
   nuts, chopped

1   Preheat the oven to 180°C/350°F/gas 4. Grease and line a 30 x 23 x 6cm/12 x 9 x 2½in baking tin.

2   Melt the butter and 350g/12oz of the chocolate together and leave to cool. Chop the remaining chocolate and set aside.

3   Put the caster sugar, light brown sugar, eggs and vanilla extract in a mixing bowl and whisk using an electric hand mixer or a whisk until the mixture is very light and has doubled in size.

4   While still whisking, slowly pour in the melted chocolate and butter mixture. Add the flour, chopped chocolate, walnuts, pecans and pistachios and fold them together, using a large metal spoon. Pour the cake mixture into the tin.

5   Bake for 25–30 minutes until the brownie has formed a crust and a skewer inserted into the middle of the brownie comes out clean. Remove the brownie from the oven and leave to cool in the tin before cutting into 16 slices.

251 SOURED CREAM GINGERBREAD

PREPARATION TIME 30 minutes   **COOKING TIME** 1–1¼ hours   **SERVES** 10

250g/9oz butter, chopped, plus extra
   for greasing
500g/1lb 2oz/3⅓ cups plain/all-purpose flour,
   plus extra for dusting
1 tsp salt
1 tsp ground ginger
1 tsp ground cinnamon
1 tsp mixed/pumpkin pie spice
1 tsp baking powder
1 tsp bicarbonate of soda/baking soda
finely grated zest of 1 lemon and
   1 tbsp of the juice

175g/6oz treacle
200g/7oz golden syrup
200g/7oz/scant 1 cup dark soft
   brown sugar
145ml/4¾fl oz/scant ⅔ cup sour cream
2 large eggs, lightly beaten
100g/3½oz stem/preserved ginger in syrup,
   drained and chopped
150g/5½oz cream cheese
400g/14oz/2⅔ cups icing/powdered
   sugar, sifted

1 Preheat the oven to 180°C/350°F/gas 4. Grease a 23cm/9in ring tin and dust with flour.
2 Sift the flour, salt, spices, baking powder and bicarbonate of soda into a mixing bowl, add the lemon zest and stir with a wooden spoon. Put 170g/6oz of the butter in a saucepan with the treacle, syrup and dark brown sugar and heat gently until the butter has melted and the sugar dissolved. Cool slightly, then beat into the dry ingredients with the sour cream, eggs and stem ginger. Scrape the mixture into the tin using a spatula.
3 Bake for about 1–1¼ hours until the cake springs back when pressed lightly and a skewer inserted into the cake comes out clean. Remove the cake from the oven and leave to stand for 5 minutes, then turn out on to a wire rack.
4 Put the cream cheese, icing sugar, remaining butter and the lemon juice in a mixing bowl and beat using an electric hand mixer or wooden spoon to form a smooth, thick icing/frosting. Spread over the cake using a round-bladed knife and leave to set before serving.

252 APPLE & PECAN GINGERBREAD

PREPARATION TIME 20 minutes   **COOKING TIME** 1–1¼ hours   **MAKES** 20 slices

175g/6oz butter, chopped, plus extra
    for greasing
500g/1lb 2oz/3⅓ cups plain/all-purpose flour
1 tsp salt
1 tsp ground ginger
1 tsp ground cinnamon
1 tsp mixed/pumpkin pie spice
1 tsp baking powder
1 tsp bicarbonate of soda/baking soda
140g/5oz treacle
200g/7oz/scant 1 cup dark soft brown sugar

200g/7oz golden syrup
300ml/10½fl oz/scant 1¼ cups milk
2 tbsp natural/plain yogurt
2 large eggs, lightly beaten
100g/3½oz/½ cup sultanas/golden raisins
6 pieces of stem/preserved ginger in syrup,
    drained and finely chopped
3 large cooking/baking apples, peeled, cored
    and thinly sliced
100g/3½oz/¾ cup pecan nuts
3 tbsp of the stem ginger syrup

1 Preheat the oven to 180°C/350°F/gas 4. Grease and line a 40 x 20 x 6cm/16 x 8 x 2½in baking tin.
2 Sift the flour, salt, spices, baking powder and bicarbonate of soda into a mixing bowl and stir with a wooden spoon. Put the butter, treacle, sugar and syrup in a saucepan and heat gently until the butter has melted and the sugar has dissolved. Leave to cool slightly, then beat into the dry ingredients with the milk, yogurt, eggs, sultanas and stem ginger. Scrape the mixture into the tin using a spatula.
3 Place some of the apple slices in 2 rows overlapping at one end of the tin. Place a row of pecans next to the apples and then repeat with rows of apple slices and pecans until the cake is covered.
4 Bake for about 1–1¼ hours until the cake springs back when pressed lightly and a skewer inserted into the middle of the cake comes out clean.
5 Remove the cake from the oven and leave to stand for 5 minutes, then turn out on to a wire rack. Heat the ginger syrup in a small saucepan, then brush the glaze over the top of the cake with a pastry brush. Leave to cool.

253 VANILLA FLAPJACKS

PREPARATION TIME 15 minutes   **COOKING TIME** 25–30 minutes   **MAKES** 12 flapjacks

115g/4oz butter, chopped, plus extra
    for greasing
3 tbsp golden syrup

85g/3oz/scant ⅓ cup caster/superfine sugar
250g/9oz/2½ cups porridge/rolled oats
1 tsp vanilla extract

1 Preheat the oven to 180°C/350°F/gas 4. Grease an 18 x 18 x 5cm/7 x 7 x 2in baking tin.
2 In a saucepan, gently heat the butter, syrup and sugar for 5 minutes until the butter melts and the sugar dissolves. Remove from the heat and stir in the oats and vanilla extract. Scrape the oat mixture into the tin and spread it out with the back of a spoon.
3 Bake for 20–25 minutes until golden brown. Remove the flapjack from the oven and leave to cool in the tin, then cut into 12 slices.

Note: If serving to a coeliac, check that they are able to eat oats, as although oats are generally gluten free, some coeliacs are also allergic to oats.

254 SULTANA FLAPJACKS

PREPARATION TIME 15 minutes   **COOKING TIME** 25–30 minutes   **MAKES** 12 flapjacks

115g/4oz butter, chopped, plus extra
    for greasing
3 tbsp golden syrup
85g/3oz/scant ⅓ cup caster/superfine sugar

250g/9oz/2½ cups porridge/rolled oats
55g/2oz/scant ⅓ cup sultanas/golden raisins
finely grated zest of 1 large lemon
1 tsp vanilla extract

1 Preheat the oven to 180°C/350°F/gas 4. Grease an 18 x 18 x 5cm/7 x 7 x 2in baking tin.
2 In a saucepan, gently heat the butter, syrup and sugar for 5 minutes until the butter melts and the sugar dissolves. Remove from the heat and stir in the oats, sultanas, lemon zest and vanilla extract. Scrape the oat mixture into the tin and spread it out with the back of a spoon.
3 Bake for 20–25 minutes until golden brown. Remove the flapjack from the oven and leave to cool in the tin, then cut into 12 slices.

Note: If serving to a coeliac, check that they are able to eat oats, as although oats are generally gluten free, some coeliacs are also allergic to oats.

255 NUTTY FLAPJACKS

PREPARATION TIME 15 minutes   **COOKING TIME** 30–35 minutes   **MAKES** 12 flapjacks

130g/4½oz butter, chopped, plus extra
    for greasing
4 tbsp golden syrup
85g/3oz/⅓ cup light soft brown sugar
250g/9oz/2½ cups porridge/rolled oats
200g/7oz/1⅓ cups unsalted mixed nuts

1 tsp vanilla extract
1 tbsp crunchy peanut butter
55g/2oz/⅓ cup icing/powdered sugar, sifted
1 tbsp milk

1 Preheat the oven to 180°C/350°F/gas 4. Grease an 18 x 18 x 5cm/7 x 7 x 2in baking tin.
2 In a saucepan, gently heat 115g/4oz of the butter, 3 tablespoons of the syrup and the light brown sugar for 5 minutes until the butter has melted and the sugar has dissolved. Remove from the heat and stir in the oats, nuts and vanilla extract. Scrape the oat mixture into the tin and spread it out with the back of a spoon.
3 Bake for 20–25 minutes until golden brown. Remove the flapjack from the oven and leave to cool in the tin.
4 Heat the peanut butter, icing sugar, milk and remaining butter and syrup in a saucepan for a few minutes until the butter has melted and you have a smooth toffee icing/frosting. Spoon over the top of the flapjack, still in the tin, and leave to cool, then cut into 12 slices.

Note: If serving to a coeliac, check that they are able to eat oats, as although oats are generally gluten free, some coeliacs are also allergic to oats.

256 CHOCOLATE FLAPJACKS

PREPARATION TIME 15 minutes   **COOKING TIME** 25–30 minutes   **MAKES** 12 flapjacks

115g/4oz butter, chopped, plus extra
  for greasing
3 tbsp golden syrup
85g/3oz/⅓ cup light soft brown sugar
250g/9oz/2½ cups porridge/rolled oats

1 tsp vanilla extract
100g/3½oz/⅔ cup white chocolate chips (gf)
100g/3½oz/⅔ cup plain/semisweet
  chocolate chips (gf)

1 Preheat the oven to 180°C/350°F/gas 4. Grease an 18 x 18 x 5cm/7 x 7 x 2in baking tin.
2 In a saucepan, gently heat the butter, syrup and sugar for 5 minutes until the butter melts and the sugar dissolves. Remove from the heat and leave to cool a little, then stir in the oats, vanilla extract and 40g/1½oz each of both types of chocolate chips. Scrape the oat mixture into the tin and spread it out with the back of a spoon. Sprinkle the remaining chocolate chips over the top of the flapjack.
3 Bake for 20–25 minutes until golden brown. Remove the flapjack from the oven and leave to cool in the tin, then cut into 12 slices.

Note: If serving to a coeliac, check that they are able to eat oats, as although oats are generally gluten free, some coeliacs are also allergic to oats.

257 CREAM SLICES

PREPARATION TIME 20 minutes   **COOKING TIME** 15–20 minutes   **MAKES** 8 slices

butter, for greasing
flour, for dusting
500g/1lb 2oz block puff pastry
1 medium egg, beaten
2 tbsp caster/superfine sugar

4 tbsp blackcurrant jam/jelly
375ml/13fl oz/1½ cups double/heavy cream,
   whipped to stiff peaks
icing/powdered sugar, for dusting

1   Preheat the oven to 190°C/375°F/gas 5. Lightly grease a 30cm/12in square baking tray.
2   Sift flour on to a clean work surface and roll the pastry out to a 30 x 20cm/12 x 8in rectangle, 5mm/¼in thick, using a rolling pin. Using a sharp knife, trim the edges of the pastry so that the rectangle has straight sides and then cut lengthways down the middle of the pastry to give 2 sheets.
3   Using the rolling pin to help, lift both pieces of pastry on to the baking tray, leaving about 2.5cm/1in between them. Using a pastry brush, brush the tops of the pastry pieces with some of the beaten egg, then sprinkle with the caster sugar.
4   Bake for 15–20 minutes until golden brown and crisp. Remove the slices from the oven and leave to cool on the tray, then cut each slice crossways into 8 equal slices. Spread the jam over half the pastry slices and cover with a layer of whipped cream. Top each one with a second pastry slice and dust with icing sugar to serve.

258 STICKY PECAN SLICE

PREPARATION TIME 20 minutes   **COOKING TIME** 35–45 minutes   **MAKES** 12 slices

55g/2oz butter, chopped, plus extra
   for greasing
flour, for dusting
1 recipe quantity Shortcrust Pastry
   (see page 23)
85g/3oz/1 cup fresh breadcrumbs,
   made from day-old bread

300g/10½oz/2 cups pecan nuts,
   coarsely chopped
juice and finely grated zest of 1 lemon
350g/12oz golden syrup

1   Preheat the oven to 180°C/350°F/gas 4. Lightly grease and line a 30 x 20cm/12 x 8in loose-bottomed cake tin.
2   Sift flour on to a clean work surface and roll the pastry out to 5mm/¼in thick using a rolling pin. Line the cake tin with the pastry, making sure it comes up the sides of the tin, as this will hold the pecan filling in. Trim the edges of the pastry with a sharp knife.

3 Put the breadcrumbs, pecans and lemon zest in a mixing bowl. Put the butter, lemon juice and syrup in a saucepan and heat gently until the butter has melted, then pour the lemon syrup over the breadcrumb mixture. Leave to cool for a few minutes, then spoon the mixture into the pastry case/shell.

4 Bake for 30–40 minutes until the pastry is golden brown and the filling is set. Remove the slice from the oven and leave to cool in the tin before cutting into 12 slices.

259 PLUM & CINNAMON SLICE

PREPARATION TIME 20 minutes   **COOKING TIME** 25–30 minutes   **MAKES** 8 slices

butter, for greasing
flour, for dusting
500g/1lb 2oz block puff pastry
4 tbsp ground almonds
1 tbsp icing/powdered sugar
1 tbsp vegetable oil
100g/3½oz marzipan, chilled in the freezer
    for 30 minutes and then grated

1 tsp ground cinnamon
10 plums, halved and pitted
55g/2oz/⅓ cup flaked/sliced almonds
2 tbsp clear honey
milk, for glazing

1 Preheat the oven to 190°C/375°F/gas 5. Grease a 30cm/12in square baking tray.

2 Sift flour on to a clean work surface and roll the pastry out to a 30 x 20cm/12 x 8in rectangle, 5mm/¼in thick, using a rolling pin. Transfer the pastry to the baking tray, using the rolling pin to help lift it, and score a line 2cm/¾in from the edge of the pastry all the way around with a knife. Do not cut all the way through the pastry.

3 Put the ground almonds, icing sugar and oil into a blender and whizz to form a smooth paste. Spread the almond paste inside the scored lines and sprinkle with the grated marzipan and ground cinnamon. Place the plum halves on top in rows, cut side down, sprinkle with the flaked almonds and drizzle with the honey. Brush the edges of the pastry with milk using a pastry brush.

4 Bake for 25–30 minutes until the pastry is golden brown and the plums are tender when pierced with a knife. Remove from the oven and leave to cool in the tin, then cut into 8 slices.

260 BAKEWELL SLICE

PREPARATION TIME 20 minutes   **COOKING TIME** 25–30 minutes   **MAKES** 16 slices

175g/6oz butter, softened, plus extra
   for greasing
85g/3oz/heaped ½ cup plain/all-purpose
   flour, sifted, plus extra for dusting
1 recipe Shortcrust Pastry (see page 23)
4 tbsp raspberry jam/jelly

140g/4½oz/heaped ½ cup caster/
   superfine sugar
175g/6oz/1½ cups ground almonds
3 egg yolks
55g/2oz/½ cup flaked/sliced almonds

1 Preheat the oven to 180°C/350°F/gas 4. Lightly grease and line a 30 x 20cm/12 x 8in Swiss/jelly roll tin.
2 Sift flour on to a clean work surface and roll the pastry out to 5mm/¼in thick using a rolling pin. Line the tin with the pastry and trim the edges with a sharp knife.
3 Spread the jam over the pastry base. Put the butter and sugar in a mixing bowl and beat using an electric hand mixer or wooden spoon until the mixture is light and creamy. Add the ground almonds, egg yolks and flour and beat again. Spread the topping over the jam.
4 Sprinkle over the flaked almonds and bake for 25–30 minutes until golden brown. Remove from the oven and leave to cool in the tin, then cut into 16 slices.

261 MINCEMEAT & APPLE SLICE

PREPARATION TIME 20 minutes   **COOKING TIME** 1 hour–1 hour 10 minutes   **MAKES** 10 slices

225g/8oz butter, softened, plus extra
   for greasing
225g/8oz/scant 1 cup caster/superfine sugar
4 large eggs, lightly beaten
225g/8oz/1½ cups self-raising flour

2 tsp ground cinnamon
2 dessert apples, peeled, cored and grated
400g/14oz mincemeat
55g/2oz/⅓ cup flaked/sliced almonds
icing/powdered sugar, for dusting

1 Preheat the oven to 180°C/350°F/gas 4. Grease and line a 20cm/8in loose-bottomed square cake tin.
2 Put the butter and sugar in a mixing bowl and beat using an electric hand mixer or wooden spoon until the mixture is light. Beat in the eggs. Sift in the flour and ground cinnamon and fold them into the mixture with the grated apple and mincemeat, using a large metal spoon. Scrape the mixture into the tin using a spatula. Sprinkle the top with the flaked almonds.
3 Bake for 1 hour–1 hour 10 minutes until golden brown and firm to touch. If the nuts start to brown too much, cover with a sheet of baking parchment. Remove the slice from the oven and leave to stand for 5 minutes, then turn out on to a wire rack and leave to cool. Dust with icing sugar and cut into 10 slices.

262 ALL-IN-ONE GOOSEBERRY CRUMBLE SLICE

PREPARATION TIME 30 minutes   **COOKING TIME** 30–35 minutes   **MAKES** 16 slices

350g/12oz butter, softened, plus extra
   for greasing
225g/8oz/1 cup light soft brown sugar
4 large eggs, lightly beaten
225g/8oz/1½ cups self-raising flour, sifted
1 tsp vanilla extract
400g/14oz cooked/preserved gooseberries

200g/7oz cream cheese
100ml/3½fl oz/scant ½ cup double/
   heavy cream
140g/5oz/1 cup plain/all-purpose flour, sifted
115g/4oz/1 cup ground almonds
2 tbsp caster/superfine sugar

1   Preheat the oven to 180°C/350°F/gas 4. Grease and line a 40 x 20 x 6cm/16 x 8 x 2½in baking tin.
2   Beat 225g/8oz of the butter, the brown sugar, eggs, self-raising flour and vanilla with an electric hand mixer or wooden spoon. Scrape into the tin. Scatter the gooseberries on top.
3   In a separate bowl, beat the cream cheese and cream with an electric hand mixer or a wooden spoon until there are no lumps, then spoon the mixture over the gooseberries.
4   Put the flour and ground almonds in a bowl and rub in the remaining butter to make large crumble pieces. Mix in the caster sugar. Sprinkle the topping over the cake.
5   Bake for 30–35 minutes until the crumble topping is golden brown and the cream cheese layer has set. Remove from the oven and leave to cool in the tin, then cut into 16 slices.

263 RASPBERRY FRANGIPANE SLICE

PREPARATION TIME 30 minutes   **COOKING TIME** 30–35 minutes   **MAKES** 16 slices

350g/12oz butter, softened, plus extra
   for greasing
280g/10oz/heaped 1 cup caster/superfine sugar
4 large eggs, lightly beaten
225g/8oz/1½ cups self-raising flour, sifted
400g/7oz/2¾ cups raspberries

200g/7oz cream cheese
55g/2oz amaretti biscuits/cookies
85g/3oz/¾ cup ground almonds
1 tsp almond extract
55g/2oz/⅓ cup plain/all-purpose flour, sifted
30g/1oz marzipan, finely chopped

1   Preheat the oven to 180°C/350°F/gas 4. Grease and line a 40 x 20 x 6cm/16 x 8 x 2½in baking tin.
2   Put 225g/8oz of the butter and 225g/8oz/scant 1 cup of the caster sugar in a mixing bowl and beat using an electric hand mixer or wooden spoon until the mixture is light and creamy. Add the eggs gradually, beating after each addition. Add the self-raising flour and gently fold it in, using a large metal spoon. Scrape the mixture into the tin using a spatula. Scatter the raspberries over the top and place teaspoons of cream cheese among them.

3 In a separate bowl, beat the remaining butter and sugar as before. Put the amaretti biscuits in a plastic bag and crush them with a rolling pin, then add to the creamed mixture with the remaining ingredients. Cover the cake with teaspoons of the almond topping.

4 Bake for 30–35 minutes until the topping is golden brown and the cake is firm to touch. Remove from the oven and leave to cool in the tin, then cut into 16 slices.

264 PEACH STREUSEL SLICE

PREPARATION TIME 30 minutes   **COOKING TIME** 30–35 minutes   **MAKES** 16 slices

350g/12oz butter, softened, plus extra
    for greasing
280g/10oz/heaped 1 cup caster/
    superfine sugar
4 large eggs, lightly beaten
350g/12oz/2⅓ cups self-raising flour, sifted

4 ripe peaches, stones removed and
    flesh sliced
200g/7oz cream cheese
1 tsp vanilla extract
100ml/3½fl oz/scant ½ cup double/
    heavy cream
85g/3oz/¾ cup ground almonds

1 Preheat the oven to 180°C/350°F/gas 4. Grease and line a 40 x 20 x 6cm/16 x 8 x 2½in baking tin.

2 Follow step 2 in recipe 263, using 225g/8oz/1½ cups of the flour. Place the peach slices on top of the mixture instead of the raspberries and cream cheese.

3 In a separate bowl, beat the cream cheese, vanilla extract and cream with an electric hand mixer or wooden spoon until smooth, then spoon the mixture over the peach slices.

4 In a separate bowl, beat the remaining butter and sugar as before. Fold in the remaining flour and the ground almonds. Cover the cake with teaspoons of the almond topping.

5 Bake for 30–35 minutes until the crumble topping is golden brown and the cake is firm. Remove from the oven and leave to cool in the tin, then cut into 16 slices.

265 SOURED CREAM & APPLE SLICE

PREPARATION TIME 30 minutes   **COOKING TIME** 45–50 minutes   **MAKES** 16 slices

6 eating apples, peeled, cored and sliced
1 tbsp light soft brown sugar
2 tsp ground cinnamon
350g/12oz butter, softened, plus extra
    for greasing
280g/10oz/heaped 1 cup caster/
    superfine sugar

4 large eggs, lightly beaten
225g/8oz/1½ cups self-raising flour
100ml/3½fl oz/scant ½ cup sour cream
85g/3oz/¾ cup ground almonds
55g/2oz/heaped ⅓ cup flaked/sliced almonds
55g/2oz/⅓ cup plain/all-purpose flour

1. Simmer the apple slices with 150ml/5fl oz/scant ⅔ cup water, the light brown sugar and 1 teaspoon of the ground cinnamon for about 20 minutes until the apples are soft. Leave to cool.
2. Preheat the oven to 180°C/350°F/gas 4. Grease and line a 40 x 20 x 6cm/16 x 8 x 2½in baking tin. Follow step 2 in recipe 263. Place the cooked apples on top of the mixture instead of the raspberries and cream cheese, and spoon the sour cream over the apples.
3. In a separate bowl, beat the remaining butter and sugar as before. Mix in the ground almonds, flaked almonds and plain flour and top the cake with the crumble. Bake for 45–50 minutes. Remove from the oven and leave to cool in the tin, then cut into 16 slices.

266 MILLIONAIRE'S SHORTBREAD

PREPARATION TIME 30 minutes, plus chilling   **COOKING TIME** 20–25 minutes   **MAKES** 18 slices

280g/10oz butter, softened, plus extra
  for greasing
85g/3oz/⅓ cup caster/superfine sugar
225g/8oz/1½ cups plain/all-purpose
  flour, sifted
55g/2oz/heaped ½ cup desiccated/dried
  shredded coconut
70g/2½oz/⅓ cup light soft brown sugar
175ml/5½fl oz/⅔ cup condensed milk

a little purple or pink food colouring paste
100g/3½oz white chocolate, melted
  and cooled slightly
2 tsp vegetable oil
100g/3½oz plain/semisweet chocolate,
  melted and cooled slightly
2 tbsp bought crystallized violets,
  to decorate (optional)

1. Preheat the oven to 190°C/375°F/gas 5. Grease and line a 25 x 20cm/10 x 8in cake tin.
2. Put 185g/6½oz of the butter and the caster sugar in a mixing bowl and beat using an electric hand mixer or wooden spoon until the mixture is light and creamy. Add the flour and coconut, then bring the mixture together with your hands to form a soft dough. Press the dough into the tin with your hands, covering the base evenly.
3. Bake for 12–15 minutes until golden brown. Remove the shortbread from the oven and leave to cool in the tin.
4. In a saucepan, simmer the remaining butter, the brown sugar and condensed milk for 8–10 minutes until the sugar has dissolved, then bring the mixture to the boil and remove from the heat. Pour over the shortbread and leave until cold, then refrigerate for 1 hour.
5. Add a little colouring paste to the white chocolate and stir well with a spoon until the chocolate is an even pink or purple colour. Add 1 teaspoon of the vegetable oil each to both the coloured and plain chocolate and mix well. Place spoonfuls of the coloured and plain chocolate alternately on top of the caramel. Using a fork, swirl the chocolates together so that the whole surface of the caramel is covered with chocolate and you have a pretty, feathered pattern. Sprinkle the crystallized violets over the top, if using, and set aside for 1 hour until the chocolate has set, then cut into 18 slices.

267 CHOCOLATE PEPPERMINT SLICE

PREPARATION TIME 20 minutes, plus chilling   **COOKING TIME** 3 to 5 minutes   **MAKES** 18 slices

185g/6½oz butter, chopped, plus extra
    for greasing
400g/14oz chocolate-covered digestive
    biscuits/graham crackers, roughly broken
3 tbsp golden syrup
4 tbsp cocoa powder
100g/3½oz/heaped 1 cup desiccated/dried
    shredded coconut
200g/7oz plain/semisweet chocolate,
    broken into pieces

PEPPERMINT LAYER
200g/7oz/1⅓ cups icing/powdered
    sugar, sifted
2 tbsp butter
2 tbsp milk
a few drops of peppermint extract
green food colouring

1 Grease and line a 30 x 20cm/12 x 8in Swiss/jelly roll tin.
2 Put the broken biscuits in a food processor and pulse to fine crumbs. Alternatively, put them in a plastic bag and crush with a rolling pin. Heat 150g/5½oz of the butter, the syrup and cocoa in a large saucepan for 3–5 minutes until the butter has melted and the sugar has dissolved. Add the biscuit crumbs and coconut and stir well with a wooden spoon to make sure that all the crumbs are coated in the butter mixture. Press the biscuit mixture into the tin and refrigerate for 30 minutes.
3 In a separate bowl, beat the peppermint layer ingredients using an electric hand mixer or wooden spoon to make a smooth cream. Remove the tin from the refrigerator and spread the mint cream over the biscuit base. Refrigerate again for 30 minutes.
4 When the mint layer has set, melt the chocolate and remaining butter together and stir to form a smooth icing/frosting. Leave to cool a little, then spread over the mint layer and leave to set before cutting into 18 slices.

Chapter 5

CELEBRATION CAKES & COOKIES

This chapter contains some simple but stunning ideas for creating cakes and biscuits for special occasions, whether a children's birthday party, Christmas, Easter or even a wedding. While looking impressive, the cakes and cookies in this chapter are also very easy to prepare, using a few simple ideas such as fresh flower centrepieces, ribbons and edible glitter. Delight your Christmas visitors with a slice of traditional Iced Christmas Cake, flavoured with amaretto or brandy. Celebrate Valentine's Day with Valentine Ribbon Hearts for your friends and family or a Chocolate Heart Gateau for your loved one. There are decorated cupcakes to welcome a baby and to celebrate a retirement, 18th Birthday Cupcakes and St Patrick's Day Cupcakes, spooky cakes and cookies for Halloween, and Bonfire Night Treacle Cookies to munch while watching fireworks. With a Giant Birthday Cookie, Cinnamon Orange Stollen and delicious Easter Egg Cupcakes, this chapter contains something for every occasion.

268 1ST BIRTHDAY CAKE

PREPARATION TIME 40 minutes   **COOKING TIME** 35–40 minutes   **SERVES** 10

350g/12oz butter, softened, plus extra
   for greasing
350g/12oz/1⅓ cups caster/superfine sugar
6 large eggs, lightly beaten
350g/12oz/2⅓ cups self-raising flour, sifted

1 tsp vanilla extract
2 recipe quantities Vanilla Buttercream
   (see page 24)
a few drops of food colouring of choice
sugar sprinkles, to decorate

1 Preheat the oven to 180°C/350°F/gas 4. Grease and line a 40 x 20 x 6cm/16 x 8 x 2½in baking tin.

2 Put the butter and sugar in a mixing bowl and beat using an electric hand mixer or wooden spoon until the mixture is light and creamy. Add the eggs gradually, beating after each addition. Add the flour and vanilla extract and gently fold them into the mixture, using a large metal spoon. Scrape the mixture into the tin using a spatula.

3 Bake for 35–40 minutes until the cake springs back when pressed lightly and a skewer inserted into the middle of the cake comes out clean. Remove the cake from the oven and leave to stand for 5 minutes, then turn out on to a wire rack and leave to cool.

4 Using the full width and length of the cake, cut out a large number '1' using a sharp knife. (Keep the cut-out bits and either cut into squares ready to ice another day or use in a trifle.) Transfer the cake to a large, foil-covered board the size of the cake tin.

5 Reserve a quarter of the buttercream in a separate bowl and carefully cover the cake with the remainder, making sure the sides and top are all covered. Decorate the top of the cake with the sprinkles. Stir your food colouring into the remaining buttercream until the colour is uniform. Spoon the icing/frosting into an icing bag fitted with a 13mm/½in star nozzle and pipe small stars around the outline of the top and the bottom of the cake. Leave the icing to set before serving.

18TH BIRTHDAY CUPCAKES

PREPARATION TIME 40 minutes　　**COOKING TIME** 15–20 minutes　　**MAKES** 24 cakes

225g/8oz butter, softened

225g/8oz/scant 1 cup caster/superfine sugar

4 large eggs, lightly beaten

225g/8oz/1½ cups self-raising flour, sifted

2 tbsp natural/plain yogurt

finely grated zest of 2 lemons

2 tbsp lemon curd

food colouring paste of your choice

55g/2oz ready-to-roll icing

icing/powdered sugar, for dusting

2 recipe quantities Vanilla Buttercream
  (see page 24)

TO DECORATE

sugar sprinkles

edible glitter

1　Preheat the oven to 180°C/350°F/gas 4. Put 24 cake cases/liners in two 12-hole bun tins.

2　Put the butter and caster sugar in a mixing bowl and beat using an electric hand mixer or wooden spoon until the mixture is light and creamy. Add the eggs gradually, beating after each addition. Add the flour, yogurt, lemon zest and lemon curd and gently fold them into the mixture, using a large metal spoon. Spoon the mixture into the cake cases.

3　Bake for 15–20 minutes until the cakes spring back when pressed lightly and a skewer inserted into the middle of a cake comes out clean. Remove the cakes from the oven, turn out on to a wire rack and leave to cool.

4　Dip a cocktail stick/toothpick into the food colouring paste and wipe it on the ready-to-roll icing, then knead the icing until the colour is uniformly even. Repeat, if necessary, to achieve the desired depth of colour. Sift icing sugar on to a clean work surface and roll out the icing to 5mm/¼in thick using a rolling pin. Cut out the numbers '1' and '8', each slightly smaller than the size of the surface of the cupcakes, using number cutters or cardboard templates and a knife.

5　Spoon the buttercream into an icing bag fitted with a 13mm/½in plain nozzle and pipe a swirl on top of each cupcake. Cover each cake with sprinkles and place on a tiered cake stand. Place the '1' and '8' on two of the cupcakes in the centre of your display and dust all the cakes with edible glitter.

PREPARATION TIME I hour   **COOKING TIME** 25–30 minutes   **SERVES** 10

225g/8oz butter, softened, plus extra
    for greasing
225g/8oz/scant I cup caster/superfine sugar
4 large eggs, lightly beaten
225g/8oz/1½ cups self-raising flour, sifted
I tbsp instant coffee granules dissolved
    in I tbsp boiling water, then cooled
100g/3½oz plain/semisweet
    chocolate, grated
I recipe quantity Vanilla Buttercream
    (see page 24)
icing/powdered sugar, for dusting

450g/1lb ready-to-roll icing
a few drops of food colouring of choice
½ quantity Royal Icing (see page 24)

TO DECORATE
3.5cm/1½in high floral foam dome on
    a plastic base with self-adhesive pad
flowers to match your icing colour
1.5m x 3cm/5ft x 1¼in ribbon
long wooden cocktail stick/toothpick or
    lollipop/popsicle stick

1 Preheat the oven to 180°C/350°F/gas 4. Grease and base-line two 20cm/8in sandwich cake tins.

2 Put the butter and sugar in a mixing bowl and beat using an electric hand mixer or wooden spoon until the mixture is light and creamy. Add the eggs gradually, beating after each addition. Add the flour, coffee liquid and grated chocolate and gently fold them into the mixture, using a large metal spoon. Divide the mixture between the tins using a spatula.

3 Bake for 25–30 minutes until the cakes spring back when pressed lightly. Remove from the oven and leave to stand for 5 minutes, then turn out on to a wire rack to cool.

4 Sandwich the cakes together with a third of the buttercream and cover the top and sides of the cake with the remainder.

5 Sift icing sugar on to a clean work surface and roll out the ready-to-roll icing to 5mm/¼in thick using a rolling pin. Lift the icing on top of the cake, using the rolling pin to help, and smooth down with your hands to ensure there are no creases. Trim the icing around the bottom of the cake with a sharp knife. Add the food colouring to the royal icing and stir until the colour is uniform. Spoon it into an icing bag fitted with a 13mm/½in star nozzle and pipe stars around the base and the edge of the top of the cake.

6 Just before you wish to serve the cake, soak the foam in water. Cut the flowers so that they have 2.5cm/1in stems and press them into the foam. Place the foam on top of the cake, sticking it down with the self-adhesive pad. Wrap the ribbon around the cake and tie in a bow. Write a 21st birthday message on a small piece of card, secure it on a long stick and poke it into the centre of the flowers.

271 GINGERBREAD MAN CUPCAKES

PREPARATION TIME 40 minutes   **COOKING TIME** 15–20 minutes   **MAKES** 12 cakes

115g/4oz butter, softened
115g/4oz/scant ½ cup caster/superfine sugar
2 large eggs, lightly beaten
115g/4oz/¾ cup self-raising flour
1 tsp ground ginger
1 tsp ground cinnamon
55g/2oz plain/semisweet chocolate, melted
    and cooled slightly

36 sugar-coated chocolate beans
12 small gingerbread men, either made
    following the recipe on page 297, but
    using a smaller cutter, or store-bought
1 recipe quantity Vanilla Buttercream
    (see page 24)
sugar sprinkles, to decorate

1   Preheat the oven to 180°C/350°F/gas 4. Put 12 cake cases/liners in a 12-hole bun tin.
2   Put the butter and sugar in a mixing bowl and beat using an electric hand mixer or
    wooden spoon until the mixture is light and creamy. Add the eggs gradually, beating after
    each addition. Sift in the flour, ginger and ground cinnamon and gently fold them into the
    mixture, using a large metal spoon. Spoon the mixture into the cake cases.
3   Bake for 15–20 minutes until the cakes spring back when pressed lightly and a skewer
    inserted into the middle of a cake comes out clean. Remove the cakes from the oven, turn
    out on to a wire rack and leave to cool.
4   Use the melted chocolate to attach 3 chocolate beans to each gingerbread man as
    buttons. Leave the chocolate to set. Spoon the buttercream into an icing bag fitted with a
    13mm/½in star nozzle and pipe a swirl of icing on top of each cake. Stand a gingerbread
    man upright in the centre of each cake so that his feet are fixed into the icing. Shake a few
    sprinkles over the icing to decorate.

272 CHOCOLATE BOX CAKE

PREPARATION TIME 40 minutes   **COOKING TIME** 25–30 minutes   **SERVES** 10

225g/8oz butter, softened, plus extra
    for greasing
225g/8oz/scant 1 cup caster/superfine sugar
4 large eggs, lightly beaten
200g/7oz/1⅓ cups self-raising flour
4 tbsp cocoa powder
½ recipe quantity Chocolate Buttercream
    (see page 24)
1 recipe quantity Chocolate Ganache

(see page 22)
30 assorted chocolates, wrapped
    or unwrapped
1.5m x 5cm/5ft x 2in ribbon

1   Preheat the oven to 180°C/350°F/gas 4. Grease and base-line two 20cm/8in sandwich cake tins.

2   Put the butter and sugar in a mixing bowl and beat using an electric hand mixer or wooden spoon until the mixture is light and creamy. Add the eggs gradually, beating after each addition. Sift in the flour and cocoa and gently fold them into the mixture, using a large metal spoon. Divide the mixture between the tins using a spatula.

3   Bake for 25–30 minutes until the cakes spring back when pressed lightly and a skewer inserted into the middle of each cake comes out clean. Remove the cakes from the oven and leave to stand for 5 minutes, then turn out on to a wire rack and leave to cool.

4   Sandwich the cakes together with the buttercream and then cover the top and sides with the ganache. Arrange the chocolates on the cake, making sure they cover the whole top, and mixing different colours and shapes. Leave the ganache to set completely.

5   Wrap the ribbon around the cake and tie it neatly in a bow. Remove the ribbon before cutting the cake into slices to serve.

273 BIRTHDAY PRESENT CAKE

PREPARATION TIME 1 hour   **COOKING TIME** 35–40 minutes   **SERVES** 10

225g/8oz butter, softened, plus extra
  for greasing
225g/8oz/scant 1 cup caster/superfine sugar
4 large eggs, lightly beaten
225g/8oz/1½ cups self-raising flour, sifted
finely grated zest of 2 lemons
2 tbsp natural/plain yogurt

1 recipe quantity Vanilla Buttercream
  (see page 24)
3 tbsp lemon curd
icing/powdered sugar, for dusting
450g/1lb ready-to-roll icing
1.5m x 3cm/5ft x 1¼in wide coloured ribbon
edible glitter, for dusting

1   Preheat the oven to 180°C/350°F/gas 4. Grease and line a 20cm/8in loose-bottomed square cake tin.

2   Put the butter and sugar in a mixing bowl and beat using an electric hand mixer or wooden spoon until the mixture is light and creamy. Add the eggs gradually, beating after each addition. Add the flour, lemon zest and yogurt and gently fold them into the mixture, using a large metal spoon. Scrape the mixture into the tin using a spatula.

3   Bake for 35–40 minutes until the cake springs back when pressed lightly and a skewer inserted into the middle of the cake comes out clean. Remove the cake from the oven and leave to stand for 5 minutes, then turn out on to a wire rack and leave to cool.

4   Cut the cake in half horizontally using a sharp knife and sandwich the halves together with a third of the buttercream and the lemon curd. Cover the top and sides of the cake with the remaining buttercream, saving 1 tablespoon to fix the ribbons to the cake.

5   Sift icing sugar on to a clean work surface and, using a rolling pin, roll out the ready-to-roll icing to 5mm/¼in thick. Using the rolling pin to help, lift the icing on top of the cake and smooth down with your hands to ensure there are no creases. Trim the icing around the bottom of the cake with a sharp knife so that you have a neat parcel shape.

6   Cut 2 lengths of the ribbon each long enough to reach over the cake and place on top of the cake, crossing in the centre. Fix the ribbons to the bottom of each side of the cake with a small amount of buttercream. Tie the remaining ribbon in a bow and fix in the centre of the ribbon cross with another dab of buttercream. Dust the cake with edible glitter. When you are ready to cut the cake, remove the ribbons.

274 STRAWBERRY ICE CREAM BIRTHDAY CAKE

PREPARATION TIME 40 minutes, plus freezing/chilling   **COOKING TIME** 25–30 minutes   **SERVES** 10

1 litre/35fl oz/4 cups strawberry
   ice cream, softened
350g/12oz butter, softened, plus extra
   for greasing
350g/12oz/1⅓ cups caster/superfine sugar
6 large eggs, lightly beaten

350g/12oz/2⅓ cups self-raising flour, sifted
1 tsp vanilla extract
200g/7oz white chocolate, melted
   and cooled slightly
5 strawberries, halved
10 white chocolate truffles

1   Line two 20cm/8in sandwich cake tins with cling film/plastic wrap, letting the film come over the top. Divide the ice cream between the tins and freeze for 1 hour. Lift the ice cream out of the tins, using the film, cover with another layer of cling film and return to the freezer.

2   Preheat the oven to 180°C/350°F/gas 4. Wash both tins, then grease and base-line both washed tins and a third tin of the same size.

3   Put the butter and sugar in a mixing bowl and beat using an electric hand mixer or wooden spoon until the mixture is light and creamy. Add the eggs gradually, beating after each addition. Add the flour and vanilla extract and gently fold them into the mixture, using a large metal spoon. Divide the mixture between the tins using a spatula.

4   Bake for 25–30 minutes until the cakes spring back when pressed lightly and a skewer inserted into the middle of each cake comes out clean. Remove the cakes from the oven and leave to stand for 5 minutes, then turn out on to a wire rack and leave to cool.

5   Cover one of the cakes with the melted chocolate and top with the strawberries and white chocolate truffles.

6   Remove the ice cream layers from the freezer 10 minutes before you are ready to serve the cake so that they soften a little. Stack up the cake and ice-cream layers, finishing with the decorated cake layer. Add candles, if wished, and serve immediately.

275 ROSE & VIOLET BIRTHDAY CAKE

PREPARATION TIME 40 minutes   **COOKING TIME** 25–30 minutes   **SERVES** 10

225g/8oz butter, softened, plus extra
   for greasing
225g/8oz/scant 1 cup caster/superfine sugar
4 large eggs, lightly beaten
200g/7oz/1⅓ cups self-raising flour
4 tbsp cocoa powder
a few drops of pink food colouring

2 tbsp rose syrup or rosewater
½ recipe quantity Vanilla Buttercream
   (see page 24)
2 tbsp rose or raspberry jam/jelly
1 recipe quantity Chocolate Ganache
   (see page 22)
10 rose and violet cream chocolates

1 Preheat the oven to 180°C/350°F/gas 4. Grease and base-line two 20cm/8in sandwich cake tins.

2 Put the butter and sugar in a mixing bowl and beat using an electric hand mixer or wooden spoon until the mixture is light and creamy. Add the eggs gradually, beating after each addition. Sift in the flour and cocoa and gently fold them into the mixture, using a large metal spoon. Divide the mixture between the tins using a spatula.

3 Bake for 25–30 minutes until the cakes spring back when pressed lightly and a skewer inserted into the middle of each cake comes out clean. Remove the cakes from the oven and leave to stand for 5 minutes, then turn out on to a wire rack and leave to cool.

4 Stir the food colouring and rose syrup into the buttercream until the colour is uniform. Sandwich the cakes together with the jam, then the buttercream. Cover the top and sides of the cake with the ganache and place the rose and violet chocolates alternately around the top of the cake. Leave to set before serving.

276 STRAWBERRY WINDMILL CAKE

PREPARATION TIME 30 minutes   **COOKING TIME** 25–30 minutes   **SERVES** 8

225g/8oz butter, softened, plus extra
   for greasing
225g/8oz/scant 1 cup caster/superfine sugar
4 large eggs, lightly beaten
200g/7oz/1⅓ cups self-raising flour
4 tbsp cocoa powder
3 tbsp almond liqueur, such as amaretto

600ml/21fl oz/scant 2½ cups double/heavy
   cream, whipped to stiff peaks
400g/14oz/2⅔ cups strawberries,
   hulled and halved
3 tbsp strawberry jam/jelly
icing/powdered sugar, for dusting

1 Preheat the oven to 180°C/350°F/gas 4. Grease and base-line two 20cm/8in sandwich cake tins.

2 Put the butter and caster sugar in a mixing bowl and beat using an electric hand mixer or wooden spoon until the mixture is light and creamy. Add the eggs gradually, beating after each addition. Sift in the flour and cocoa and gently fold them into the mixture, using a large metal spoon. Divide the mixture between the tins using a spatula.

3 Bake for 25–30 minutes until the cakes spring back when pressed lightly and a skewer inserted into the middle of each cake comes out clean. Remove the cakes from the oven and leave to stand for 5 minutes, then turn out on to a wire rack and leave to cool.

4 Cut each cake in half horizontally with a sharp knife. Drizzle 1 tablespoon of the amaretto over one cake layer and cover with a third of the cream. Top with a third of the strawberries and 1 tablespoon of the jam. Repeat with the next 2 cake layers. Cut the top layer of cake into 6 equal segments and place on top of the cake at 45-degree angles as though like windmill sails, adjusting the strawberries so that they lie in between the sails. Dust with icing sugar to serve.

277 CHOCOLATE COCONUT BIRTHDAY CAKE

PREPARATION TIME 30 minutes   **COOKING TIME** 25–30 minutes   **SERVES** 8

225g/8oz butter, plus extra for greasing
225g/8oz/1½ cups self-raising flour, sifted,
    plus extra for dusting
225g/8oz/scant 1 cup caster/superfine sugar
4 large eggs, lightly beaten
250g/9oz/3 cups desiccated/dried
    shredded coconut

100g/3½oz/heaped ½ cup milk
    chocolate chips
2 tsp ground cinnamon
300g/10½oz white chocolate, melted
    and cooled slightly
sugar-coated chocolate beans, to decorate

1 Preheat the oven to 180°C/350°F/gas 4. Grease a 23cm/9in ring tin and dust with flour.

2 Put the butter and sugar in a mixing bowl and beat using an electric hand mixer or wooden spoon until the mixture is light. Add the eggs gradually, beating after each addition. Add the flour, 100g/3½oz/1 cup of the coconut, the chocolate chips and ground cinnamon and fold into the mixture, using a large metal spoon. Scrape the mixture into the tin using a spatula.

3 Bake for 25–30 minutes until the cake springs back when pressed lightly. Remove from the oven and leave to stand for 5 minutes, then turn out on to a wire rack to cool.

4 Cover the top of the cake with half the melted chocolate. Mix the remaining chocolate and coconut and spoon over the top of the cake. Decorate with the chocolate beans and candles if you wish.

278 STRAWBERRY & TRUFFLE CHOCOLATE CELEBRATION CAKE

PREPARATION TIME 40 minutes   **COOKING TIME** 25–30 minutes   **SERVES** 10

225g/8oz butter, softened, plus extra
   for greasing
225g/8oz/scant 1 cup caster/superfine sugar
4 large eggs, lightly beaten
200g/7oz/1⅓ cups self-raising flour
4 tbsp cocoa powder

½ recipe quantity Chocolate Buttercream
   (see page 24)
200g/7oz plain/semisweet chocolate,
   melted and cooled slightly
10 strawberries
10 chocolate truffles

1   Preheat the oven to 180°C/350°F/gas 4. Grease and base-line two 20cm/8in sandwich cake tins.
2   Put the butter and sugar in a mixing bowl and beat using an electric hand mixer or wooden spoon until the mixture is light and creamy. Add the eggs gradually, beating after each addition. Sift in the flour and cocoa and gently fold them into the mixture, using a large metal spoon. Divide the mixture between the tins using a spatula.
3   Bake for 25–30 minutes until the cakes spring back when pressed lightly. Remove the cakes from the oven and leave to stand for 5 minutes, then turn out on to a wire rack to cool.
4   Sandwich the cakes together with the buttercream. Cover the top of the cake with the melted chocolate and arrange the strawberries and truffles alternately around the edge.

279 GIANT BIRTHDAY COOKIE

PREPARATION TIME 30 minutes   **COOKING TIME** 25–30 minutes   **SERVES** 10

250g/9oz butter, plus extra for greasing
400g/14oz/1⅔ cups caster/superfine sugar
2 large eggs, lightly beaten
2 tsp vanilla extract
550g/1lb 4oz/3⅔ cups plain/all-purpose flour

1 tsp baking powder
100g/3½oz/heaped ½ cup plain/semisweet
   chocolate chips
½ quantity Royal Icing (see page 24)
sweets/candies and edible silver balls

1   Preheat the oven to 180°C/350°F/gas 4. Grease a 30cm/12in fluted square flan tin.
2   Put the butter and sugar in a mixing bowl and beat using an electric hand mixer or wooden spoon until the mixture is light and creamy. Beat in the eggs and vanilla extract. Sift in the flour and baking powder and add the chocolate chips. Mix together with your hands to form a soft dough and press it into the tin evenly with the back of a spoon.
3   Bake for 25–30 minutes until golden brown and just firm. Remove from the oven and leave to cool in the tin, then transfer to a serving plate. Put a third of the royal icing in an icing bag fitted with a 3mm/⅛in plain nozzle and write a message in the centre of the cookie. Put the remaining icing in a bag with a 5mm/¼in star nozzle and pipe stars around the

edge. Press the sweets and silver balls into the icing to decorate. Pipe small stars around the message and press a sweet into each. Leave the icing to set before serving.

280 FLOWERPOT CAKES

PREPARATION TIME 40 minutes   **COOKING TIME** 15–20 minutes   **MAKES** 16 cakes

115g/4oz butter, softened
115g/4oz/scant ½ cup caster/superfine sugar
2 large eggs, lightly beaten
115g/4oz/¾ cup self-raising flour, sifted
1 tsp vanilla extract

a few drops of green food colouring
1 recipe quantity Vanilla Buttercream
(see page 24)
16 large sugar flowers
16 sugar leaves

1 Preheat the oven to 180°C/350°F/gas 4. Wash sixteen 3cm/1¼in brand-new terracotta flowerpots and leave to dry, then put a cake case/liner in each one, using your fingers to fold and smooth the paper down so that it fits around the sides of the pots.
2 Put the butter and sugar in a mixing bowl and beat using an electric hand mixer or wooden spoon until the mixture is light and creamy. Add the eggs gradually, beating after each addition. Add the flour and vanilla extract and gently fold them into the mixture, using a large metal spoon. Spoon the mixture into the cake cases using a teaspoon.
3 Place the flowerpots on a baking tray and bake for 15–20 minutes until the cakes spring back when pressed lightly and a skewer inserted into the middle of a cake comes out clean. Remove the cakes from the oven and transfer to a wire rack to cool.
4 Stir the food colouring into the buttercream until the colour is uniform. Spoon it into an icing bag fitted with a 5mm/¼in star nozzle. Pipe a swirl of buttercream on top of each cake. If you do not have an icing bag, spread a thick layer of icing over each cake using a round-bladed knife.) Top each cake with a sugar flower and leaf.

281 GIFT TAG COOKIES

PREPARATION TIME 30 minutes, plus chilling   **COOKING TIME** 12–15 minutes   **MAKES** 10 cookies

115g/4oz butter, softened, plus extra
    for greasing
55g/2oz/¼ cup caster/superfine sugar
175g/6oz/heaped 1 cup plain/all-purpose
    flour, sifted, plus extra for dusting
1 tbsp milk (optional)
300g/10½oz/2 cups icing/powdered
    sugar, sifted

TO DECORATE
edible gel writing pen
sugar-coated chocolate beans or
    small sweets/candies
2m x 3mm/6ft 6in x ⅛in ribbon

1 Put the butter and sugar in a mixing bowl and beat using an electric hand mixer or wooden spoon until the mixture is light and creamy. Add the flour and mix with your hands to form a soft dough, adding the milk if the mixture is too dry. Wrap the dough in cling film/plastic wrap and refrigerate for 1 hour.

2 Preheat the oven to 180°C/350°F/gas 4. Grease two 30cm/12in square baking trays.

3 Sift flour on to a clean work surface and roll the dough out to about 1cm/⅜in thick using a rolling pin. Cut out 5 large rectangles and 5 large rounds, with a cutter or knife, gathering up the trimmings and re-rolling as necessary. Place the cookies on the baking trays and, using a skewer or cocktail stick/toothpick, make a 5mm/¼in hole near one edge of each cookie.

4 Bake for 12–15 minutes until golden brown and just firm. Remove the cookies from the oven and leave to cool on the trays for a few minutes, then transfer to a wire rack to cool.

5 In a bowl, mix the icing sugar with 2–3 tablespoons water to make a smooth icing/frosting and spread it over the cookies. Use the skewer or cocktail stick to reopen the holes if they closed during baking or if they fill with icing. Leave the icing to set, then write names on the gift tags with the gel pen and decorate around the edge of each tag with chocolate beans. Cut the ribbon into 20cm/8in lengths, thread one length through the hole on each cookie and attach to your present.

282 FRESH FLOWER CAKE

PREPARATION TIME 40 minutes   **COOKING TIME** 25–30 minutes   **SERVES** 10

225g/8oz butter, softened, plus extra
   for greasing
225g/8oz/scant 1 cup caster/superfine sugar
4 large eggs, lightly beaten
200g/7oz/1⅓ cups self-raising flour
4 tbsp cocoa powder
1 recipe quantity Chocolate Buttercream
   (see page 24)
1 recipe quantity Chocolate Ganache
   (see page 22)

TO DECORATE
chocolate truffles and chocolate buttons
3.5cm/1½in high floral foam dome on a
   plastic base with self-adhesive pad
fresh flowers of your choice

1 Preheat the oven to 180°C/350°F/gas 4. Grease and base-line two 20cm/8in sandwich
cake tins.

2 Put the butter and caster sugar in a mixing bowl and beat using an electric hand mixer or
wooden spoon until the mixture is light and creamy. Add the eggs gradually, beating after
each addition. Sift in the flour and cocoa and gently fold them into the mixture, using a
large metal spoon. Divide the mixture between the tins using a spatula.

3 Bake for 25–30 minutes until the cakes spring back when pressed lightly and a skewer
inserted into the middle of each cake comes out clean. Remove the cakes from the oven
and leave to stand for 5 minutes, then turn out on to a wire rack and leave to cool.

4 Sandwich the cakes together with half of the buttercream and then cover the top and
sides of the cake with the ganache, working gently with a palette knife to smooth it evenly.

5 Gently lift the cake on to a serving plate or cake stand. Spoon the remaining buttercream
into an icing bag fitted with a 13mm/½in star nozzle and pipe around the edge of the
top and around the base of the cake. Press chocolate buttons all around the edge of the
buttercream where it sandwiches the cakes together. Use the remaining buttons and the
truffles to decorate the top, leaving the centre free for the flowers. Leave to set.

6 When you are ready to display the cake, soak the floral foam in water for a few minutes.
Cut the flower stems down to 2.5cm/1in long and press them into the foam, covering the
entire dome to the top with flowers. Remove the backing paper on the self-adhesive pad
on the base of the plastic tray and stick the dome in the centre of the top of the cake.

283 JELLYBEAN CAKE

PREPARATION TIME 40 minutes **COOKING TIME** 25–30 minutes **SERVES** 8

225g/8oz butter, plus extra for greasing
225g/8oz/scant 1 cup caster/superfine sugar
4 large eggs, lightly beaten
225g/8oz/1½ cups self-raising flour
4 tbsp cocoa powder
90g/3¼oz/½ cup plain/semisweet
   chocolate chips

3 tbsp natural/plain yogurt
½ recipe quantity Vanilla Buttercream
   (see page 24)
1 recipe quantity Chocolate Ganache
   (see page 22)
jelly beans, to decorate

1 Preheat the oven to 180°C/350°F/gas 4. Grease and base-line two 20cm/8in sandwich cake tins.
2 Put the butter and sugar in a mixing bowl and beat using an electric hand mixer or wooden spoon until the mixture is light. Add the eggs gradually, beating after each addition. Sift in the flour and cocoa and gently fold them into the mixture with the chocolate chips and yogurt, using a large metal spoon. Divide the mixture between the tins using a spatula.
3 Bake for 25–30 minutes until the cakes spring back when pressed lightly. Remove from the oven and leave to stand for 5 minutes, then turn out on to a wire rack to cool.
4 Sandwich the cakes together with the buttercream and cover the top and sides of the cake with the ganache. Arrange the jelly beans in a pattern around the edge of the top of the cake. Leave the ganache to set.

284 CHILDREN'S PARTY CUPCAKES

PREPARATION TIME 30 minutes **COOKING TIME** 15–20 minutes **MAKES** 24 cakes

225g/8oz butter, softened
225g/8oz/scant 1 cup caster/superfine sugar
4 large eggs, lightly beaten
225g/8oz/1½ cups self-raising flour
4 tbsp cocoa powder
100g/3½oz/heaped ½ cup milk
   chocolate chips

3 tbsp natural/plain yogurt
a few drops of food colouring of choice
2 recipe quantities Vanilla Buttercream
   (see page 24)
sweets/candies and edible glitter,
   to decorate

1 Preheat the oven to 180°C/350°F/gas 4. Put 24 cake cases/liners in two 12-hole bun tins.
2 Put the butter and sugar in a mixing bowl and beat using an electric hand mixer or wooden spoon until the mixture is light and creamy. Add the eggs gradually, beating after each addition. Sift in the flour and cocoa and gently fold them into the mixture with the chocolate chips and yogurt, using a large metal spoon. Spoon the mixture into the cake cases.

3 Bake for 15–20 minutes until the cakes spring back when pressed lightly. Remove the cakes from the oven, turn out on to a wire rack and leave to cool.

4 Stir the food colouring into the buttercream until the colour is uniform. Spoon the buttercream into an icing bag fitted with a 13mm/½in star nozzle and pipe swirls on top of each cake, then add a sweet and a sprinkle of edible glitter.

285 CHOCOLATE BROWNIE BIRTHDAY STACK

PREPARATION TIME 40 minutes   **COOKING TIME** 25–30 minutes   **SERVES** 16

250g/9oz butter, plus extra for greasing
350g/12½oz plain/semisweet chocolate
200g/7oz/¾ cup caster/superfine sugar
200g/7oz/¾ cup light soft brown sugar
5 large eggs
1 tsp vanilla extract

200g/7oz/1⅓ cups plain/all-purpose flour, sifted
200g/7oz white chocolate, melted and cooled slightly
sweets/candies, to decorate

1 Preheat the oven to 180°C/350°F/gas 4. Grease a 30 x 23 x 6cm/12 x 9 x 2½in baking tin.

2 Melt the butter and plain chocolate together and leave to cool. Put both sugars, the eggs and vanilla in a bowl and whisk using an electric hand mixer or a whisk until very light and doubled in size. While still whisking, slowly pour in the chocolate and butter mixture. Fold in the flour, using a large metal spoon, then scrape the mixture into the tin using a spatula.

3 Bake for 25–30 minutes until the brownie has formed a crust and a skewer inserted into the middle comes out clean. Remove from the oven, leave to cool in the tin, then cut into 16 slices. Stack the slices on a plate, drizzle with white chocolate and decorate with sweets.

286 CHRISTENING CAKE

PREPARATION TIME 1 hour   **COOKING TIME** 25–30 minutes   **SERVES** 10

225g/8oz butter, softened, plus extra for greasing
225g/8oz/scant 1 cup caster/superfine sugar
4 large eggs, lightly beaten
225g/8oz/1½ cups self-raising flour, sifted
1 tsp vanilla extract
1 recipe quantity Vanilla Buttercream (see page 24)
2 tbsp raspberry jam/jelly
icing/powdered sugar, for dusting

450g/1lb ready-to-roll icing
a few drops of food colouring
½ quantity Royal Icing (see page 24)

TO DECORATE
3.5cm/1½in high floral foam dome on a plastic base with self-adhesive pad
flowers in your colour of choice
1.5m x 3cm/5ft x 1¼in wide ribbon in your colour of choice

1   Preheat the oven to 180°C/350°F/gas 4. Grease and base-line two 20cm/8in sandwich cake tins.

2   Put the butter and sugar in a mixing bowl and beat using an electric hand mixer or wooden spoon until the mixture is light and creamy. Add the eggs gradually, beating after each addition. Add the flour and vanilla extract and gently fold them into the mixture, using a large metal spoon. Divide the mixture between the tins using a spatula.

3   Bake for 25–30 minutes until the cakes spring back when pressed lightly and a skewer inserted into the middle of each cake comes out clean. Remove the cakes from the oven and leave to stand for 5 minutes, then turn out on to a wire rack and leave to cool.

4   Sandwich the cakes together with a third of the buttercream and the jam and use the remainder to cover the top and sides. Sift icing sugar on to a clean work surface and roll out the ready-to-roll icing to 5mm/¼in thick using a rolling pin. Lift the icing on top of the cake, using the rolling pin to help, and smooth down with your hands to ensure there are no creases. Trim the icing around the bottom of the cake with a sharp knife.

5   Stir your choice of food colouring into the royal icing until the colour is uniform, then spoon it into an icing bag fitted with a 13mm/½in star nozzle. Pipe stars around the base and the edge of the top of the cake.

6   When you are ready to display the cake, soak the floral foam in water for a few minutes. Cut the flower stems down to 2.5cm/1in long and press them into the foam, covering the entire dome to the top with flowers. Remove the backing paper on the self-adhesive pad on the base of the plastic tray and stick the dome in the centre of the top of the cake. On a 7.5 x 4cm/3 x 1½in piece of card, neatly write the name of the child being christened. Using a craft knife or small sharp scissors, cut a slit on each side of the card, wide enough to thread the ribbon through, with the ribbon lying behind the name. Tie the ribbon around the sides of the cake so that the child's name is at the front.

287 WELCOME BABY CUPCAKES

PREPARATION TIME 40 minutes   **COOKING TIME** 15–20 minutes   **MAKES** 24 cakes

225g/8oz butter, softened

225g/8oz/scant 1 cup caster/superfine sugar

4 large eggs, lightly beaten

225g/8oz/1½ cups self-raising flour, sifted

2 tbsp natural/plain yogurt

1 tsp vanilla extract

a few drops of food colouring

2 recipe quantities Vanilla Buttercream (see page 24)

TO DECORATE

edible glitter

baby-themed cake decorations (optional)

1   Preheat the oven to 180°C/350°F/gas 4. Put 24 cake cases/liners in two 12-hole bun tins.

2   Put the butter and sugar in a mixing bowl and beat using an electric hand mixer or wooden spoon until the mixture is light and creamy. Add the eggs gradually, beating after

each addition. Add the flour, yogurt and vanilla extract and gently fold them into the mixture, using a large metal spoon. Spoon the mixture into the cake cases.

3 Bake for 15–20 minutes until the cakes spring back when pressed lightly. Remove the cakes from the oven, turn out on to a wire rack and leave to cool.

4 Stir your choice of food colouring into the buttercream until the colour is uniform. Spoon the buttercream into an icing bag fitted with a 13mm/½in plain nozzle and pipe a swirl on top of each cake. Decorate with edible glitter and baby decorations, if wished.

288 COUNTRY WEDDING CAKE

PREPARATION TIME 2½ hours   **COOKING TIME** 45 minutes   **SERVES** 60–70 (small slices)

680g/1lb 8oz butter, softened, plus extra for greasing
680g/1lb 8oz/2¾ cups caster/superfine sugar
12 large eggs, lightly beaten
680g/1lb 8oz/4½ cups self-raising flour, sifted
juice and finely grated zest of 8 lemons
4 tbsp icing/powdered sugar, sifted, plus extra for dusting
3 recipe quantities Vanilla Buttercream (see page 24)
8 tbsp lemon curd
1.3kg/3lb ready-to-roll icing

2 recipe quantities Royal Icing (see page 24)

TO DECORATE
silver dragées and white chocolate truffles
3.5cm/1½in high floral foam dome on a plastic base with self-adhesive pad
white and cream flowers of choice
6m x 3mm/19ft 6in x ⅛in ribbons in cream, silver and white
edible glitter

1 Preheat the oven to 180°C/350°F/gas 4. Grease and line three springform cake tins, the first measuring 17cm/7in, the second 20cm/8in and the third 23cm/9in.

2 Put the butter and sugar in a very large mixing bowl and beat using an electric hand mixer or wooden spoon until the mixture is light and creamy. Add the eggs gradually, beating after each addition. Add the flour and lemon zest and gently fold them into the mixture, using a large metal spoon. Divide the mixture between the tins proportionally.

3 Bake the cakes for about 25, 35 and 45 minutes respectively, until each cake springs back when pressed lightly and a skewer inserted into the middle of each cake comes out clean. (Note that if you are not using a fan oven, cakes on the bottom shelf may take longer to cook than the given times.)

4 Just before the cakes come out of the oven, heat the lemon juice with the icing sugar in a saucepan until the icing sugar has dissolved, then boil for 1 minute to create a syrup. Remove the cakes from the oven and pour the syrup over them in proportional amounts. Leave the cakes to cool, then turn out on to a wire rack.

5 Cut each cake in half horizontally using a sharp knife and sandwich together with some of

the buttercream and all the lemon curd. Use nearly all the remaining buttercream to cover each cake with a thin coat, reserving just a little for step 7.

6 Put the largest cake on a 30cm/12in round cake board. Divide the ready-to-roll icing into thirds, then take some icing from one ball and add it to another, giving you 3 balls of increasing size. Sift icing sugar on to a clean work surface and roll out the largest ball to 5mm/¼in thick using a rolling pin. Lift the icing over the largest cake using the rolling pin to help you. Using your hands, smooth down the top and sides of the icing, making sure there are no creases. Trim the bottom edges of the icing with a sharp knife. Repeat with the other 2 cakes and their icing.

7 Stack the cakes in size order, handling them as gently as possible to minimize fingerprints and using the reserved buttercream to secure them.

8 Spoon the royal icing into a large icing bag fitted with a 13mm/½in star nozzle (you may have to do this in batches) and pipe stars of icing around the base of the cake and to cover the joins between each cake. Pipe a row of stars around the edge of the top cake. Decorate the icing stars with the silver dragées and white chocolate truffles, making sure they are evenly spaced. Leave the icing to set.

9 When you are ready to display the cake, soak the floral foam in water for a few minutes. Cut the flower stems down to 2.5cm/1in long and press them into the foam, covering the entire dome to the top with flowers. Cut the 3 ribbons into quarters and drape the 12 lengths over the top of the cake and down the sides to give 24 ribbons equally spaced around the cake. Remove the backing paper on the self-adhesive pad on the base of the plastic tray and stick the flower dome in the centre of the top of the cake, where the ribbons cross. Dust the cake with edible glitter before serving.

289 BIRTHDAY ROSE MUFFINS

PREPARATION TIME 20 minutes   **COOKING TIME** 15–20 minutes   **MAKES** 10 muffins

280g/10oz/scant 2 cups plain/
  all-purpose flour
2 tsp baking powder
1 tsp bicarbonate of soda/baking soda
115g/4oz/scant ½ cup caster/
  superfine sugar
250ml/9fl oz/1 cup milk
125ml/4fl oz/½ cup crème fraîche

115g/4oz butter, melted and cooled
2 large eggs, lightly beaten
3 tbsp rose syrup or rosewater
200g/7oz/1⅓ cups icing/powdered
  sugar, sifted
30 small sugar roses, to decorate
a few drops of pink food colouring

1 Preheat the oven to 180°C/350°F/gas 4. Put 10 muffin cases/liners in a 12-hole muffin tin.

2 Sift the flour, baking powder and bicarbonate of soda into a mixing bowl, add the caster sugar and stir well with a wooden spoon.

3 In a separate bowl, whisk together the milk, crème fraîche and melted butter with an electric hand mixer or a whisk, add the eggs and 1 tablespoon of the rose syrup and whisk again. Pour the liquid into the bowl containing the dry ingredients and fold in with a large metal spoon. Do not overmix: the mixture should be thick and slightly lumpy. Spoon the mixture into the muffin cases.

4 Bake for 15–20 minutes until the muffins spring back when pressed lightly and a skewer inserted into the middle of a muffin comes out clean. Remove the muffins from the oven, turn out on to a wire rack and leave to cool.

5 In a bowl, mix the remaining rose syrup with the icing sugar and a few drops of food colouring to form a smooth icing, adding a little water if it is too stiff. Spread some of the icing over each muffin using a round-bladed knife and top the muffins with 3 sugar roses, adding candles if wished.

290 WEDDING CUPCAKES

PREPARATION TIME 1 hour, plus soaking   **COOKING TIME** 15–20 minutes   **MAKES** 48 cakes

200g/7oz/heaped 1 cup sultanas/golden raisins
200ml/7fl oz/scant 1 cup almond liqueur,
   such as amaretto
450g/1lb butter, softened
450g/1lb/1¾ cups caster/superfine sugar
8 large eggs, lightly beaten
450g/1lb/3 cups self-raising flour

2 tsp baking powder
1 tbsp almond extract
200g/7oz/1⅓ cups flaked/sliced almonds
4 recipe quantities Vanilla Buttercream
   (see page 24)
48 silver sugar almonds and
   edible glitter, to decorate

1 Soak the sultanas in the amaretto overnight. Preheat the oven to 180°C/350°F/gas 4. Put 48 cake cases/liners in four 12-hole bun tins.

2 Put the butter and sugar in a mixing bowl and beat using an electric hand mixer or wooden spoon until the mixture is light and creamy. Add the eggs gradually, beating after each addition. Sift in the flour and baking powder and gently fold them into the mixture with the almond extract, flaked almonds and fruit, using a large metal spoon. Spoon the mixture into the cake cases.

3 Bake for 15–20 minutes until the cakes spring back when pressed lightly. Remove the cakes from the oven, turn out on to a wire rack and leave to cool.

4 Spoon the buttercream into a large icing bag fitted with a 13mm/½in star nozzle (you may have to do this in batches) and pipe a large swirl of buttercream on each cake. Place a silver sugar almond in the centre of each cake and sprinkle with edible glitter.

291 GOLDEN WEDDING ANNIVERSARY CAKE

PREPARATION TIME I hour **COOKING TIME** 25–30 minutes **SERVES** 8–10

225g/8oz butter, plus extra for greasing
225g/8oz/scant I cup caster/superfine sugar
4 large eggs, lightly beaten
225g/8oz/1½ cups self-raising flour, sifted
finely grated zest of 2 lemons
I recipe quantity Vanilla Buttercream
(see page 24)
3 tbsp passion fruit curd
icing/powdered sugar, for dusting
450g/1lb ready-to-roll icing

a few drops of yellow food colouring
½ quantity Royal Icing (see page 24)

TO DECORATE
60g/2oz marzipan
2 small sheets edible gold leaf
3.5cm/1½in high floral foam dome on
a plastic base with self-adhesive pad
yellow and golden flowers
1.5m x 3cm/5ft x 1¼in wide gold ribbon

1 Preheat the oven to 180°C/350°F/gas 4. Grease and base-line two 20cm/8in sandwich cake tins.

2 Put the butter and sugar in a mixing bowl and beat using an electric hand mixer or wooden spoon until the mixture is light and creamy. Add the eggs gradually, beating after each addition. Add the flour and lemon zest and gently fold them into the mixture, using a large metal spoon. Divide the mixture between the tins using a spatula.

3 Bake for 25–30 minutes until the cakes spring back when pressed lightly. Remove from the oven, turn out on to a wire rack and leave to cool. Sandwich together with a third of the buttercream and the passion fruit curd. Cover the cake with the remaining buttercream.

4 Sift icing sugar on to a clean work surface and roll out the ready-to-roll icing to 5mm/¼in thick using a rolling pin. Lift the icing on top of the cake, using the rolling pin to help, and smooth down with your hands to make sure there are no creases. Trim the icing around the bottom of the cake with a sharp knife.

5 Stir the food colouring into the royal icing until the colour is uniform, then spoon it into an icing bag with a 13mm/½in star nozzle and pipe stars around the base and top of the cake.

6 Roll out the marzipan to 5mm/¼in thick with the rolling pin on the dusted work surface. Crumble the gold leaf sheets on top and roll again to press them into the marzipan. Cut out the numbers '5' and '0' using large number cutters or a sharp knife. Using a pastry brush, lightly brush a very small amount of water on to the top cake where you want to place the numbers, which should be offset to one side, then press them into place.

7 When you are ready to display the cake, soak the floral foam in water for a few minutes. Cut the flower stems down to 2.5cm/1in long and press them into the foam, covering the entire dome to the top with flowers. Remove the backing paper on the self-adhesive pad on the base of the plastic tray and stick the flower dome behind the numbers on the top cake. Wrap the golden ribbon around the cake and tie in a bow.

292 VALENTINE RIBBON HEARTS

PREPARATION TIME 25 minutes, plus chilling   **COOKING TIME** 12–15 minutes   **MAKES** 12 cookies

115g/4oz butter, softened, plus extra
   for greasing
55g/2oz/¼ cup caster/superfine sugar
175g/6oz/heaped 1 cup plain/all-purpose
   flour, sifted, plus extra for dusting

1 tbsp milk (optional)
3m x 3mm/10ft x ⅛in ribbon

1   Put the butter and sugar in a mixing bowl and beat using an electric hand mixer or wooden spoon until the mixture is light and creamy. Add the flour and mix together with your hands to form a soft dough, adding the milk if the mixture is too dry. Wrap in cling film/plastic wrap and refrigerate for 1 hour.

2 Preheat the oven to 180°C/350°F/gas 4. Grease two 30cm/12in square baking trays.

3 Sift flour on to a clean work surface and roll the dough out to about 1cm/⅜in thick using a rolling pin. Cut out 12 heart shapes using a large heart cutter or a cardboard template and a knife, gathering up the trimmings and re-rolling as necessary. Place the cookies on the baking trays and, using a skewer or cocktail stick/toothpick, make two 5mm/¼in holes at the top of the cookies on either side of the centre of the heart.

4 Bake for 12–15 minutes until golden brown and just firm. Remove the cookies from the oven and use the skewer or cocktail stick to reopen any holes that have closed during cooking while the cookies are still warm. Leave to cool on the trays for a few minutes, then transfer to a wire rack using a palette knife to cool. Cut the ribbon into twelve 25cm/10in lengths. Thread a ribbon through each hole and tie in a bow at the front of each cookie.

293 CHOCOLATE HEART GATEAU

PREPARATION TIME 30 minutes   **COOKING TIME** 25–30 minutes   **SERVES** 10–12

350g/12oz butter, softened, plus extra
    for greasing
350g/12oz/1⅓ cups caster/superfine sugar
6 large eggs, lightly beaten
280g/10oz/scant 2 cups self-raising flour
55g/2oz/⅓ cup cocoa powder
300ml/10½fl oz/1¼ cups double/heavy
    cream, whipped to stiff peaks

2 tbsp strawberry jam/jelly
400g/14oz/2⅔ cups strawberries,
    hulled and sliced
200g/7oz plain/semisweet chocolate, melted
    and cooled slightly

1 Preheat the oven to 180°C/350°F/gas 4. Grease and base-line two 30cm/12in heart-shaped cake tins.

2 Put the butter and sugar in a mixing bowl and beat using an electric hand mixer or wooden spoon until the mixture is light and creamy. Add the eggs gradually, beating after each addition. Sift in the flour and cocoa and gently fold them into the mixture, using a large metal spoon. Divide the mixture between the tins using a spatula.

3 Bake for 25–30 minutes until the cakes spring back when pressed lightly and a skewer inserted into the middle of each cake comes out clean. Remove the cakes from the oven and leave to stand for 5 minutes, then turn out on to a wire rack and leave to cool.

4 Place one of the cakes on a serving plate or board. Cover the top of the cake with the whipped cream, jam and strawberry slices, retaining about 30 slices for decoration. Place the second cake on top and cover with the melted chocolate. Arrange the reserved strawberry slices around the edge of the cake. Leave the chocolate to set before serving.

294 VALENTINE CUPCAKES

PREPARATION TIME 40 minutes   **COOKING TIME** 15–20 minutes   **MAKES** 24 cakes

225g/8oz butter, softened
225g/8oz/scant 1 cup caster/superfine sugar
4 large eggs, lightly beaten
225g/8oz/1½ cups self-raising flour
4 tbsp cocoa powder
3 tbsp natural/plain yogurt
24 chocolate-covered soft caramels

1 recipe quantity Chocolate Ganache
   (see page 22)

TO DECORATE
heart-shaped sugar sprinkles
edible silver balls

1 Preheat the oven to 180°C/350°F/gas 4. Put 24 cake cases/liners in two 12-hole bun tins.
2 Put the butter and sugar in a mixing bowl and beat using an electric hand mixer or wooden spoon until the mixture is light and creamy. Add the eggs gradually, beating after each addition. Sift in the flour and cocoa and gently fold them into the mixture with the yogurt, using a large metal spoon.
3 Put a spoonful of cake mixture into each cake case. Place a chocolate-covered caramel in the centre of each cake and top with a further spoonful of cake mixture, so that the caramel is completely covered.
4 Bake for 15–20 minutes until the cakes spring back when pressed lightly and a skewer inserted into the middle of a cake comes out clean. Remove the cakes from the oven, turn out on to a wire rack and leave to cool.
5 Cover each cake with ganache and sprinkle over the heart-shaped sprinkles and silver balls to decorate. Leave the ganache to set before serving.

295 ST PATRICK'S DAY CUPCAKES

PREPARATION TIME 40 minutes   **COOKING TIME** 15–20 minutes   **MAKES** 12 cakes

115g/4oz butter, softened
115g/4oz/scant ½ cup caster/superfine sugar
2 large eggs, lightly beaten
115g/4oz/¾ cup self-raising flour, sifted
1 recipe quantity Vanilla Buttercream
   (see page 24)

TO DECORATE
55g/2oz/heaped ½ cup desiccated/dried
   shredded coconut
a few drops of green food colouring
orange-coloured sugar-coated chocolate
   beans or orange sweets/candies
12 mini Irish flags on cocktail sticks/
   toothpicks

1 Preheat the oven to 180°C/350°F/gas 4. Put 12 cake cases/liners in a 12-hole bun tin.
2 Put the butter and sugar in a mixing bowl and beat using an electric hand mixer or wooden spoon until the mixture is light and creamy. Add the eggs gradually, beating after each addition. Add the flour and gently fold it into the mixture, using a large metal spoon. Spoon the mixture into the cake cases.
3 Bake for 15–20 minutes until the cakes spring back when pressed lightly and a skewer inserted into the middle of a cake comes out clean. Remove the cakes from the oven, turn out on to a wire rack and leave to cool.
4 Cover each cake with buttercream using a round-bladed knife. Mix the desiccated coconut with the green food colouring so that the coconut is uniformly coloured green, then sprinkle some of the coconut over each cake. Top with the orange chocolate beans or sweets and fix a mini Irish flag in the centre of each cake.

296 EASTER EGG CUPCAKES

PREPARATION TIME 40 minutes   **COOKING TIME** 15–20 minutes   **MAKES** 24 cakes

225g/8oz butter
225g/8oz/scant 1 cup caster/superfine sugar
4 large eggs, lightly beaten
225g/8oz/1½ cups self-raising flour
4 tbsp cocoa powder
3 tbsp natural/plain yogurt

100g/3½oz Easter egg or milk chocolate, broken into small pieces
a few drops of yellow food colouring
2 recipe quantities Vanilla Buttercream (see page 24)
sugar or chocolate eggs, to decorate

1 Preheat the oven to 180°C/350°F/gas 4. Put 24 cake cases/liners in two 12-hole bun tins.
2 Put the butter and sugar in a mixing bowl and beat using an electric hand mixer or wooden spoon until the mixture is light and creamy. Add the eggs gradually, beating after each addition. Sift in the flour and cocoa and gently fold them into the mixture with the yogurt and Easter egg pieces or chocolate, using a large metal spoon. Spoon the mixture into the cake cases.
3 Bake for 15–20 minutes until the cakes spring back when pressed lightly and a skewer inserted into the middle of a cake comes out clean. Remove the cakes from the oven, turn out on to a wire rack and leave to cool.
4 Stir the food colouring into the buttercream until the colour is uniform. Spoon the buttercream into an icing bag fitted with a 13mm/½in star nozzle and pipe swirls on top of the cakes. Decorate each cake with a few sugar or chocolate eggs.

297 SIMNEL CAKE

PREPARATION TIME 45 minutes   **COOKING TIME** 1¾–2 hours   **SERVES** 10

175g/6oz butter, softened, plus extra
    for greasing
175g/6oz/¾ cup light soft brown sugar
3 large eggs, lightly beaten, plus
    1 large egg yolk (optional)
225g/8oz/1½ cups plain/all-purpose flour
1 tsp baking powder
2 tsp ground cinnamon
1 tsp mixed/pumpkin pie spice
400g/14oz/2 cups sultanas/golden raisins
100g/3½oz/½ cup glacé/candied
    cherries, halved

100g/3½oz/½ cup mixed/candied peel
finely grated zest of 1 orange
finely grated zest of 1 lemon
icing/powdered sugar, for dusting
450g/1lb marzipan
3 tbsp apricot jam/jelly

TO DECORATE
sugar flowers
1.5m x 3cm/5ft x 1¼in yellow ribbon

1 Preheat the oven to 160°C/325°F/gas 3. Grease and line a deep 20cm/8in springform cake tin.

2 Put the butter and light brown sugar in a mixing bowl and beat using an electric hand mixer or wooden spoon until the mixture is light and creamy. Add the whole eggs gradually, beating after each addition. Sift in the flour, baking powder, ground cinnamon and mixed spice and gently fold them into the mixture with the sultanas, cherries, mixed peel and orange and lemon zests. Spoon half the cake mixture into the tin.

3 Sift icing sugar on to a clean work surface and cut the marzipan in half. Roll out one half to 5mm/¼in thick using a rolling pin and cut out a circle of marzipan the size of the cake tin, saving the trimmings for later. Place the marzipan on top of the bottom layer of the cake mixture in the tin and cover with the remaining cake mixture.

4 Bake for 1¾–2 hours until a skewer inserted into the middle of the cake comes out clean. Remove the cake from the oven and leave to cool in the tin.

5 Roll out the remaining marzipan as before and cut out a second circle the size of your cake tin. Retain the trimmings again. Warm the jam in a small saucepan, then remove the cake from the tin, brush the top with some of the jam and cover with the marzipan.

6 Roll the marzipan trimmings into 11 small balls to represent the 11 apostles and place around the edge of the cake, securing with a little more of the jam. If wished, brush the top of the marzipan lightly with a little of the egg yolk, using a pastry brush, and place under a hot grill for a few minutes until the marzipan starts to brown. Fix the sugar flowers between the balls with the remaining jam and tie the ribbon around the cake.

298 GLAZED EASTER COOKIES

PREPARATION TIME 25 minutes, plus chilling   **COOKING TIME** 12–15 minutes   **MAKES** 12 cookies

115g/4oz butter, softened, plus extra
    for greasing
55g/2oz/¼ cup caster/superfine sugar
175g/6oz/heaped 1 cup plain/all-purpose
    flour, sifted, plus extra for dusting
55g/2oz marzipan, chilled then grated
55g/2oz/⅓ cup sultanas/golden raisins
1 tsp almond extract

200g/7oz/1⅓ cups icing/powdered
    sugar, sifted
a few drops of yellow food colouring

TO DECORATE
sugar flowers
edible silver balls

1 Put the butter and caster sugar in a mixing bowl and beat using an electric hand mixer or wooden spoon until the mixture is light and creamy. Add the flour, grated marzipan, sultanas and almond extract and mix together with your hands to form a soft dough. Wrap in cling film/plastic wrap and refrigerate for 1 hour.
2 Preheat the oven to 180°C/350°F/gas 4. Grease two 30cm/12in square baking trays.
3 Sift flour on to a clean work surface and roll the dough out to about 1cm/⅜in thick, using a rolling pin. Cut out 12 rounds using a 7.5cm/3in round cutter, gathering up the trimmings and re-rolling as necessary. Place the cookies on the baking trays.
4 Bake for 12–15 minutes until golden brown and just firm. Remove the cookies from the oven and leave to cool on the trays for a few minutes, then transfer to a wire rack with a palette knife to cool.
5 Mix the icing sugar with 1–2 tablespoons water and the food colouring to make a runny icing/frosting. Spoon over the cookies and decorate with the sugar flowers and silver balls.

299 MOTHER'S DAY ROSE PETAL SPONGE

PREPARATION TIME 35 minutes   **COOKING TIME** 25–30 minutes   **SERVES** 10

225g/8oz butter, softened, plus extra
    for greasing
225g/8oz/scant 1 cup caster/superfine sugar
4 large eggs, lightly beaten
225g/8oz/1½ cups self-raising flour
1 tsp baking powder
1 tsp vanilla extract
115g/4oz/scant 1 cup pistachio nuts,
    finely chopped

1 recipe quantity Rose Petal Paste
    (see page 24)
250ml/9fl oz/1 cup double/heavy cream,
    whipped to stiff peaks
115g/4oz/¾ cup icing/powdered sugar, sifted
1–2 tbsp rose syrup or rosewater
1 recipe quantity Frosted Rose Petals
    (see page 22), to decorate

1 Preheat the oven to 180°C/350°F/gas 4. Grease and base-line two 20cm/8in sandwich cake tins.

2 Put the butter and sugar in a mixing bowl and beat using an electric hand mixer or wooden spoon until the mixture is light and creamy. Add the eggs gradually, beating after each addition. Sift in the flour and baking powder and gently fold them into the mixture with the vanilla extract and two-thirds of the pistachios, using a large metal spoon. Divide the mixture between the tins using a spatula.

3 Bake for 25–30 minutes until the cakes spring back when pressed lightly and a skewer inserted into the middle of each cake comes out clean. Remove the cakes from the oven and leave to stand for 5 minutes, then turn out on to a wire rack and leave to cool.

4 Fold the rose petal paste into the whipped cream, using a large metal spoon and use to sandwich the cakes together. Mix the icing sugar with the rose syrup to form a smooth icing/frosting and spread over the top of the cake. Sprinkle over the remaining chopped pistachios and decorate with the frosted rose petals.

300 FATHER'S DAY BISCUITS

PREPARATION TIME 25 minutes, plus chilling   **COOKING TIME** 12–15 minutes   **MAKES** 10 biscuits

115g/4oz butter, softened, plus extra
    for greasing
55g/2oz/¼ cup caster/superfine sugar
175g/6oz/heaped 1 cup plain/all-purpose
    flour, sifted, plus extra for dusting
1 tbsp milk (optional)

200g/7oz/1⅓ cups icing/powdered
    sugar, sifted
a few drops of food colouring of choice

TO DECORATE
flat, fizzy fruit-liquorice strips
sugar-coated chocolate beans

1 Put the butter and caster sugar in a mixing bowl and beat using an electric hand mixer or wooden spoon until the mixture is light and creamy. Add the flour and mix together with your hands to form a soft dough, adding the milk if the mixture is too dry. Wrap in cling film/plastic wrap and refrigerate for 1 hour.

2 Preheat the oven to 180°C/350°F/gas 4. Grease two 30cm/12in square baking trays.

3 Sift flour on to a clean work surface and roll the dough out to about 1cm/⅜in thick using a rolling pin. Cut out 10 tie shapes of your choice (bow ties, thin ties or fat ties), gathering up the trimmings and re-rolling as necessary. Place the biscuits on the baking trays.

4 Bake for 12–15 minutes until golden brown and just firm. Remove from the oven and leave to cool on the trays for a few minutes, then transfer to a wire rack with a palette knife to cool.

5 Mix the icing sugar with the food colouring and 1–2 tablespoons water to form a smooth icing/frosting and spread some over each biscuit. Decorate with the liquorice strips to make striped ties and the chocolate beans to make spotted ties. Leave the icing to set.

301 BONFIRE NIGHT TREACLE COOKIES

PREPARATION TIME 15 minutes   **COOKING TIME** 14–18 minutes   **MAKES** 18 cookies

125g/4½oz butter, softened, plus extra
   for greasing
350g/12oz/2⅓ cups self-raising flour
a pinch salt
½ tsp bicarbonate of soda/baking soda
1 tsp ground ginger

1 tsp ground cinnamon
200g/7oz/heaped ¾ cup caster/
   superfine sugar
1 tbsp golden syrup
1 tbsp treacle
1 large egg, beaten

1 Preheat the oven to 180°C/350°F/gas 4. Grease two 30cm/12in square baking trays.
2 Sift the flour, salt, bicarbonate of soda, ginger and ground cinnamon into a mixing bowl, add the sugar and stir with a wooden spoon. Put the butter, syrup and treacle in a saucepan and heat gently until the butter has melted. Cool slightly, then stir into the dry ingredients. Beat in the egg to make a soft dough.
3 Divide the dough into 18 walnut-size pieces and place on the baking trays, leaving about 5cm/2in between them to allow for spreading.
4 Bake for 12–15 minutes until golden brown and just firm. Remove the cookies from the oven and leave to cool on the trays for a few minutes, then transfer to a wire rack with a palette knife to cool.

302 HALLOWEEN CUPCAKES

PREPARATION TIME 40 minutes   **COOKING TIME** 15–20 minutes   **MAKES** 12 cakes

115g/4oz butter, softened
115g/4oz/scant ½ cup caster/superfine sugar
2 large eggs, lightly beaten
115g/4oz/¾ cup self-raising flour, sifted
a few drops each of green and orange
   food colourings

1 recipe quantity Vanilla Buttercream
   (see page 24)
Halloween sweets/candies and chocolates,
   to decorate

1 Preheat the oven to 180°C/350°F/gas 4. Put 12 cake cases/liners in a 12-hole bun tin.
2 Put the butter and sugar in a mixing bowl and beat using an electric hand mixer or wooden spoon until the mixture is light and creamy. Add the eggs gradually, beating after each addition. Add the flour and gently fold it into the mixture, using a large metal spoon.
3 Divide the cake mixture between 2 bowls and colour one green and one orange using a few drops of the food colourings. Spoon the orange cake mixture into half the cake cases and the green cake mixture into the other half.
4 Bake for 15–20 minutes until the cakes spring back when pressed lightly and a skewer

inserted into the middle of a cake comes out clean. Remove the cakes from the oven, turn out on to a wire rack and leave to cool.

5 Remove the cake cases from each cake and turn upside down. Divide the buttercream between 2 bowls and colour one green and one orange, using more of the food colourings. Spread orange icing over the green cakes and green icing over the orange cakes and top each cake with some Halloween sweets and chocolates.

303 HALLOWEEN GHOST COOKIES

PREPARATION TIME 25 minutes, plus chilling   **COOKING TIME** 12–15 minutes   **MAKES** 10 cookies

115g/4oz butter, softened, plus extra
    for greasing
55g/2oz/¼ cup caster/superfine sugar
175g/6oz/heaped 1 cup plain/all-purpose
    flour, plus extra for dusting

1 tsp ground cinnamon
1 tbsp milk (optional)
200g/7oz/1⅓ cups icing/powdered
    sugar, sifted
20 plain/semisweet chocolate chips

1 Put the butter and caster sugar in a mixing bowl and beat using an electric hand mixer or wooden spoon until the mixture is light and creamy. Sift in the flour and ground cinnamon and mix together with your hands to form a soft dough, adding the milk if the mixture is too dry. Wrap in cling film/plastic wrap and refrigerate for 1 hour.

2 Preheat the oven to 180°C/350°F/gas 4. Grease two 30cm/12in square baking trays.

3 Sift flour on to a clean work surface and roll the dough out to about 1cm/⅜in thick using a rolling pin. Cut out 10 ghost shapes using a cutter or a cardboard template and a knife, gathering up the trimmings and re-rolling as necessary. Place the cookies on the baking trays.

4 Bake for 12–15 minutes until golden brown and just firm. Remove the cookies from the oven and leave to cool on the trays for a few minutes, then transfer to a wire rack with a palette knife to cool.

5 Mix the icing sugar with 1–2 tablespoons water to make a runny icing/frosting. Using a round-bladed knife, cover each cookie in icing and decorate with 2 chocolate chips for eyes. Leave the icing to set before serving.

304 CANDY CANE CAKE

PREPARATION TIME 50 minutes   **COOKING TIME** 2½–3 hours   **SERVES** 15

225g/8oz butter, softened, plus extra
    for greasing
250g/9oz/1 cup caster/superfine sugar
4 large eggs, lightly beaten

225g/8oz/1½ cups self-raising flour
1 tsp ground cinnamon
400g/14oz/2 cups sultanas/golden raisins
200g/7oz/1 cup glacé/candied cherries, halved

2 tbsp orange liqueur, such as Cointreau
1 tbsp golden syrup
450g/1lb marzipan
2 tbsp apricot jam/jelly

1 recipe quantity Royal Icing (see page 24)
8 candy canes
1.5m x 5cm/5ft x 2in red ribbon

1   Preheat the oven to 150°C/300°F/gas 2. Grease and line a deep 20cm/8in springform cake tin. Wrap the sides in a double layer of brown paper and tie with string.
2   Put the butter and sugar in a mixing bowl and beat using an electric hand mixer or wooden spoon until the mixture is light and creamy. Add the eggs gradually, beating after each addition. Sift in the flour and ground cinnamon and gently fold them into the mixture with the sultanas, cherries, Cointreau and syrup, using a large metal spoon. Scrape the mixture into the tin using a spatula.
3   Bake for 2½–3 hours until a skewer comes out clean with no cake mixture on it. Remove the cake from the oven and leave to cool in the tin, then turn out.
4   Apply the marzipan and royal icing to the cake following step 6 in recipe 305. Arrange the candy canes around the side of the cake and fix them in place by wrapping the ribbon around the cake and tying it in a bow at the front.

305 ICED CHRISTMAS CAKE

PREPARATION TIME 50 minutes, plus soaking   **COOKING TIME** 2½–3 hours   **SERVES** 15

1kg/2lb 4oz/5½ cups mixed fruit (sultanas, raisins, currants)
200g/7oz/1 cup glacé/candied cherries, halved
125ml/4fl oz/½ cup almond liqueur, such as amaretto, plus extra for feeding the cake
225g/8oz butter, softened, plus extra for greasing
175g/6oz/1 cup lightly packed dark muscovado sugar
55g/2oz/¼ cup caster/superfine sugar
4 large eggs, lightly beaten
55g/2oz/⅓ cup self-raising flour
175g/6oz/heaped 1 cup plain/all-purpose flour
1 tsp ground cinnamon

1 tsp mixed/pumpkin pie spice
¼ tsp freshly grated nutmeg
200g/7oz/1½ cups mixed unsalted nuts, roughly chopped
finely grated zest of 2 lemons
1 tbsp treacle
icing/powdered sugar, for dusting
450g/1lb marzipan
2 tbsp apricot jam/jelly
1 recipe quantity Royal Icing (see page 24)
Christmas figures and edible glitter, to decorate

1   Soak the mixed fruit and glacé cherries in the amaretto overnight.
2   Preheat the oven to 150°C/300°F/gas 2. Grease and line a 23cm/9in loose-bottomed square cake tin. Wrap the sides in a double layer of brown paper and tie with string.

3 Put the butter, muscovado sugar and caster sugar in a mixing bowl and beat using an electric hand mixer or wooden spoon until the mixture is light and creamy. Add the eggs gradually, beating after each addition. Sift in the self-raising and plain flours and spices and gently fold them into the mixture with the nuts, lemon zest, treacle, soaked fruits and amaretto, using a large metal spoon. Scrape the mixture into the tin using a spatula.

4 Bake for about 2½–3 hours until a skewer comes out clean with no cake mixture on it. (If the top of the cake starts to brown too much, cover it with a piece of baking parchment.) Remove the cake from the oven and leave to cool in the tin, then turn out.

5 Wrap the cake in greaseproof paper and cling film/plastic wrap and store in a sealed tin. Open once a week, prick the surface with a skewer and pour over 1–2 tablespoons of the amaretto. The more weeks you do this, the richer the cake will become. A month is ideal.

6 When you are ready to serve, sift icing sugar on to a clean work surface and roll out the marzipan to 5mm/¼in thick using a rolling pin. Heat the jam in a small saucepan and brush it over the cake, then cover with the marzipan, flattening down the top and sides with your hands. Cover the marzipan with royal icing forked into 'snow' and position the Christmas figures in the centre. Dust the cake with edible glitter and leave the icing to set before serving.

306 YULE LOG

PREPARATION TIME 30 minutes   **COOKING TIME** 10–12 minutes   **SERVES** 8

butter, for greasing
3 large eggs
85g/3oz/⅓ cup caster/superfine sugar
85g/3oz/heaped ½ cup self-raising flour
1 tsp baking powder

55g/2oz plain/semisweet chocolate, melted and cooled slightly
1 recipe quantity Chocolate Buttercream (see page 24)
icing/powdered sugar, for dusting

1 Preheat the oven to 180°C/350°F/gas 4. Grease and line a 30 x 20cm/12 x 8in Swiss/jelly roll tin.

2 Put the eggs and sugar in a mixing bowl and whisk together using an electric hand mixer or a whisk until the mixture is creamy and pale yellow and the whisk leaves a trail when lifted up. Sift in the flour and baking powder and add the melted chocolate, then fold them in, using a large metal spoon. Scrape the mixture into the tin using a spatula.

3 Bake for 10–12 minutes until the cake springs back when pressed lightly. Remove the cake from the oven and leave for a few minutes.

4 Put a sheet of baking parchment on a clean work surface. Turn the cake out on to the paper, cover with a damp dish towel and leave for 10 minutes. Remove the towel and paper and cut away the edges of the cake to neaten it. Roll up the cake from a short end using the paper to help you and leave to cool completely. (The paper will end up inside the cake.)

5 When the cake has cooled, unroll it. Spread a third of the buttercream over the cake. Roll the Swiss roll up again using the paper to help you but this time not rolling it inside the cake and place on a serving plate. Cover with the remaining buttercream and use a fork to make patterns in the cream resembling bark. Dust with icing sugar.

307 CHRISTMAS CLOUD CAKE

PREPARATION TIME 40 minutes   **COOKING TIME** 1 hour 5 minutes   **SERVES** 8

butter, for greasing
4 large egg whites
½ tsp cream of tartar
250g/9oz/1 cup caster/superfine sugar
225g/8oz/¾ cup mincemeat (gf)
2 tbsp almond liqueur, such as amaretto

1 eating apple, peeled, cored and grated
400g/14oz/2 cups preserved cherries
400ml/14fl oz/1½ cups double/heavy cream,
    whipped to stiff peaks
seeds of 1 pomegranate

1 Preheat the oven to 140°C/275°F/gas 1. Grease and base-line a 20cm/8in springform cake tin.

2 Put the egg whites in a clean, dry bowl and whisk with an electric hand mixer or a whisk until they form stiff peaks. Add the cream of tartar and whisk again, then add the sugar, a little at a time, whisking to form a glossy meringue. Pour the meringue into the cake tin, pushing it up the sides to make a well in the centre to contain the filling.

3 Bake for 1 hour until crisp. Remove the meringue from the oven and leave to cool in the tin.

4 Heat the mincemeat with the amaretto, grated apple and a quarter of the cherries in a saucepan over a gentle heat for 5 minutes. Leave to cool completely, then fold into the whipped cream. Remove the cake from the tin and place on a serving plate. Fill with the mincemeat mixture and top with the remaining cherries and the pomegranate seeds.

308 CINNAMON ORANGE STOLLEN

PREPARATION TIME 30 minutes, plus soaking and rising   **COOKING TIME** 25–30 minutes   **SERVES** 10

55g/2oz/⅓ cup raisins
55g/2oz/⅓ cup sultanas/golden raisins
55g/2oz/¼ cup glacé/candied cherries,
    chopped
55g/2oz/⅓ cup toasted flaked/sliced almonds
55g/2oz/⅓ cup mixed/candied peel
100ml/3½fl oz/scant ½ cup orange liqueur,
    such as Cointreau
150ml/5fl oz/scant ⅔ cup warm milk
3 tbsp clear honey

2 tsp fast action dried yeast
450g/1lb/3 cups plain/all-purpose flour,
    plus extra for dusting
4 tsp ground cinnamon
finely grated zest of 1 orange
115g/4oz butter, melted and cooled,
    plus extra for greasing and brushing
1 large egg, lightly beaten
150g/5½oz marzipan
2 tsp icing/powdered sugar, for dusting

1 Put the raisins, sultanas, cherries, flaked almonds and mixed peel in a bowl with the Cointreau. Cover and leave to soak overnight.

2 The next day, put the warm milk, honey and yeast in a cup and leave for 10–20 minutes until foamy. Sift the flour and 2 teaspoons of the ground cinnamon into a large mixing bowl, add the orange zest, melted butter and egg and mix with your hands to form a dough. Add the soaked fruit and nuts.

3 Sift flour on to a clean work surface and turn the dough out of the bowl. Knead vigorously with your hands until you have a soft, pliable dough. Put the dough back in the bowl and cover with a damp dish towel. Leave to rise in a warm place for 1–1½ hours or until the dough has doubled in size.

4 Tip the dough on to the floured work surface and punch it a few times to knock the air out of it, then roll it out into a 30 x 15cm/12 x 6in rectangle. Roll the marzipan into a 30cm/12in long sausage shape with your fingertips and place in the centre of the dough. Fold the sides of the dough together over the marzipan, pressing them together well to seal the dough. Grease a 30cm/12in square baking tray and place the loaf on the tray. Cover with a damp dish towel and leave to rise in a warm place for 30 minutes until it has doubled in size.

5 Preheat the oven to 190°C/375°F/gas 5. Bake for 25–30 minutes until the bread sounds hollow when you pick it up with an oven glove and tap it underneath. Remove the loaf from the oven and brush with a little melted butter. Mix the icing sugar with the remaining ground cinnamon and dust over the stollen. Serve warm or cold.

309 TWELFTH NIGHT CAKE

PREPARATION TIME 25 minutes, plus soaking **COOKING TIME** 1½–1¾ hours **SERVES** 10

55g/2oz/⅓ cup mixed/candied peel
115g/4oz/heaped ½ cup raisins
115g/4oz/heaped ½ cup sultanas/
   golden raisins
115g/4oz/½ cup dried apricots, chopped
100g/3½oz/½ cup glacé/candied cherries,
   chopped
3 tbsp orange liqueur, such as Cointreau
225g/8oz butter, softened, plus extra
   for greasing

225g/8oz/scant 1 cup caster/superfine sugar
4 large eggs, lightly beaten
250g/9oz/1⅔ cups self-raising flour
1 tsp ground cinnamon
1 tsp mixed/pumpkin pie spice
1 tsp ground ginger
1 whole blanched almond
icing/powdered sugar, for dusting

1 Put the mixed peel, raisins, sultanas, apricots and cherries in a bowl with the Cointreau. Cover and leave to soak overnight.

2 Preheat the oven to 160°C/325°F/gas 3. Grease and line a 20cm/8in springform cake tin.

3 Put the butter and caster sugar in a mixing bowl and beat using an electric hand mixer or wooden spoon until the mixture is light and creamy. Add the eggs gradually, beating after

each addition. Sift in the flour, ground cinnamon, mixed spice and ginger and gently fold them into the mixture with the soaked fruit and whole almond, using a large metal spoon. Scrape the mixture into the tin using a spatula.

4 Bake for 1½–1¾ hours until the cake springs back when pressed lightly and a skewer inserted into the middle of the cake comes out clean. Remove the cake from the oven and leave to cool in the tin, then turn out.

5 When you serve the cake on Twelfth Night, tradition has it that whoever gets the almond (originally a bean) in their slice, becomes the king or queen of the festivities for the day.

310 AMARETTO GINGERBREAD NUT RING

PREPARATION TIME 30 minutes, plus soaking **COOKING TIME** 60–70 minutes **SERVES** 10

100g/3½oz/½ cup raisins

100g/3½oz/½ cup glacé/candied cherries, halved

125ml/4fl oz/½ cup almond liqueur, such as amaretto

225g/8oz butter, softened, plus extra for greasing

125g/4½oz/scant 1 cup plain/all-purpose flour, plus extra for dusting

125g/4½oz/heaped ½ cup dark soft brown sugar

2 large eggs, lightly beaten

2 tbsp golden syrup

2 tbsp treacle

100g/3½oz/⅔ cup self-raising flour

1 tsp bicarbonate of soda/baking soda

125ml/4fl oz/½ cup milk

4 pieces of stem/preserved ginger in syrup, finely chopped

400g/14oz/2⅔ cups combined pistachio and brazil nuts

250g/9oz/1 cup caster/superfine sugar

150g/5½oz cream cheese

400g/14oz/2⅔ cups icing/powdered sugar, sifted

2 tbsp of the stem ginger syrup

1 Put the raisins and cherries in a bowl with the amaretto. Cover and leave to soak overnight. Preheat the oven to 160°C/325°F/gas 3. Grease a 23cm/9in ring tin and dust with flour.

2 Put 125g/4½oz of the butter and the dark brown sugar in a mixing bowl and beat using an electric hand mixer or wooden spoon until the mixture is light and creamy. Add the eggs gradually, beating after each addition, then add the syrup and treacle and beat again. Sift in the plain and self-raising flours and the bicarbonate of soda and fold them into the mixture with the milk, soaked fruit, amaretto and chopped stem ginger, mixing well. Scrape the mixture into the tin using a spatula.

3 Bake for 50–60 minutes until the cake springs back when pressed lightly and a skewer inserted into the cake comes out clean. Remove the cake from the oven and leave to cool in the tin, then turn out on to a serving plate.

4 Dry-fry the nuts in a frying pan for 3–5 minutes. Grease a large baking tray with butter and sprinkle the nuts over the tray. Heat the caster sugar in a heavy-based saucepan for

about 5 minutes until the sugar has dissolved and starts to turn golden. Remove from the heat immediately and pour the caramel over the nuts. Leave to cool.

5 Whisk together the cream cheese, icing sugar, remaining butter and ginger syrup in a bowl to form a smooth icing. Cover the cake with the icing, using a round-bladed knife. Break the caramel nuts into shards and use to decorate the top of the ring.

311 SNOWFLAKE COOKIES

PREPARATION TIME 25 minutes, plus chilling **COOKING TIME** 12–15 minutes **MAKES** 10 cookies

115g/4oz butter, softened, plus extra
    for greasing
55g/2oz/¼ cup light muscovado sugar
175g/6oz/heaped 1 cup plain/all-purpose
    flour, plus extra for dusting

1 tbsp ground cinnamon
1 tbsp milk (optional)
1 tbsp icing/powdered sugar, sifted
edible glitter (optional), to decorate

1 Put the butter and muscovado sugar in a mixing bowl and beat using an electric hand mixer or wooden spoon until the mixture is light and creamy. Sift in the flour and 1 teaspoon of the ground cinnamon and mix together with your hands to form a soft dough, adding the milk if the mixture is too dry. Wrap in cling film/plastic wrap and refrigerate for 1 hour.

2 Preheat the oven to 180°C/350°F/gas 4. Grease two 30cm/12in square baking trays.

3 Sift flour on to a clean work surface and roll the dough out to about 1cm/⅜in thick using a rolling pin. Cut out 10 snowflake shapes using different-size snowflake cutters, gathering up the trimmings and re-rolling as necessary. Alternatively, for more elaborate snowflakes, cut out the centre of each cookie with a smaller snowflake cutter to leave you with snowflake outlines; the cut-outs make small biscuits. (If you do not have snowflake cutters, use a 10cm/4in star cutter for the cookies and a 6cm/2⅓in star cutter for the holes, if making, or use cardboard templates and a knife.) Place the cookies on the baking trays.

4 Bake for 12–15 minutes until golden brown and just firm. Remove the cookies from the oven and leave to cool on the trays for a few minutes, then transfer to a wire rack with a palette knife to cool. Mix the remaining ground cinnamon and the icing sugar together and dust them over the cookies. Decorate with edible glitter, if using.

312 RIBBONED CHRISTMAS TREE COOKIES

PREPARATION TIME 25 minutes, plus chilling   **COOKING TIME** 12–15 minutes   **MAKES** 10 cookies

115g/4oz butter, softened, plus extra
   for greasing
55g/2oz/¼ cup light muscovado sugar
175g/6oz/heaped 1 cup plain/all-purpose
   flour, plus extra for dusting

1 tsp ground cinnamon
1 tbsp milk (optional)
6 tbsp icing/powdered sugar, sifted
edible silver balls, to decorate
2m x 3mm/6ft 6in x ⅛in ribbon

1 Put the butter and muscovado sugar in a mixing bowl and beat using an electric hand mixer or wooden spoon until the mixture is light and creamy. Sift in the flour and ground cinnamon and mix together with your hands to form a soft dough, adding the milk if the mixture is too dry. Wrap in cling film/plastic wrap and refrigerate for 1 hour.

2 Preheat the oven to 180°C/350°F/gas 4. Grease two 30cm/12in square baking trays.

3 Sift flour on to a clean work surface and roll the dough out to about 1cm/⅜in thick using a rolling pin. Cut out 10 large festive shapes, such as reindeer and stars, using cutters or cardboard templates and a knife, gathering up the trimmings and re-rolling as necessary. Place the cookies on the baking trays and, using a skewer or cocktail stick/toothpick, make a 5mm/¼in hole in the centre of the top of each cookie.

4 Bake for 12–15 minutes until firm. Remove the cookies from the oven and, while the cookies are still on the baking trays, use the skewer or cocktail stick to reopen any holes

that have closed during cooking while the cookies are still warm. Transfer to a wire rack with a palette knife to cool.

5   Mix the icing sugar with 1 tablespoon water to make a stiff icing/frosting. Spoon into an icing bag fitted with a 3mm/⅛in plain nozzle and pipe lines on to the reindeer to make a saddle and bridle and a white line around the edge of each star. Decorate with silver balls and leave to set. Cut the ribbon into 20cm/8in lengths, thread one length through the hole on each cookie and tie in a knot. Hang the cookies from your Christmas tree for no longer than 5 days if you intend to eat them.

313 CHRISTMAS GLAZED FRUIT CAKE

PREPARATION TIME 50 minutes, plus soaking   **COOKING TIME** 2½–3 hours   **SERVES** 15

1kg/2lb 4oz/5½ cups mixed fruit (sultanas, raisins, currants)

200g/7oz/1 cup glacé/candied cherries, halved

100g/3½oz/¾ cup flaked/sliced almonds

125ml/4fl oz/½ cup brandy, plus extra for feeding the cake

225g/8oz butter, softened, plus extra for greasing

175g/6oz/1 cup lightly packed dark muscovado sugar

55g/2oz/¼ cup caster/superfine sugar

4 large eggs, lightly beaten

175g/6oz/heaped 1 cup plain/all-purpose flour

55g/2oz/⅓ cup self-raising flour

1 tsp ground cinnamon

1 tsp mixed/pumpkin pie spice

¼ tsp freshly grated nutmeg

finely grated zest of 2 oranges

1 tbsp treacle

3 tbsp apricot jam/jelly

juice of 1 lemon

400g/14oz/1¾ cups mixed glacé/candied fruits

1   Soak the mixed fruit, cherries and flaked almonds in the brandy in a bowl overnight.

2   Preheat the oven to 150°C/300°F/gas 2. Grease and line a 23cm/9in loose-bottomed square cake tin.

3   Put the butter, muscovado sugar and caster sugar in a large mixing bowl and beat using an electric hand mixer or wooden spoon until the mixture is light and creamy. Add the eggs and whisk again. Sift in the plain and self-raising flours and the spices and gently fold in with the orange zest, treacle, soaked fruits and nuts and brandy. Scrape the mixture into the tin using a spatula.

4   Bake for 2½–3 hours until a skewer comes out clean with no cake mixture on it. (If the top of the cake starts to brown too much, cover it with a piece of baking parchment.) Remove the cake from the oven and leave to cool in the tin, then turn out.

5   Wrap the cake in greaseproof paper and cling film/plastic wrap and store in a sealed tin. Open once a week, prick the surface with a skewer and pour over 1–2 tablespoons brandy. The more weeks you do this, the richer the cake will become. One month is ideal.

6 When you are ready to serve the cake, heat the jam with the lemon juice in a small saucepan and brush some over the top of the cake with a pastry brush. Arrange the glacé fruits in a decorative pattern on top of the cake and brush with some more of the glaze.

314 CHRISTMAS GLAZED SPICE BISCUITS

PREPARATION TIME 30 minutes   **COOKING TIME** 14–18 minutes   **MAKES** 18 biscuits

115g/3½oz butter, chopped, plus extra
    for greasing
250g/9oz/1⅔ cups plain/all-purpose flour
1 tsp baking powder
1 tsp bicarbonate of soda/baking soda
1 tsp ground cinnamon
1 tsp ground ginger
¼ tsp grated nutmeg

100g/3½oz/scant 1 cup ground almonds
2 tbsp golden syrup
2 tbsp clear honey
finely grated zest of 1 orange plus
    1–2 tbsp of the juice
150g/5½oz/1 cup icing/powdered
    sugar, sifted
1 egg white, beaten

1 Preheat the oven to 180°C/350°F/gas 4. Grease two 30cm/12in square baking trays.
2 Sift the flour, baking powder, bicarbonate of soda and spices into a mixing bowl and stir together with the ground almonds using a wooden spoon. Put the butter, syrup and honey in a saucepan and heat gently until the butter melts. Cool slightly, then stir into the dry ingredients with the orange zest.
3 Divide the dough into 18 walnut-size balls and place on the baking trays, leaving about 5cm/2in gaps for spreading. Press each biscuit down slightly using your fingers.
4 Bake for 12–15 minutes until golden brown and firm. Remove the biscuits from the oven and leave to cool on the trays for a few minutes, then transfer to a wire rack with a palette knife to cool.
5 Mix together the icing sugar, orange juice and egg white and spoon over the biscuits. Leave the icing/frosting to set, then apply a second coat – it will be quite translucent. Leave the second coat to set before serving.

315 GOLD LEAF COOKIES

PREPARATION TIME 20 minutes   **COOKING TIME** 14–18 minutes   **MAKES** 20 cookies

85g/3oz butter, plus extra for greasing
85g/3oz/⅓ cup caster/superfine sugar
300g/10½oz white chocolate, melted
    and cooled slightly
250g/9oz/1⅔ cups self-raising flour

100g/3½oz/⅔ cup plain/all-purpose flour
2 large eggs, lightly beaten
3 small sheets edible gold leaf,
    to decorate

1 Preheat the oven to 180°C/350°F/gas 4. Grease two 30cm/12in square baking trays.
2 Heat the butter and sugar in a large saucepan until the butter has melted and the sugar has dissolved. Add two-thirds of the melted chocolate and leave to cool. Sift the self-raising and plain flours into the saucepan, add the eggs and beat well with a wooden spoon.
3 Place 20 large spoonfuls of the mixture on to the baking trays, leaving about 5cm/2in between them to allow for spreading.
4 Bake for 12–15 minutes until golden brown and just firm. Remove the cookies from the oven and leave to cool on the trays for a few minutes, then transfer to a wire rack with a palette knife to cool. Spread each cookie with a little of the remaining melted chocolate and top with a small piece of gold leaf to decorate.

316 CHINESE NEW YEAR LUCKY BUNS

PREPARATION TIME 40 minutes   **COOKING TIME** 15–20 minutes   **MAKES** 12 buns

115g/4oz butter, softened
115g/4oz/scant ½ cup caster/superfine sugar
2 large eggs, lightly beaten
115g/4oz/¾ cups self-raising flour, sifted
1 tsp red food colouring

1 recipe quantity Vanilla Buttercream
  (see page 24)
gold chocolate coins and red sugar
  sprinkles, to decorate

1 Preheat the oven to 180°C/350°F/gas 4. Put 12 cake cases/liners in a 12-hole bun tin.
2 Put the butter and sugar in a mixing bowl and beat using an electric hand mixer or wooden spoon until the mixture is light and creamy. Add the eggs gradually, beating after each addition. Add the flour and food colouring and gently fold them into the mixture, using a large metal spoon. Spoon the mixture into the cake cases.
3 Bake for 15–20 minutes until the buns spring back when pressed lightly and a skewer inserted into the middle of a bun comes out clean. Remove the buns from the oven, turn out on to a wire rack and leave to cool.
4 Spread buttercream over the buns using a round-bladed knife and decorate with the chocolate coins and sprinkles. Make sure your guests unwrap the coins before eating them.

317 SCANDINAVIAN MAY DAY DOUGHNUTS

PREPARATION TIME 20 minutes   **COOKING TIME** 15–25 minutes   **MAKES** 15 doughnuts

2 large eggs, plus 4 large egg whites
400g/14oz/1⅔ cups caster/superfine sugar
175g/6oz/heaped 1 cup plain/all-purpose flour
4 tsp ground cinnamon

½ tsp freshly grated nutmeg
finely grated zest of 1 large lemon
1½ litres/52fl oz/6 cups vegetable oil,
  for deep-frying

1 In a bowl, whisk together the whole eggs and 175g/6oz/scant ¾ cup of the sugar until light and foamy. Sift in the flour, 2 teaspoons of the ground cinnamon and the nutmeg and fold in with the lemon zest. Put the egg whites in a clean, dry bowl and whisk with an electric hand mixer or a whisk until they form stiff peaks, and fold into the mixture. Spoon the mixture into an icing bag fitted with a 13mm/½in star nozzle.

2 Heat the oil in a deep saucepan to 190°C/375°F or until a cube of bread dropped into the hot oil browns in 30 seconds. Pipe five lines or circles of mixture into the hot oil and cook for 5–8 minutes, turning once, until the doughnuts are golden brown on both sides. Remove the doughnuts from the oil with a slotted spoon and drain on paper towels to remove the excess oil, then keep warm while you fry the remainder.

3 Mix the remaining sugar and ground cinnamon on a plate and coat the warm doughnuts in it.

318 FUNFETTI MARDI GRAS CUPCAKES

PREPARATION TIME 40 minutes   **COOKING TIME** 15–20 minutes   **MAKES** 24 cakes

225g/8oz butter
225g/8oz/scant 1 cup caster/superfine sugar
4 large eggs, lightly beaten
225g/8oz/1½ cups self-raising flour, sifted
3 tbsp natural/plain yogurt
3 tbsp rainbow sugar sprinkles

2 recipe quantities Vanilla Buttercream
   (see page 24)
a few drops each of red and yellow
   food colouring
brightly coloured sweets/candies, popping
   candy and edible glitter, to decorate

1 Preheat the oven to 180°C/350°F/gas 4. Put 24 cake cases/liners in two 12-hole bun tins.

2 Put the butter and sugar in a mixing bowl and beat using an electric hand mixer or wooden spoon until the mixture is light and creamy. Add the eggs gradually, beating after each addition. Add the flour, yogurt and sprinkles and gently fold them into the mixture, using a large metal spoon. Spoon the mixture into the cake cases.

3 Bake for 15–20 minutes until the cakes spring back when pressed lightly. Remove the cakes from the oven, turn out on to a wire rack and leave to cool.

4 Divide the buttercream between 2 bowls. Stir one food colouring into each of the bowls until the colour is uniform. Spoon the icing/frosting into a piping bag fitted with a 13mm/½in star nozzle, putting the red icing on one side and the yellow on the other. Pipe a swirl of 2-tone icing on each cupcake and decorate with the sweets, popping candy and edible glitter.

319 4TH OF JULY STARRY CUPCAKES

PREPARATION TIME 40 minutes   **COOKING TIME** 15–20 minutes   **MAKES** 24 cakes

225g/8oz butter, softened
225g/8oz/scant I cup caster/superfine sugar
4 large eggs, lightly beaten
225g/8oz/1½ cups self-raising flour, sifted
3 tbsp natural/plain yogurt
I tsp vanilla extract
125g/4½oz ready-to-roll icing
red and blue food colouring pastes

icing/powdered sugar, for dusting
2 recipe quantities Vanilla Buttercream
   (see page 24)

TO DECORATE
red and blue sugar sprinkles
edible glitter

1 Preheat the oven to 180°C/350°F/gas 4. Put 24 cake cases/liners in two 12-hole bun tins.
2 Put the butter and caster sugar in a mixing bowl and beat using an electric hand mixer or wooden spoon until the mixture is light and creamy. Add the eggs gradually, beating after each addition. Add the flour, yogurt and vanilla extract and gently fold them into the mixture, using a large metal spoon. Spoon the mixture into the cake cases.
3 Bake for 15–20 minutes until the cakes spring back when pressed lightly and a skewer inserted into the middle of a cake comes out clean. Remove the cakes from the oven, turn out on to a wire rack and leave to cool.
4 Divide the ready-to-roll icing in half and colour one half red and the other blue using the food colouring pastes (see recipe 269 for the method). Sift icing sugar on to a clean work surface and roll the red and blue icings out to 5mm/¼in thick, using a rolling pin. Cut out 12 red and 12 blue stars, using a 2.5cm/1in star cutter.
5 Spoon the buttercream into an icing bag fitted with a 15mm/⅝in plain nozzle and pipe a swirl on to each cupcake. Decorate with the red and blue sprinkles and top each cake with a red or blue star. Sprinkle over the edible glitter to make the stars sparkle.

320 VEG PATCH RETIREMENT CUPCAKES

PREPARATION TIME I hour   **COOKING TIME** 15–20 minutes   **MAKES** 24 cakes

225g/8oz butter
225g/8oz/scant I cup caster/superfine sugar
4 large eggs, lightly beaten
225g/8oz/1½ cups self-raising flour
4 tbsp cocoa powder
2 tbsp natural/plain yogurt
90g/3¼oz/½ cup milk chocolate chips
140g/5oz ready-to-roll icing

red, green and orange food
   colouring pastes
I tsp green food colouring
2 recipe quantities Vanilla Buttercream
   (see page 24)
55g/2oz milk chocolate, finely grated

1 Preheat the oven to 180°C/350°F/gas 4. Put 24 cake cases/liners in two 12-hole bun tins.

2 Put the butter and sugar in a mixing bowl and beat using an electric hand mixer or wooden spoon until the mixture is light and creamy. Add the eggs gradually, beating after each addition. Sift in the flour and cocoa and gently fold them into the mixture with the yogurt and chocolate chips, using a large metal spoon. Spoon the mixture into the cake cases.

3 Bake for 15–20 minutes until the cakes spring back when pressed lightly. Remove the cakes from the oven, turn out on to a wire rack and leave to cool.

4 Divide the ready-to-roll icing into 4 equal pieces and colour one red, one green and one orange (see recipe 269 for the method). Leave the remaining piece white. Roll the red icing into small balls for tomatoes. Roll half the green icing into small balls and press them flat with your fingertips to make leaves. Fold one leaf in half as the lettuce heart, then wrap a further 3 or 4 leaves around the heart to make lettuces. To make cauliflowers, use the same process for the lettuces but use a ball of white icing in the centre and wrap the green leaves around it. Mark dots in the white ball with a cocktail stick/toothpick. Divide the orange icing into 4 pieces and roll into balls. Press the balls to flatten the top and bottom slightly. Make indents vertically around the sides with a knife to form pumpkins.

5 Stir the green food colouring into the buttercream until the colour is uniform. Spread a thick layer of the buttercream over each cake using a round-bladed knife. Sprinkle the grated chocolate over each cupcake and place a sugar vegetable in the centre. Spoon the remaining buttercream into an icing bag fitted with a 15mm/⅝in plain nozzle and pipe small green dots on the tomatoes and pumpkins as stalks and stems. To make your cakes extra special, print out or draw pictures of small seed packets, cut them out and fix them to cocktail sticks with glue or adhesive tape, then poke one into each cake.

321 THANKSGIVING SPICED PUMPKIN CAKE

PREPARATION TIME 30 minutes   **COOKING TIME** 40–50 minutes   **SERVES** 10

175g/6oz butter, softened, plus extra
   for greasing
175g/6oz/scant ¾ cup caster/superfine sugar
3 large eggs, lightly beaten
225g/8oz/1½ cups self-raising flour
1 tsp ground ginger
½ tsp ground cloves
2 tsp ground cinnamon
125ml/4fl oz/½ cup sour cream
200g/7oz canned unsweetened
   pumpkin purée

85g/3oz/heaped ⅓ cup raisins
finely grated zest of 1 large lemon
115g/4oz/heaped ⅔ cup pecan nuts, chopped

FOR THE ICING
150g/5¼oz cream cheese
85g/3oz butter
400g/14oz/2⅔ cups icing/powdered
   sugar, sifted
1 tbsp lemon juice

1 Preheat the oven to 180°C/350°F/gas 4. Grease and line a 20cm/8in springform cake tin.

2 Put the butter and caster sugar in a mixing bowl and beat using an electric hand mixer or wooden spoon until the mixture is light and creamy. Add the eggs gradually, beating after each addition. Sift in the flour and spices and gently fold them into the mixture with the sour cream, pumpkin purée, raisins, lemon zest and half the pecans, using a large metal spoon. Scrape the mixture into the tin using a spatula.

3 Bake for 40–50 minutes until the cake springs back when pressed lightly and a skewer inserted into the middle of the cake comes out clean. Remove the cake from the oven and leave to stand for 5 minutes, then turn out on to a wire rack and leave to cool.

4 Put the icing ingredients in a mixing bowl and beat using an electric hand mixer or wooden spoon to form a smooth icing/frosting. Cover the cake with the icing, sprinkle with the remaining pecans and leave to set before serving.

Chapter 6

CHILDREN'S CAKES & COOKIES

Encouraging children to cook from a young age gives them an essential understanding of food and the confidence to cook for themselves in later life. This chapter is aimed at getting children to put on an apron, get out a mixing bowl and wooden spoon and learn to bake. Most of the recipes are simple and suitable for you to cook with your children. There are also some lovely ideas for children's parties, such as Ladybird Cakes, Fairy Toadstool Meringues and Magnifying Glass Biscuits, with clear peppermint that children can look through. At Christmas time, delight your children with Christmas Tree Biscuits to decorate the tree or Snowman Cupcakes to leave out for Santa. Why not let them help you bake treats for their lunchbox, such as Granola Bars, Lemon Fairy Cakes or Apple Flapjacks? And, after school, let them settle down to homework with a slice of warm Banana Bread or freshly baked cookies and a glass of milk. Whatever your children love, there will be something to tempt them here.

322 RAINBOW CAKE

PREPARATION TIME 25 minutes   **COOKING TIME** 25–30 minutes   **SERVES** 8

225g/8oz butter, softened, plus extra
    for greasing
225g/8oz/scant 1 cup caster/superfine sugar
4 large eggs, lightly beaten
200g/7oz/1⅓ cups self-raising flour
4 tbsp cocoa powder

1 tsp vanilla extract
1 recipe quantity Chocolate Buttercream
    (see page 24)
sugar-coated chocolate beans in rainbow
    colours, to decorate

1. Preheat the oven to 180°C/350°F/gas 4. Grease and base-line two 20cm/8in sandwich cake tins.
2. Put the butter and sugar in a mixing bowl and beat using an electric hand mixer or wooden spoon until the mixture is light and creamy. Add the eggs gradually, beating after each addition. Sift in the flour and cocoa and gently fold them into the mixture with the vanilla extract, using a large metal spoon. Divide the mixture between the tins using a spatula.
3. Bake for 25–30 minutes until the cakes spring back when pressed lightly and a skewer inserted into the middle of each cake comes out clean. Remove the cakes from the oven and leave to stand for 5 minutes, then turn out on to a wire rack and leave to cool.
4. Sandwich the cakes together with half the buttercream and cover the top of the cake with the remainder. Place the coloured chocolate beans on the cake in rings following the rainbow colours: a red ring around the edge of the cake, then a smaller ring of orange beans, then yellow and so on.

323 BANANA BREAD

PREPARATION TIME 15 minutes   **COOKING TIME** 50–60 minutes   **SERVES** 8

115g/4oz butter, softened, plus extra
    for greasing
175g/6oz/¾ cup dark soft brown sugar
2 large eggs, lightly beaten
3 ripe bananas, peeled and mashed
    with a fork

225g/8oz/1½ cups self-raising flour
1 tsp baking powder
55g/2oz/⅓ cup sultanas/golden raisins
115g/4oz/scant 1 cup chopped
    pecan nuts

1. Preheat the oven to 180°C/350°F/gas 4. Grease and line a 24 x 12cm/9½ x 4½in loaf tin.
2. Put the butter and sugar in a mixing bowl and beat using an electric hand mixer or wooden spoon until the mixture is light and creamy. Add the eggs gradually, beating after each addition, then beat in the mashed bananas. Sift in the flour and baking powder and

gently fold them into the mixture with the sultanas and pecans, using a large metal spoon. Scrape the mixture into the tin using a spatula.

3 Bake for 50–60 minutes until the loaf springs back when pressed lightly and a skewer inserted into the middle of the loaf comes out clean. Remove the loaf from the oven and leave to stand for 5 minutes, then turn out on to a wire rack and leave to cool.

324 COCONUT AND RASPBERRY SWISS ROLL

PREPARATION TIME 20 minutes   **COOKING TIME** 10–15 minutes   **SERVES** 6

butter, for greasing
3 large eggs
85g/3oz/⅓ cup caster/superfine sugar
85g/3oz/heaped ½ cup self-raising
   flour, sifted
55g/2oz/heaped ½ cup desiccated/dried
   shredded coconut

3 tbsp icing/powdered sugar, sifted
250ml/9fl oz/1 cup double/heavy cream,
   whipped to stiff peaks
300g/10½oz/2 cups raspberries

1 Preheat the oven to 180°C/350°F/gas 4. Grease and line a 30 x 20cm/12 x 8in Swiss/jelly roll tin.

2 Put the eggs and caster sugar in a mixing bowl and whisk together using an electric hand mixer or a whisk until the mixture is creamy and pale yellow and the whisk leaves a trail when lifted up. Add the flour and half the desiccated coconut and fold them in, using a large metal spoon. Scrape the mixture into the tin using a spatula.

3 Bake for 10–15 minutes until the cake springs back when pressed lightly. Remove the cake from the oven and leave for a few minutes.

4 Put a sheet of baking parchment on a clean work surface. Dust with the icing sugar and sprinkle with the remaining coconut. Turn the cake out on to the sugar- and coconut-covered paper, cover with a damp dish towel and leave to cool for 10 minutes. Remove the dish towel and lining paper and cut away the edges of the cake to neaten it. Roll the cake up from a short end using the sugar- and coconut-covered paper to help you, then leave to cool completely. (The paper will end up rolled inside the cake.)

5 Unroll the cake, spread the whipped cream over and cover with the raspberries. Roll the Swiss roll up, using the paper to help you but this time not rolling it inside the cake, and place on a serving plate. As the Swiss roll contains fresh cream, it should be eaten straight away or stored in a lidded container in the refrigerator.

325 STRAWBERRY & BLUEBERRY MUFFINS

PREPARATION TIME 15 minutes   **COOKING TIME** 20–25 minutes   **MAKES** 10 muffins

250g/9oz/1⅔ cups self-raising flour
1 tsp baking powder
1 tsp bicarbonate of soda/baking soda
100g/3½oz/heaped ⅓ cup caster/
    superfine sugar
150g/5½oz/1 cup blueberries

finely grated zest of 1 lemon
150ml/5fl oz/scant ⅔ cup milk
4 tbsp natural/plain yogurt
100g/3½oz butter, melted and cooled
3 tbsp strawberry jam/jelly
2 large eggs, lightly beaten

1 Preheat the oven to 180°C/350°F/gas 4. Put 10 muffin cases/liners in a 12-hole muffin tin.
2 Sift the flour, baking powder and bicarbonate of soda into a mixing bowl, add the sugar, blueberries and lemon zest and stir well with a wooden spoon.
3 In a separate bowl, whisk together the milk, yogurt, melted butter and jam with an electric hand mixer or a whisk, add the eggs and whisk again. Pour the liquid into the bowl containing the dry ingredients and fold in with a large metal spoon. Do not overmix: the mixture should be thick and slightly lumpy. Spoon the mixture into the muffin cases.
4 Bake for 20–25 minutes until the muffins spring back when pressed lightly and a skewer inserted into the middle of a muffin comes out clean. Remove the muffins from the oven, turn out on to a wire rack and leave to cool.

326 LOLLIPOP CUPCAKES

PREPARATION TIME 20 minutes   **COOKING TIME** 15–20 minutes   **MAKES** 12 cakes

115g/4oz butter, softened
115g/4oz/scant ½ cup caster/superfine sugar
2 large eggs, lightly beaten
115g/4oz/¾ cup self-raising flour, sifted
2 tbsp natural/plain yogurt
12 lollipop/popsicle sticks
200g/7oz plain/semisweet chocolate,
    melted and cooled slightly

TO DECORATE
sugar sprinkles
edible silver balls

1 Preheat the oven to 180°C/350°F/gas 4. Put 12 cake cases/liners in a 12-hole bun tin.
2 Put the butter and sugar in a mixing bowl and beat using an electric hand mixer or wooden spoon until the mixture is light and creamy. Add the eggs gradually, beating after each addition. Add the flour and yogurt and gently fold them into the mixture, using a large metal spoon. Spoon the mixture into the cake cases.
3 Bake for 15–20 minutes until the cakes spring back when pressed lightly and a skewer

inserted into the middle of a cake comes out clean. Remove the cakes from the oven, turn out on to a wire rack and leave to cool.

4 Remove the cakes from their cases and press a lollipop stick into the top of each one. Put a sheet of greaseproof paper on the work surface. Hold each cake by the stick over the bowl of melted chocolate and spoon over several spoonfuls of the chocolate so that each cake is covered. Lay the lollipops on their sides on the greaseproof paper and cover the chocolate with sprinkles and silver balls. Leave the chocolate to set before serving.

327 CHOCOLATE FUDGE CUPCAKES

PREPARATION TIME 20 minutes   **COOKING TIME** 15–20 minutes   **MAKES** 24 cakes

225g/8oz butter, softened
225g/8oz/1 cup dark soft brown sugar
4 large eggs, lightly beaten
175g/6oz/heaped 1 cup self-raising flour
55g/2oz/⅓ cup cocoa powder

1 recipe quantity **Chocolate Buttercream**
   (see page 24)
100g/3½oz white chocolate buttons
55g/2oz milk chocolate, melted and
   cooled slightly

1   Preheat the oven to 180°C/350°F/gas 4. Put 24 cake cases/liners in two 12-hole bun tins.
2   Put the butter and sugar in a mixing bowl and beat using an electric hand mixer or wooden spoon until the mixture is light and creamy. Add the eggs gradually, beating after each addition. Sift in the flour and cocoa and gently fold them into the mixture, using a large metal spoon. Spoon the mixture into the cake cases.
3   Bake for 15–20 minutes until the cakes spring back when pressed lightly and a skewer inserted into the middle of a cake comes out clean. Remove the cakes from the oven, turn out on to a wire rack and leave to cool.
4   Spoon the buttercream into an icing bag fitted with a 13mm/½in star nozzle and pipe a large star on the top of each cake. (If you do not have an icing bag, cover each cake with a layer of buttercream using a round-bladed knife.) Place several chocolate buttons on each cake and drizzle over the melted chocolate in thin lines using a fork. Leave to set before serving.

328 CHOCOLATE CHIP BUNS

PREPARATION TIME 20 minutes   **COOKING TIME** 15–20 minutes   **MAKES** 24 buns

225g/8oz butter, softened
225g/8oz/scant 1 cup caster/superfine sugar
4 large eggs, lightly beaten
200g/7oz/1⅓ cups self-raising flour
55g/2oz/heaped ¼ cup cocoa powder
3 tbsp natural/plain yogurt
100g/3½oz/heaped ½ cup white
   chocolate chips

100g/3½oz/heaped ½ cup plain/semisweet
   chocolate chips
200g/7oz milk chocolate, melted
   and cooled slightly
mini sugar-coated chocolate beans,
   to decorate

1   Preheat the oven to 180°C/350°F/gas 4. Put 24 cake cases/liners in two 12-hole bun tins.
2   Put the butter and sugar in a mixing bowl and beat using an electric hand mixer or wooden spoon until the mixture is light and creamy. Add the eggs gradually, beating after each addition. Sift in the flour and cocoa and gently fold them into the mixture with the

yogurt, using a large metal spoon. Add the white and plain chocolate chips and mix again. Spoon the mixture into the cake cases.

3 Bake for 15–20 minutes until the buns spring back when pressed lightly and a skewer inserted into the middle of a bun comes out clean. Remove the buns from the oven, turn out on to a wire rack and leave to cool.

4 Spread some melted chocolate over each bun using a round-bladed knife and decorate with the mini chocolate beans. Leave to set before serving.

329 LADYBIRD CUPCAKES

PREPARATION TIME 40 minutes   **COOKING TIME** 15–20 minutes   **MAKES** 12 cakes

115g/4oz butter, softened
115g/4oz/scant ½ cup caster/superfine sugar
2 large eggs, lightly beaten
115g/4oz/¾ cup self-raising flour
4 tbsp cocoa powder
2 tbsp natural/plain yogurt

200g/7oz plain/semisweet chocolate, melted and cooled slightly
icing/powdered sugar, for dusting
250g/9oz red ready-to-roll icing
2 heaped tbsp plain/semisweet chocolate chips

1 Preheat the oven to 180°C/350°F/gas 4. Put 12 cake cases/liners in a 12-hole bun tin.

2 Put the butter and caster sugar in a mixing bowl and beat using an electric hand mixer or wooden spoon until the mixture is light and creamy. Add the eggs gradually, beating after each addition. Sift in the flour and cocoa and gently fold them into the mixture with the yogurt, using a large metal spoon. Spoon the mixture into the cake cases.

3 Bake for 15–20 minutes until the cakes spring back when pressed lightly and a skewer inserted into the middle of a cake comes out clean. Remove the cakes from the oven, turn out on to a wire rack and leave to cool.

4 Reserve a small amount of the melted chocolate to use for the decoration and spread the rest over the cakes, using a round-bladed knife.

5 Sift icing sugar on to a clean work surface and roll the ready-to-roll icing out to 5mm/¼in thick using a rolling pin. Cut out circles the same size as the top of your cupcakes using a round cutter. Remove a strip from each circle that is about 1cm/⅜in wide at its widest point, and discard. Cut what remains of each circle in half from the flat end. Place the halves on top of each cupcake at an angle, so that their rounded ends stick out beyond the cake case, to resemble an open pair of wings, with the flat edges set slightly in from the edge of the cake to leave space for the eyes. Stick 2 chocolate chips in place for eyes and attach 2 or 3 more to each wing with melted chocolate for the spots.

330 PIGLET CUPCAKES

PREPARATION TIME 40 minutes   **COOKING TIME** 15–20 minutes   **MAKES** 12 cakes

115g/4oz butter, softened
115g/4oz/scant ½ cup caster/superfine sugar
2 large eggs, lightly beaten
115g/4oz/¾ cup self-raising flour, sifted
2 tbsp natural/plain yogurt
2 tbsp raspberry jam/jelly
a few drops of red food colouring

1 recipe quantity Vanilla Buttercream
    (see page 24)
12 pink marshmallows
2 heaped tbsp plain/semisweet
    chocolate chips
55g/2oz pink ready-to-roll icing

1   Preheat the oven to 180°C/350°F/gas 4. Put 12 cake cases/liners in a 12-hole bun tin.
2   Put the butter and sugar in a mixing bowl and beat using an electric hand mixer or
    wooden spoon until light and creamy. Add the eggs gradually, beating after each addition.
    Add the flour, yogurt and jam and gently fold into the mixture, using a large metal spoon.
3   Spoon the mixture into the cake cases and bake for 15–20 minutes until the cakes spring
    back when pressed lightly and a skewer inserted into the middle of a cake comes out
    clean. Remove the cakes from the oven, turn out on to a wire rack and leave to cool.
4   Stir the food colouring into the buttercream until the colour is uniform, then cover the
    top of each cake with the buttercream, using a round-bladed knife to make a smooth
    surface. Place a pink marshmallow in the middle of each cake and 2 chocolate chips
    above it for eyes. Using a little of the buttercream, attach 2 chips in the centre of the
    marshmallow for the nostrils.
5   Cut the ready-to-roll icing into quarters, then cut each quarter into six pieces to give
    24 pieces. Roll each piece into a small ball approximately 1cm/⅜in in diameter. Press each
    ball flat between your fingers and then pinch together at one end to form an ear shape.
    Add 2 ears to each cake. Leave the buttercream to set before serving.

331 BUMBLEBEE CUPCAKES

PREPARATION TIME 40 minutes   **COOKING TIME** 15–20 minutes   **MAKES** 12 cakes

115g/4oz butter, softened
115g/4oz/scant ½ cup caster/superfine sugar
1 tbsp clear honey
2 large eggs, lightly beaten
115g/4oz/¾ cup self-raising flour
2 tsp ground cinnamon
100g/3½oz/heaped ½ cup white
    chocolate chips

a few drops of yellow food colouring
1 recipe quantity Vanilla Buttercream
    (see page 24)
icing/powdered sugar, for dusting
125g/4½oz black ready-to-roll icing
1 tbsp plain/semisweet chocolate chips
6 sheets edible rice paper

1 Preheat the oven to 180°C/350°F/gas 4. Put 12 cake cases/liners in a 12-hole bun tin.

2 Put the butter, sugar and honey in a mixing bowl and beat using an electric hand mixer or wooden spoon until the mixture is light and creamy. Add the eggs gradually, beating after each addition. Sift in the flour and ground cinnamon and gently fold them into the mixture with the white chocolate chips, using a large metal spoon. Spoon the mixture into the cake cases.

3 Bake for 15–20 minutes until the cakes spring back when pressed lightly and a skewer inserted into the middle of a cake comes out clean. Remove the cakes from the oven, turn out on to a wire rack and leave to cool.

4 Stir the food colouring into the buttercream until the colour is uniform, then cover each cupcake with the yellow buttercream using a round-bladed knife.

5 Sift icing sugar on to a clean work surface and roll the black icing out to 5mm/¼in thick. Cut 24 strips of icing measuring 8 x 1cm/3¼ x ⅜in and place 2 parallel on each cake to make the bee's stripes. Add 2 chocolate chips for the bee's eyes. Divide each sheet of rice paper into 4 and cut out wing shapes. Press 2 wings into the buttercream between the stripes. Leave the buttercream to set before serving.

332 SUGAR MICE CUPCAKES

PREPARATION TIME 20 minutes   **COOKING TIME** 15–20 minutes   **MAKES** 12 cakes

115g/4oz butter, softened
115g/4oz/scant ½ cup caster/superfine sugar
2 large eggs, lightly beaten
115g/4oz/¾ cup self-raising flour
4 tbsp cocoa powder
2 tbsp natural/plain yogurt

a few drops of pink food colouring
1 recipe quantity Vanilla Buttercream
   (see page 24)
12 sugar mice
edible silver balls, to decorate

1   Preheat the oven to 180°C/350°F/gas 4. Put 12 cake cases/liners in a 12-hole bun tin.
2   Put the butter and sugar in a mixing bowl and beat using an electric hand mixer or wooden spoon until the mixture is light and creamy. Add the eggs gradually, beating after each addition. Sift in the flour and cocoa and gently fold them into the mixture with the yogurt, using a large metal spoon. Spoon the mixture into the cake cases.
3   Bake for 15–20 minutes until the cakes spring back when pressed lightly and a skewer inserted into the middle of a cake comes out clean. Remove the cakes from the oven, turn out on to a wire rack and leave to cool.
4   Stir the food colouring into the buttercream until the colour is uniform, then cover the top of each cake with the icing using a round-bladed knife. Place a sugar mouse in the centre of each cake and decorate the rest of the cake with silver balls.

333 CHOCOLATE BUTTERFLY CAKES

PREPARATION TIME 20 minutes   **COOKING TIME** 15–20 minutes   **MAKES** 24 cakes

225g/8oz butter, softened
225g/8oz/scant 1 cup caster/superfine sugar
4 large eggs, lightly beaten
175g/6oz/heaped 1 cup self-raising flour

55g/2oz/⅓ cup cocoa powder
1 recipe quantity Vanilla Buttercream
   (see page 24)
2 chocolate flake bars, crumbled

1   Preheat the oven to 180°C/350°F/gas 4. Put 24 cake cases/liners in two 12-hole bun tins.
2   Put the butter and sugar in a mixing bowl and beat using an electric hand mixer or wooden spoon until the mixture is light and creamy. Add the eggs gradually, beating after each addition. Sift in the flour and cocoa and gently fold them into the mixture, using a large metal spoon. Spoon the mixture into the cake cases.
3   Bake for 15–20 minutes until the cakes spring back when pressed lightly and a skewer inserted into the middle of a cake comes out clean. Remove the cakes from the oven, turn out on to a wire rack and leave to cool.
4   Cut a shallow, cone-shaped piece out of the top of each cake and fill the hole left with a

spoonful of buttercream. Cut each removed piece in half and place 2 halves on each cake a little apart and at an angle to make wings. Sprinkle over the chocolate to decorate.

334 LEMON FAIRY CAKES

PREPARATION TIME 20 minutes   **COOKING TIME** 15–20 minutes   **MAKES** 24 cakes

225g/8oz butter, softened
225g/8oz/scant 1 cup caster/superfine sugar
4 large eggs, lightly beaten
225g/8oz/1½ cups self-raising flour, sifted
3 tbsp lemon curd

juice and finely grated zest of 1 lemon
300g/10½oz/2 cups icing/powdered
  sugar, sifted
edible silver balls and sugar sprinkles,
  to decorate

1   Preheat the oven to 180°C/350°F/gas 4. Put 24 cake cases/liners in two 12-hole bun tins.
2   Put the butter and caster sugar in a mixing bowl and beat using an electric hand mixer or wooden spoon until the mixture is light and creamy. Add the eggs gradually, beating after each addition. Add the flour, lemon curd and lemon zest and gently fold them into the mixture, using a large metal spoon. Spoon the mixture into the cake cases.
3   Bake for 15–20 minutes until the cakes spring back when pressed lightly and a skewer inserted into the middle of a cake comes out clean. Remove the cakes from the oven, turn out on to a wire rack and leave to cool.
4   In a bowl, mix the icing sugar, lemon juice and 1–2 tablespoons water to make a smooth, thick icing/frosting, and spread over the cakes. Sprinkle over the silver balls and sprinkles.

335 SAILING BOAT CUPCAKES

PREPARATION TIME 40 minutes   **COOKING TIME** 15–20 minutes   **MAKES** 10 cakes

115g/4oz butter, softened
115g/4oz/scant ½ cup caster/superfine sugar
2 large eggs, lightly beaten
50g/2oz/⅓ cup plain/semisweet
  chocolate chips

115g/4oz/¾ cup self-raising flour, sifted
1 quantity Vanilla Buttercream (see page 24)
a few drops of blue food colouring
10 sheets edible rice paper
10 cocktail sticks/toothpicks

1   Preheat the oven to 180°C/350°F/gas 4. Put 10 cake cases/liners in a 12-hole bun tin and 10 mini foil cases in a 12-hole mini-muffin tin.
2   Put the butter and sugar in a mixing bowl and beat using an electric hand mixer or wooden spoon until the mixture is creamy. Add the eggs gradually, beating after each addition. Add the chocolate chips and flour and fold them into the mixture, using a large metal spoon. Put a large spoonful of mixture into each cake case and 2 teaspoons into each foil case.

3 Bake for 12–15 minutes (small) and 15–20 minutes (large) until the cakes spring back when pressed lightly. Remove from the oven, turn out on to a wire rack and leave to cool.

4 Reserve 2 tablespoons of the buttercream and stir the food colouring into the remainder until the colour is uniform. Cover the large cakes with the blue buttercream and then dot with small amounts of the reserved white buttercream. Use a fork to form the buttercream into peaks to make waves. Place a small cake in its foil case in the middle of each cake. Cut the rice paper into 20 small triangles and thread 2 sails on to each cocktail stick. Put a mast and sails into the middle of each mini-muffin. Leave the buttercream to set before serving.

336 SPICED SUGAR COOKIES

PREPARATION TIME 20 minutes, plus chilling   **COOKING TIME** 10–15 minutes   **MAKES** 10 cookies

115g/4oz butter, softened, plus extra
    for greasing
55g/2oz/¼ cup caster/superfine sugar
140g/5oz/1 cup plain/all-purpose flour,
    plus extra for dusting

4 tbsp cocoa powder
1 tsp ground cinnamon
100g/3½oz/heaped ½ cup chocolate chips
1 tbsp milk (optional)
2 tbsp demerara sugar

1 Put the butter and caster sugar in a mixing bowl and beat using an electric hand mixer or wooden spoon until the mixture is light and creamy. Sift in the flour, cocoa and ground cinnamon, add the chocolate chips, and mix together with your hands to form a soft dough, adding the milk if the mixture is too dry. Wrap in cling film/plastic wrap and refrigerate for 1 hour.

2 Preheat the oven to 180°C/350°F/gas 4. Grease two 30cm/12in square baking trays.

3 Sift flour on to a clean work surface and roll the dough out to 1cm/⅜in thick with a rolling pin. Cut out 10 squares using a 7.5cm/3in fluted cutter, gathering up the trimmings and re-rolling as necessary. Place the cookies on the baking trays and sprinkle with the demerara.

4 Bake for 10–15 minutes until firm. Remove the cookies from the oven and leave to cool on the trays for a few minutes, then transfer to a wire rack with a palette knife to cool.

337 WHITE CHOCOLATE COOKIES

PREPARATION TIME 15 minutes   **COOKING TIME** 14–18 minutes   **MAKES** 20 cookies

125g/4½oz butter, plus extra for greasing
200g/7oz/¾ cup caster/superfine sugar
350g/12oz/heaped 2 cups plain/
    all-purpose flour
1 tsp bicarbonate of soda/baking soda

2 tbsp golden syrup
1 tsp vanilla extract
1 large egg, lightly beaten
200g/7oz white chocolate, chopped

1 Preheat the oven to 180°C/350°F/gas 4. Grease and line two 30cm/12in square baking trays. Put the sugar in a mixing bowl and sift in the flour and bicarbonate of soda. Mix together with a wooden spoon. Put the butter and syrup in a saucepan and heat gently until the butter melts. Cool slightly, then beat into the dry ingredients with the vanilla extract, egg and chopped chocolate.

2 Divide the dough into 20 walnut-size balls and place on the baking trays, leaving about 5cm/2in between them to allow for spreading. Press each cookie down slightly with a fork.

3 Bake for 12–15 minutes until golden brown. Remove from the oven and leave to cool on the trays for a few minutes, then transfer to a wire rack to cool.

338 CHOCOLATE CHECKERBOARD COOKIES

PREPARATION TIME 20 minutes, plus chilling   **COOKING TIME** 12–15 minutes   **MAKES** 15 cookies

115g/4oz butter, softened, plus extra
   for greasing
55g/2oz/¼ cup caster/superfine sugar

175g/6oz/heaped 1 cup plain/all-purpose
   flour, sifted, plus extra for dusting
4 tbsp cocoa powder, sifted
1 tbsp milk

1 Put the butter and sugar in a mixing bowl and beat using an electric hand mixer or wooden spoon until the mixture is light and creamy. Add the flour and mix together with your hands to form a soft dough.

2 Divide the dough in half in the bowl, and remove one half. Add the cocoa and milk to the bowl and mix them into the dough with your hands.

3 Dust the work surface with flour. Divide the plain and cocoa-flavoured dough pieces in half and roll each one with your fingers into equal-size sausage shapes about 2cm/¾in thick and 15cm/6in long. Place 1 plain sausage next to a chocolate sausage and then top with the remaining 2 in reverse order to make a checkerboard effect. Press the dough together firmly with your hands. Wrap in cling film/plastic wrap and refrigerate for 1 hour.

4 Preheat the oven to 180°C/350°F/gas 4. Grease two 30cm/12in square baking trays. Cut the dough into 15 slices and place on the baking trays.

5 Bake for 12–15 minutes until golden brown. Remove the cookies from the oven and leave to cool on the trays for a few minutes, then transfer to a wire rack with a palette knife to cool.

339 THUMBPRINT COOKIES WITH RASPBERRY JAM

PREPARATION TIME 15 minutes **COOKING TIME** 15–18 minutes **MAKES** 24 cookies

175g/6oz butter, softened
85g/3oz/heaped ½ cup icing/powdered
    sugar, sifted
225g/8oz/1½ cups plain/all-purpose
    flour, sifted

1 tsp vanilla extract
1 tbsp milk (optional)
8 tbsp raspberry jam/jelly

1 Preheat the oven to 180°C/350°F/gas 4. Put 24 cake cases/liners into two 12-hole bun tins.

2 Put the butter and sugar in a mixing bowl and beat using an electric hand mixer or wooden spoon until the mixture is light and creamy. Add the flour and vanilla extract and mix together with your hands to form a soft dough, adding the milk if the mixture is too dry.

3 Put large spoonfuls of dough into each cake case. Press down in the middle of each one with your thumb to make a dent and fill with 1 teaspoon of the jam.

4 Bake for 15–18 minutes until golden brown. Remove the cookies from the oven and leave to cool on the trays for a few minutes, then transfer to a wire rack with a palette knife to cool.

340 MELTING MOMENTS

PREPARATION TIME 15 minutes   **COOKING TIME** 15–18 minutes   **MAKES** 20 biscuits

115g/4oz butter, softened, plus extra
   for greasing
2 tbsp golden syrup
85g/3oz/⅓ cup caster/superfine sugar
1 large egg, lightly beaten

1 tsp almond extract
300g/10½oz/2 cups self-raising flour
85g/3oz/scant 1 cup porridge/rolled oats
10 glacé/candied cherries, halved

1   Preheat the oven to 180°C/350°F/gas 4. Grease two 30cm/12in square baking trays.

2   Put the butter, syrup and sugar in a mixing bowl and beat using an electric hand mixer or wooden spoon until the mixture is light and creamy. Beat in the egg and almond extract. Sift in the flour and mix together with your hands to form a soft dough.

3   Divide the dough into 20 walnut-size pieces and roll into balls with your hands. Roll each ball in the oats to cover it. Place on the baking trays, leaving about 5cm/2in between them to allow for spreading. Press each ball down flat with the back of a fork and top each with half a glacé cherry.

4   Bake for 15–18 minutes until crisp and golden brown. Remove the biscuits from the oven and leave to cool on the trays for a few minutes, then transfer to a wire rack with a palette knife to cool.

341 LEMON SANDWICH COOKIES

PREPARATION TIME 20 minutes, plus chilling   **COOKING TIME** 12–15 minutes   **MAKES** 8 cookies

175g/6oz butter, softened, plus extra
   for greasing
55g/2oz/¼ cup caster/superfine sugar
175g/6oz/heaped 1 cup plain/all-purpose
   flour, sifted, plus extra for dusting

juice and finely grated zest of
   1 small lemon
1 tbsp milk (optional)
200g/7oz/1⅓ cups icing/powdered
   sugar, sifted
2 tbsp condensed milk

1   Put 115g/4oz of the butter and the caster sugar in a mixing bowl and beat using an electric hand mixer or wooden spoon until the mixture is light and creamy. Add the flour and lemon zest and mix together with your hands to form a soft dough, adding the milk if the mixture is too dry. Wrap in cling film/plastic wrap and refrigerate for 1 hour.

2   Preheat the oven to 180°C/350°F/gas 4. Grease two 30cm/12in square baking trays.

3   Sift flour on to a clean work surface and roll the dough out to about 1cm/⅜in thick using a rolling pin. Cut out 16 rounds using a 5cm/2in fluted round cutter, gathering up the trimmings and re-rolling as necessary. Place the cookies on the baking trays.

4 Bake for 12–15 minutes until crisp and golden brown. Remove the cookies from the oven and leave to cool on the trays for a few minutes, then transfer to a wire rack with a palette knife to cool.

5 In a bowl, mix together the remaining butter with the icing sugar, lemon juice and condensed milk using an electric hand mixer or a wooden spoon to form a smooth icing/frosting. Sandwich the cookies together in pairs with the icing.

342 DUCK POND COOKIES

PREPARATION TIME 40 minutes, plus chilling   **COOKING TIME** 12–15 minutes   **MAKES** 16 cookies

115g/4oz butter, softened, plus extra
   for greasing
55g/2oz/¼ cup caster/superfine sugar
175g/6oz/heaped 1 cup plain/all-purpose
   flour, sifted, plus extra for dusting
1 tbsp milk (optional)

150g/5½oz yellow ready-to-roll icing
a few drops of red food colouring
300g/10½oz/2 cups fondant icing
   sugar, sifted
a few drops of blue food colouring

1 Put the butter and caster sugar in a mixing bowl and beat using an electric hand mixer or wooden spoon until the mixture is light and creamy. Add the flour and mix together with your hands to form a soft dough, adding the milk if the mixture is too dry. Wrap in cling film/plastic wrap and refrigerate for 1 hour.

2 Preheat the oven to 180°C/350°F/gas 4. Grease two 30cm/12in square baking trays.

3 Sift flour on to a clean work surface and roll the dough out to about 1cm/⅜in thick using a rolling pin. Cut out 16 circles using a 5cm/2in round cutter, gathering up the trimmings and re-rolling as necessary. Transfer the cookies to the baking trays using a palette knife.

4 Bake for 12–15 minutes until golden brown. Remove from the oven and leave to cool on the trays for a few minutes, then transfer to a wire rack with a palette knife to cool.

5 Pinch off about a 1cm/⅜in cube of the ready-to-roll icing and form the remainder into small duck shapes with your fingers. Colour the pinched-off bit with the red food colouring to make orange icing and use this to make beaks for the ducks.

6 Mix together the fondant icing sugar with 2–3 tablespoons water and the blue food colouring to form a smooth icing/frosting. Spoon the blue icing over the cooled cookies, covering them completely. Place a sugar duck in the middle of each cookie and leave the icing to set before serving.

343 FRIED EGG BISCUITS

PREPARATION TIME 20 minutes, plus chilling   **COOKING TIME** 12–15 minutes   **MAKES** 16 biscuits

115g/4oz butter, softened, plus extra
   for greasing
55g/2oz/¼ cup caster/superfine sugar
175g/6oz/heaped 1 cup plain/all-purpose
   flour, sifted, plus extra for dusting

1 tbsp milk (optional)
300g/10½oz/2 cups fondant icing sugar, sifted
16 round yellow jellies

1 Put the butter and caster sugar in a mixing bowl and beat using an electric hand mixer or wooden spoon until the mixture is light and creamy. Add the flour and mix together with your hands to form a soft dough, adding the milk if the mixture is too dry. Wrap in cling film/plastic wrap and refrigerate for 1 hour.

2 Preheat the oven to 180°C/350°F/gas 4. Grease two 30cm/12in square baking trays.

3 Sift flour on to a clean work surface and roll the dough out to about 1cm/⅜in thick using a rolling pin. Cut out 16 fried-egg shapes using a knife, gathering up the trimmings and re-rolling as necessary. Transfer the biscuits to the baking trays using a palette knife.

4 Bake for 12–15 minutes until golden brown. Remove the biscuits from the oven and leave to cool on the trays for a few minutes, then transfer to a wire rack with a palette knife to cool.

5 In a bowl, mix the fondant icing sugar with 2–3 tablespoons water to make a smooth icing/frosting. Spoon the icing over each biscuit so that the top and sides are covered, and top each with a yellow jelly to represent the yoke.

344 GINGERBREAD MEN

PREPARATION TIME 20 minutes   **COOKING TIME** 12–15 minutes   **MAKES** 16 biscuits

70g/2½oz butter, softened, plus extra
   for greasing
185g/6½oz/1¼ cups plain/all-purpose flour,
   plus extra for dusting
1 tsp bicarbonate of soda/baking soda
1 tsp ground ginger
1 tsp mixed/pumpkin pie spice
finely grated zest of 1 small orange

1 large egg, lightly beaten
85g/3oz/⅓ cup light soft brown sugar
2 tbsp golden syrup
55g/2oz milk chocolate, melted and
   cooled slightly
mini sugar-coated chocolate beans,
   to decorate

1 Preheat the oven to 180°C/350°F/gas 4. Grease two 30cm/12in square baking trays.

2 Sift the flour, bicarbonate of soda, ginger and mixed spice into a mixing bowl and add the orange zest. Rub the butter into the flour with your fingertips until it resembles fine

breadcrumbs, then add the egg, sugar and syrup and mix together with your hands to form a soft dough.

3 Sift flour on to a clean work surface and roll the dough out to about 1cm/⅜in thick using a rolling pin, and adding a little more flour to the dough if it is too soft to roll. Cut out 16 biscuits using a 13cm/5in gingerbread-man cutter. Transfer the biscuits to the baking trays using a palette knife.

4 Bake for 12–15 minutes until golden brown. Remove the biscuits from the oven and leave to cool on the trays for a few minutes, then transfer to a wire rack with a palette knife to cool.

5 Use the melted chocolate to attach the chocolate beans for eyes and buttons. Leave to set before serving.

345 MAGNIFYING GLASS BISCUITS

PREPARATION TIME 20 minutes, plus chilling   **COOKING TIME** 12–15 minutes   **MAKES** 8 biscuits

20 clear boiled peppermint sweets/candies
115g/4oz butter, softened, plus extra for greasing
55g/2oz/¼ cup caster/superfine sugar

175g/6oz/heaped 1 cup plain/all-purpose flour, sifted, plus extra for dusting
1 tbsp milk (optional)

1 Remove the wrappers from the peppermints and blitz them to a fine dust in a blender or food processor.

2 Put the butter and sugar in a mixing bowl and beat using an electric hand mixer or wooden spoon until the mixture is light and creamy. Add the flour and mix together with your hands to form a soft dough, adding the milk if the mixture is too dry. Wrap in cling film/plastic wrap and refrigerate for 1 hour.

3 Preheat the oven to 180°C/350°F/gas 4. Grease and line two 30cm/12in square baking trays, or use a silicone mat to make absolutely sure these delicate cookies won't stick.

4 Sift flour on to a clean work surface and roll the dough out to about 1cm/⅜in thick using a rolling pin. Cut out eight 10cm/4in rounds with a handle to look like magnifying glasses, using a knife. Transfer the biscuits to the baking trays using a palette knife.

5 Using a round cutter smaller than the circle of the magnifying glass, cut out a round from the centre of each biscuit. (You can re-roll these cut-outs to make more biscuits, if wanted.) Fill each hole with a layer of the peppermint dust, ensuring there are no gaps.

6 Bake for 12–15 minutes until the biscuits are golden brown and the peppermint dust has melted. Remove the biscuits from the oven and leave to cool completely on the trays so that the sugar 'glass' solidifies.

346 DINOSAUR BISCUITS

PREPARATION TIME 20 minutes, plus chilling   **COOKING TIME** 12–15 minutes   **MAKES** 10 biscuits

115g/4oz butter, softened, plus extra
   for greasing
55g/2oz/¼ cup caster/superfine sugar
175g/6oz/heaped 1 cup plain/all-purpose
   flour, plus extra for dusting
1 tsp ground cinnamon

finely grated zest of 1 orange
1 tbsp milk (optional)
1 tbsp icing/powdered sugar, sifted
mini sugar-coated chocolate beans,
   to decorate

1 Put the butter and caster sugar in a mixing bowl and beat using an electric hand mixer or wooden spoon until the mixture is light and creamy. Sift in the flour and ground cinnamon and add the orange zest. Mix together with your hands to form a soft dough, adding the milk if the mixture is too dry. Wrap in cling film/plastic wrap and refrigerate for 1 hour.
2 Preheat the oven to 180°C/350°F/gas 4. Grease two 30cm/12in square baking trays.
3 Sift flour on to a clean work surface and roll the dough out to about 1cm/⅜in thick using a rolling pin. Cut out 10 biscuits using dinosaur cutters or a cardboard template and a knife, gathering up the trimmings and re-rolling as necessary. Transfer the biscuits to the baking trays using a palette knife.
4 Bake for 12–15 minutes until golden brown. Remove the biscuits from the oven and leave to cool on the trays for a few minutes, then transfer to a wire rack with a palette knife to cool.
5 Mix the icing sugar with 1 teaspoon water to make a smooth, thick icing/frosting. Use the icing to attach the chocolate beans as eyes on each dinosaur.

347 DOMINO BISCUITS

PREPARATION TIME 20 minutes, plus chilling   **COOKING TIME** 12–15 minutes   **MAKES** 18 biscuits

115g/4oz butter, softened, plus extra
   for greasing
55g/2oz/¼ cup caster/superfine sugar
175g/6oz/heaped 1 cup plain/all-purpose
   flour, sifted, plus extra for dusting
1 tbsp milk (optional)

300g/10½oz/2 cups icing/powdered
   sugar, sifted

TO DECORATE
18 matchstick chocolates
chocolate chips

1 Put the butter and caster sugar in a mixing bowl and beat using an electric hand mixer or wooden spoon until the mixture is light and creamy. Add the flour and mix together with your hands to form a soft dough, adding the milk if the mixture is too dry. Wrap in cling film/plastic wrap and refrigerate for 1 hour.

2 Preheat the oven to 180°C/350°F/gas 4. Grease two 30cm/12in square baking trays.

3 Sift flour on to a clean work surface and roll the dough out to about 1cm/⅜in thick using a rolling pin. Cut out eighteen 7.5 x 4cm/3 x 1¼in rectangles using a knife or cutter, gathering up the trimmings and re-rolling as necessary. Transfer the biscuits to the baking trays using a palette knife.

4 Bake for 12–15 minutes until golden brown. Remove the biscuits from the oven and leave to cool on the trays for a few minutes, then transfer to a wire rack with a palette knife to cool.

5 Mix the icing sugar with 2–3 tablespoons water to make a smooth, thick icing/frosting. Spoon the icing over each biscuit so that the top and sides are covered. While the icing is still wet, cut the matchstick chocolates to the width of each biscuit and place in the centre to divide your biscuits into 2 halves. Decorate each side of the biscuit with up to 6 chocolate chips to represent the dots on the dominoes.

348 STAINED GLASS BISCUITS

PREPARATION TIME 20 minutes, plus chilling   **COOKING TIME** 12–15 minutes   **MAKES** 12 biscuits

12 cola-flavoured boiled sweets/candies
115g/4oz butter, softened, plus extra for greasing
55g/2oz/¼ cup caster/superfine sugar

175g/6oz/heaped 1 cup plain/all-purpose flour, sifted, plus extra for dusting
1 tbsp milk (optional)

1 Remove any wrappers from the boiled sweets and blitz them to a fine dust in a blender or food processor.

2 Put the butter and sugar in a mixing bowl and beat using an electric hand mixer or wooden spoon until the mixture is light and creamy. Add the flour and mix together with your hands to form a soft dough, adding the milk if the mixture is too dry. Wrap in cling film/plastic wrap and refrigerate for 1 hour.

3 Preheat the oven to 180°C/350°F/gas 4. Grease and line two 30cm/12in square baking sheets, or use a silicone mat to make absolutely sure these delicate cookies won't stick.

4 Sift flour on to a clean work surface and roll the dough out to about 1cm/⅜in thick using a rolling pin. Cut out 12 biscuits using a 7.5cm/3in heart-shaped cutter, gathering up the trimmings and re-rolling as necessary. Transfer the biscuits to the baking trays using a palette knife. Using a smaller star- or heart-shaped cutter, cut away a star or heart from the centre of each biscuit. Fill each hole with 1 teaspoon of the sweet dust, ensuring there are no gaps.

5 Bake for 12–15 minutes until golden brown and the sweet dust has melted. Remove the biscuits from the oven and leave to cool completely on the trays so that the sugar 'glass' solidifies.

349 FACE BISCUITS

PREPARATION TIME 20 minutes, plus chilling   **COOKING TIME** 12–15 minutes   **MAKES** 18 biscuits

115g/4oz butter, softened, plus extra
   for greasing
55g/2oz/¼ cup caster/superfine sugar
175g/6oz/heaped 1 cup plain/all-purpose
   flour, sifted, plus extra for dusting
1 tbsp milk (optional)

300g/10½oz/2 cups icing/powdered
   sugar, sifted

TO DECORATE
sugar-coated chocolate beans
liquorice or sugar sprinkles

1   Put the butter and caster sugar in a mixing bowl and beat using an electric hand mixer or
    wooden spoon until the mixture is light and creamy. Add the flour and mix together with
    your hands to form a soft dough, adding the milk if the mixture is too dry. Wrap in cling
    film/plastic wrap and refrigerate for 1 hour.
2   Preheat the oven to 180°C/350°F/gas 4. Grease two 30cm/12in square baking trays.
3   Sift flour on to a clean work surface and roll the dough out to about 1cm/⅜in thick using
    a rolling pin. Cut out 18 biscuits using a 5cm/2in round cutter, gathering up the trimmings
    and re-rolling as necessary. Transfer the biscuits to the baking trays using a palette knife.
4   Bake for 12–15 minutes until golden brown. Remove the biscuits from the oven and
    leave to cool on the trays for a few minutes, then transfer to a wire rack with a palette
    knife to cool.
5   In a bowl, mix the icing sugar with 2–3 tablespoons water to make a smooth icing/
    frosting. Spoon the icing over each biscuit so that the top and sides are covered. Use the
    sweets/candies to make faces, with chocolate beans for eyes and mouths and chopped
    liquorish or sprinkles for hair.

350 ICE CREAM SANDWICH BISCUITS

PREPARATION TIME 20 minutes   **COOKING TIME** 10–12 minutes   **MAKES** 8 biscuits

140g/5oz butter, softened, plus extra
   for greasing
125g/4½oz/heaped ½ cup light soft
   brown sugar
100g/3½oz/heaped ⅓ cup caster/
   superfine sugar

1 large egg, lightly beaten
1 tsp vanilla extract
250g/9oz/scant 2 cups plain/all-purpose flour
1 tsp baking powder
100g/3½oz/heaped ½ cup milk chocolate chips
500ml/17fl oz/2 cups vanilla ice cream

1   Preheat the oven to 180°C/350°F/gas 4. Grease two 30cm/12in square baking trays.
2   Put the butter, light brown sugar and caster sugar in a mixing bowl and beat using an
    electric hand mixer or wooden spoon until the mixture is light and creamy. Beat in the

egg and vanilla extract. Sift in the flour and baking powder and add the chocolate chips. Mix together with your hands to form a soft dough.

3   Divide the dough into 16 walnut-size balls and place on the baking trays, leaving about 5cm/2in between them to allow for spreading. Press each biscuit down slightly with your fingers or a fork.

4   Bake for 10–12 minutes until golden brown. Remove the biscuits from the oven and leave to cool on the trays for a few minutes, then transfer to a wire rack with a palette knife to cool.

5   Remove the ice cream from the freezer 5 minutes before you want to assemble the biscuits so that it has softened a little and is easy to use. When the biscuits are completely cold, sandwich together pairs of biscuits with a few tablespoons of ice cream in each. Serve the biscuits immediately.

351 SUNFLOWER BISCUITS

PREPARATION TIME 30 minutes, plus chilling   **COOKING TIME** 12–15 minutes   **MAKES** 8 biscuits

115g/4oz butter, softened, plus extra
   for greasing
55g/2oz/¼ cup caster/superfine sugar
175g/6oz/heaped 1 cup plain/all-purpose
   flour, sifted, plus extra for dusting
1 tbsp milk (optional)

300g/10½oz/2 cups icing/powdered
   sugar, sifted
a few drops of yellow food colouring
100g/3½oz/heaped ½ cup plain/semisweet
   chocolate chips

1   Put the butter and caster sugar in a mixing bowl and beat using an electric hand mixer or wooden spoon until the mixture is light and creamy. Add the flour and mix together with your hands to form a soft dough, adding the milk if the mixture is too dry. Wrap in cling film/plastic wrap and refrigerate for 1 hour.

2   Preheat the oven to 180°C/350°F/gas 4. Grease two 30cm/12in square baking trays.

3   Sift flour on to a clean work surface and roll the dough out to about 1cm/⅜in thick using a rolling pin. Cut out 8 biscuits using a large flower cutter or a cardboard template and a knife, gathering up the trimmings and re-rolling as necessary. Transfer the biscuits to the baking trays using a palette knife.

4   Bake for 12–15 minutes until golden brown. Remove the biscuits from the oven and leave to cool on the trays for a few minutes, then transfer to a wire rack with a palette knife to cool.

5   In a bowl, mix the icing sugar with 2–3 tablespoons water and the food colouring to make a smooth, thick icing/frosting. Spoon the icing over each biscuit so that the top and sides are covered and place some chocolate chips in the middle of each biscuit to make the centre of the sunflowers. Leave the icing to set before serving.

PREPARATION TIME 30–35 minutes **COOKING TIME** 1–1¼ hours **MAKES** 20 meringues

butter, for greasing
3 large egg whites

175g/6oz/scant ¾ cup caster/superfine sugar
a few drops of red food colouring

1 Preheat the oven to 140°C/275°F/gas 1. Grease and line two 30cm/12in square baking trays.
2 Put the egg whites and sugar in a heatproof bowl set over a pan of simmering water.
   It is important that the bottom of the bowl does not touch the water. Using an electric
   hand whisk, whisk the egg whites and sugar over the heat for 5 minutes until they form
   stiff peaks. Remove the bowl from the heat and whisk for another 5–10 minutes until the
   meringue is stiff. It is best if an adult helps with this stage due to the boiling water.

3　Spoon a third of the meringue into a separate bowl. Colour the remaining meringue with the red food colouring, stirring until the colour is uniform.

4　Spoon the red meringue into an icing bag fitted with a 2cm/¾in plain nozzle and pipe large ovals of meringue on to the trays a little distance apart for the mushroom caps. Spoon the white meringue into another piping bag fitted with a 1cm/⅜in plain nozzle and pipe the toadstool stalks under the caps and also small white dots on the caps.

5　Bake for about 1–1¼ hours until dried and crisp. Remove the meringues from the oven and leave to cool on the trays before serving.

353 GRANOLA BARS

PREPARATION TIME 15 minutes　**COOKING TIME** 30–35 minutes　**MAKES** 14 bars

150g/5½oz butter, chopped, plus extra
　　for greasing
150g/5½oz/⅔ cup light soft brown sugar
3 tbsp golden syrup
70g/2½oz/scant 1 cup desiccated/dried
　　shredded coconut
150g/5½oz/1 cup self-raising flour, sifted

200g/7oz/2 cups toasted muesli
2 large eggs, lightly beaten
100g/3½oz/½ cup chopped mixed raw nuts
200g/7oz/2 cups porridge/rolled oats
55g/2oz/¾ cup pumpkin seeds
55g/2oz/⅓ cup chopped dried apricots
finely grated zest of 2 lemons

1　Preheat the oven to 180°C/350°F/gas 4. Grease and line a 30 x 20cm/12 x 8in Swiss/jelly roll tin.

2　Put the butter, sugar and syrup in a saucepan and heat gently until the butter has melted.

3　Put all the remaining ingredients into a mixing bowl and pour in the butter mixture. Stir well to coat, then spoon into the tin and bake for 25–30 minutes until golden brown.

4　Remove from the oven and leave in the tin to cool, then cut into 14 bars to serve.

354 JAM TARTS

PREPARATION TIME 20 minutes, plus chilling　**COOKING TIME** 12–15 minutes　**MAKES** 20 tarts

115g/4oz chilled butter, chopped, plus extra
　　for greasing
225g/8oz/1½ cups plain/all-purpose flour,
　　sifted, plus extra for dusting

2 tbsp caster/superfine sugar
200g/7oz raspberry or strawberry
　　jam/jelly

1　Preheat the oven to 180°C/350°F/gas 4. Lightly grease two 12-hole shallow bun tins.

2　Put the flour in a mixing bowl. Rub the butter into the flour with your fingertips until the mixture resembles fine breadcrumbs. Stir in the sugar and add 3–4 tablespoons cold water, a little at a time, until the mixture comes together to form a soft dough. Wrap the dough in cling film/plastic wrap and refrigerate for 30 minutes.

3 Sift flour on to a clean work surface and roll the dough out to about 5mm/¼in thick using a rolling pin. Cut out 20 rounds using a 7.5cm/3in round cutter, gathering up the trimmings and re-rolling as necessary. Place the rounds in the bun tins and put 1 heaped teaspoon of the jam into each pastry case/shell.

4 Bake for 12–15 minutes until the pastry is golden brown. Remove the tarts from the oven and leave to cool in the tins for a few minutes, then transfer to a wire rack to cool.

355 RAISIN & CINNAMON PINWHEELS

PREPARATION TIME 15 minutes   **COOKING TIME** 15–20 minutes   **MAKES** 8 pastries

15g/½oz butter, melted and cooled,
    plus extra for greasing
flour, for dusting
250g/9oz block puff pastry
2½ tbsp light soft brown sugar

1 tsp ground cinnamon
55g/2oz/¼ cup raisins
1 medium egg, beaten
3 tbsp icing/powdered sugar, sifted

1 Preheat the oven to 180°C/350°F/gas 4. Lightly grease two 30cm/12in square baking trays.

2 Sift flour on to a clean work surface and roll out the pastry into a 20cm/8in square using a rolling pin. Brush with the melted butter, using a pastry brush, and sprinkle over the brown sugar, ground cinnamon and raisins. Starting at one side, roll the pastry up like a Swiss/jelly roll and press down firmly.

3 Cut the roll into 8 slices and roll each slice out into a round about 1cm/⅜in deep. Place the rounds on the baking trays and brush with the beaten egg.

4 Bake for 15–20 minutes until crisp and golden. Remove the pastries from the oven and transfer to wire racks with a palette knife to cool. In a small bowl, mix the icing sugar with 1–2 teaspoons water to form a smooth icing/frosting. Drizzle the icing in thin lines over the pinwheels. Leave to set before serving.

356 CHOCOLATE CRISPY SQUARES

PREPARATION TIME 20 minutes, plus chilling   **COOKING TIME** 2–3 minutes   **MAKES** 16 squares

55g/2oz butter, chopped, plus extra
    for greasing
200g/7oz orange milk chocolate (gf),
    broken into pieces
3 tbsp golden syrup

1 tbsp cocoa powder, sifted
250g/9oz/8⅓ cups rice crispies (gf)
100g/3½oz/heaped ½ cup white
    chocolate chips (gf)
55g/2oz/⅓ cup pistachio nuts, chopped

1 Grease a 20cm/8in loose-bottomed square cake tin.

2 Put the butter, orange chocolate, golden syrup and cocoa in a saucepan and heat gently until melted. Remove from the heat and stir in the rice crispies until they are well coated.

3 Press the mixture into the tin using the back of a spoon and leave to cool for a few minutes. Sprinkle over the chocolate chips and nuts and refrigerate for 2 hours until the chocolate has set. Cut into 16 squares using a sharp knife and place into cake cases/liners.

357 CORNFLAKE SPRINKLE CAKES

PREPARATION TIME 15 minutes   **COOKING TIME** 2–3 minutes   **MAKES** 20 cakes

55g/2oz butter, chopped
3 tbsp golden syrup

250g/9oz/8⅓ cups cornflakes (gf)
sugar sprinkles, to decorate

1 Put 20 cake cases/liners in two 12-hole bun tins.

2 Put the butter and syrup in a saucepan and heat gently, stirring, until melted. Remove from the heat, add the cornflakes and stir well, making sure they are well coated.

3 Put a large spoonful of the cornflake mixture into each cake case and decorate with the sprinkles. Leave to set for 1 hour before serving.

358 CHOCOLATE EGG NESTS

PREPARATION TIME 15 minutes, plus chilling   **COOKING TIME** 2–3 minutes   **MAKES** 20 nests

15g/½oz butter, chopped
2 tbsp golden syrup
250g/9oz caramel-filled chocolate (gf),
  broken

2 tbsp cocoa powder, sifted
250g/9oz/8⅓ cups cornflakes (gf)
60 sugar-coated mini chocolate eggs

1 Put 20 cake cases/liners in two 12-hole bun tins.

2 Put the butter, syrup, chocolate and cocoa in a saucepan and heat gently, stirring, until melted. Remove from the heat and stir in the cornflakes until they are well coated.

3 Put a large spoonful of the cornflake mixture into each cake case and place 3 mini eggs in the centre of each nest. Refrigerate for 1 hour before serving.

359 CHOCOLATE REFRIGERATOR CAKE

PREPARATION TIME 20 minutes, plus chilling   **COOKING TIME** 2–3 minutes   **MAKES** 16 squares

115g/4oz butter, chopped, plus extra
   for greasing
500g/1lb 2oz plain/semisweet chocolate,
   broken into pieces
300g/10½oz ginger biscuits/cookies,
   roughly broken
55g/2oz/scant 2 cups cornflakes

100g/3½oz/½ cup glacé/candied
   cherries, halved
55g/2oz/⅓ cup flaked/sliced almonds
55g/2oz/⅓ cup pistachio nuts
100g/3½oz white chocolate, melted
   and cooled slightly

1   Grease a 20cm/8in loose-bottomed square cake tin.
2   Melt the butter and plain chocolate together and leave to cool slightly.
3   Put the broken ginger biscuits in a plastic bag and crush into small pieces with a rolling pin. Put the biscuit bits, cornflakes, cherries, almonds and pistachios in a mixing bowl, add the melted butter mixture and stir well, making sure everything is coated in chocolate. Scrape into the tin and smooth the top with a spatula. Refrigerate for 30 minutes.
4   Drizzle the melted white chocolate over the cake, using a fork to make thin, decorative lines. Refrigerate for a further 30 minutes to set, then cut into 16 squares.

360 LEMON & RASPBERRY SLICE

PREPARATION TIME 20 minutes   **COOKING TIME** 25–30 minutes   **MAKES** 20 slices

225g/8oz butter, softened, plus extra
   for greasing
225g/8oz/scant 1 cup caster/
   superfine sugar
4 large eggs, lightly beaten
225g/8oz/1½ cups self-raising flour, sifted

finely grated zest of 2 lemons,
   plus 2–3 tbsp of the juice
200g/7oz/1½ cups raspberries
300g/10½oz/2 cups icing/powdered
   sugar, sifted
a few drops of pink food colouring

1   Preheat the oven to 180°C/350°F/gas 4. Grease and line a 38 x 25 x 6cm/15 x 10 x 2½in baking tin.
2   Put the butter and sugar in a mixing bowl and beat using an electric hand mixer or wooden spoon until the mixture is light and creamy. Add the eggs gradually, beating after each addition. Add the flour and gently fold it in with the lemon zest, using a large metal spoon. Add the raspberries and fold in gently. Scrape the mixture into the tin using a spatula.
3   Bake for 25–30 minutes until the cake springs back when pressed lightly and a skewer inserted into the middle of the cake comes out clean. Remove the slice from the oven and leave to cool in the tin.

4   In a bowl, mix the icing sugar with the lemon juice to make a smooth, thick icing/frosting. (You may not need all of the lemon juice.) Cover the slice with three-quarters of the icing. Add the food colouring to the remaining icing and then drizzle the pink icing over the top of the slice, using a small spoon to form pretty patterns on the white icing. Leave to set, then cut into 20 slices to serve.

361 APPLE FLAPJACKS

PREPARATION TIME 20 minutes   **COOKING TIME** 25–30 minutes   **MAKES** 10 flapjacks

115g/4oz butter, plus extra for greasing
3 tbsp golden syrup
85g/3oz/⅓ cup light muscovado sugar
250g/9oz/2½ cups porridge/rolled oats

1 large cooking/baking apple, peeled,
    cored and grated
2 tsp ground cinnamon
115g/4oz/⅔ cup sultanas/golden raisins

1   Preheat the oven to 180°C/350°F/gas 4. Grease a 20cm/8in loose-bottomed square cake tin.
2   Put the butter, syrup and sugar in a saucepan and heat for about 5 minutes until the sugar has dissolved and the butter has melted. Cool a little, then stir in the oats, grated apple, ground cinnamon and sultanas. Spoon the oat mixture into the tin.
3   Bake for 20–25 minutes until the flapjack is golden brown. Remove the flapjack from the oven and leave to cool in the tin, then cut into 10 slices to serve.

Note: If serving to a coeliac, check that they are able to eat oats, as although oats are generally gluten free, some coeliacs are also allergic to oats.

362 CHOCOLATE COCONUT KISSES

PREPARATION TIME 15 minutes   **COOKING TIME** 12–15 minutes   **MAKES** 18 cakes

butter, for greasing
200g/7oz/2½ cups desiccated/dried
    shredded coconut
200ml/7fl oz/scant 1 cup condensed milk

150g/5½oz/1 cup self-raising flour, sifted
1 tsp vanilla extract
100g/3½oz/heaped ½ cup plain/semisweet
    chocolate chips

1   Preheat the oven to 180°C/350°F/gas 4. Grease two 30cm/12in square baking trays.
2   Put all the ingredients in a mixing bowl and stir well with a wooden spoon. Using 2 teaspoons, place 18 walnut-size mounds of the coconut mixture on the trays a small distance apart.
3   Bake for 12–15 minutes until golden brown. Remove the cakes from the oven and transfer to a wire rack to cool.

363 SIMPLE CHOCOLATE BROWNIES

PREPARATION TIME 20 minutes   **COOKING TIME** 25–30 minutes   **MAKES** 16 brownies

250g/9oz butter, chopped, plus extra
    for greasing
400g/14oz plain/semisweet chocolate,
    broken into pieces
200g/7oz/¾ cup caster/superfine sugar
200g/7oz/¾ cup dark soft brown sugar

5 large eggs
1 tsp vanilla extract
200g/7oz/1⅓ cups plain/all-purpose
    flour, sifted
100g/3½oz/heaped ½ cup white
    chocolate chips

1 Preheat the oven to 180°C/350°F/gas 4. Grease and line a 30 x 23 x 6cm/12 x 9 x 2½in baking tin.
2 Melt the butter and 350g/12oz of the plain chocolate together for about 5 minutes, then leave to cool. Chop the remaining plain chocolate and set aside.
3 Put the caster sugar, dark brown sugar, eggs and vanilla extract in a mixing bowl and whisk using an electric hand mixer or a whisk until the mixture is very light and has doubled in size. While still whisking, slowly pour in the melted chocolate and butter mixture until it is all incorporated. Fold in the flour, the remaining plain chocolate and the white chocolate chips. Pour the cake mixture into the tin.
4 Bake for 25–30 minutes until the brownie has formed a crust and a skewer inserted into the middle of the cake comes out clean. Remove from the oven and leave to cool in the tin, then cut into 16 slices.

364 SNOWMAN CUPCAKES

PREPARATION TIME 40 minutes   **COOKING TIME** 15–20 minutes   **MAKES** 12 cakes

115g/4oz butter, softened
115g/4oz/scant ½ cup caster/superfine sugar
2 large eggs, lightly beaten
115g/4oz/¾ cup self-raising flour
4 tbsp cocoa powder
100g/3½oz mint chocolate, chopped
1 quantity Vanilla Buttercream (see page 24)

TO DECORATE
55g/2oz orange ready-to-roll icing
mini sugar-coated chocolate beans
    or chocolate chips
red fizzy liquorice strips/twists

1 Preheat the oven to 180°C/350°F/gas 4. Put 12 cake cases/liners in a 12-hole bun tin.
2 Put the butter and sugar in a mixing bowl and beat using an electric hand mixer or wooden spoon until the mixture is light and creamy. Add the eggs gradually, beating after each addition. Sift in the flour and cocoa and gently fold them into the mixture with the mint chocolate, using a large metal spoon. Spoon the mixture into the cake cases.

3 Bake for 15–20 minutes until the cakes spring back when pressed lightly and a skewer inserted into the middle of a cake comes out clean. Remove the cakes from the oven, turn out on to a wire rack and leave to cool.

4 Cover each cake in buttercream, smoothing the surface with a round-bladed knife.

5 Use the ready-to-roll icing to make 2cm/¾in carrot shapes for the snowmen's noses and place one in the middle of each cake. Use the chocolate beans or chips to make eyes and mouths. Cut 2 strips of the liquorice and place crossed over on the bottom of each cake to make a scarf for the snowman. Leave the buttercream to set before serving.

365 CHRISTMAS TREE BISCUITS

PREPARATION TIME 20 minutes, plus chilling   **COOKING TIME** 12–15 minutes   **MAKES** 10 biscuits

115g/4oz butter, softened, plus extra
    for greasing
55g/2oz/¼ cup caster/superfine sugar
175g/6oz heaped 1 cup plain/all-purpose
    flour, plus extra for dusting
2 tsp ground cinnamon

1 tbsp milk (optional)
200g/7oz/1⅓ cups icing/powdered
    sugar, sifted
a few drops of green food colouring
sweets/candies, to decorate

1 Put the butter and sugar in a mixing bowl and beat using an electric hand mixer or wooden spoon until the mixture is light and creamy. Sift in the flour and ground cinnamon and mix together with your hands to form a soft dough, adding the milk if the mixture is too dry. Wrap in cling film/plastic wrap and refrigerate for 1 hour.

2 Preheat the oven to 180°C/350°F/gas 4. Grease and line two 30cm/12in square baking trays.

3 Sift flour on to a clean work surface and roll the dough out to about 1cm/⅜in thick using a rolling pin. Cut out 10 biscuits using a Christmas-tree cutter or a cardboard template and a knife, gathering up the trimmings and re-rolling as necessary. Transfer the biscuits to the baking trays using a palette knife.

4 Bake for 12–15 minutes until golden brown. Remove the biscuits from the oven and leave to cool on the trays for a few minutes, then transfer to a wire rack with a palette knife to cool.

5 Mix the icing sugar with 1–2 tablespoons water and the food colouring to make a smooth green icing/frosting. Cover each biscuit with green icing using a round-bladed knife and decorate with the sweets. Leave the icing to set before serving.

INDEX